THE ASHGATE RESEARCH COMPANION
TO THOMAS LOVELL BEDDOES

'*The Ashgate Research Companion to Thomas Lovell Beddoes* convenes a valuable collection of critical perspectives and resources for research, magnetized by the gorgeous intensities of this morbidly enchanting writer. With a comprehensive introduction and a detailed bibliography, editors Ute Berns and Michael Bradshaw advance the resurgence of interest in this experimenter in literary form, worker of exceptional imagination, and vivid register of the phantasmagoria of historical tumult and crisis. The precocious *Brides' Tragedy* and the obsessive *Death's Jest-Book* command the fullest attention; we are invited as well to consider Beddoes' arresting, haunting lyrics, the conflicts of his homosexual passions, his adventures in science, and his contentious revolutionary activism. Working productively across boundaries of genre, gender, nation, period, and discipline (and, in consequence, the whole terrain of existential selfhood), this company of critics and scholars proves a most worthy companion to the extraordinary Mr. Beddoes'.

—Susan J. Wolfson, Professor of English, Princeton University

ASHGATE
RESEARCH
COMPANION

The *Ashgate Research Companions* are designed to offer scholars and graduate students a comprehensive and authoritative state-of-the-art review of current research in a particular area. The companion's editor brings together a team of respected and experienced experts to write chapters on the key issues in their speciality, providing a comprehensive reference to the field.

The Ashgate Research Companion to Thomas Lovell Beddoes

Edited by

UTE BERNS
Free University of Berlin, Germany

and

MICHAEL BRADSHAW
Manchester Metropolitan University, UK

ASHGATE

Published by
Ashgate Publishing Limited
Gower House
Croft Road
Aldershot
Hampshire GU11 3HR
England

Ashgate Publishing Company
Suite 420
101 Cherry Street
Burlington, VT 05401-4405
USA

Ashgate website: http://www.ashgate.com

British Library Cataloguing in Publication Data
The Ashgate research companion to Thomas Lovell Beddoes. -
(The nineteenth century series)
    1. Beddoes, Thomas Lovell, 1803-1849 – Criticism and interpretation
    I. Berns, Ute II. Bradshaw, Michael, 1966- III. Research companion to Thomas Lovell
    Beddoes
    828.7'09

Library of Congress Cataloging-in-Publication Data
The Ashgate research companion to Thomas Lovell Beddoes / edited by Ute Berns and
    Michael Bradshaw.
       p. cm. — (The nineteenth century series)
    Includes bibliographical references and index.
    ISBN 978-0-7546-6009-5 (alk. paper)
    1. Beddoes, Thomas Lovell, 1803-1849—Criticism and interpretation. I. Berns, Ute. II.
Bradshaw, Michael, 1966-

PR4098.A8 2007
821'.7—dc22

2007019865

ISBN: 978-0-7546-6009-5

Printed and bound in Great Britain by MPG Books Ltd, Bodmin, Cornwall.

Contents

The Nineteenth Century Series
General Editors' Preface

The aim of the series is to reflect, develop, and extend the great burgeoning of interest in the nineteenth century that has been an inevitable feature of recent years, as that former epoch has come more sharply into focus as a locus for our understanding not only of the past but of the contours of our modernity. It centres primarily upon major authors and subjects within Romantic and Victorian literature. It also includes studies of other British writers and issues, where these are matters of current debate: for example, biography and autobiography, journalism, periodical literature, travel writing, book production, gender, non-canonical writing. We are dedicated principally to publishing original monographs and symposia; our policy is to embrace a broad scope in chronology, approach and range of concern, and both to recognize and cut innovatively across such parameters as those suggested by the designations 'Romantic' and 'Victorian'. We welcome new ideas and theories, while valuing traditional scholarship. It is hoped that the world which predates yet so forcibly predicts and engages our own will emerge in parts, in the wider sweep, and in the lively streams of disputation and change that are so manifest an aspect of its intellectual, artistic, and social landscape.

Vincent Newey
Joanne Shattock
University of Leicester

Notes on Contributors

David M. Baulch is Associate Professor of English at the University of West Florida. He has published articles in *Studies in Romanticism, Word and Image, European Romantic Review, The Wordsworth Circle,* and other journals. He is currently preparing a critical edition of Beddoes's *The Brides' Tragedy,* a book on William Blake, and a study focused on Romanticism, revolution, and the psychoanalytic subject.

Ute Berns was Senior Lecturer in the Department of English Literature at the Technical University of Berlin; she is now a Research Fellow in the interdisciplinary project 'Cultures of Performance' at the Free University of Berlin. She has published articles on Beddoes and is currently working on an English monograph on the playwright. She has also written on other British writers of the nineteenth and twentieth centuries, such as Maturin and Charlotte Brontë, and is author of the study *Mikropolitik im Englischen Gegenwartsdrama* (Wissenschaftlicher Verlag Trier, 1997).

Michael Bradshaw is the editor of *Death's Jest-Book: The 1829 text* (Carcanet / Routledge, 2003), the author of *Resurrection Songs: The Poetry of Thomas Lovell Beddoes* (Ashgate, 2001), and the co-editor of *Thomas Lovell Beddoes, Selected Poetry* (Carcanet, 1999), and has written a number of shorter essays on the poet in journals and edited collections. He has also published on George Darley, Walter Savage Landor, John Keats, and Mary Shelley. He is currently Principal Lecturer in English at the Manchester Metropolitan University.

Frederick Burwick still teaches at UCLA, although he has also enjoyed visiting positions in Germany at the universities of Würzburg, Siegen, Göttingen, and Bamberg. Author and editor of twenty books and a hundred articles and reviews, he dedicates his research to problems of perception, illusion, and delusion in literary representation and theatrical performance. He has directed many student productions of Romantic plays, including *Death's Jest-Book*. His book *The Haunted Eye* (1987) concludes with a chapter on Thomas Lovell Beddoes and Georg Büchner. His *Poetic Madness and the Romantic Imagination* (1996) won the Outstanding Book of the Year Award of the American Conference on Romanticism. He has been named Distinguished Scholar by both the British Academy (1992) and the Keats-Shelley Association (1998).

Alan Halsey is a poet, publisher, and bookseller. He has written several critical articles and pamphlets on Beddoes and is the editor of *Death's Jest-Book; or, The Day Will Come* (West House, 2003). He is also the author of the Beddoes entry in the New *DNB* (2004). His book *Marginalien* (2005) includes excerpts from an unfinished study, *An Anatomy of 'Death's Jest-Book'*. His other books include *The Text of Shelley's Death* (1995, repr. 2001), *A Robin Hood Book* (2006) and *Not Everything Remotely: Selected Poems 1978–2005* (2006).

Raphael Hörmann is working on a doctoral thesis in Comparative Literature on nineteenth-century German and English revolutionary literature at the University of Glasgow, entitled *Authoring the Revolution, 1819–1848: Radical German and British Literature and the Shift from Political to Social Revolution*.

Diane Long Hoeveler is Professor of English and Coordinator of Women's Studies at Marquette University, Milwaukee, Wisconsin. She is the author of *Romantic Androgyny: The Women Within* (1990) and *Gothic Feminism* (1998); co-author of *Charlotte Brontë* (1997); and co-editor of the MLA's *Approaches to Teaching Jane Eyre* (1993) and *Approaches to Teaching Gothic Fiction* (2003). In addition, she has co-edited *Comparative Romanticisms* (1998), *Women of Color* (2001), *The Historical Dictionary of Feminism* (1996; 2004), *Romanticism: Comparative Discourses* (2006), and *Interrogating Orientalism* (2006). Her new book is *Genre Riffs: Literary Adaptations in a Hyperbolic Key*.

Andrew James Johnston is Professor of Medieval and Early Modern English Literature at the Freie Universität Berlin. He is the author of *Clerks and Courtiers: Chaucer, Middle English Literature and the State Formation Process* (2001) and co-editor of *Anglo-Romanische Kulturkontakte von Humanismus bis Postkolonialismus* (2002) and *Language and Text: Current Perspectives on English and Germanic Historical Linguistics and Philology* (2006). He is currently completing a book entitled *Performing the Middle Ages from* Beowulf *to* Shakespeare. Though his research focuses mainly on medieval and Renaissance literature, he has also written essays on Bertolt Brecht, J.R.R. Tolkien, and the work of film-makers David Fincher and Lars von Trier. He has published two novels in German.

Nat Leach is Assistant Professor of English at Cape Breton University and has forthcoming publications on Lord Byron and Joanna Baillie.

Jerome J. McGann is John Stewart Bryan University Professor at the University of Virginia, and Thomas Holloway Professor of Victorian Media and Culture and Director of the Victorian Centre at Royal Holloway College, University of London. Widely acknowledged as the foremost scholar of Romanticism of his generation, his most recent books include: *Radiant Textuality: Literature after the World Wide Web* (Palgrave Macmillan, 2001), and *Byron and Romanticism* (Cambridge University Press, 2002).

Christopher Moylan is an Associate Professor of English at New York Institute of Technology. His literary scholarship includes a number of publications and conference papers on T.L. Beddoes, including most recently '"For Luz is a Good Joke": T.L. Beddoes and Jewish Mysticism,' in *Romanticism and the Jews*, ed. Sheila Spector (Palgrave Macmillan, 2003). He also publishes poetry and art criticism.

Michael O'Neill is Chairman of the Department of English Studies and Professor of English at the University of Durham. His recent books on Romantic literature include *Romanticism and the Self-Conscious Poem* (Oxford University Press, 1997) and *The Human Mind's Imaginings: Conflict and Achievement in Shelley's Poetry* (Oxford University Press, 1989).

Marjean D. Purinton is Professor of English and Associate Chair of the Department of English at Texas Tech University, where she also teaches in the Women's Studies and Comparative Literature Programs. She is the author of *Romantic Ideology Unmasked: The Mentally Constructed Tyrannies in Dramas of William Wordsworth, Lord Byron, Percy Shelley and Joanna Baillie*, and of the forthcoming *Staging Grotesques and Ghosts: Techno-Gothic British Romantic Drama*. She has written numerous articles about Romantic drama; and her essay on Beddoes's *The Brides' Tragedy* has been nominated for the Nineteenth-Century Studies Association Best Article Award. She has also written about the teaching of Romantic drama. She is a member of the Advisory Board for the International Conference on Romanticism, a member of the Advisory / Editorial Board for *British Women Playwrights around 1800*, and the British Literature Consulting Editor for the *South Central Review*. She is the recipient of SCMLA and NEH Research Grants, and her teaching contributions have been recognized by the MLA.

Shelley Rees wrote a doctoral dissertation on Beddoes, 'Gender and Desire in Thomas Lovell Beddoes' *The Brides' Tragedy* and *Death's Jest-Book*', at the University of North Texas and now teaches writing at The Oklahoma School of Science and Mathematics. She is the author of 'Melveric and Wolfram: A Love Story', and the editor of the *Thomas Lovell Beddoes Society Journal*.

Acknowledgements

Ute Berns would like to thank Manfred Pfister and Frank Gertich, as well as the interdisciplinary research project 'Cultures of Performance' at the Free University of Berlin, especially Irmgard Maassen and Kirstin Müller. Her thanks also go to the former Department of English at the Technical University of Berlin and to Kuno Schuhmann in particular.

Michael Bradshaw would like to thank all the staff of the English Department at Manchester Metropolitan University, especially Jess Edwards, Jeffrey Wainwright, Julie Wilkinson, and Sue Zlosnik. He is grateful to the English Research Institute at MMU for a term of sabbatical leave in 2004.

We are both indebted to our students past and present, at the Technical University of Berlin and MMU respectively. We would like to thank the Thomas Lovell Beddoes Society. And many thanks go to Ann Donahue at Ashgate Publishing for her much-appreciated advice and support. The editors are, above all, grateful to the dedicated team of contributing scholars who made this volume possible—diverse in background, method and style, but united in a common passion for the work of an extraordinary writer.

Our special thanks belong to our families: Holmer and Arthur; Desdemona, Jacob, and Ruby.

Ute Berns and Michael Bradshaw
Berlin and Manchester, 2006

Prologue:
'Prince of Morticians':
Authors on Beddoes, 1823–2002

This is the Beddoes of reputation and myth. Novelists and poets as well as biographers and literary critics have been consistently intrigued by the strange body of death-obsessed work left by the self-styled anatomist poet, and several— such as Pound and Ashbery, for example—have used images both of the poet and from his texts to enhance the macabre or antiquarian temper in their own creative work. This collage of short quotations illustrates Beddoes's deceptively persistent presence in the changing literary imagination.

> This Drama [*The Brides' Tragedy*] is undoubtedly one of the most promising performances of this 'poetical age'. There are, indeed, few things which, *as mere poetry*, surpass it.
>
> Bryan Waller Procter (1823)[1]

> He is a fine, open-hearted, ingenuous, accomplished and gentlemanly youth; and we . . . pronounce him a promising poet,—we tie a wreath of laurel round his forehead,— and may it remain there till displaced to make room for a bolder branch of the sacred tree.
>
> John Wilson (1823)[2]

> If you have a few shillings to spare, buy the Brides' Tragedy immediately. It is worth all the Tragedies Byron ever wrote or ever will write—with mawkish Mirandola to boot.
>
> George Darley (1823)[3]

> I am food for *what I am good* for—worms . . . I ought to have been among other things a good poet; Life was too great a bore on one peg & that a bad one.
>
> Thomas Lovell Beddoes (1849)[4]

---

1   Review of *The Brides' Tragedy*, in *The London Magazine*, 7 (1823), 169–72 (p. 169).
2   Review of *The Brides' Tragedy*, 'Notices of the Modern British Dramatists, No. II. Beddoes', in *Blackwood's Edinburgh Magazine*, 14, 83 (1823), 723–29 (p. 724).
3   Cited in Claude Colleer Abbott, *The Life and Letters of George Darley, Poet and Critic* (London: Oxford University Press, 1928), p. 28.
4   *The Works of Thomas Lovell Beddoes*, ed. with an introduction H.W. Donner (London: Oxford University Press, 1935; repr. New York: AMS Press, 1978), p. 683.

To destroy, with so many authors the most painful and difficult of tasks, was to him not less easy than to produce: a passage of a scene, if, on a comprehensive view, it appeared superfluous or misplaced, was never spared from destruction for its own inherent beauty.

Thomas Forbes Kelsall (1851)[5]

Nearly two centuries have elapsed since a work of the same wealth of genius as Death's Jest-Book hath been given to the world.

Walter Savage Landor (1853)[6]

Don't fear but that your zeal and the marvellous power of the man will eventually raise up the whole Beddoes again out of the Luz, the bookful of beauty and something beyond, which you have rescued. . . .

Robert Browning (1868)[7]

[Beddoes's] noble instinct for poetry could never carry him in practice beyond the production of a few lofty and massive fragments of half-formed verse which stand better by themselves when detached from the incoherent and disorderly context. . . .

A.C. Swinburne (1875)[8]

Few collections of letters exist in which the discussion of literary topics holds so prominent a place as it does in these of Beddoes. If any excuse were needed for bringing them before the public, it would be more than supplied by Mr. Swinburne who . . . remarked . . . that Beddoes' 'brilliant correspondence on poetical questions gives to me a higher view of his fine and vigorous intelligence than any other section of his literary remains.'

Edmund Gosse (1893)[9]

His mature blank verse is perfect. It is not an artificial concoction galvanized into a semblance of life; it simply lives.

Lytton Strachey (1907)[10]

5   *The Poems Posthumous and Collected of Thomas Lovell Beddoes, with a Memoir*, 2 vols (London: William Pickering, 1851), p. xviii.
6   *Last Fruit off an Old Tree* (1853); quoted in John Forster, *Walter Savage Landor* (London: Chapman and Hall, 1869), p. 475.
7   Letter to T.F. Kelsall, in *The Browning Box: or, The Life and Works of Thomas Lovell Beddoes as reflected in letters by his friends and admirers*, ed. H.W. Donner (London: Oxford University Press, 1935), p. 111.
8   *George Chapman: A Critical Essay* (London: Chatto & Windus, 1875), p. 77.
9   'Prefatory Note' in *The Letters of Thomas Lovell Beddoes*, ed. with notes by Edmund Gosse (London: Matthews and Land, 1894).
10 'The Last Elizabethan' (1907), in *Books and Characters, French and English* (London: Chatto & Windus, 1922), p. 240.

When we come to what should be the universally known first stanza of 'Dream Pedlary' what words can possibly do justice to its movement and music? what prosody of the very greatest . . . can be held superior to it? . . . Not even in Shelley before, or Tennyson after, is there anything more significant of the recovered mastery of prosodic music.

George Saintsbury (1910)[11]

It is a pity that his blank verse is best in fragments; but the gods are jealous.

Oliver Elton (1924)[12]

Each scene goes its own way, the whole remains fragmentary. But one cannot emphasize enough how strongly almost every passage comes across when taken on its own; drive, powerful moods, intellectually riveting speeches, and tones of real pathos convey a sense of poetry that comes naturally and draws on lavish resources.

Grete Moldauer (1924)[13]

It is indeed preposterous to call him a great poet and yet he has written what only the greatest poets can equal—and that only when they are at their best. His intensity is astonishing—not to say appalling.

Royall H. Snow (1928)[14]

Beddoes became a magnificent failure; . . . he confused the alphabet of imagery, and made thoughts go forth as nonsense.

Edmund Blunden (1931)[15]

And when we think how still and cold the plays of Beddoes or of Sir Henry Taylor lie, in spite of all their beauty . . .

Virginia Woolf (1932)[16]

---

11   *A History of English Prosody* (London: Macmillan, 1910), III, 150.
12   *A Survey of English Literature 1780–1830* (1912; London: Edward Arnold, 1928), p. 302.
13   Editors' translation from the original German. '. . . *jede Szene* [*geht*] *ihre eigenen Wege, das Ganze bleibt Stückwerk. Trotzdem kann nicht genug betont werden, wie stark fast jede Stelle, als einzelnes genommen, wirkt; Schwung, Stimmungskraft, geistvoll fesselnde Reden und Töne von echtem Pathos geben den Teilen den Hauch ungekünstelter, aus dem Vollen schöpfender Dichtung.' Thomas Lovell Beddoes* (Wien and Leipzig: Wilhelm Braunmüller, 1924), p. 135.
14   *Thomas Lovell Beddoes: Eccentric and Poet* (New York: Covici-Friede, 1928), p. 2.
15   'Beddoes and His Contemporaries', in *Votive Tablets: Studies Chiefly Appreciative of English Authors and Books* (London: Coloden-Sanderson, 1931), pp. 292–303 (p. 297).
16   '*Aurora Leigh*', in *The Common Reader, Second Series* (London: The Hogarth Press, 1932), p. 213.

His polished, cutting words betray an eloquent speaker highly sensitive to form. His poetic power enabled him to win his readers for his political ideas through gripping images and pithy dramatic scenes.

Carl August Weber (1935)[17]

Beddoes had learned to suffer hardship and wrong without a murmur, but it was not because he did not feel them; it was that he felt them too strongly, and to this we owe the power of his verse. He could not help writing, for that was his only means of liberation.

H.W. Donner (1935)[18]

'Death's Jest Book' is not by any standards a coherent drama; but it is at least a colossal anthology of dramatic poetry on the theme of death and immortality; and we can see it now as one of the greatest poems of the nineteenth century.

Edwin Muir (1935) [19]

Curious, is it not, that Mr Eliot / has not given more time to Mr Beddoes / (T.L.) prince of morticians / where none can speak his language. . . .

Ezra Pound (1947)[20]

Thomas Lovell Beddoes / Could never walk through meadows / Without getting the glooms / And thinking of tombs.

W.H. Auden (1952)[21]

Beddoes should have been a great poet, but failed for want of a subject . . . Only death met the desire of his imagination, but a poet cannot demonstrate his creative exuberance in a celebration of death alone.

Harold Bloom (1962)[22]

---

17   Discussing TLB's German political prose; editors' translation from the original German. '*In scharf geschliffenen Worten sprach hier ein Wortgewandter, dem die Form nicht gleichgültig war, dem aus dichterischer Gestaltungskraft die Fähigkeit erwuchs, in packenden Bildern und straffer dramatischer Szene die Leser für seine politischen Ideen zu begeistern.*' *Bristols Bedeutung für die englische Romantik und die deutsch-englisch Beziehungen* (Halle: Max Niemayer, 1935; repr. Walluf: Sändig, 1973), pp. 213–14.

18   Discussing TLB c. 1837–38, *Thomas Lovell Beddoes: The Making of a Poet* (Oxford: Basil Blackwell, 1935; repr. Folcroft, 1970), p. 324.

19   [Review of] 'T.L. Beddoes, *The Works of Beddoes* ed. H.W. Donner and *Thomas Lovell Beddoes* by H.W. Donner', in *The Truth of Imagination: Some Uncollected Reviews and Essays by Edwin Muir*, ed. P.H. Butter (Aberdeen: Aberdeen University Press 1988), pp. 52 and 55.

20   From Canto LXXX, in *The Cantos of Ezra Pound* (London: Faber and Faber, 1964), p. 531.

21   From 'Academic Graffiti' (1952, 1970), in *Collected Poems*, ed. Edward Mendelson (London: Faber and Faber, 1994).

22   *The Visionary Company: A Reading of English Romantic Poetry* (London and New York: Faber and Faber, 1962), p. 428.

If he had been as interested in life as he was in death he might have been a very great poet. As it is he remains the most tantalizing of all our writers; a man of genius who wrote nothing that is commonly remembered.

Ian Jack (1963)[23]

Beddoes, identifying . . . invisible and underlying reality with death, seems . . . to have hit a bullseye that many of his contemporaries saw but tried not to hit.

Northrop Frye (1968)[24]

Only a poet of eldritch talents, alive to the cutting edge of the dramatic monologue, would have been able to imagine the relations of speech to silence as tellingly as Beddoes does.

Christopher Ricks (1984)[25]

'Nor do I suppose the name would mean anything to you. Not at all a fashionable poet, at present . . .' / 'I wish very much I knew your poet'. / 'Then look for him. He's not totally obscure. Just a little off the beaten path'.

Robertson Davies (1988)[26]

The posthumous spyglass / Of the author lies, alert. The works / Of Thomas Lovell Beddoes fall open / And are sick and alive, books of iron, and faintly gilded / In the dim light of the early nineteenth century.

John Ashbery (1990)[27]

Browning missed his chance to adjust our sense of his century and to make public one of the most curious and still misprized voices of his time, who belongs with Shelley on the one hand, and with Wilde on the other, as a radical presence who gradually gets language on his own terms.

Michael Schmidt (1998)[28]

The gold in Beddoes is inextricably entangled in the ore of the pays. It is not just that he is a 'poet of fragments'; it is that the fragments don't separate easily from the matrix, and when they do, something is found wanting: they need their rough natural setting to register fully, even as it partially obscures them.

John Ashbery (2000)[29]

---

23   *English Literature, 1815–32* (*The Oxford History of English Literature*) (London: Oxford University Press, 1963), p. 144.
24   *A Study of English Romanticism* (London: Harvester, 1983), p. 85.
25   'Thomas Lovell Beddoes: "A Dying Start"', in *The Force of Poetry* (Oxford: Clarendon Press, 1984), pp. 135–62 (p. 162).
26   *The Lyre of Orpheus*, in *The Cornish Trilogy* (Harmondsworth: Penguin, 1991), p. 939.
27   'October at the Window', in *April Galleons* (London: Paladin, 1990).
28   *Lives of the Poets* (London: Weidenfeld & Nicolson, 1998), p. 403.
29   'Olives and Anchovies: The Poetry of Thomas Lovell Beddoes', in *Other Traditions* (Cambridge, Mass., and London: Harvard University Press, 2000), pp. 23–44 (p. 32).

'Beddoes sought enlightenment through medicine, that most socially beneficial of sciences, and through support of radical egalitarian movements, but each of these avenues led him back to the same conclusion, that man was a botched creation whose proper domain was darkness and whose only salvation was death'.

Reginald Hill (2002)[30]

---

30   *Death's Jest-Book* (London: HarperCollins, 2003), p. 498.

Introduction

At the peak of his mid-Victorian celebrity, Robert Browning is said to have announced that should he ever be made Professor of Poetry at Oxford University, he would make Thomas Lovell Beddoes the subject of his inaugural address.[1] Likely as this may have seemed at the time, Browning never attained the distinction, and the lecture was never given. Browning's statement is often cited in memorials and re-evaluations of Beddoes, as if a famous author's unfulfilled intention were a valuable endorsement rather than a back-handed compliment: to read this anecdote yet again produces a melancholy sensation, seeming to epitomize the stalled reputation, the unread texts, and all the special pleading involved in championing a 'minor'. Never short of occasional praise, and still numbering the great and good among his admirers and promoters, Beddoes yet seemed destined to be the perennial also-ran of late Romanticism, the 'eccentric and poet', the 'man of genius who wrote nothing that is commonly remembered'.[2]

But just before the turn of the twenty-first century, a great poet of our own era—John Ashbery, an admirer and critic of long standing—finally made good that promise of Browning's and delivered a prestigious public lecture on Beddoes.[3] Now, more than a century after Browning and Edmund Gosse planned Beddoes's assimilation into the main current of literary reading and discussion, the work of recovery has gained new momentum. Over the last decade, and especially in the last four or five years, the strange works of Thomas Lovell Beddoes have attracted unprecedented attention: several new editions of key works have been published; scholarly and critical studies continue to proliferate, in print, online, and at

---

1 The anecdote is frequently cited: see e.g., D.F. Hannigan, 'Thomas Lovell Beddoes: "A Forgotten Oxford Poet", *The Westminster Review*, 149 (1898), 484–92; Kelsall mentioned the lecture to Browning in a letter of 1867; and H.W. Donner states that Browning's intention was 'well known', in *The Browning Box: or, The Life and Works of Thomas Lovell Beddoes as reflected in letters by his friends and admirers*, ed. H.W. Donner (London: Oxford University Press, 1935), pp. 98 and 162.

2 Quotations from Royall H. Snow and Ian Jack, both cited above in Prologue. The association with Browning continues to be cited as a recommendation: TLB is 'the obvious link between Shelley and Browning', in James R. Thompson, *Thomas Lovell Beddoes* (Boston: Twayne, 1985), p. 123. But John Heath-Stubbs considers the possible detrimental effect of Browning's half-hearted involvement in the transmission of TLB's texts: 'Most of his poetry remained in manuscript, locked away—the fact is symbolic—in Browning's bureau, like a suppressed memory in the mind', in *The Darkling Plain: A Study of the Later Fortunes of Romanticism in English Poetry from George Darley to W.B. Yeats* (London: Eyre & Spottiswoode, 1950), p. 22.

3 Ashbery's Norton Lecture on TLB is published as 'Olives and Anchovies: The Poetry of Thomas Lovell Beddoes', in *Other Traditions* (Cambridge, Mass., and London: Harvard University Press, 2000), pp. 23–44.

international conferences; there has even been a stage production of Beddoes's defining work, *Death's Jest-Book*, long presumed hostile to theatrical performance or even downright unstageable. Some of these events will be considered in more detail below.

Now that the texts are in print once more, Beddoes's poetry and drama are actually being taught, and not only at postgraduate level, but are, in fact, finding their way onto undergraduate literature curricula, a crucial condition of lasting canonical status. In the midst of this volatile and exciting climate, there are of course no guarantees that his reputation will not fade once again.

This volume assembles contributions by a diverse team of scholars working on the many versions of Thomas Lovell Beddoes—Beddoes as dramatist, Beddoes as scientist, Beddoes as lyrical poet, Beddoes as revolutionary activist, Beddoes as psychological case study, Beddoes as gay writer, Beddoes as literary reviver and ventriloquist . . . Beddoes is relevant to so many contexts of Romantic and nineteenth-century literature that we feel his continuing presence in academic conversation is not only desirable but also important. This volume has the intentions of consolidating this current momentum, taking stock of the diversity of recent and ongoing work, and charting some future directions in the interpretation of Beddoes's texts and contexts. Most importantly, we would like to reach scholars and students who are not yet very familiar with Beddoes in the hope that this collection may help to convey the richness and complexity of his writing, thus showing him to be a rewarding subject for further analysis. To that end, the volume concludes with a fully comprehensive bibliography of writings by, about, and relevant to Thomas Lovell Beddoes. The book is a deliberate intervention into the canon of European Romanticism; we hope it may also help to inspire future readers and scholars to engage with the author and to experience, in Browning's phrase, 'the marvellous power of the man'.[4]

This introduction contains three major sections. The first is a brief biographical sketch, which aims not to be exhaustively detailed but, rather, to offer a general frame in which to situate the various works discussed in detail by the contributors; alternative, more comprehensive and authoritative 'lives' of the poet are referenced here and in the general bibliography at the end. The second section is a review of the major critical reactions to Beddoes that have been published since his lifetime, attempting to outline certain distinct tendencies in groups of critics, rather than to itemize them chronologically. Since this critical history, intersecting with theatre history, has led to and is paralleled by the eventual staging of *Death's Jest-Book*, that event will be included in this survey. Finally, there is a section devoted to introduction proper, which indicates how the present collection of critical essays fits into this matrix, summarizing the major argument of each and indicating its methodology and style.

This collection is not a fully comprehensive account of all current scholarship on Beddoes, but it does include as many different perspectives as possible. We aim to take stock of the rapidly altered situation of Beddoes studies in the early twenty-

---

4 Letter to Kelsall, in *The Browning Box*, p. 111.

first century and, simultaneously, set an agenda for the years to come, focusing, among other things, on such distinctive themes as political and revolutionary history. Moreover, we wish to advocate a more fully internationalized approach that pays greater heed to Beddoes's German contexts than before.

I   The life of Beddoes

Thomas Lovell Beddoes was born in Clifton near Bristol, on 30 June 1803, the son of Dr Thomas Beddoes and Anna Maria, née Edgeworth.[5] By this time Thomas Beddoes Senior was well known as an experimental scientist and teacher of science, and alternatively revered or reviled as a radical democrat and Jacobin sympathizer. His statements on the French Revolution eventually led to his giving up his Chair at Oxford University. He set up the Pneumatic Institute in Bristol Hotwells and later Clifton, a laboratory based at his home, devoted to research into the medical properties of the inhalation of gases, and related matters of progressive science. It is thought (and often cited as a partial explanation of his son's morbid preoccupations) that he educated his children in comparative anatomy with displays and dissections of human and animal bodies. Thomas Beddoes died in 1808, while Thomas Lovell was still a small boy, leaving a legal guardianship and the income of several properties to support his children.[6] Thomas Lovell's mother was, of course, the sister of Maria Edgeworth, and her influence on the poet, together with the influence of her singular family, must not be underestimated in the traditional marking out of Thomas Lovell as the inheritor of his father's gruff radicalism and way with dead bodies. Anna Edgeworth was acknowledged as an intelligent and principled woman, and her having taken the children on a prolonged visit to Edgeworthtown in Ireland in 1808 provided Thomas Lovell with a strongly flavoured alternative to the house-cum-laboratory in Clifton: in Ireland, as well as being read to by his novelist aunt Maria, he came to know his maternal grandfather Richard Lovell Edgeworth, a celebrated eccentric and free-thinker to rival Dr Beddoes, a radical educational reformer and inventor.

Thomas Lovell Beddoes was sent away to boarding school by his guardian Davies Giddy (or Gilbert), first to Bath Grammar School and then to Charterhouse, where he had a hectic and turbulent career as a school-boy ring-leader, rebel, and sometime poet. It is reported by a younger contemporary, Charles Dacres Bevan, that the young Beddoes devised a slang language that long survived him in the school, and that when he bestowed a nickname on an elder or peer, whether benign

---

5   To date there are two full-length biographies of TLB: Snow's *Thomas Lovell Beddoes: Eccentric and Poet* (1928), cited above; and H.W. Donner, *Thomas Lovell Beddoes: The Making of a Poet* (Oxford: Basil Blackwell, 1935; repr. Folcroft, 1970). A new biography is being written by John Baker. There is also a biographical essay by Gerald McDaniel, available online in the Thomas Lovell Beddoes website: <http://www.beddoes.org>.

6   A comprehensive account of Dr Thomas Beddoes Senior's life, including his scientific and political activities, can be found in Dorothy A. Stansfield, *Thomas Beddoes, MD, 1760–1808: Chemist, Physician, Democrat* (Dordrecht: D. Reidel, 1984).

or contemptuous, it tended to stick. The manuscript of Beddoes's juvenile prose romance 'Scaroni; or, the Mysterious Cave' is still in the possession of Charterhouse School Library. He published a macabre narrative poem, *The Improvisatore*, in 1821.

Beddoes continued his private war on authority at Pembroke College, Oxford, where he also wrote and had published *The Brides' Tragedy* (1822), the second and last major publication of his lifetime; *The Brides' Tragedy* was well received by critics, with extremely positive reviews appearing in *The London Magazine* and *Blackwood's*. Beddoes derived the plot of *The Brides' Tragedy* from an Oxford ballad in which a privileged student murders his secret lower-class bride in order to marry a noblewoman:[7] although the play does have a certain patchy quality, particularly in female characterization, Beddoes's protagonist Hesperus is a superb creation, uttering brilliantly imagined verse as he wrestles both with grisly supernatural temptations and with the influence of his generic ancestors in Renaissance drama. Beddoes's handling of the tragic structure is deft and confident, as we watch Hesperus transmute rapidly from romantic lover and faithful son to criminal psychopath: he dies from sniffing a bouquet of poisoned flowers offered by his wife's mother, with invisible demons clutching at him in a Faustus-like damnation. Over the next few years Beddoes took up residence in London and became acquainted with Bryan Waller Procter, also known as the poet 'Barry Cornwall'; Beddoes also made some lengthy visits to a new friend, Thomas Forbes Kelsall, in Southampton, where he worked energetically at several new tragedies. Kelsall was to be a lifelong friend and supporter—although his wife never came to share his affection for the irascible Beddoes—and eventually became his literary executor and the crucial figure in the transmission of Beddoes's writing. If it had not been for Kelsall's belief and commitment, very few of Beddoes's works would have survived at all. Fragments of three tragedies date from 1823–24: *The Last Man*, *Love's Arrow Poisoned*, and *Torrismond*; *The Second Brother*, which survives as a fairly substantial four-act 'torso' of a play, was probably written in 1824–25. A striking and wrongly overlooked text, it contains all the main ingredients of Beddoes's dramatic style—fratricidal enmity, betrayal and treachery, violent transformations, death, and immortality—and is regarded by Donner as the forerunner of *Death's Jest-Book*, having been abandoned shortly before Beddoes departed for Germany.[8]

Beddoes's mother died in Florence in 1824, shortly before he arrived to see her. While in Italy he became acquainted with Walter Savage Landor, an exile and literary misfit for whom he found a lasting and reciprocated sympathy. After some travelling between Bristol, London, and Oxford, Beddoes left England for the German states in July 1825. It is worth noting that when Beddoes left England, he effectively turned his back on a literary scene that held out much promise for him. This decision may have been partly determined by Beddoes's desire to put some

---

7   'Lucy' from *The Midlands Minstrel* (1822) is reproduced in Donner's *Works*, pp. 707–11.

8   *The Making of a Poet*, p. 157. A completed version of *The Second Brother* was staged by the Maddermarket Theatre in Norwich in 1935.

distance between himself and his family and escape to a country with a much more lenient legislation on 'sodomy'.[9] At the same time, his choice of the University of Göttingen is a measure of his intellectual commitment to his new chosen career—medicine.

It was in July 1825 that Beddoes left England for Germany, to immerse himself in a frenzy of scientific study at the University of Göttingen, as he described to Kelsall in December:

> Up at 5, Anatomical reading till 6—Translation from English into German till 7—prepare for Blumenbach's lecture till 9—Stromeyer's lecture on Chemistry till 10. 10 to ½ p. 12, Practical Zootomy—½ p. 12 to 1 English into German or German literary reading with a pipe—1 to 2 Anatomical lecture. 2 to 3 anatomical reading. 3 to 4 Osteology. 4 to 5 Lecture in German language. 5 to 6 dinner and light reading in Zootomy, Chem. or Anat^y. 6 to 7, this hour often wasted in a visit, sometimes Anatomical reading till 8. Then coffee and read Greek till 10. 10 to 11, write a little Death's Jest Book w^h is a horrible waste of time, but one must now & then throw away the dregs of the day; read Latin sometimes or even continue the Anatomy—and at 11 go to bed. (Works, pp. 608–09)

Beddoes showed considerable scientific talent as well as avid commitment, winning the admiration of eminent professors such as Blumenbach in Göttingen and, later, Schönlein in Würzburg. His new tragedy, 'for w^h I have a very jewel of a name—DEATH'S JESTBOOK' (p. 604), although in some ways the inheritor of his literary success of 1822–23, was conceived and began to grow in this new distinctive environment of intensive scientific and linguistic study. As Beddoes explains in his surviving letters to Procter and Kelsall, the Jest-Book combined a number of his personal ambitions and preoccupations, and marked a vigorous new beginning after the self-conscious endeavours as an English professional poet. In his 'Preface' to Death's Jest-Book, Beddoes deliberately sets out to antagonize the critics and start the English tragedy out of its complacent slumber;[10] he also set himself the task of satirizing death itself, as he boasts in these often-quoted lines from a verse letter

---

9   Paul Derks discusses the period between 1750 and the early decades of the nineteenth century as a time when Enlightenment tolerance and pietistic tendencies of introspection created an environment conducive to a comparatively open exploration of homosexual identities *avant la lettre*. Alternatives to heterosexual monogamy, frequently mediated through literary texts, were debated and considered as options almost within the realm of the possible. Derks points out instances of people actually trying to 'live' these alternatives. In his chronology, the backlash ironically set in at about the time when TLB emigrated to Germany. Paul Derks, *Die Schande der heiligen Päderastie: Homosexualität und Öffentlichkeit in der deutschen Literatur 1750–1850* (Berlin: Rosa Winkel, 1990), p. 11.

10   See *Works*, pp. 530–35.

to Procter, which evoke the wild comic spirit of the new drama as he originally conceived it:

> *... I have been*
> *Giving some negro minutes of the night*
> *Freed from the slavery of my ruling spright*
> *Anatomy the grim, to a new story*
> *In whose satiric pathos we will glory.*
> *In it Despair has married wildest Mirth*
> *And to their wedding-banquet all the earth*
> *Is bade to bring its enmities and loves*
> *Triumphs and horrors: ...*
> *But he who fills the cups and makes the jest*
> *Pipes to the dancers, is the fool o' the feast.*
> *Who's he? I've dug him up and decked him trim*
> *And made a mock, a fool, a slave of him*
> *Who was the planet's tyrant: dotard Death:*
> *Man's hate and dread: not with a stoical breath*
> *To meet him like Augustus standing up,*
> *Nor with grave saws to season the cold cup*
> *Like the philosopher nor yet to hail*
> *His coming with a verse or jesting tale*
> *As Adrian did and More: but of his night*
> *His moony ghostliness and silent might*
> *To rob him, to uncypress him i' the light*
> *To unmask all his secrets; make him play*
> *Momus o'er wine by torchlight is the way*
> *To conquer him and kill; ...*
> *For death is more 'a jest' than Life: you see*
> *Contempt grows quick from familiarity.*
> *I owe this wisdom to Anatomy— (pp. 614–15)*

Death's Jest-Book; or, The Fool's Tragedy is impossible to summarize briefly. It is an immense text, written in blank verse and comic prose and interspersed with a large number of dramatic lyrics, especially in the later revisions. It concerns two brothers' revenge against a corrupt duke, insurrection and civil war, and fratricidal jealousy; it involves a scene of necromancy, including an on-stage resurrection in the third act. Beddoes sent this letter to Procter from Göttingen in March 1826, in the early days of composition. Eventually *Death's Jest-Book* was to move far away from this satirical mission. The gradual evolution of Beddoes's great work from this recklessly ambitious inception, which seems to invite defeat and disillusion, has been analyzed by various critics. Having completed a fair copy by the end of 1828, Beddoes sent his new work to three friends in February 1829; they were

Procter, Kelsall, and J.G.H. Bourne, a former college friend, now a barrister (and later a novelist). Kelsall reacted positively, or at least supportively, and advised publication; but Bourne, and especially Procter, reacted very negatively, expressed deep disapproval, and recommended serious revision.[11] Beddoes fell into a depression. The *Jest-Book* was intermittently revised and expanded, and was never printed in any form until after his death.[12] Two of Beddoes's finest non-dramatic poems, 'Doomsday' and 'Dream Pedlary', date from the aftermath of this crisis, around 1830.

Beddoes's four years at Göttingen were characterized by intensive scientific and literary study, and also chequered with episodes of drunken rowdiness, which caused him further brushes with authority. Beddoes made his first suicide attempt in 1829 and was eventually sent down from the university in August 1829; his fine collection of books was later auctioned to defray some of his unpaid debts.

Beddoes continued his medical studies in the Bavarian university town of Würzburg. He continued to study anatomy and physiology and graduated MD in 1831. It was in Bavaria that Beddoes's political activism began in earnest; he became increasingly involved in the regional radical politics, joining the campaign for unification of the German states under a constitutional Prussian monarchy. Becoming a full member of the *Germania Burschenschaft*, he rose to a position of prominence in the organization unprecedented for a foreigner. He was a noted public speaker, and wrote some fine articles on European political themes for the *Bayerisches Volksblatt*, including themes such as the passage of the Reform Bill in the British Houses of Parliament, the Polish revolt against Russian rule, and the French government of Périer in the aftermath of the revolution of July 1830.

Having studiously antagonized the civic and academic authorities of Würzburg, Beddoes was deported from Bavaria in 1832, receiving a hero's send-off from fellow activists; he then travelled to Switzerland to join the growing community of European exiles and radicals, and matriculated in the university. He went first to Zürich and continued his career as an advocate of liberal causes; he was recommended for a chair in Anatomy in 1835 but was never appointed. He left Zürich in 1839, moving on to Berlin and then Frankfurt, and in 1844 went to Basel, where his friend Alfred Frey worked in the hospital, and where he met Konrad Degen. Beddoes formed a close relationship with Degen, and encouraged his theatrical interests by staging a production of Shakespeare's *Henry IV* as a vehicle for Degen's acting talent.[13]

---

11   See Kelsall's letter to Browning, June 1868: 'Your regret that TLB. did not send to the press DJB. when first completed, was always mine: & I urged that step at the time both to him & his . . . advisers Procter & Bourne, precisely for the reasons you express—but the two, conscious of his inestimable power, aimed at a perfecter offspring,—with a lamentable result.—He himself, I think w^d have liked to free his mind from some of its poetic foetuses . . .'. *The Browning Box*, pp. 108–09.

12   For some widely differing interpretations of this key crisis in TLB's writing career, see: Donner, *The Making of a Poet*, Ch. IX, 'The Poet'; Ian Jack, *English Literature, 1815–32*, pp. 140–41; Michael Bradshaw, *Resurrection Songs: The Poetry of Thomas Lovell Beddoes* (Aldershot and Burlington: Ashgate, 2001), pp. 103–05; and essays by Burwick and Halsey in this volume.

13   See Donner, *The Making of a Poet*, pp. 313–16.

During this time, *Death's Jest-Book* continued to grow and to change radically: Beddoes re-conceived his 'Fool's Tragedy' as an expansive lyrical drama, full of digression and ironic nuance. He completed a vastly expanded first act, which contains nine new songs, including two fine dirges sung by voices 'from the Waters': 'As sudden thunder / Pierces night' and 'The swallow leaves her nest'. The programme of revision was never completed, but even as a work-in-progress it represents a radical change of direction; Beddoes adopted a new sub-title, 'The Day Will Come'. In the 1830s, Beddoes was also working on a volume of prose tales and lyrics to be called *The Ivory Gate*, after the origin of false dreams in classical myth: miscellaneous lyrics and prose fragments survive. Rather than being a new departure as such, however, *The Ivory Gate* seems to have been intended to include the reconceived *Jest-Book*, the lifelong project that Beddoes, try as he might, could not escape from.

Beddoes made his last trip to England in 1846, making visits to London and to Shropshire, still the home of his extended family and from where he drew a rent from his property. He stayed for about ten months, a miserable time beset with depression and illness and misanthropic withdrawal from family and friends. By the time he left to return to Switzerland, he was widely considered insane, and his departure was a relief to many. In Frankfurt in the winter of 1847–48, Beddoes caught a serious infection while performing a dissection. He returned to Basel without Degen in 1848. Frey had him admitted to the hospital, where Beddoes made an attempt on his life. He first tried to kill himself with his surgical skill by opening an artery in his left leg, which was later amputated below the knee due to the spread of gangrene. Beddoes finally put his knowledge of drugs to effective use: on 26 January 1849, he left his hospital bed to buy the poison curare. He was found in his room later that day. Beddoes's friend Frey communicated to the family in England a bowdlerized version of a natural death from an apoplexy. Though this version was doubted by many, a full account of the facts only came to light in 1883, when Browning and Gosse opened the box of Beddoes's papers together, Beddoes's last letter having been brought home by his brother and included in the box of manuscripts by Kelsall.[14] The sense of dread and bogus versions of Beddoes's death can be traced in the critical literature far into the twentieth century.[15]

---

14   After the poet's death, his brother, his cousin Zoë King, and Kelsall visited Basel, and the information obtained by them raised the probability of suicide. Even after the facts were established, however, Gosse's entry for the *Dictionary of National Biography* (1885–1900) preserves the bogus story that TLB concocted to reassure his family, that he had initially injured his leg in a riding accident; after registering a slight hesitation, Gosse accepts the official version that TLB died of the subsequent infection. A corrected entry for the new edition of the *DNB* (2004) has now been written by Alan Halsey. Gosse reports having experienced a feeling of dread before opening the papers with his colleague, as if the box might contain a secret or scandal best left undisturbed: this uncanny atmosphere that seemed to linger around the texts themselves he later attributes to the imminent discovery of TLB's suicide; see Introduction to *Works*, pp. l–li, and *The Browning Box*, p. 136.

15   In 1928 Snow still adhered to this version; it seems to matter to him to disprove the prospect of actual suicide, even though—unlike Gosse—he acknowledges that TLB

The other aspect of Beddoes's life that his nineteenth-century inheritors found difficult to deal with was his likely homosexuality. Beddoes's early biographers, Kelsall, Snow, and Donner, are all hesitant to approach the topic explicitly. But reading between the lines of their works, one can detect a clear enough intuition that Beddoes was gay, and led a gay life in Europe: for example, Snow's solemn evaluation of the troubling impact Beddoes had on the wives and families of his English friends and relatives on his final visit to England in 1846, and his association with the nineteen-year-old Degen, 'a nice-looking young man dressed in a blue blouse, fine expression, and of a natural dignity of manner', are circumstantial evidence not only that Beddoes was indeed gay but also that this has been covertly acknowledged for a considerable time.[16]

The year after Beddoes's death, his untiring supporter and champion Thomas Forbes Kelsall published an edition of *Death's Jest-Book*;[17] followed shortly afterwards by *The Poems Posthumous and Collected of Thomas Lovell Beddoes*, which included his memoir of the poet, the most important source for biographical information.[18] It was Procter who introduced Kelsall to Browning; Kelsall had a cordial correspondence with Browning and soon resolved to bequeath him Beddoes's papers. There are signs in Browning's letters, however, that he may have tired of the Beddoes project

---

had made an attempt: 'There is no reason to doubt the honesty of [Frey's letter to William Minton Beddoes] . . . One must, in the face of such evidence, allow Beddoes the sorry comfort of a natural death, after his having failed to accomplish an unnatural one. Beddoes made mistakes but he never made them blindly. The end was taken out of his hands, and he did not die a suicide'. Thomas Lovell Beddoes: Eccentric and Poet, pp. 96–97.

16   Zoë King's description of Degen, quoted by Snow, pp. 87–91. The contents of TLB's own German letters to Tobler might be cited as a more direct testimony, especially the provocatively blasphemous passage in the first letter, which seems to thrive on sexual innuendo: 'O Leonhard, I would gladly take up the pen, if I could convince myself that a beam of Heavenly Light had touched your heart as well, that you too had renounced the sinful desires and appetites of the flesh: but I do fear that you still stand far—very far—away from this blessing. How I long to offer you a helping hand—not, like once, to perform unholy acts—but to lift you from the cesspool of iniquity, to which you tried to draw me, too, in vain (thank God). However, youth, I forgive you, and more; I wish to work with you until your are pierced by the beam of the Divine . . . But you must change, I know you will soon overcome the evil spirit within yourself, fall to your knees, and pray with a thankful ejaculation of semen . . . I hope I deceived you with the religious content of this page, which I didn't know how to fill in a better way'. H.W. Donner, 'T.L. Beddoes to Leonhard Tobler: Eight German Letters', *Studia Neophilologica*, 35.2 (1963), 227–35 (p. 234; editors' translation).

17   *Death's Jest-Book; or, The Fool's Tragedy* (London: William Pickering, 1850) was published anonymously and contains cuts and amendments made overtly by Kelsall on grounds of taste.

18   *The Poems Posthumous and Collected of Thomas Lovell Beddoes, with a Memoir*, ed. T.F. Kelsall, 2 vols (London: William Pickering, 1851).

and was happy enough to defer to Gosse as the next prominent editor.[19] Gosse played a valuable role in exposing Beddoes to a popular readership with his *Poetical Works* (1890);[20] but in fact it was neither he nor Browning who made the most lasting contribution to the state of the texts, but James Dykes Campbell, who accomplished a full transcription of all extant works around 1886 but did not live to make a definitive edition—the work which was eventually completed by Donner in the 1930s.

II Critical history

The critical evaluation of Beddoes is changing. If this introduction were being written five years ago, Beddoes's far less prominent place in the canons of literature and Romanticism would make a material difference to the way he ought to be framed for continuing reading, study and discussion. The cautions would be deeper and more pronounced, the note of critical apology for devoting substantial publishing space to Beddoes would probably still persist. Recent scholarly and theatrical events encourage us to believe, however, that Beddoes's status is undergoing a major international shift and that he may yet come to prominence as the widely acknowledged and important voice in nineteenth-century writing we feel he should be. For the numerous admirers of Beddoes's writing, with its involved imagery, imaginative intensity and complex irony, this re-evaluation is long overdue, so why is it taking place now? Though questions like these remain unanswerable in principle, two general considerations may be put forward. Arguably, the rediscovery of Beddoes's demanding work has been aided by recent efforts critically to re-read national canons and question their criteria of exclusion. Beddoes's life and death in particular supply good grounds for believing that his texts have long been shunned for its author's suspected homosexuality and ascertained suicide. A related tendency that may have recently worked in Beddoes's favour is a new sensitivity to the crucial contribution made by voices on the margin, voices hard to classify, to our perception of a given period and the cultural forces active in it. Beddoes's uniting or, alternatively, struggling with the roles of poet and scientist, political radical, and sexual deviant in the life of an exile holds out a number of perspectives inevitably destined to question the priorities of any of his chosen cultural environments.

As we will argue presently, Beddoes's alleged change in canonical status, work-in-progress as it is, is shaped in many respects by the determination to situate his work and its complex poetics in a more adequate way by drawing on new theoretical and historical or cultural contexts. Having said this, we must point out

---

19   See, e.g., Browning's reaction to being bequeathed all the Beddoes papers: 'I have many precious M.S.S, which I, too, am anxious should only belong, after my death, to the appreciative. Wherever I bestow these,—the papers of Beddoes shall likewise be laid up . . .'. *The Browning Box*, p. 116.

20   *The Poetical Works of Thomas Lovell Beddoes*, ed. with a Memoir by Edmund Gosse (London: Dent, 1890).

immediately that the manifest difficulty in placing this strange author runs like a thread through earlier criticism too. Yet many of the earlier debates, enlightening as they are, tended to be guided by a general concern with periodization. Though profiting from this work, more recent studies have outlined a contrasting agenda based on the assumption that there are contexts more specific and illuminating to refer to than the homogenizing idea of the literary 'period'. Moreover, they have begun to pay closer attention to the political pressures operating in these contexts.

Thus widening the frame of the discussion by working with and towards a far more heterogeneous notion of 'period', and by vigorously pluralizing the theoretical inroads into that period, recent criticism of Beddoes has opened up new vistas even where it has revisited apparently familiar topics. After briefly narrating the early stages and some chronological peculiarities of Beddoes's critical history, we will take a closer look at the illuminating attempts, old and new, to somehow 'place' this extraordinary author. From there we will move on to survey crucial or recurring issues of the critical discussion, focusing also on some previously neglected aspects. A preview of the present collection of essays will fall into place against this framework.

There are good reasons for arguing that the erratic history of Beddoes criticism, especially during and immediately after his lifetime, a history that is bound up with the textual history of his work, has contributed in no small degree to the perceived problem of placing the poet. The earliest reaction to Beddoes's writing dates from 1821 and is a review of his extravagantly grisly *The Improvisatore, in three fyttes*, now usually regarded as juvenilia: the reviewer is appalled by the young Beddoes's shock tactics: '*Fits* indeed! hysterical decidedly. Let the reader judge from this battle-piece . . . Have we not "supped full of horrors?"'[21] Indeed, on many readers' first acquaintance, the most striking feature of Beddoes's writing is its obsession with violence, death, and decay: this early review begins a lasting intertextual habit of using Beddoes's characteristic macabre as a critical vocabulary with which to evaluate him. The striking difference in tone in all of the reviews attracted by *The Brides' Tragedy*, published just the following year, indicates how fast Beddoes had developed as a writer and how skilful he could be at accommodating his vision to a popular taste, if he chose to. Bryan Waller Procter, John Wilson, and George Darley, all well-known critics at that time, consistently praised the tragedy and indicated that a bright future lay ahead for the young author. Darley cites Beddoes at length in his 'Letter to the Dramatists of the Day', partly to put his mediocre contemporaries to shame in being so bested by a young boy:

> I am almost tempted to confess after the perusal of our Minor's poem,
> that I have been premature in pronouncing the decline of English
> poetry from the Byronian epoch: and to express my confidence that

---

21 Anon., review of *The Improvisatore*, in *The Monthly Review; or Literary Journal*, enlarged, 95 (1821), 218–19.

> tragedy has once again put forth a scion worthy of the stock from
> which Shakespeare and Marlow sprung.[22]

An anonymous reviewer for *The Gentleman's Magazine* wrote of Beddoes's 'fine originality', stating that 'a brighter promise (not Chatterton excepted) was never offered by youthful genius'.[23] Critics were divided on the question of whether Beddoes could really write for the stage, or whether he was essentially a lyric poet not suited to drama; they identified certain flaws and implied an arch sense of indulging youthful excess; but they were all highly positive about the author's talent.[24] Urged on by this considerable success with a tough, and at times vindictive, literary press, Beddoes worked fast at writing several new plays, but never published another full-length work in his life.[25] There is therefore a long hiatus in published critical assessments, from 1823 until 1851, when Kelsall included a memoir of the poet's life with his edition of *The Poems Posthumous and Collected*. As a consequence, Beddoes's most substantial work *Death's Jest-Book*, first intended for publication in 1829, was not appreciated on a par with that of its contemporaries. By the time the continuously revised text was posthumously published and discussed, it had already become a 'contemporary' of Elizabeth Barrett Browning's *Aurora Leigh*, and thus brought with it the pervading sense of pastness described by Virginia Woolf when comparing the two.[26] Reviews of Kelsall's and Gosse's editions of the major works appeared intermittently in the latter half of the century: occasional reviews and memorial articles vary widely in the amount of sympathy they seem willing to extend to the writer of disturbingly erotic and macabre works, which have begun to seem distasteful: 'If Beddoes was misled into producing bad work, so was many another, but none was so far misled as he'.[27] Nineteenth-century assessments of Beddoes may almost be divided up into ardent and sympathetic supporters on the one hand, and those intent on exposing his flaws and faults on the other.

While the critical fate of Beddoes's work in the nineteenth century is determined not least by the wide gap occurring in the first half of it, critical appreciation in the twentieth century owes much of its shape to the opposite phenomenon—a sudden abundance in the 1930s. Three seminal publications in 1935 effectively dictated the direction of critical work on Beddoes for the remainder of the century and beyond.

---

22 'John Lacy' (George Darley), 'A Sixth Letter to the Dramatists of the Day', *The London Magazine*, 8 (1823), 645–52 (p. 648).
23 Anon., 'Reviews of Miscellaneous Publications', *The Gentleman's Magazine*, 93.2 (1823), 347.
24 The other reviews of *The Brides' Tragedy* are: Procter (anon.), in *The London Magazine*, 7 (1823), 169–72; Anon., 'On Ancient and Modern Tragedy', *The Album*, 3.5 (1823), 1–31; and Wilson (anon.), 'Notices of the Modern British Dramatists, No. II. Beddoes', *Blackwood's Edinburgh Magazine*, 14.83 (1823), 723–29.
25 *The Last Man, Love's Arrow Poisoned, Torrismond* and *The Second Brother* date from the period in between the publication of *The Brides' Tragedy* and TLB's departure for Germany in the summer of 1825.
26 See Prologue above.
27 Anon., review of the Gosse edn, *The Athenaeum*, 3296 (1890), 881.

H.W. Donner edited the definitive *Works*, printing every known text by the author, editing a large number of texts from James Dykes Campbell's transcription (c. 1886) that had never seen the light before, and including translations from and original writings in German. This edition has never been improved upon; for its sheer comprehensiveness and attention to detail, it seems certain to remain the standard scholarly text, and most of the essays in this volume have used it as their principal source.[28] In the same year, Donner published his critical biography, *Thomas Lovell Beddoes: The Making of a Poet*, which narrates the poet's life with humanity and compassion; the way Donner charts the emotional fortunes of his protagonist very often has a tragic temper, and this may have contributed to Beddoes's faltering reputation as an outcast wanderer, a casualty in the margins of his historical epoch. At least as significant as this biography as a resource for new work is *The Browning Box*, Donner's edited collection of the correspondence between literary executors and editors after the poet's death. With such a fractured set of literary 'remains', it is important to have a clear sense of the transmission history, and Donner's collection readily provides this, as well as valuable notes on the key players. Donner's lasting influence is still felt, not only in the extraordinary quality of his scholarship and our continuing reliance on his *Works* but also in the association between Beddoes and Uppsala, where articles on the poet have been and continue to be published by the journal *Studia Neophilologica*.

If the erratic publication history, as well as the stops and starts of the displaced critical debates dependent on it, go some way towards accounting for the widely perceived difficulty of properly situating Beddoes in the nineteenth century, this largely external factor is complemented by a conspicuous feature intrinsic to his voice—the so called 'archaism' of his style. This prominent feature of his texts has been interpreted very differently, according to the observer's historical point of view. For example, the idea that Beddoes was addicted to period pastiche and unable to find an authentic voice from his own age is as familiar as it is frequently expressed; and yet it was not until the twentieth century that critics first began to make this argument, the classic instance being 'The Last Elizabethan', an essay by Lytton Strachey published in 1907.[29] Ezra Pound's essay 'Beddoes and Chronology' (1913) extends the debate beyond simplistic ventriloquism to consider what might now be called self-conscious displacement or stylistic self-fashioning, leaving the question of where—or when—Beddoes belongs interrogatively open:

> *Can a man write poetry in a purely archaic dialect? Presumably he*
> *can, and Beddoes has done so; but would not this poetry, his poetry be*
> *more effective, would not its effectiveness be much more lasting if he*
> *had used real speech instead of a language which may have been used*

---

28   See Note on Texts below.

29   Lytton Strachey, 'The Last Elizabethan' (1907), in *Book and Characters, French and English* (1922), pp. 225–52. Barnette Miller was probably the first critic to cite Webster and Tourneur as influences on TLB's style, also in the very early twentieth century, in 'Thomas Lovell Beddoes', *The Sewanee Review*, 11 (1903), 305–36 (pp. 323 ff.).

> on the early Victorian stage, but certainly had no existence in the life
> of his era?[30]

F.L. Lucas continued the debate on period and archaism, comparing Beddoes to Chatterton in his apparent inability to write well in a contemporary idiom, and the freedoms that he found in the past: Beddoes is most *himself* when 'masquerading as a Jacobean'.[31] But the relatively late appearance of this issue, and what is now a standard line on Beddoes's dramatic style, indicates how acceptable and even commonplace the practice of Elizabethan/Jacobean revival was in the England of the 1820s—and a sense of this context paradoxically puts Beddoes securely 'back' in his own generation. Writers such as Charles Lamb, Bryan Waller Procter, and Henry Hart Milman did much to keep Renaissance styles and generic forms before a reading public; when *The Brides' Tragedy* was published in 1822, notwithstanding some reservations and ironies, none of its contemporary critics asked why Beddoes was borrowing from the past, since most of Darley's wretched 'Dramatists of the Day' were doing this as well; there were no jibes about ventriloquism or masquerade. It was partly the loss of this sense of popular context that contributed to the widespread concern with archaism in early twentieth-century assessments, when for a time Beddoes's aesthetic obsession with verse tragedy was incorrectly thought to be exceptional.

Critical discussion of Beddoes's dramas needs to move on from 'the last Elizabethan', which he never was, and to re-discover the complexity of Beddoes's representation of history, for example in the multi-layered ironic anachronisms of *Death's Jest-Book*. Beddoes's complex relationship with and use of forebears from the English Renaissance remains an important area for further study, precisely because it does not divorce him from his nineteenth-century contemporaries, as was once thought, but places his work squarely 'in his own day'.[32] Terence Hoagwood is not the only one to claim that, intentionally or not, Romantic plays' 'ideological content and political importance are customarily displaced symbolically and dispersed across exotic, magical, or historically removed surface content'.[33] The analysis of the stylistic disguises or 'archaisms', as well as the mediaeval locations and magical feats, in Beddoes work may well take its cue from the recent interest in Romantic drama as

---

30   Ezra Pound, 'Beddoes and Chronology' (1913), in *Selected Prose, 1909–1965*, ed. William Cookson (London: Faber and Faber, 1973), pp. 348–53 (p. 351).

31   F.L. Lucas, 'Death's Jester', *Life and Letters*, 5 (1930), 219–45 (p. 235).

32   Other studies of TLB's relationship with Renaissance drama include: Donner, *The Making of a Poet*, esp. Chs 3, 4 and 8, a substantial discussion which unfortunately tends to assume 'indiscriminate borrowing from old plays' (p. 92); and a study of source material in Charles Alva Hoyt, *Studies in Thomas Lovell Beddoes* (unpublished doctoral dissertation, Columbia University, 1961). An alternative approach based on intertextual dialogue rather than passive influence can be found in Bradshaw, *Resurrection Songs*, pp. 54–57.

33   'Prolegomenon for a Theory of Romantic Drama', *Wordsworth Circle*, 23.2 (1992), 49–64 (p. 51).

a genre under pressure, a genre best analyzed in relation to its contemporary history and culture.[34]

Yet reference to contemporary culture indicates only one of the directions today's critics may wish to follow. Eleanor Wilner (1975), for instance, identifying some of the confusion that surrounds Beddoes's use of the Elizabethans, actually suggests a very different approach for breaking out of the restrictions imposed by the antiquarian model:

> It is this adoption of Elizabethan language and conventions by Beddoes that has cloaked for so many his modernity and led them to see him as archaic, simply because he had a vision for which a form did not yet exist. Beddoes, in trying to embody that vision, invented the expressionist drama in English through his manipulation of the Elizabethan conventions in such a way as to both mock the significance of the tradition which they embodied, and overthrow the sense of reality of his own day.[35]

This approach to Beddoes's Elizabethanism as an expressionist means for transcending the period in which the work was produced, and for 'overthrow[ing] the sense of reality of his own day', tallies with other voices pointing to Beddoes's proto-Modernist sensibility which we will return to in a moment.

As already indicated, questions of periodization in the narrow sense have also contributed to the debate on how best to situate Beddoes and his texts. No matter how the lines are drawn, the author's biography almost invariably straddles the border between Romanticism and Victorianism. Hence, the Modernists' enquiry into a language that had 'no existence in the life of [the author's] era' gave way, in the second half of the century, to a number of attempts to make sense of Beddoes's poetry and drama within the mainstream of English literature with Romanticism as the most obvious category for an alignment. John Heath-Stubbs (1950) writes of Beddoes as one of a group of belated Romantics, including Hood and Darley, 'born too late into an uncongenial world' and unable to make the necessary compromise with the world of Victorian propriety.[36] Ian Jack returned to the theme of 'belatedness' and its impact on canonical status in his assessment of Beddoes of 1963: in an influential argument, Jack suggests that the failure to publish *Death's Jest-Book* in 1829 had an arresting effect on Beddoes's writing from which he never recovered; the analogy is made with Keats's bolder decision to publish of *Endymion*, when he risked all the pains of venomous rejection, but was then able to develop into the poet of *Hyperion* and the great odes.[37] An essay by Harold Bloom in *The*

---

34   See n. 67 below.
35   Eleanor Wilner, *Gathering the Winds: Visionary Imagination and Radical Transformation of Self and Society* (Baltimore and London: The Johns Hopkins University Press, 1975), p. 83.
36   Heath-Stubbs, *The Darkling Plain*, p. 22.
37   Jack, p. 141.

Visionary Company (1961) attempted to accommodate Beddoes to the 'high' Romantic paradigm of imagination as apocalyptic fusion: the inclusion of Beddoes in this study was a positive statement in itself, and yet Bloom seems to take an essentially negative line on Beddoes's achievement, foregrounding self-defeat and making a familiar easy connection with the poet's undoubted biographical misfortunes:

> *Beddoes, in despair of his time and of himself, chose to waste his genius on a theme that baffled his own imagination. The postulate of Beddoes's poetry is a world in which every metaphor resolves itself as another figure of death. For Beddoes the separation between subject and object is bridged not by any imaginative act . . . but by dying.*[38]

As Beddoes's status in the canon of Romantic literature continues to change quickly, it becomes important to re-assess in more detail his relationships with forebears and contemporaries. Michael O'Neill's reading of Beddoes's relationship with his most admired poetic mentor, P.B. Shelley, in terms of the 'immortality' of literary reputation, is one recent intertextual study (1999) pursuing this rewarding line of inquiry.[39]

If Bloom's essay has epitomized the Romantic Beddoes, Christopher Ricks makes the case for Beddoes as a significant Victorian author. Editing *The New Oxford Book of Victorian Verse* (1987), Ricks takes the bold step of opening the volume with Thomas Lovell Beddoes, represented by nine poems and followed by Alfred, Lord Tennyson. Referring to the reign of Queen Victoria (1837–1901) as an editorial guideline, Ricks admits that Beddoes' is 'the only truly tricky case' of the volume.[40] Yet he points out that *Death's Jest-Book* was under revision up to 1849 and argues, furthermore, that some of Beddoes's early poems are included 'because none of them was published until 1851, when they contributed powerfully to Victorian not to Georgian literature, and because Beddoes was for half his adult life a Victorian'.[41] In fact, Ricks's editorial practice acts on his own earlier appreciation of Beddoes in *The Force of Poetry* (1984) as someone who 'did not invent the dramatic monologue, but was alive to its essential pressures, the silent interlocutor', thus occupying a significant position in relation to a major development in Victorian poetry.[42]

---

38   Harold Bloom, *The Visionary Company: A Reading of English Romantic Poetry* (London and New York: Faber and Faber, 1962), p. 434.

39   Michael O'Neill, '"A Storm of Ghosts": Beddoes, Shelley, Death and Reputation', *Cambridge Quarterly*, 28.2 (1999), 102–15.

40   Christopher Ricks, Introduction to *The New Oxford Book of Victorian Verse* (Oxford: Oxford University Press, 1987), p. xxxi.

41   Ibid., p. xxxi.

42   An analogous quotation is included in Prologue above, 'A Dying start', p. 155. A similar observation on the proximity of TLB's poetry to the dramatic monologue is made by Franz Wieselhuber (who does not acknowledge Ricks), in 'Thomas Lovell Beddoes', in *Beyond the Suburbs of the Mind: Exploring English Romanticism*, ed. Michael Gassenmeier and Norbert H. Platz. (Essen: Verlag die blaue Eule, 1987) p. 179.

Beyond these arguments in favour of Beddoes's nineteenth-century alignments, a strong case for the proto-Modernist features of his work may also be made. Northrop Frye is the critic who has done most to highlight Beddoes's affinity with modern and specifically Modernist literature and theory. Frye's essay 'Yorick: The Romantic Macabre' (1968) makes a compelling argument that Beddoes's dramatic style anticipates the European theatre of the absurd in its experimental performance of human alienation.[43] Frye's reading of the *Jest-Book* is significant also because he acknowledges the importance of Beddoes's comedy, another strong contrast with Bloom. Frye's crucial observations on the modern aspects of Beddoes's work are corroborated by the Modernists themselves: Pound not only wrote a critical appreciation of Beddoes but also included him as a ghostly presence in Canto LXXX (quoted in the Prologue above). There is also evidence in Pound's annotations to Eliot's *The Waste Land* that he encouraged in his friend a taste for Beddoes.[44] Christopher Ricks's close analysis of Beddoes's verse and syntax (1982–84) also suggests affinities with Pound and Eliot.[45]

We may even speculate whether Beddoes's revival in the twentieth century would ever have taken place if it had not been for the serious attention the Modernists paid to his work. Irrespective of subject matter and genre, it is Beddoes's language, dense with complex imagery, that has arguably appealed most to a Modernist poetics. Even more informative for the Modernist context than Saintsbury's praise quoted above may be his statement that, 'except Donne, there is perhaps no English poet more difficult to write about, so as to preserve the due pitch of enthusiasm on the one hand and criticism on the other, than Thomas Lovell Beddoes . . .'.[46] As if to develop this comparison, Grete Moldauer discusses Beddoes as a self-confessed lover of conceits, claiming that he does not express but rather represents feeling in an often abstract fashion, drawing on a language that becomes poetic 'through the thoughts and associations of sentiments it knows how to enforce, through novel combinations of quality and contrastive effects'.[47] Moldauer deploys this characterization to place Beddoes outside the Romantic 'mainstream'. Implicitly, however, she also situates Beddoes within Eliot's powerful paradigm of a 'dissociation of sensibility' (1921), developed in his attempt to free poets from Donne to Cowley—to the detriment of the Romantics—from 'coddl[ing] antiquarian affection' in order to re-evaluate them

---

43   Northrop Frye, 'Yorick: The Romantic Macabre', in *A Study of English Romanticism* (New York: Random House, 1968; repr. London: Harvester, 1983), pp. 51–85.

44   See *The Waste Land: A facsimile and transcript of the original drafts including the annotations of Ezra Pound*, ed. Valerie Eliot (London: Faber and Faber, 1971; repr. 1980), pp. 10–11.

45   Christopher Ricks, 'Thomas Lovell Beddoes: "A dying start"', *Grand Street*, 1 (1982), 32–48; and 3 (1984), 90–102; repr. in *The Force of Poetry* (Oxford: Oxford University Press, 1984), pp. 135–62.

46   George Saintsbury, *A History of Nineteenth Century Literature, 1780–1900* (1896; London: Macmillan, 1906), p. 114.

47   Grete Moldauer, *Thomas Lovell Beddoes* (Wien and Leipzig: Wilhelm Braunmüller, 1924), p. 43; editors' translation.

'in the direct current of English poetry'.[48] One might even argue that Beddoes's recovery by Modernist critics owes much to their simultaneous rediscovery of Metaphysical poetry. Drawing heavily on the metaphysical tradition and Cowley in particular, Beddoes dismayed his contemporaries but delighted the Modernists, many of whose sensibilities he shared.[49]

Irrespective of how plausible individual attempts to locate Beddoes within the established periods of English literary history may be, it seems that Beddoes's work highlights the very problem of periodization itself, just as much as the problem of national canon-formation. After all, the necessary complement to the 'English' Beddoes—the author of Elizabethan pastiche tragedies and Shelleyan Romantic lyrics—is of course Beddoes as naturalized German, the author of German political and satirical tracts, the translator of Schiller and Walter von der Vogelweide, the eulogist of David Friedrich Strauss, and the emulator of the Romantic ironist Ludwig Tieck.[50] In this role, he is a writer also of the repressive *Restaurationsperiode* as well as of the revolutionary German *Vormärz* up to 1848. This makes Beddoes, despite his interest in the German *Klassik* and early Romanticists, an immediate contemporary of such eminent nineteenth-century figures as Heinrich Heine, Georg Büchner, Christian Dietrich Grabbe, and the authors of the 'Junges Deutschland'. Considering that Beddoes moved to Germany in his early twenties and produced the largest part of his work there, we have as yet a very unsatisfactory understanding of the extent of his engagement with German culture. Weber's diligent study of the political context of Beddoes's time in Germany (1935) or Grete Moldauer's appreciation of his style and literary relations to German authors (1924)—both written in German—have often been passed by.[51] Assessments customarily rely on the ground-breaking researches of Donner and on Jon W. Lundin's documentation of Beddoes's reading in the Göttingen years.[52] Anne Harrex's article on the evidence of German philosophy and aesthetics in *Death's Jest-Book* still stands out for the depth of its insight, enlarging on Donner's view of the operation of 'Romantic irony'

---

48   T.S. Eliot, 'The Metaphysical Poets' (1921), in *Selected Prose of T.S. Eliot*, ed. with an introduction by Frank Kermode (London: Faber and Faber, 1980), pp. 64, 66.

49   Having read the manuscript version of *Death's Jest-Book*, Bryan Waller Procter accused TLB of the use of conceits; TLB admits in reply that he is, 'alas, a little partial' to this stylistic device, recalling that 'Cowley was the first poetical writer I learned to understand' (letter, 19 April 1829, *Works*, p. 642).

50   TLB's translations of 'Philosophic Letters of Schiller', first published in 1825, Works, pp. 549–59; TLB's German poetry (Works, pp. 143–52 and 701–06) includes his satirical 'anti-Strauss greeting', 'Antistraussianischer Gruss an einen Herrn Antistes' (1839).

51   Carl August Weber, *Bristols Bedeutung für die Englische Romantik und die Deutsch-Englischen Beziehungen* (1935; Tübingen: Max Niemeyer, 1973). Though this study appeared in the same year as Donner's key publications, Donner makes great use of Weber's study and praises his 'brilliant research', responsible not least for the identification of TLB's political prose in the *Bayerisches Volksblatt*; see also Grete Moldauer, *Thomas Lovell Beddoes*.

52   Jon W. Lundin, 'T.L. Beddoes at Göttingen', *Studia Neophilologica*, 43 (1971), 484–99.

in the drama.[53] The contemporary critic who has done most work on the German contexts is Frederick Burwick, whose comparative study of Beddoes's grotesque and the writing of Georg Büchner significantly opts to narrate Beddoes not from the familiar Romantic Bristol of the 1790s but, rather, beginning in Zürich in 1836, which is a statement in itself.[54] Taking our cue from there, we believe that the perception of Beddoes in a European framework will not only broaden our understanding of his texts but also illuminate the intercultural contours of nineteenth-century writing. Though he did not command and influence a wide contemporary audience like Coleridge, who had spent time in Göttingen almost thirty years earlier, Beddoes's texts testify to his significant role as cultural mediator—a role calling for further exploration. Recent research by Christopher Moylan into Beddoes's knowledge and use of Jewish doctrine offers a glimpse of the fascinating diversity of his intercultural appropriations.[55]

Despite a certain 'centralizing' tendency in some of the studies discussed—attempting, for instance, to pull Beddoes towards major literary categories—there have always been critical strands with a focus on specific topics, and, as may already have been noticed, recent scholarship in particular has begun to engage more boldly with the large number of available contexts for interpretation and the issues emerging from them. One enduring critical theme that has just been broached in the Modernist context is the form and structure of Beddoes's work. Critics of Beddoes often have an instinctive preference either for his lyrical poems or for his dramatic blank verse. Notable champions of his blank verse include Strachey and Pound, whereas H.W. Donner is keenly interested in the metrical qualities of Beddoes's lyricism throughout his biography. Formal features discussed more recently include Beddoes's dextrous linguistic creativity, worth the sustained attention of the editors of the OED;[56] as well as the overall shape of his work. 'It is difficult to read through', wrote F.L. Lucas of Beddoes's *oeuvre* as a whole, 'I have done so twice, and never shall again. But I return with ever fresh astonishment to his fragments'.[57] Due to a combination of editorial accident (such as the eventual loss of the 'Browning box' of manuscripts) and his own piecemeal writing habits, many of Beddoes's texts

---

53 Anne Harrex, '*Death's Jest-Book* and the German Contribution', *Studia Neophilologica*, 39 (1967), 15–37 and 302–18.

54 Frederick Burwick, 'Death's Fool: Beddoes and Büchner', in *The Haunted Eye: Perception and the Grotesque in English and German Romanticism* (Heidelberg: Carl Winter, 1987), pp. 274–300. Burwick's research also includes studies of TLB's political context and his journalistic work; c.f. 'Beddoes, Bayern und die Burschenschaften', *Comparative Literature*, 21.4 (1969), pp. 289–306, and 'Beddoes and the Schweizerischer Republikaner, *Studia Neophilologica* 44.1 (1972), pp. 90–112.

55 Christopher Moylan, '"For Luz is a Good Joke": Thomas Lovell Beddoes and Jewish Eschatology', in *British Romanticism and the Jews*, ed. Sheila Spector (New York: Palgrave, 2002), pp. 93–103.

56 Greg Crossan, 'Thomas Lovell Beddoes's *Death's Jest-Book*: An *OED* Oversight', *Notes & Queries*, 247 (2002), 486–89, and 'Unnoticed Words in Beddoes for *OED*', Notes & Queries, 248 (2003), 446–53.

57 F.L. Lucas, 'Death's Jester', *Life and Letters*, 5 (1930), 219–45 (p. 245).

exist in a state of complex disarray; and ever since the earliest reviewers drew attention to a certain unevenness and neglect of form in *The Brides' Tragedy*, critics have been interested by Beddoes's propensity to generate radiant moments of poetry that are never resolved into a coherent whole.[58] The indeterminate qualities of Beddoes's writing have been discussed in the most recent monograph on the author, *Resurrection Songs* by Michael Bradshaw, which connects the conceptual preoccupations of Beddoes's work with the idea of fragmentation.[59]

Beddoes's use of dramatic genre and his relation to the stage is yet another topic with an impressive tradition, moreover one that is gaining renewed force. Strachey's essay from early 1907 is significant for a most untypical interest in the stage. Strachey attests to a hope that *Death's Jest-Book* will one day be performed, not now in the 'melancholy condition' of the theatre in 1907, but at some future date: 'Then, and only then, shall we be able to make the true measure of Beddoes' genius'.[60] All of Beddoes's dramas, including unfinished texts such as *The Last Man* and *The Second Brother*, have at one time or another been designated closet drama, 'mental theatre', or otherwise unsuited to the stage, either by design or by indisputable temperament. The large number of critics who round on *Death's Jest-Book* in particular as 'un-performable', except presumably in the interior space of the reading experience, is evidence that Beddoes's reputation has been deeply influenced by a tradition of disparagement towards the Romantics' attempts to write drama.[61] Typified by David V. Erdman's influential reading of Byron's ambivalent and troubled relationship with the theatre, 'Byron's Stage Fright' (1939), there has existed a long-standing presumption that the Romantics could not 'do' drama for reasons intrinsically rooted in what made them Romantic in the first place—the constant preoccupation with subjective experience and internal reflection, the desire for uninterrupted intensity, the general frame of mind that finds its definitive expression in the lyric poem.[62] In light of this problem, the exact sense in which Beddoes's writing may be considered 'dramatic' has been the subject of much critical debate; the debate continues among recent commentators. James R. Thompson (1985) favours the 'mental theatre' model and interprets Beddoes's dramas in terms of subjective monodrama, writing of *The Brides' Tragedy*:

---

58   Donner calls TLB 'a poet of fragments', in Introduction to *Works*, p. xxiii.
59   See *Resurrection Songs*, esp. Ch. 2.
60   Strachey, pp. 244 and 245.
61   Barnette Miller serves as quite an aggressive early example of the dismissive attitude to the prospect of TLB as poet of the stage: 'Beddoes, in a letter dated February, 1829, says that it should be the typical aim of a dramatist to produce a drama to be acted, and that its fitness for this purpose is the most thorough test. It is scarcely to be credited that he thought "Death's Jest Book" practical for presentation on the stage, for his perception of his own shortcomings was ordinarily so keen, it is not likely that he was deceived in this instance. He must therefore have written "Death's Jest Book" solely for his own amusement'. Miller, p. 327.
62   David V. Erdman, 'Byron's Stage Fright: The History of his Ambition and Fear of Writing for the Stage', *English Literary History*, 6 (1939), 219–43.

The action ... is metaphorical, not sociohistorical. The work 'dramatizes' in the largest sense, Beddoes's spiritual, thence aesthetic predicament; the choice of drama provides an occasion for poetic eloquence and a reassuring, traditionally significant container, for a radically pessimistic vision. . . .[63]

He goes on to argue that *Death's Jest-Book* can be read as an expansive 'monodramatic' experiment, citing *Faust* and *Manfred* as analogies.[64] Alan Richardson (1988) also discusses the connection between an immaterial 'stage' and Romantic subjectivity;[65] while Daniel P. Watkins (1989) offers a materialist reading of *The Brides' Tragedy* as a dramatization of anxieties of gender and social class, in which Romantic drama as 'a literary form in crisis' is fraught with the tensions between past and present.[66]

Since then, the notion of the closet, now perceived as ranging from a mental space to the concrete space of private readings, and investigations into reader-response patterns and political agency, have crucially expanded the notion of the closet or mental theatre.[67] At the same time, critics have drawn attention to the theatre of Romanticism and its real stages as a site where issues of gender and nation took shape, while a new understanding of the relation of licensed and unlicensed plays and theatrical locations has opened up new contexts for situating individual plays and performances. We believe that the analysis of Beddoes's major texts is destined to benefit greatly from this resurgent interest in Romantic drama. In fact, in 2003 a version of *Death's Jest-Book* was put on stage, thus forming the first ever stage production of Beddoes's central dramatic work.[68] The very act of producing this

---

63   James R. Thompson, *Thomas Lovell Beddoes* (Boston: Twayne, 1985), p. 33
64   Thompson, p. 61.
65   Alan Richardson, '*Death's Jest-Book*: "Shadows of Words"', in *A Mental Theater: Poetic Drama and Consciousness in the Romantic Age* (University Park, Penn., and London: Pennsylvania State University Press, 1988), pp. 154–73.
66   Daniel P. Watkins, 'Thomas Lovell Beddoes's The Brides' Tragedy and the Situation of Romantic Drama', *Studies in English Literature 1500–1900*, 29 (1989), 699–712 (p. 710).
67   For some significant developments in the interpretation of dramatic performance in Romantic culture, see e.g.: Catherine B. Burroughs, *Closet Stages: Joanna Baillie and the Theater Theory of British Romantic Women Writers* (Philadelphia: University of Pennsylvania Press, 1997); Frederick Burwick, *Illusion and the Drama: Critical Theory of the Enlightenment and Romantic Drama* (University Park: Pennsylvania State University Press, 1991), and 'The Romantic Drama', in *A Companion to Romanticism*, ed. Duncan Wu (Oxford: Blackwell, 1998), pp. 323–32; Jeffrey N. Cox and Michael Gamer (eds), *In the Shadows of Romance: Romantic Tragic Drama in Germany, England and France* (Athens: Ohio University Press, 1987); Thomas C. Crochunis (ed.), Joanna Baillie, *Romantic Dramatist: Critical Essays* (New York: Routledge, 2004); and Daniel P. Watkins, *A Materialist Critique of English Romantic Drama* (Gainesville: University Press of Florida, 1993). See also essays by Berns and Leach in this collection.
68   Prior to this, we only know of the production of a version of TLB's fragment *The Second Brother* undertaken by the Maddermarket Theatre in Norwich: see Anon., 'Review of a performance of *The Second Brother* at the Maddermarket Theatre, Norwich', *The Times* (London), 2 April 1935, p. 12.

play constitutes a break with mainstream critical opinion, which has deemed the text unstageable, and it is no accident that two respected scholars of the Romantic period, Jerome J. McGann and Frederick Burwick, were involved in the event. These performances, complete with orchestra and special effects, totally revitalize the debate about Beddoes's theatricality.[69] It remains to be seen how this will bear, not least, on the question of Beddoes's relation to the tradition and contemporary development of German play-writing.

If traditional assumptions about mental theatre as devoted to internal dialogue and self-exegesis tend to foster analysis in psychological and psychoanalytic terms, these approaches have been encouraged, in Beddoes's case, by the poet's unsparing representation of death and decay. Early psychological stirrings can be observed in John Sparrow's essay of 1930, when he states that as a child Beddoes received practical lessons in morbid anatomy from his father, a theme taken up less cryptically by H.W. Donner in 1935.[70] One of Donner's most lasting critical judgements in his biography of Beddoes was the alleged 'skeleton complex', according to which the poet supposedly received from his father's progressive scientific practices a horror of the human body and its decay and dissolution, producing in the subject a trauma which sought expression and exorcism in his imaginative writing—a thought argued more subtly than its later ironic treatment as a loose conflation of life and works may seem to allow.[71] In Donner's view, it was the discovery of Romantic irony among the German writers and its importation into the developing *Jest-Book* that resolved this crisis. Less subtly, Daniela Tandecki holds Beddoes's exposure to death and dying responsible for the negation of life in his work and for his suicide.[72] And a blunt use of psychoanalysis can be found in a full-blown forensic diagnosis of the poet by Hiram Kellogg Johnson (1943), who astonishingly judges a sexually repressed Beddoes to be 'without humor'.[73] The psychoanalytic tradition continued with Charles Alva Hoyt's Freudian reading of father-son

---

69   C.f. *Death's Jest-Book: A posthumous theatrical travesty, in three acts*, translated by Jerome McGann, from the original dramatical fantasia by Thomas Lovell Beddoes (Belper: Thomas Lovell Beddoes Society, 2003). Both McGann and Burwick write critical accounts of the process of bringing Beddoes to the stage below. The production was staged in Los Angeles, New York, and Grasmere, throughout 2003. See Michael Bradshaw, 'Review of the Performance of Death's Jest-Book' (NASSR, August 2003, Fordham University), *European Romantic Review*, 15.2 (2004), 387–90.

70   John Sparrow, 'Dr Beddoes', *Farrago*, 3 (1930), 135–48.

71   Donner actually traces a line from TLB's childhood familiarity with death through a literary fashion for the morbid, which TLB emulated in his schoolboy Gothic prose tale *Scaroni* (1818) and then *The Improvisatore* (1821), and connects this with TLB's avowed attempts to revitalize the English tragedy in the 1820s, until the theme was eventually reinforced by his own scientific pursuits at Göttingen and Würzburg. See *The Making of a Poet*, p. 201.

72   Daniela Tandecki, 'Die Totentänze des Thomas Lovell Beddoes—*Death's Jest-Book* und die Verneinung des Lebens', *Tanz und Tod in Kunst und Literatur*, ed. Franz Link (Berlin: Duncker and Humblot, 2003), pp. 189–99.

73   Hiram Kellogg Johnson, 'Thomas Lovell Beddoes: A Psychiatric Study', *The Psychiatric Quarterly*, 17 (1943), 446–69 (p. 469).

conflict in Beddoes's drama (1963),[74] and in Eleanor Wilner's rich Jungian study of Beddoes's mythic symbolism (1975). There is a psychoanalytic strain but also an engaging political imagination in Geoffrey Wagner's highly suggestive memorial essay, 'Centennial of a Suicide' (1949), which interprets Beddoes's 'world o' th' dead' as a ghostly imprint of Marxist social equality.[75] Frances Wilson, drawing on Julia Kristeva, has recently offered a study of melancholia in Beddoes's work.[76]

It is tempting to assume that the remarkable psychological and psychoanalytic interest critics have taken in Beddoes's work may be indirectly related also to the author's own medical studies, then including such disciplines as anthropology, psychology, and mental pathology. In fact, the relation between his literary and scientific ambitions forms an object of intriguing reflections in Beddoes's own correspondence. Beddoes is uniquely placed among writers influenced by 'Romantic science', being at once the inheritor of the 'factitious airs' and 1790s stimulant therapies of Dr Beddoes of Clifton, and also a highly trained and brilliant anatomist in his own right, with first-hand experience of the teaching of Friedrich Blumenbach; the medical theories of two distinct generations and traditions meet in his life and work. The groundwork laid down by Donner and Lundin has recently been expanded by Christopher Moylan's discussion of Beddoes interest in contemporary anthropology and psychology (1991) and by Marjean D. Purinton's reading of the *Brides' Tragedy* as expressive of different theories of madness (2003).[77] Ute Berns explores Beddoes's research interest in the German life-sciences from embryology to pre-Darwinian theories of evolution and traces how he negotiates these theories—including their political and aesthetic challenges—in the poem 'Isbrand's Song' (2006).[78] With the current high levels of interest in the scientific discourse of the period fruitfully intersecting with its imaginative writing, it seems certain that work on Beddoes's science and medicine will continue to develop.

Beddoes's sexuality and politics—associated not least by their shared deviance vis-à-vis a repressive culture—present further aspects of his life and work that demand to be addressed in the future. The representations of sexuality in Beddoes's texts offer a rich area for investigation and invite approaches ranging from biographical and cultural criticism to gender-informed or psychoanalytic

---

74 'Theme and Imagery in the Poetry of Thomas Lovell Beddoes', *Studia Neophilologica*, 35 (1963), 85–103.

75 Geoffrey Wagner, 'Centennial of A Suicide: Thomas Lovell Beddoes', *Horizon*, 19 (1949), 417–35.

76 '"Strange Sun": Melancholia in the Writings of Thomas Lovell Beddoes', in *Untrodden Regions of the Mind: Romanticism and Psychoanalysis* (New York and London: Associated University Presses, 2002), pp. 127–42.

77 Christopher Moylan, 'T.L. Beddoes, Romantic Medicine, and the Advent of Therapeutic Theater', *Studia Neophilologica*, 69 (1991), 181–88; and more recently: 'In the air: T.L. Beddoes and Pneumatic Medicine', *Studia Neophilologica*, 73 (2001), 48–54; and Marjean D. Purinton, 'Staging the Physical: Romantic Science Theatricalized in T.L. Beddoes's *The Brides' Tragedy*', *European Romantic Review*, 14 (2003), 81–95.

78 Ute Berns, 'Thomas Lovell Beddoes and the German Sciences of Life', *Poetica* (Munich) 38 (2006), 1–2, 137–65.

readings of his work. Some new studies of gender and eroticism in Beddoes's writing have begun to elucidate this aspect that, as has been noted above, was consistently suppressed in earlier scholarship. Shelley Rees has traced patterns of homoerotic desire in *The Brides' Tragedy* and *Death's Jest-Book*,[79] and Stephen Guy-Bray has attributed ideas of autoeroticism to 'Pygmalion', an overlooked and exquisitely intricate narrative poem that Beddoes claimed to have written in a single morning.[80] If issues of gender and sexuality in Beddoes are in need of further development, this holds even more for the political implications of Beddoes's life and texts. The early elucidation of the political background undertaken by Weber has been complemented not only by Donner but also more recently by Burwick. Lately, Ute Berns has discussed the relevance of Marx's reflections in *The Eighteenth Brumaire* on revolution and the spectral quality of history for reading revolution and the ghosts of the past in *Death's Jest-Book*.[81]

As this survey has demonstrated, the turn of the century has seen a proliferation of new critical contexts, theoretical and historical. Recent discussions have highlighted aspects such as the indeterminacy in Beddoes's fragmented work, his intertextual relation to a major canonical forebear, or the melancholy pervading his writing; and they analyze the negotiation of contemporary discourses on medicine, gender, and politics in Beddoes's texts, as well as their intercultural horizons. The challenge now is to keep up this momentum, to bring Beddoes further into the mainstream of British nineteenth-century literary studies, as well as into a German and, indeed, a European perspective. However, if Beddoes's longstanding marginal status had any compensating features, it was that his readers were able to retain a sense of his resistance to being placed in the familiar slots of the Romantic or Victorian, of his stubborn uniqueness. We believe that this unwieldy quality of his texts should be accounted for rather than levelled out. What we need is a Beddoes criticism informed enough to investigate his connectedness with the great and diverse currents of nineteenth-century cultures — literary, philosophical, scientific, political, psychosexual etc. — as they are both determined by and cut across national boundaries; only a spectrum of perspectives as wide as this will do justice to the position from which Beddoes offers his critique of the period in which he wrote and to which he contributed his own texts. At the same time, the complexity of Beddoes's speaking position as it is so stunningly transformed into the body of his work will usefully interrogate some of the comfortable standards of the British canon.

---

79 Shelley Rees, 'Gender and Desire in Thomas Lovell Beddoes' *The Brides' Tragedy* and *Death's Jest-Book*' (unpublished doctoral dissertation, University of North Texas, 2002), and 'Melveric and Wolfram: A Love Story', *Thomas Lovell Beddoes Society Journal*, 8 (2002), 14–25.

80 Letter to Kelsall, April 1825, *Works*, p. 601; Stephen Guy-Bray, 'Beddoes, Pygmalion and the Art of Onanism', *Nineteenth-Century Literature*, 52 (1998), 446–70.

81 Ute Berns, 'The Politics of Revolution in Thomas Lovell Beddoes' *Death's Jest-Book*', *Romantic Voices, Romantic Poetics*, ed. Christoph Bode and Katharina Rennhak (Trier: Wissenschaftlicher Verlag Trier, 2005), pp. 97–107.

III   Synopses

The articles collected in this volume are intended to intervene in and advance the ongoing debate. They preserve the variety of approaches that characterize the most recent work on Beddoes, bringing together a high attention to formal detail and, among other things, an interest in political and medical culture, European perspectives, and the dramatic genre. A majority of the contributors concentrate on *Death's Jest-Book*, thus reflecting the central status of this text among Beddoes's writings, but his other dramatic works and his political prose are covered as well, the letters forming an important point of reference in several of the essays. This predominance of dramatic texts over lyrical poetry seriously questions the prejudice that drama was uncongenial to Beddoes, while testifying to the rising profile of dramatization within Romantic studies. Besides, partiality for the drama in Beddoes's work is more inclusive than may appear at first sight. A number of Beddoes's most substantial lyrics are inserted into the plays from which they draw much of their meaning—a fact that led Susan J. Wolfson and Peter J. Manning actually to anthologize those poems with some of the scenic dialogue in which they occur (2000);[82] and several essays include detailed discussions of poems that appear in the plays. Considering that Beddoes is often known only through his anthologized poetry, the essays of this volume help to redress the balance.

The first of the two sections is devoted to articles tackling *Death's Jest-Book*, and issues of history, politics, and medicine open the debate. Michael O'Neill investigates the relation of poetry and agency in the drama, giving his full attention to Beddoes's powerful language as a means to transgress limits, delineate new spaces, and place the reader on the verge of revolutionary change. Describing how Beddoes's language 'yokes heterogeneous things . . . violently together', with the 'metaphorical vehicle displacing the literal plot as the focus of attention', the author seems to revive some of the Modernist fascination for Beddoes's poetic art, while transcending the Modernist critical framework. O'Neill focuses on Isbrand as both a character in the text and a character self-consciously commentating on the text; a character whose ambition to create both in language and in history betrays his close kinship with his author while warding off their identification. In this reading Isbrand's poem 'Squats on a toadstool', with its speaking voice insistently asking 'what shall I be?' epitomizes the agency of poetry explored throughout play. Analogously, the blurring of the categories of life and death—or present, past, and future—in the political plot is shown to display the text's historical self-awareness 'on the threshold of imaginative breakthrough', while subjecting solipsistic self-assertion to incessant irony.

David M. Baulch takes a psychoanalytical angle on the depiction of self and history when addressing the ubiquitous presence of death in *Death's Jest-Book*.

---

82   'We present the songs for which Beddoes is most admired, not independently but in the dramatic contexts for which he intended them and by which they are (sometimes subversively, satirically) inflected', *Selected Poems of Hood, Praed and Beddoes*, ed. Susan J. Wolfson and Peter J. Manning (Harmondsworth: Penguin, 2000), p. 254.

Introducing his exploration of revolution and return in Beddoes play, he juxtaposes Eros as the revolutionary force of Shelley's *Prometheus Unbound* with Thanatos as the revolutionary force of *Death's Jest-Book*. The different stages of Beddoes's understanding of Thanatos in his letters and in his play are shown to resemble yet transcend those of Freud and result in a conception similar to the Lacanian re-reading of Freud's death-drive as 'the unsymbolizable void of the Real'. In this perspective, Beddoes's reanimations of the dead are regarded as an attempt to bring Thanatos back into the symbolic order in a play in which 'life is ultimately a perverse epiphenomenon of death'. The author analyzes Beddoes's tragedy as a form of therapeutic drama intended to cure the pathologies that death inspires. He reads the revolution represented in this drama as the compulsive return to death as the ahistorical void of the real and discovers structural analogies in Marx's theory of revolution. Rather than interpreting the play as an allegory about innate human aggression, however, Baulch emphasizes Beddoes's engagement with a paradoxical principle of structure that holds the potential of a critique of ideology in its encompassing Lacanian sense.

The next essay on *Death's Jest-Book* is an experimental re-framing of the drama by Michael Bradshaw, who contrastingly moves the emphasis away from matters of mortality and the supernatural and instead foregrounds the theme of the state and 'body politic' in Beddoes's drama of rebellion and insurgency. Bradshaw introduces this discussion with a close analysis of a pivotal exchange between Isbrand and Melveric on the question of spying, from Act III of the *Jest-Book*, re-read in terms of modern espionage, and Foucaultian surveillance. Suggesting a generally muted quality in earlier political estimations of Beddoes's writings, Bradshaw then goes on to relate this imagination of political power to the author's direct experiential knowledge of political and intellectual repression and resistance in his new residence within the German Confederation: when Beddoes was completing the first version of the drama, radical sentiment in a university such as Göttingen was regarded by the Austrian higher state as 'a severe threat to the stability of monarchical government'. A complementary context is then identified in the motif of the disguised ruler on the Renaissance stage, with examples from Marston, Middleton, and Shakespeare; Beddoes's adaptation of this dramatic device in the characterization of the Duke articulates the pervasiveness of the state machinery, a 'conflation of internalized self-regulation and external invasion.' The complex representation of political control in *Death's Jest-Book*, shot through with contemporary radical sympathies, is offered as an example of how *Death's Jest-Book* continues to reward shifts in contextual orientation.

Raphael Hörmann continues the investigation into the politics of *Death's Jest-Book* by relating it to the revolutionary discourses in Germany between 1820 and 1840, and the writing of Heinrich Heine, Ludwig Börne, and Georg Büchner in particular. For Hörmann, the 1829 version of *Death's Jest-Book* calls for a political revolution that is concerned, above all, with the question of civil liberties in the neo-absolutist German states. In this perspective, comparisons with the motif of Belsazar and the spectres of aristocracy in Heine, respectively, suggest that the restoration of monarchy towards the end of *Death's Jest-Book* 'rings as hollow as the attempted Restoration of the pre-revolutionary order after 1815 in the real world'. As the revolutionary discourse in the 1830s gradually moves towards the concept of a social revolution, Hörmann reveals a similar development in a piece of political prose called 'Die Gespenster' that is attributed to Beddoes, drawing on the writing of Börne to help elucidate this political shift. The author then argues that a scene in the later, revised version of *Death's Jest-Book* should also be understood as propagating such a move towards social concerns, supporting his claim by close comparison with a scene from Büchner's *Leonce and Lena*. Hörmann refers to Beddoes's late poem 'Lines written in Switzerland' to propose the conclusion that the poet finally settles for the perspective of a social revolution.

Frederick Burwick, drawing on a wide range of archival research, examines the role of the pathological imagination, especially in its relation to the representation of homosexuality in *Death's Jest-Book*, which he holds responsible for much of the discouraging criticism the manuscript version received from its first readers. Burwick sketches Beddoes's initiation into German culture and university life, as well as the merging of his literary and scientific interests. Surveying both the older school of speculative science under the sway of *Naturphilosophie* and the work of the empirically-minded scientists devoted to physiological and anatomical investigation, he uncovers strong traces of the whole spectrum in Beddoes's dramatic text. Contemporary discourses of cell theory and electricity, *Scheintod*, and hallucination are shown to destabilize the boundary of life and death in a drama that constantly opposes the fake and real, whether it be death, ghosts, or invisibility. In this 'dramatic brew mixed of lore and science, magic and medicine', medical practice and the effects of drugs combine with tales of the vampire, just as anatomical detail such as 'the bone of Luz' is deciphered as a coded wink of the homosexual. Burwick concludes that the manner in which Beddoes deploys contemporary science as well as the occult in his drama testifies to his 'assertive and independent stance on issues of morality and sexual relations'.

The three essays to follow concentrate on the dramatic qualities of *Death's Jest-Book*, taking up different angles and positioning the play in different literary traditions. Nat Leach delineates the ethics of Beddoes's 'mental theatre'. He situates Beddoes's drama between the idealized space of the closet on the one hand and the public stage on the other, only to deconstruct the absolute distinction between the two. Rather than reading the text as inherently anti-theatrical, he traces in it a modern sensibility of the ethical implications of all representation, as it has been theorized by Lévinas, Derrida, and Blanchot. Drawing on Lévinas's reading of death as an ethical moment in which alterity breaks through the totalizing representations of the self, Leach analyzes *Death's Jest-Book* as signifying 'the resistance of alterity and death to representation, exposing the gaps in its own dramatic construction'. According to Leach, the play thus radicalizes the problem of the theatrical body and its relation to the mind also tackled by other Romantic dramatists. A closer view of Beddoes's representation of revolution, the body, and language convinces Leach that in displaying the inescapable alterity that haunts the mental space and the theatre alike, and resides even in language itself, the dramatist moves beyond the drama of Baillie and Byron. The author argues that the body represented in

Death's Jest-Book haunts 'not only the Romantic mind but literature itself', standing at the beginning of a modernism that exposes the textual past as a set of mere material signifiers. Body and word alike are taken to ethically signal an unreadably other space within the soul.

By contrast, Ute Berns breaks with the scholarly habit of reading *Death's Jest-Book* as a closet play in the tradition of the 'mental theatre'. Instead, she relates the *Fool's Tragedy* and its generic ambiguities—its tragic conventions on the one hand and its foolery as well as references to a great variety of popular genres on the other—to the contemporary British theatrical culture. Drawing on British and German political discourse, she argues in a first step that Beddoes's conception of the avenger, a revolutionary Bonapartist, skilfully modernizes the Early Modern revenge tragedy. Rather than 'killing the king' in person, the avenger remodels the constitution of the body politic. In a second step, Berns points out that specific aspects of *Death's Jest-Book* draw on the contemporary harlequinade, thus investing a play apparently lacking a plebeian element with the social energy of a popular genre. The actor Edmund Kean, himself bridging the gulf between harlequin and Shakespearean tragedian, is suggested as a model for Beddoes's protagonist. In this perspective, *Death's Jest-Book*, fusing elements of legitimate and illegitimate theatre, undertakes a bold attempt to remodel the British body theatrical. This attempt is related both to the earlier experiments with theatre and drama in the circle of Leigh Hunt, on the periphery of which Beddoes moved while still in England, and to the literary and theatrical scene of the German *Vormärz*.

Alan Halsey, recent editor of the later version of *Death's Jest-Book*, begins by reflecting on the process of actually reading the play and on the difference between reading the early and late text in particular. If the early version is still a functioning five-act tragedy, the author argues, then there are good grounds for assuming that Beddoes did not want to publish it because it did not yet match his radical intentions for the novel form of theatre he discusses in his letters. This new kind of theatre emerges, rather, in the later version, which approximates a psychic theatre of disembodied voices, in which Halsey recognizes a próto-Modernist project akin to Artaud's Theatre of Cruelty. Pointing out their similarly estranged position vis-à-vis their respective contemporary theatre, Halsey stages a dialogue between Artaud and Beddoes on Balinese theatre and Greek masks. Making frequent reference to *Death's Jest-Book*, Halsey discusses the significance of death and 'cruelty' for both dramatists, the role of mental turmoil and the double, as well as their shared sense 'of the discontinuities of thought and the self'. Returning to the different versions of *Death's Jest-Book*, Halsey suggests that Beddoes, finding death 'as invulnerable a target for satire as one could ask', swerved to hit 'the nearest available target', the five-act tragedy itself, thus finally undermining the very model and language he had started out from.

The second section of the volume opens up the discussion to include Beddoes's political prose, his other dramatic texts, and critical appreciations that draw on his work as a whole. Andrew James Johnston concentrates on Beddoes's radical German prose that appeared in the democratic newspaper *Bayerisches Volksblatt* in 1831 and 1832. A brief survey of the impact of the French Revolution of July

1830 on Europe and of the debate of the Reform Bill in Britain helps the author to situate Beddoes's interest in the political situation of Britain, France, and Poland. Approaching the prose itself, Johnston finds that it keeps turning over its problems 'through metaphorically recasting them as it proceeds', thus by-passing the strong drive for closure characteristic of partisan journalism. In Johnston's view, Beddoes's 'essentially poetic approach' combines the capacity to write lucid, straightforward passages with the attempt to recreate on the textual level the political confusion described. The author demonstrates that Beddoes's satire of leading figures of contemporary reactionary politics—Wellington, Périer, Chateaubriand—draws on the trope of the living dead, a trope closely bound up also with the representation of history as a hybrid intermingling of past and present. Pointing out affinities to and differences from Marx's relegation of histrionic resurrections of the past in order to conceive the new revolutionary subject, Johnston recognizes in Beddoes both the revolutionary desire to leave the past behind and the acknowledgment of the staying-power of history. From this tension, Johnston argues, the political prose engenders the spectre of history itself 'as the realm of the living dead, a world of vampires constantly transgressing the borders of the present'.

Turning towards Beddoes's neglected dramatic fragments *The Second Brother* and *Torrismond*, Marjean D. Purinton explores the intersecting fields of science and the supernatural under the heading of the 'techno-gothic', as they help to articulate forbidden topics and disturbing issues in Romantic culture. In a period in which 'medicine was theatricalized and theatre was medicalized', the dramatic fragments should be interpreted, according to Purinton, as objects of instruction or, more specifically, appendages with a pedagogical purpose, figuring medical discourse and inviting the audience to practice their anatomical gaze. However, Purinton reads the fragments as negotiating not only medical discourse in general but also ideas and topics from Beddoes's father's progressive medical text *Hygëia* in particular. Thus she highlights representations of drugs and hypochondria/hysteria, or infection/contagion and the anxieties inspired by death in the fragments. In these discursive fields, the author argues, the dramatic forms of ghostliness help to stage cultural dualisms such as health and disease, sobriety and drunkenness, etc., just as features of the grotesque insistently question the legibility of the performing body. Purinton demonstrates how the dramatic fragments can be made to yield significant medical semiotics and insights that cast the audience into the role of the anatomist/physician and contribute to the contemporary cultural move towards 'the medicalization of body and spirit'.

Shelley Rees and Diane Long Hoeveler, choosing different angles and texts, both discuss Beddoes's representation of gender. Rees argues that in *The Brides' Tragedy* Beddoes draws on the myth of Cupid and Psyche as told by Apuleius. Yet whereas the classical source celebrates the perfect union between masculine and feminine, an ideal also cherished in male Romantic poetry, Rees traces its alteration and ultimate rejection in Beddoes' play. She identifies Floribel as 'a Romantic version of Psyche' and Hesperus, 'her lover/destroyer', as Cupid. Naturalizing and feminizing Floribel as a refuge from his own patriarchal environment, Hesperus turns against her as soon as he catches a glimpse of her as an 'independent other' who exposes his own vulnerability. The author locates the analogy between Hesperus and the mythical Cupid in their initial immaturity, which is epitomized in their unattainable desire for absolute control of the object. She points out, however, that Cupid's subsequent emotional growth is not matched by Hesperus. Unlike Psyche's lover, who turns away from his jealous mother Venus and dedicates himself to his bride, Floribel's husband merges with the vindictive and jealous Venus figure. And whereas the gods intervene to immortalize Psyche, Hesperus is seen to render Floribel immortal by killing her. As Hesperus repeats the gesture of idolizing the feminine with his second bride, Olivia, thus depriving her, too, of her humanity, Rees interprets the protagonist as 'a Cupid who allows the jealous Venus to slaughter his brides'.

Diane Long Hoeveler discusses the role of the dying brides and the death-fetish in Beddoes's texts. Selecting passages from across his work, she relates them to the contemporary popular concern with death and burial practices on the one hand, and the ideological agenda of Gothic literature on the other. Situating Beddoes in the tradition of masculinist Gothic anti-Catholicism, she argues that the poet deployed pre-Christian as well as Germanic literary sources both to 'critique the failure of the female body to redeem humanity' and to develop and valorize the death-fetish. Beddoes's obsession with death, and especially violent female death—the latter is understood to signify the control of female fertility—are shown to build on distinct though intersecting sources. Hoeveler provides a survey of relevant thematic material from the ballad tradition as it reaches back before Christianity, and traces several of these ballad motifs in Renaissance drama, invoking further contextual material in the German folk tradition and Märchen. With reference to Beddoes's biography and letters, Hoeveler diagnoses a frustrated desire for faith and a loathing of the flesh. The former is held accountable for his anti-Jesuit attacks that mask the lack of eschatological answers in his own life and his secret fascination with a male brotherhood. The latter is seen to lie at the root of his demonizing the fertility of the 'mother-bride' and the promise of a life after death, while 'nostalgically mourn[ing] the demise of such a system of belief'.

Concluding the preceding debates, Christopher Moylan asks how the poet managed to inscribe his life and work 'with the obscurity of the little known, little read, and little understood'. In pursuit of this self-effacement, Moylan focuses on Beddoes's writing on death, arguing that Beddoes's reflections on the paradoxical nature of death and the afterlife tend to serve the purpose of effacing or displacing crucial topics. Foremost among these, Moylan singles out the repression of desire, a 'splitting of effect and idea', that leads to repeated patterns of tragic love in *Death's Jest-Book*. Rather than using its 'thinly disguised homosexual encounters' as a key to the text, however, Moylan highlights 'the disruptive quality of desire', destructive or monstrous, as it is transformed into dramatic substitutions and reversals. Moylan finds this desire associated with states outside categorization or meaning and thus linked to the fool Homunculus Mandrake, himself an appearance from beyond the symbolic order. Both are analyzed with relation to the Lacanian 'second death', describing the termination of the relation of the self to the symbolic order that simultaneously allows the self to stay 'in contact with the fantasmatic kernel of its being'. Moylan regards this refusal of closure in the dramatized identity formations, the poetic form, and in Beddoes's self-establishment as poet as crucial for the resistance to his reception, emphasizing, however, that 'the process of effacement casts its own spell'.

The Epilogue turns to the stage production of *Death's Jest-Book* in 2003 and moves from the scholarly perspective to that of two people involved in the production. Jerome J. McGann describes the history of the stage-script he produced for this event. This history goes back to the University of Chicago in the 1970s, when theatre people concerned with Brecht, Artaud, and anti-realist plays became interested in staging Romantic drama, including *Death's Jest-Book*. McGann describes his difficulties with putting together a functioning acting version of *Death's Jest-Book* at the time, and elucidates some of the principles guiding his adaptation of Beddoes's text for the stage nearly thirty years later. Frederick Burwick, as stage-director, comments on the production itself. He describes his own changes to McGann's script, most notably his re-insertion of the lyrics, and recalls his collaboration with Brian Holmes, who wrote the music for the songs as well as an overture and choral reprise for the finale. Burwick points out which motifs the production focused on, elucidates how the 'supernatural' scenes were realized on stage, and comments on how individual actors interpreted their roles. The material presented in the epilogue is thus shaped by a participatory point of view. It ranges from factual description and impressionistic memories to anecdotal observation, thus offering a glimpse of this other, artistic revival of Beddoes in a historic theatrical event.

IV Note on Texts

The standard edition of Beddoes, for all writings—drama, poetry, and prose, is still *The Works of Thomas Lovell Beddoes*, edited by H.W. Donner (1935);[83] this edition has been used as the principal textual source for most essays in this collection. Where an author departs from Donner 1935 for a particular reason, preferring an alternative text, such as Kelsall (1850, 1851), Gosse (1890), Colles (1907), or Donner (1950), this will be indicated in the notes. But Donner's *Works* is the 'default', and therefore does not require constant referencing: act-scene-line references, line numbers or page numbers as appropriate, will be given in parentheses after quotations. Where appropriate, authors have used Donner's terminology to distinguish between the principal acknowledged versions of *Death's Jest-Book*, 'β' and 'γ', referencing as follows: (β: III, iii, 710–13).[84] The bibliography includes a full list of published editions of Beddoes.

---

83   Donner's *Works* exists in two editions: the 1935 original, *The Works of Thomas Lovell Beddoes*, ed. with an introduction by H.W. Donner (London: Oxford University Press, 1935); and a reprint made by AMS Press (New York: AMS Press, 1978).

84   Donner's terminology: the α text (1828) is the first fair copy; the β text (1829) is TLB's transcription for the press; the γ text (1830–44) is a capacious term that includes all later drafts and additions, representing at least two major phases of revision. See Donner's detailed account of the manuscripts and transcripts of *DJ-B* in the Introduction to *Works*, esp. pp. xxxiii–xliii.

'The latch-string of a new world's wicket':

Poetry and Agency in *Death's Jest-Book;*

or, The Fool's Tragedy[1]

Michael O'Neill

Conversing with Homunculus Mandrake's Boy, Isbrand says, 'But go on, boy, I am but a commentator on this world: to the text again' (II, i, 87).[2] The remark illustrates the reflexive play of Isbrand's and his creator's ironic linguistic intelligence in the 1829 version of the drama, on which this essay will concentrate. Isbrand presents himself here as someone who is 'a commentator on this world', and he urges the Boy to take him back 'to the text', back, that is, to events and realities. The comedy of this self-presentation derives from Isbrand's insouciant assumption of the critic's role, and from the gap between the speaker's show of humility and his evident desire, expressed elsewhere in the play, not only to 'comment' on the world's 'text' but also to rewrite it. At his most overweening he asserts, 'I have a bit of FIAT in my soul, / And can myself create my little world' (V, i, 38): this 'little world' made cunningly sets itself in opposition to the world of limits and matter, as Isbrand trusts in 'A will above my will' (V, i, 53) to make possible his own semi-mocking version of perfectibility, a 'comparative philosophy' that will allow him 'means, bye and bye, of flying higher' (V, i, 68, 71). These cavalier assertions recall his self-communing question at I, i, 208–9, when he asks: 'Art thou alone? Why, so should be / Creators and destroyers'. Here, as later, he sounds like one who would change history; 'creators' flowers into self-important existence across the line-ending and passes into 'destroyers' with Napoleonic aplomb.

And yet Isbrand has already referred to himself as a 'tragic fool', assuming the space allotted by the play's sub-title ('The Fool's Tragedy'), and he goes on to mimic the accents of a Hamlet rather than a Lenin: 'I'll go brood / And strain my burning

---

1   The author would like to thank Anita O'Connell, who worked as his research assistant for a few months in 2006, for help with formatting and checking references.

2   The play is quoted from the reading text of the 1829 press copy included by H.W. Donner in his *Plays and Poems of Thomas Lovell Beddoes*, ed. with intro. by H.W. Donner (London: Routledge and Kegan Paul, 1950); hereafter *Plays and Poems*. Donner provided a text of this press copy in this edition 'so that it is now possible to read it exactly as Beddoes had intended it to be printed in 1829' (p. vii). All other writings by TLB are quoted from *The Works of Thomas Lovell Beddoes*, ed. H.W. Donner (London: Oxford University Press, 1935), referred to parenthetically in the text as *Works*.

and distracted soul / Against the naked spirit of the world / Till some portent's begotten' (I, i, 207, 209). Rather like Hamlet when he asserts 'That would be scanned', in the scene where, sword unsheathed, he finds Claudius at his prayers, Isbrand says that he will 'go brood'.[3] But, before we attach too restrictively the meaning 'meditate (esp. resentfully)' (OED) to 'brood', Isbrand wrests from the word its procreative suggestions as he develops an image that implies sexual conquest of 'the world' (an implication played down in the wording of the 1830–44 version). Even should this conquest be attained, however, the result will only be for some 'portent' to be 'begotten'. The speech implies that the begetting of portents may be the most that we can expect of the poet as 'tragic fool', if we take Isbrand's words to reflect, however ironically, on Beddoes's own aspirations for poetry. Isbrand cannot be taken unequivocally as Beddoes's surrogate, and one may feel Jerome McGann is daring to the point of over-simplification by giving, in his recent stage version of *Death's Jest-Book*, many of Isbrand's lines (including 'Squats on a toad-stool under a tree') to a character he calls 'Beddoes, *Poet and Mountebank*'.[4] But Isbrand does provoke such an identification in places, especially when he reflects on writing, imagining, for example, how death may 'write with a lipless grin on the innocent first page' of the recording angel's book, '"Here begins Death's Jest-book"' (II, iii, 127–28, 129). The internal rhyming, there, jests at the idea that 'innocence' can separate itself from death's 'lipless grin'.

The episode with which this essay began demonstrates the play's staging of imagined collisions between different realms: text and commentary, world and play. It introduces, moreover, in however implicit a fashion, the question of agency. Throughout *Death's Jest-Book*, Beddoes uses language so that it 'beckons to new places', to borrow a line from William Carlos William's *Paterson*, Book II, imaginative spaces between the material world and a world of, or symbolized by, death; between flesh and spirit; between ruined worlds and worlds in formation; between, to quote from the same passage in *Paterson*, 'A / world lost' and 'a world unsuspected'.[5] But these spaces tend to de-create themselves, to undergo an ironized shutting-down in the moment of their opening up. The vehicles of such ambivalent spaces are images that speak of breaches between states of existence. One such image is that of the door through which passage between states appears to be possible. In Athulf's soliloquy in IV, iii, 'under the windows of Amala's apartment', he represents himself as a reformed rake turned suicidal: 'Once more I'll see thee, love, speak to thee, hear thee; / And then my soul shall cut itself a door / Out of this planet' (1–3). The first line, plangent with longing, gives way to an

---

3   *Hamlet*, III, iii, 75; quoted, as are all references to Shakespeare, from *The Norton Shakespeare, Based on the Oxford Edition*, ed. Stephen Greenblatt et al. (New York: Norton, 1997).

4   See *Death's Jest-Book: A Posthumous Theatrical Travesty, in Three Acts, Translated by Jerome McGann from 'The Original Dramatical Fantasia' by Thomas Lovell Beddoes, with Musical Score by Brian Holmes* (Belper: The Thomas Lovell Beddoes Society, 2003), p. 1.

5   William Carlos Williams, *Paterson, Books 1–V* (London: MacGibbon & Kee, 1964), Book II, section 3.

imagining of suicide conceived of in terms appropriate to heroic and yet quotidian action. Athulf's sublime carpentry will enable him to escape 'Out of this planet'. The emotional rhythm of the speech has a characteristic backwards and forwards motion, however. There is a subsequent dip into depression, 'A worthless life, / A life ridiculous! Day after day, / Folly on folly!' (6–8), where Macbeth's sense of futility in 'Tomorrow, and tomorrow, and tomorrow' (*Macbeth*, V, v, 18) is briefly reprised, before the speaker asserts, 'But I'll not repent. / Remorse and weeping shall not be my virtues' (8–9).

The resistance to repentance is striking in Beddoes, who turns away from the example set by Shelley's hero in the first act of *Prometheus Unbound*, where Prometheus asserts, on hearing again his cursing of Jupiter, 'It doth repent me; words are quick and vain' (303).[6] Speakers in Beddoes prefer, in their sardonic ways, to side with the last aspect of the advice contained in Demogorgon's line, 'Neither to change, nor falter, nor repent' (*Prometheus Unbound*, IV, 575). Isbrand dismisses the idea of reconciliation with the comment, 'Reconciled! A word out of a love tale, that's not in my language' (II, ii, 75–76): another meta-poetic comment in a work by a poet aware that 'none can speak his language' (I, ii, 144), a phrase, which read meta-poetically, has an inflection that is both self-deprecating and assertive. Yet if the characters rarely repent with conviction, they do change and falter.[7] So, after the self-loathing of the middle section of his speech ('I hate and will have vengeance on my soul', IV, iii, 17), Athulf momentarily swings from thoughts of suicide to imagining an act sponsored by 'Satirical Murder' (IV, iii, 18): 'I'll cut his throat across, make her my wife' (IV, iii, 22). This proposed way of dealing with his brother, Adalmar, and the object of his desires, Amala, contrasts sharply with the wish for his soul to 'cut itself a door / Out of this planet'. The same verb 'cut' serves both to imagine transcendence and destruction.

Elsewhere, the image of the door reinforces manipulative plotting. The Duke disguised as a pilgrim remarks to Torwald: 'Already has our slave, / The grape juice, left the side-door of the youngest / Open to me' (II, iii, 304–6). The Duke may be dissembling, but he speaks out of the heart of the play's concern with duplicity. Throughout *Death's Jest-Book*, Beddoes shows how the suspicious mind can, through the venting of its suspicions, inhabit a cloud of paranoia. As the Duke's speech develops, it matters relatively little whether the fire that flashes from his youngest son is treasonous or loving; the speech dwells, rather, on the process of wheedling

---

6   Shelley is quoted from *Percy Bysshe Shelley: The Major Works*, ed. Zachary Leader and Michael O'Neill (Oxford: Oxford University Press, 2003). For a discussion of TLB's response to Shelley, see Michael O'Neill, '"A Storm of Ghosts": Beddoes, Shelley, Death, and Reputation', *The Cambridge Quarterly*, 28.2 (1999), 102–15; and Michael Bradshaw, *Resurrection Songs: The Poetry of Thomas Lovell Beddoes* (Aldershot and Burlington: Ashgate, 2001), esp. pp. 214–19; hereafter *Resurrection Songs*.

7   Eleanor Wilner points out that TLB had 'the imagination and insight to perceive that villains do not repent'; quoted from her *Gathering the Winds: Visionary Imagination and Radical Transformation of Self and Society* (Baltimore: Johns Hopkins University Press, 1975), as excerpted in the *Journal of the Thomas Lovell Beddoes Society*, 9 (2003), 14; hereafter Wilner.

out, of discovery (307–11). Later in the scene, the Duke discloses himself to Torwald in vaultingly cosmic terms: 'On he comes, / Still as a star robed in eclipse, until / The earthy shadow slips away. Who rises? / I'm changing: now who am I?' (II, iii, 329–32). Torwald answers 'Melveric!' (II, iii, 332), yet, as often in *Death's Jest-Book*, the metaphorical vehicle displaces the literal plot as the focus of attention.

This is not an adverse criticism. For all their antagonisms, characters in the play share a collective identity. Inhabiting the same metaphysical world, they compose a complexly choric voice. Here the Duke's mode of disclosing himself speaks from and to the centre of the play's obsession with imaginings of 'change'. The image of the rising star may be Shelleyan, but it struggles to sustain a note consonant with Utopian optimism. Riddlingly, the disguised Duke will say to Adalmar, 'I will come again, / This or the next world. Thou, who carriest / The seeds of a new world, may'st understand me. / Look for me ever. There's no crack without me / In earth and all around it' (II, iii, 341–45). The Duke presents himself less as the essence of transformation than of governance here; as though mocking the rebellious instincts he senses in his sons, he presides over every 'crack', permitting yet controlling change. Although Beddoes can be read as a dramatist whose characters long to lose their egos in the larger world of death, there is a fantasizing element in them, too, in which they arrogate to themselves extraordinary powers. Yet egomania passes into savage hatred as, Cenci-like, the Duke rages against his sons in his subsequent soliloquy, seeing them not as 'sons, but contracts, / Between my lust and a destroying fiend, / Written in my dearest blood, whose date runs out, / They are become death warrants, Parricide' (II, iii, 353–56).[8] Alliteration connects opposites as contracts written in dearest blood turn into death warrants.

Melveric's outburst coexists with a sense that 'Nature's polluted' (II, iii, 364); any hint of renewal provided by the earlier image of his disclosure to Torwald as the emergence of a star from eclipse cancels itself in his lines, 'Thou art old, world, / A hoary atheistic murderous star: / I wish that thou would'st die, or could'st be slain, / Hell-hearted bastard of the sun' (II, iii, 366–69). The moment disputes the Shelleyan idealism that has trailed its clouds of glory in the earlier image and aggressively assumes a debunkingly materialist or naturalist vision. The language snarls with an attitude one might call cosmic loathing, an emotion that imparts its electrical charge to the run of adjectives in 'hoary atheistic murderous', where each word blazes darkly in relation to its predecessor: 'hoary' implies cynical age; 'atheistic' godlessness; 'murderous' brutal violence. 'Hell-hearted', one of the many compounds in Beddoes, puts to flight, or severely embarrasses, Adalmar's more ethereal description of 'love' earlier in the scene as 'a heaven wandering among men, / The spirit of gone Eden haunting earth' (II, iii, 162, 163–64).[9] And yet such

---

8   For TLB's admiration for Shelley's *The Cenci*, see his letter to Kelsall of 1 April 1826 (*Works*, p. 619).

9   See Greg Crossan, 'Thomas Lovell Beddoes's *Death's Jest-Book*: An "OED" Oversight', *Notes & Queries*, n.s. 49.4 (2002), 486–89. Crossan cites many examples of TLB's use of compounds in support of his view that, by not delving into *Death's Jest-Book*, 'OED missed the opportunity to harvest the most linguistically fecund work' produced by this poet (p. 486).

hymnings of hope, here recalling the paradisal intimations of Shelley's isle in *Epipsychidion*, an isle said to be 'Bright as that wandering Eden Lucifer' (l. 459), contribute to the symphonic music of Beddoes's play. Shelley juxtaposes 'Eden' and 'Lucifer' with witty effect; he half-obliges the reader to forget that Lucifer (as Satan) brought about the demise of 'Eden', and he constructs a post-Christian space where secular happiness is possible. But the Christian story of the Fall is allowed deliberately to cast a shadow across that happiness.

Beddoes yokes heterogeneous things more violently together than Shelley does, as in the next scene, where the image of the door or gate promotes Isbrand's fantasy of dominance. This fantasy emerges from an imagining of 'Snaky rebellion turning restless' in its 'dragon-egg' (II, iv, 3, 1).[10] From this suggestion of a 'restless' process following its own grotesque laws, which may involve an endlessly restless turning, Isbrand presents himself as a conjuror or conqueror who has history in the palm of his hand: 'All is ready now: / I hold the latch-string of a new world's wicket; / One pull—and it rolls in' (II, iv, 5–7). Isbrand imagines himself as being in a position to open a 'wicket' through which a 'new world' can enter; 'wicket' was a witty revision of the first draft's 'gate' (see *Works*, p. 414, note to l. 6) and thus links itself with the play's pervasive imagery of gates and doors. His lines create a typically liminal effect; the reader is placed on the threshold of revolutionary change, and Beddoes's own political hopes find their way into the writing.[11] But the effect is mocking and sardonic, fantastical. The very image delights self-mockingly in the disparity between 'latch-string' and 'new world'.

As elsewhere, Isbrand induces at this moment a complicated response. If he is amoral, there is, in his full-blooded devotion to vengeance, an authenticity that has dramatic force. If he is power-crazed, he is also caustically self-aware. The self-awareness is difficult to disengage from the author's own delight in language's capacity to communicate afresh, to make it new. Isbrand, for example, mocks his dreams of control as 'sweet thoughts' that 'rise dimpling to my lips, / And break the dark stagnation of my features, / Like sugar melting in a glass of poison' (II, iv, 10–12). The simile of 'sugar melting in a glass of poison' allows us to taste the speaker's saccharine ferocity and prepares us for the self-revelation, in Isbrand's next speech, that 'the heart I have / Is a strange little snake. He drinks not wine / When he'd be drunk, but poison: he doth fatten / On bitter hate, not love'

---

10   Christopher Ricks comments on these lines thus: '"Turning restless" not only as becoming restless, but also as restlessly turning. Revolution, and not just rebellion, is the word that lies curled within the shell', 'Thomas Lovell Beddoes: "A Dying Start"', in *The Force of Poetry* (Oxford: Oxford University Press, 1984), p. 140; hereafter Ricks. The sense of 'revolution' as an endless turning, one might add, disputes the hoped-for implication of a revolution that will lead to a new life.

11   For a full discussion of TLB's involvement in German politics, see chapter X, 'The Politician', in H.W. Donner's magisterial *Thomas Lovell Beddoes: The Making of a Poet* (Oxford: Blackwell, 1935), pp. 288–318. For a powerful account of the 'double Beddoes', ironizing his own hopes, compulsively building his plots around 'opposing brothers', 'consciously contrasting opposing views and tones to undermine convention, and just about everything else', see Wilner, pp. 11, 13.

(II, iv, 26–29). The supple enjambements here mimic the twists and turns of the 'strange little snake' to which Isbrand compares his heart; they suggest, too, the speaker's relishing of the strangeness with which his emotions operate. As often happens in the work, the following lines conceive of a desired outcome in terms of radical metamorphosis: at Melveric's death, Isbrand will 'Fall into ashes with the mighty joy, / Or be transformed into a winged star' (II, iv, 32–33). Decay and sidereal permanence are offered as alternatives rather than flat opposites; either way, Isbrand will experience 'all eternal heaven distilled / Down to one thick rich minute' (II, iv, 34–35).

Although Christopher Ricks is right to argue that 'Beddoes is as good a poet as he is because of the romantic, lyrical, and assuaging things in him are as real in the best of his work as the antiromantic, harsh, and feverish things', it is also the case that Beddoes can connect the 'romantic' and 'antiromantic' in ways that take from either category a clear-cut identity.[12] In the passage just quoted, the bunching of scornful and elevated feelings shows in the adjectives governing 'minute': this 'minute', possible heir to the 'bewitching' (or 'bewildering') minute in *The Revenger's Tragedy*, which affected T.S. Eliot so strongly, is 'thick' in a way that suggests murkiness as well as solidity, and 'rich' in a fashion that intimates luxuriousness as well as intensity of sensation. If Beddoes knew the relevant passage from, say, Charles Lamb's *Specimens of English Dramatic Poets* (1808), where the play's authorship is ascribed to Cyril Tourneur, he would have read the following: 'Are lordships sold to maintain ladyships, / For the poor benefit of a bewitching minute?'[13] Eliot quotes the phrase as 'bewildering minute' in 'Tradition and the Individual Talent', but his account of the whole passage bears on the doubleness that Beddoes achieves. In Beddoes, as in *The Revenger's Tragedy*, 'there is a combination of positive and negative emotions: an intensely strong attraction toward beauty and an equally intense fascination by the ugliness which is contrasted with it and which destroys it'.[14] In Beddoes the language of rapture frequently cloaks the drive towards the fulfilment of destructive will. Isbrand's idiom may be Utopian, but his inflection is sardonic; and yet the result is a double sense that the speaker is neither simply bent on destruction nor wholly deceived about his imaginings of transformation. Indeed, the effect, for all the comparison it suggests with previous tragedy, confirms the force of a famous letter Beddoes wrote in 1825 when he asserts:

> I am convinced the man who is to awaken the drama must be a bold
> trampling fellow—no creeper into worm-holes—no reviser even—
> however good. These reanimations are vampire-cold. Such ghosts as
> Marloe, Webster &c are better dramatists, better poets, I dare say, than
> any contemporary of ours—but they are ghosts—the worm is in their
> pages—& we want to see something that our great-grandsires did not

---

12   Ricks, p. 146.
13   Charles Lamb, *Specimens of English Dramatic Poets* (London: George Routledge and Sons, no date given; first published 1808), p. 150.
14   *Selected Prose of T.S. Eliot*, ed. Frank Kermode (London: Faber, 1975), p. 42.

> know. With the greatest reverence for all the antiquities of the drama,
> I still think that we had better beget than revive—attempt to give the
> literature of this age an idiosyncrasy & spirit of its own, & only raise
> a ghost to gaze on, not to live with—just now the drama is a haunted
> ruin. (Works, p. 595)

Begetting rather than revival may, in theory, be Beddoes's preferred practice, as it is Isbrand's desire with regard to the bringing into being of 'portents'. But *Death's Jest-Book* thrives on revival, returns to life, and the living, 're-animations' that are consciously 'vampire-cold'. The plot hinges on Wolfram's breaking through 'The gates of the sepulchre' towards the close of the third act, where he refuses simply to be what the Duke would have him, that is, a delusion, the 'Lie of my eyes' (III, iii, 687). Moreover, Wolfram's resurrection gives rise to a revivification of ordinary language, heightened, in the presence of the extraordinary, into self-aware wordplay. 'Is this thin air, that thrusts thy sword away?', Wolfram says to the Duke when the latter threatens him 'If thou pretendest life' (III, iii, 696, 695). 'Thin air', a stereotyped phrase for something immaterial, is mocked and rejected. As he frequently does, Beddoes places us on either side of a mirror: the ghostly takes on material existence; material existence quails in the presence of the ghostly. New life is breathed into the genre of revenge tragedy as Wolfram and the Duke fascinatingly refuse to engage in the straightforward hatred demanded by the plot. Wolfram is winningly casual in his sense of escape from the grave as a vacation, even as he is assured of achieving his aim. 'Thou returnest with me', he remarks with chilling nonchalance, 'So make no hurry. I will stay awhile / To see how the world goes, feast and be merry, / And then to work again' (III, iii, 704–7). 'Eat, drink and be merry, for tomorrow we die' is the adage undergoing witty alteration in these lines, whose speaker has, in fact, died, but is back 'To see how the world goes, feast and be merry', a line in which 'goes' implies transience as well as existence. The Duke, as if realizing belatedly that he is a character in a play composed not by a Jacobean tragedian but by a proto-Absurdist, comments wryly on the futility of his actions: 'Murder's worn out / And full of holes; I'll never make't the prison / Of what I hate, again' (III, iii, 723–25).[15] The wryness reveals itself in the wordplay. Murder is 'full of holes' because it causes physical damage and leaves the corpse prey to the 'worms' that the Duke says to Wolfram 'ate thy marrow' (III, iii, 688). It is also 'full of holes' because it is ridden with philosophical flaws; it assumes the finality of 'Death', against which there has been 'rebellion' (III, iii, 722). If the Duke's attack on murder recalls but adapts to his own disillusion a moment of Shakespearean terror, Macbeth's horrified railing against the dead for rising 'With twenty mortal murders on their crowns' (*Macbeth*, III, iv, 80), the scene ends with a further revivification of a Shakespearean antecedent, this time the episode in

---

15   Northrop Frye argues that the play brings us 'into contact with the conception of the absurd', 'Yorick: The Romantic Macabre', in *A Study of English Romanticism* (Brighton: Harvester Press, 1968), p. 85; hereafter Frye.

The Tragedy of King Lear (III, iv, 158), when Lear demands to 'keep still with my philosopher' (Edgar disguised as Poor Tom). So the Duke, after calling the man he has murdered a 'murderer of Nature', bids him 'come with me', in part to consider the 'question which haunts which' (III, iii, 727, 729, 728).

At such a moment, Beddoes dramatizes less the hope of changing the world than the capacity of language to imagine an unsettling of traditionally clear-cut categories, including emotions of hate and, as Shelley Rees has argued, repressed homosexual love.[16] The confrontation between the Duke and Wolfram concludes a scene that is both remarkably sustained and unsettling. Torwald strikes a note of conventional dread and admonition when he says of the grave-digging, 'this breaking through the walls, that sever / The quick and cold, led never yet to good' (III, iii, 205–6). The rhyme of 'sever' and 'never' might be read as an ineffectual spell designed to anathematize the play's 'breaking through the walls'. In fact, the scene brims with such 'breaking through'. Isbrand, evoking the workings of incipient rebellion, feels his way into 'The little hiding holes of cunning thought, / And each dark crack in which a reptile purpose / Hangs in its chrysalis unripe for birth' (III, iii, 90–93). That image is unpleasantly pregnant with a sense of as yet 'unripe' significance. Act III scene iii plays variations full of grotesque vitality on the theme of travels to and from the bourn of death and birth, where those nouns threaten to swap places. Unidentified by the conspirators, the Duke speaks of 'A quiet, listening, flesh-concealed soul' (109). The line may describe his own dramatic position, but it assumes a larger thematic resonance. If souls are merely 'flesh-concealed', there is only a small jump to make before they manifest themselves in unfleshly form. Isbrand's ensuing question unwittingly takes that jump when he asks scornfully, 'Are the ghosts eavesdropping?' (110).

Beddoes will not allow the question merely to be derisive in its inflections, involving us in a world in which ghosts do, in fact, eavesdrop. The eavesdropper turns out to be Mario, a figure who enjoys an uncanny, anachronistic existence. He seems literally to have survived Roman history, even as he speaks in terms that recall Antony's final words in *Antony and Cleopatra*, where Shakespeare's hero describes himself, somewhat self-flatteringly, as 'a Roman by a Roman / Valiantly vanquished' (IV, xvi, 59–60): 'A Roman am I', Mario says; 'A Roman in unroman times' (121–22). Beddoes subverts our sense of temporal stability.[17] After Mario's unexplained and not wholly explicable emergence as the champion of 'Liberty' (157), the others leave, allowing the Duke to express his desire to be 'dead / With thee, my wife!' (166–67). Throughout this speech, Beddoes uses line-endings to convey a desired movement towards death. The Duke says to his dead wife that he has 'lain by night / Upon thy grave' (167–68) and he asserts, 'Far better were I / Thy grave-fellow, than thou alive with me' (171–72). In both cases, he eroticizes death

---

16   See Shelley Rees, 'Melveric and Wolfram: A Love Story', *Newsletter of the Thomas Lovell Beddoes Society*, 8 (2002), 14–25.

17   Frye, discussing the play's 'curious treatment of historical period' (p. 65), remarks, with Mario in mind, that 'the absence of any definite historical community is one of the things that create the sense of something alive and dead at the same time', p. 66.

through the pressure of the desired falling-across the line-ending into the 'grave'. In both cases, however, the writing seesaws between the enticing prospect of death and the more arduous thought of restored life.

Other instances of a teetering on the threshold between life and death fill this hypnotically effective scene and frequently relate to questions of human agency and power. The Duke questions Death's authority: 'She died. But Death is old and half worn out: / Are there no chinks in't? Could she not come to me?' (251–52). 'Chinks' is a word favoured by a man searching for weaknesses in Death's pseudo-regal armour. The last question returns to an option—of the return of the dead— which the Duke had seemed to reject. Hearing the Duke's desire sparks off Ziba's conditional proposal to 'essay / My sires' sepulchral magic' (269–70), but Beddoes cleverly introduces suspense about the nature of this 'magic' as the Duke fiercely rebuts the 'juggling African' (279) and his 'ghost-lies' (284). It is at this point that Isbrand and Siegfried transpose the scene's master-theme into a more knowing, self-aware key. If the entire play explores the agency of poetry, Isbrand brings the efficacy of song to the fore by offering a 'ballad of my making' (312), a poem about potentiality, birth, and metempsychosis, the famous 'Squats on a toad-stool under a tree' (328). The poem brings to a startling focus the scene's and the play's preoccupation with coming into being, with the question, 'What shall I be?" (330): a question posed by and to history as well as poetry.

Beddoes gives physical presence to the barely materialized by opening the ballad with the strongly stressed and surprisingly positioned verb, 'Squats'. What follows makes up a near-nonsensical, expressive patchwork of compoundings and hyphenated possibilities. The 'bodiless childfull of life in the gloom, / Crying with frog voice' (329–30) is Beddoes's own lyric voice, calling through the 'gloom' of personal and historical uncertainty, unbodied but a 'childfull of life', lamenting its condition as a 'Poor unborn ghost' (331) but unprevented from asking and imagining 'What shall I be?' (330), aborted but alive and kicking. The diction crackles with an energy that suggests that this writing has every chance of being something new in the very act of questioning its own future identity. The ghostly shades into the grotesque; the 'bodiless' into the animal; the 'unborn' into the 'egg / That's cracking asunder' (333–34). Isbrand gives us 'the lobster's tune when he is boiled' (323) as well as a ballad sung 'boldly' from the heart (326). In lines that mime what they despise, Isbrand has already declared his dislike of 'ballads that are made to come / Round like a squirrel's cage, and round again' (324–25). His own ballad avoids any circularity, breaking into different length stanzas and unpredictable rhyme-schemes, formal devices that mirror the emphasis on compounds and hybridity. That emphasis shows in the brief fantasies of hyphenated creations: the frog-voiced speaker runs through a gamut of bizarre incarnations, whether as a mummy-crunching 'Egyptian crocodile' 'with eighteen toes, / And a snuff-taking nose' (337, 335–36) or as a grimly fetching hedgehog, a 'Little, gruntless, fairy hog' (347), or as an insinuating fellow of 'Serpent Lucifer' (353) and his 'worms' and 'snakes' (354), or as a 'new Dodo' (373) made up of all sorts of beings, extinct, one may feel, before it can be born, but linguistically alive, 'finished' (373), in the double senses of being brought to completion and being ended or over.

Michael Bradshaw remarks shrewdly that 'Self-defeat, and the sardonic embrace of defeat, are hardwired into this drama from the outset', and such an embracing can be felt at work throughout Isbrand's poetic triumph.[18] The lyric seems, as a wry sub-text, to say that poetry's agency is its ability to answer the question, 'What shall I be?' in ways that are true to its own laws of metre and rhyme; words can conjure 'a new Dodo' that was never seen on land or sea, and can delight in rhyme's insistent binding-together, as when the poem's first stanza concludes with five rhyme words—*jaw, claw, craw, caw, maw* (339–43)—that relish the hunting, eating, and digestion inseparable from physical existence. 'A noble hymn to the belly gods indeed: / Would that Pythagoras heard thee, boy!' (374–75): Siegfried's approving response makes clear that Isbrand's song accords with Pythagorean notions of metempsychosis, and underscores the fact that the song sardonically hails 'the belly gods'. Bradshaw points out that Beddoes uses the same phrase, 'the belly gods', in a letter about the salamander, 'condemned to the flames for impiety against the belly gods' by continuing to live after losing its 'stomach & intestines' (*Works*, p. 622), and he argues that in the drama Beddoes 'juxtaposes man's intimation of his own immortality with his sensation of the grossness of physical tissue'.[19] Such a juxtaposition underpins the double power of Isbrand's song. Imaginatively liberated in its use of fantasy, the song celebrates, with a grim desperate wit, the inescapability of entrapment within the physical; new life shivering for reincarnation finds an imagined home in the animal world, and the effect is to stretch to a tortuous extreme—and at the same time to collapse—the distance between the poles of desire for transformation and recognition of our creaturely condition. There is in this recognition, however, no Romantic exaltation of the natural; indeed, the 'new Dodo' has commerce with evil and death; it will be 'Devil-winged; dragon-bellied; grave-jawed, because grass / Is a beard that's soon shaved, and grows seldom again / Before it is summer' (370–72). The run of hyphenated adjectives suggests the 'new bird' (368) will be a creation of bolted-together attributes, less a metaphor than a parody of a metaphor for (say) the workings of genius conceived of in organicist terms, or for a new politics. At the same time, in serving as a grotesque embodiment of Beddoes's desire for 'fair and glorious creations' (*Works*, p. 590), the song about the 'new bird' rises, phoenix-like, out of the ashes of irony, and one can see why, in his first fair copy, Beddoes called the 'new Dodo' the 'new Phoenix' (see *Works*, p. 433, note to line 367).

The post-ballad movement in this scene is, first, one of self-reflexive humour ("'tis perhaps a little / Too sweet and tender' (376–77), says Isbrand, his tone one of mock-coyness), then, of an extended fantasy about the connection between 'earth and heaven' (390). Isbrand fears that the two 'are grown bad neighbours, / And have blocked up the common door between them' (390–91), using the image of a 'door' mockingly to evoke a pre-lapsarian state of neighbourliness between worlds that is now lost. Siegfried's sustaining of the theme is among the great passages in

---

18   *'Death's Jest Book': The 1829 Text*, ed. Michael Bradshaw (Manchester: Carcanet / Routledge, 2003), p. xv.
19   *Resurrection Songs*, p. 136.

the play, marked (yet again) by that blend of unsentimental yearning and ruthlessly sardonic mockery characteristic of Beddoes's imagination as it strains against the limits of knowable experience. Siegfried recalls a time when 'The other world was cold / And thinly-peopled, so life's emigrants / Came back to mingle with the crowds of earth' (396–98). As the eerily chummy 'mingle' indicates, haunting is whimsically explained as a desire for company and comfort—and, implicitly, Beddoes explores the imagination's claims to offer us such company and comfort in the face of our existential plight. Siegfried's next step is to suggest that death has undone so many (including 'great cities . . . transplanted thither', 399) that, in fact, 'The dead are most and merriest' (402). There is, in the writing, a pang of longing for the condition of death and even regret that 'There will be no more haunting' (403); even though the plot will show that such regret is unfounded, Siegfried's words make of 'The other world' a place of riot and merriment, which the living will never reach, and make it a place where, in an uncanny way, we might feel at home.

The tone is wry, but again the poetry triumphs in the midst of its imagining of failure. Thinking of the blocked-up 'common door', for example, momentarily holds it ajar. It is at this stage that Ziba, whose claims to be able to raise the dead have previously (as noted) been attacked by the Duke, is invited by the same figure to comment on 'what's said' (407). His following speeches detailing (for instance) the resurrection of 'the crowned flower' (444), harbinger of possible human return to life, surmount in their evocative power the Duke's initial scepticism ('This was a cheat', 448), and the droll anti-climax of Mandrake's appearance in response to Ziba's necromantic summons. At the same time, we are conscious of Ziba's and Beddoes's word-spinning reliance on analogues and metaphors. Speaking of the use of 'Ghostlily' (444) in Ziba's speech about the resurrection of the 'crowned flower', Ricks comments, 'Behind the uncanny but lucid adverb there is the spectral flower, the ghost-lily'.[20] The effect is, indeed, 'uncanny'. Beddoes makes something happen in language, the appearance of a 'ghost-lily', which lends imaginative support to the idea that it might be possible to 'raise a man' (445). And yet, deconstructing his creation, he suggests that such resurrection happens only in a verbal dimension. The debt to German Romantic Irony, with its heightenings and deflations, is apparent, but Beddoes gives that Irony his own imperturbably sardonic yet tragic inflections.[21] When the Duke asks sceptically, 'What tree is man the seed of?' (451), Ziba is superbly equal to the rhetorical challenge: 'Of a ghost', he says, firmly rounding out the Duke's question into a pentameter, before adding, in another pentameter that plays its cadenced regularity against the strangeness of the matter, 'Of his night-coming, tempest-waved phantom' (451, 452). The compound adjectives give this 'phantom' a material habitation and herald the assertion that there is 'in man, a seed-shaped bone, / Aldabaron, called by the Hebrews Luz' (456–57), from which, Ziba claims, there will emerge 'The bloody,

---

20   Ricks, p. 149.
21   For a lucid discussion of TLB and German Romantic irony, see Michael Bradshaw, *Resurrection Songs*, pp. 171–75.

soul-possessed weed called man' (460). It is, indeed, a speech intent on 'calling', definition, and redefinition, and it suspends disbelief through its occult solemnity, argument by analogy, and seductive vowel-music. Even if Ziba cannot persuade of the existence of the 'seed-shaped bone', he can convince his listener that he grasps the contradictions of 'man', at once 'bloody' and 'soul-possessed'.

'Now exorcise': the Duke's subsequent command to Ziba (530) is, implicitly, the role Beddoes imagines for poetry in *Death's Jest-Book*. The peculiar pathos inherent in the poetry's self-reflexive exploration emerges in the Duke's speech before the appearance of Wolfram. Here he questions his purpose in remaining in 'this chilly silent place' (652) and asks, 'Why laugh I not, and ridicule myself?' (651). Read as Beddoes's own commentary on the text he has created, the Duke's speech takes on added resonance, as it places the speaker in a void and voided space, caught between two worlds:

> 'Tis still, and cold, and nothing in the air
> But an old grey twilight, or of eve or morn
> I know not which, dim as futurity,
> And sad and hoary as the ghostly past,
> Fills up the space. (654–58)

The writing occupies a cave of quietude, an irresolute poise that is fully aware of the ambivalence of 'twilight'—'or of eve or morn / I know not'. By contrast with writing of this urgency, Sibylla's later wish, expressed to Death, to 'pass praying away into thee, / As twilight still does into starry night' (IV, ii, 128–29), seems a beautiful fiction, one of those calculated moments of stylistic counterpoint where Beddoes plays wish-fulfilment against underlying terror.[22] The Duke's limpid, self-questioning pentameters conjure up an exact objective correlative for the Beddoesian poetic project in *Death's Jest-Book*. Positioning itself between 'futurity' and 'the ghostly past' in manner and matter, the work manages to make us aware of its historical self-awareness, its sense of itself as liminal, on the threshold of imaginative break-through. Shakespeare and the Jacobeans belong to its 'ghostly past'; Shelleyan and German Romanticism offer clues towards 'futurity'. Ethically, the work spurns Christianity while mocking proto-Nietzschean trust in the will. Politically, it imagines the destruction of kingdoms through 'Snaky rebellion' but is only too aware that the motives for rebellion may constitute a tyranny of their own. The movement in Beddoes towards break-through, figured by a fusion of death and life in images that suggest resurrection and new life, places itself in a zone where the present is haunted, the past is ghostly, and the future dim.

It may not be wholly the case that, as H.W. Donner puts it, 'All the characters [in *Death's Jest-Book*] seem to declaim into the void', and it is certainly not the case

---

22   See Wilner for penetrating commentary on 'the peculiar duality of Beddoes' style in *The Brides' Tragedy* and elsewhere: his precious, decorative sentimentality and his compressed, instinctive, and energetic voice', p. 6.

that 'none answer the others' (the exchange between Isbrand and Siegfried after the former's ballad refutes this claim).[23] Yet it is true both that, in Ricks's terms, the play's void is 'truly a void (of fear and pathos)', and that the play's reflections on poetry's agency locate that 'agency' in a kind of 'void', the dead-centre of its own coming into being, a process that threatens to turn into stasis.[24] As the Duke's speech continues, its fear and pathos, to borrow Ricks's words, centre on the notion of solipsistic isolation—not only, one feels, of the character, but also of the play to which he belongs:

> The air I seem to breathe is still the same:
> And the great dreadful thought, that now comes o'er me,
> Must remain ever as it is, unchanged.–
> This moment doth endure for evermore;
> Eternity hath overshadowed time;
> And I alone am left of all that lived . . . (674–79)

The hugely ambitious play comes to this: an intuition that the imaginative self must suffer endless incarceration within its own constructions, that 'This moment doth endure for evermore', less as a triumph over time than as an awed response to the prospect of 'Eternity', a non-temporal realm that dwarfs the temporal and threatens to leave everything 'unchanged'. As elsewhere in the play, 'Eternity' booms with sonorous emptiness. Frye observes that 'Many of Beddoes' most remarkable images are based on the sense of the liquidness of life', contrasting these images with images of rooted mountains and rocks that represent a 'criminal titanism'.[25] But, tonally astute, Beddoes can also insinuate into assertions that time passes into Eternity as a river flows to the sea an implication of wish-fulfilment. The statement, 'I alone am left of all that lived', is compounded of fear and dread exhilaration and belongs to the 'last man complex', which afflicts and empowers the apocalyptic imaginings of Mary Shelley, among others.[26] This complex blends political fears and a post-High Romantic sense of belatedness. Beddoes himself projected a play entitled *The Last Man* and wrote in a fragment associated with the play ('Dianeme's Death-Scene') in a more optimistic vein of the self as centre of the universe; Dianeme, dying, proclaims ''Round and round the curvous atmosphere / Of my own real existence I revolve, / Serene and starry with undying love. / I am, I have been, I shall be, O glory! / An universe, a god, a living Ever' (77–81; quoted from *Works*). Arguably, for all Frye's understanding of the passage as illustrating 'a genuine sense of being at the center of reality', this confidence is over-weening.[27] By the time of *Death's Jest-*

---

23   *Plays and Poems*, p. xl.
24   Ricks, p. 156.
25   Frye, pp. 78, 79.
26   See TLB's letter of 1 April 1826, in which he expresses his pleasure that Mary Shelley has published her novel, *The Last Man* (*Works*, pp. 618, 619).
27   Frye, p. 77.

Book, Beddoes subjects solipsistic self-assertion to endless irony, and indeed, for all his crimes and wickedness, the Duke continues to engage our sympathy by dint of his awareness that to be 'a living Ever' may be a nightmare.

Wolfram's rising from the grave serves, at least, to offer the Duke ghoulish company, and the exchanges between them, already discussed, bring this remarkable scene to a questioning close. The meeting infuses the Duke's subsequent words with sceptical terror, as when he begins the next act by declaring, 'Methinks / The look of the world's a lie, a face made up / O'er graves and fiery depths; and nothing's true / But what is horrible' (IV, i, 6–9). The image here is not that of a door between adjacent realms but of a pit yawning beneath one's feet; the apparent 'look of the world's a lie', alliteration again coming to the support of intuition. Macbeth's terrified intimation that 'nothing is / But what is not' links with his experience, mentioned in the same speech, of 'horrible imaginings' (I, iii, 140–41, 137) to support the Duke's conviction that only the horrible is true. Intriguingly, the imagery of breaches between realms, dominant elsewhere, gives way here to an extended metaphor of perilous jostlings within 'Life', as the Duke offers one of the play's most striking existential pronouncements:

> . . . *Life's a single pilgrim,*
> *Fighting unarmed amongst a thousand soldiers.*
> *It is this infinite invisible*
> *Which we must learn to know, and yet to scorn,*
> *And, from the scorn of that, regard the world*
> *As from the edge of a far star.* (IV, i, 13–18)

This 'infinite invisible', for once, is not another realm but 'Life' itself. What the Duke advocates is alertness to quotidian peril that permits a scorn-underpinned detachment. The different realm explored here is an inner world, a place that allows the Duke to 'regard the world / As from the edge of a far star'. Frye is acute when he praises Beddoes's underrated powers of characterization as they show themselves in the portraiture of the Duke. For Frye, using the above speech in support of his argument, the Duke is 'constantly engaged in direct action, but his engagement is at the same time a profound detachment'.[28] With no loss of plausibility, the speech detaches itself from its believable speaker and attaches itself to that invisible, infinite, and absent presence behind and controlling a text that frequently and affectingly acts as commentator on itself.

The poetry of the fourth and fifth acts continues to delight in subversion and paradox. The Duke says, for example, of the ghostly Wolfram that 'The carcase owes to me its ruinous life, / (Between whose broken walls and cloven sides / You see the other world's grey spectral light')' (IV, i, 48–50), and that glimpse of 'the other world's grey spectral light' through a breach in nature is at the obsessive core of Beddoes's imagination in the 1829 version of the play. Later additions will

---

28   Frye, p. 71.

give the play a more lyrical quality of transcendent yearning, but the 1829 version goes out in flashes that comment sardonically yet affectingly on the longing for the 'other world'. The Duke begins 'to feel / As if I were a ghost among the men, / As all I loved are' (IV, i, 70–72), and we detect, once more, Beddoes's repressed confessional voice in the drama. Isbrand plays the Beddoesian poet again in IV, iv when he declaims his 'new ballad called "The Median Supper"' (57). This ferocious ballad serves as an example of what poetry, for Beddoes, can do; here, it embodies a vision of life as ruthless and cruel, and a stance of the spirit that is defiant and brave, albeit in a masculinist way ('And Harpagus, he is my joy', says Isbrand of the man who has unwittingly eaten his son, 'Because he wept not like a woman'; 105–6). Poetry, as embodied in this ballad, can celebrate defiance of tyranny, a defiance that is itself tainted with cruelty.

Isbrand will be stabbed by Mario as a 'usurper' (V, iv, 247), but his dying words recur to his ballad's vision of existence as conflict: 'He fetches thee, who should be dead; / There's Duke for Brother! Who has won?' (V, iv, 276–77). Isbrand's tone is needling and victorious, and his wording enjoys the grammatical ambiguity about the antecedent of 'who'. The play ends with a series of reversals and cross-overs: Wolfram asks, 'But dead and living, which are which? A question / Not easy to be solved' (V, iv, 206–7); the Deaths painted in the Dance of Death in the cloisters of the ruined cathedral (see the stage directions at the start of V, iv) themselves descend from the painting and take on life as they sing of death; and at the very close of the play, Wolfram takes the Duke, with him 'still alive, into the world o' th' dead' (V, iv, 350). The last line of the work, then, brings together the living and the dead. Yet the play does not make us feel that Beddoes the poetic conjuror has solved the question posed by Wolfram about the respective identities of 'dead and living', with all the metaphorical associations attaching to each term. Instead, the 1829 version of *Death's Jest-Book* demands to be praised for its imaginings, by turns grotesque, fantastical, lyrical, and tragic-comic, of human possibility and limits, imaginings that are always centred on their own performance, and succeed in displaying, throughout, an 'idiosyncrasy & spirit of [their] own'.

'Death and his sweetheart':
Revolution and Return in *Death's Jest-Book*

David M. Baulch

I: 'That was SHELLEY': Premature Resurrections

When it was published in 1820, Percy Bysshe Shelley's *Prometheus Unbound* found an adoring disciple in the nineteen-year-old Thomas Lovell Beddoes. Only months before Shelley's death in 1822, Beddoes inscribed his poetic allegiance to Shelley's vision in the blank leaf of his copy of Shelley's poetic drama.[1] For Beddoes, *Prometheus Unbound* was a cosmic event:

> *The bright creations of a human heart*
> *Wrought magic in the bosoms of mankind:*
> *A flooding summer burst on Poetry,*
> *Of which the crowning sun, the night of beauty,*
> *The dancing showers, the birds, whose anthems wild,*
> *Note after note, unbind the enchanted leaves*
> *Of breaking buds, eve, and flow of dawn,*
> *Were centered and condensed in his one name*
> *As in a providence—and that was SHELLEY. (ll. 8–16)*

'Lines: Written by the Author of *The Bride's Tragedy*' credits Shelley's poetry with producing the same kind of universal change that his *Prometheus Unbound* describes. At the same time, it suggests an astute critique of the relationship of the past to the present, specifically as they conspire in the revolutionary moment. In *Prometheus Unbound*, the failed hopes attached to past revolutions, from those of classical mythology to the French Revolution, are suddenly realized and crystallized in a utopian future that emerges in a return to the past.

In Shelley's drama the future depends upon Prometheus' ability to recall his own curse: his challenge to Jupiter's absolute authority and power. What he must

---

1   The date assigned to 'Lines written in the *Prometheus Unbound*' rests, according to Donner 'on Kelsall's authority' that the poem was 'written early in 1822', *Works*, pp. xxvii–viii. Kelsall states in his introduction to the piece as it appeared in *The Athenaeum* on 18 May 1833: 'When Mr. Beddoes penned this fine extravaganza, the subject of its graceful idolatry was still living', p. 796.

recover, in short, is the repressed history of his own failed revolutionary attempt. Recovery requires that Prometheus recall his curse upon Jupiter in two ways. He must recall, as in recover, the memory of what he said, and he must recall, as in take back, the sentiment of those words. Prometheus' actions are a demonstration of the paradoxical way in which revolution is a return to a dead or repressed past whose meaning, as a door to the future, is retroactively assigned by its repetition in the present. It is the paradox of the uncanny revolution, a revolution dependent upon a structure of repetition, which pervades Beddoes's own most striking work, *Death's Jest-Book*, just as in the 'Lines' Beddoes writes to Shelley in 1822. Although written before Shelley's death, Beddoes's poem only found its way into print as a much-belated tribute to the departed Shelley in 1833, but this is a task that the *past-ness* of the poem accommodates remarkably well. Beddoes's celebration takes the form of a premature revival, wherein both Shelley and the 'flooding summer' of poetry are already consigned to the past, to a moment 'that *was* Shelley'. Put another way, the lyric buries Shelley alive, for when Beddoes writes his tribute, it is as if his idol were already dead. Eleven years later, when the poem to Shelley is finally published, it is presented as if it were the headstone over the corpse of Beddoes's own long-moldering literary career.

The death of Shelley signals the death of English poetry for Beddoes, and both of these deaths coincide roughly with his own figurative death from the British literary scene. On 25 August 1824, Beddoes wrote to his friend Thomas Forbes Kelsall:

> The disappearance of Shelley from the world seems, like the tropical setting of that luminary (aside, I hate that word) to which his poetical genius alone can be compared with reference to the companions of his day, to have been followed by instant darkness and owl-season, . . . if I were the literary weather-guesser for 1825 I would safely prognosticate fog, rain, blight in due succession for it's dullard months (p. 589).

When Kelsall publishes Beddoes's tribute to Shelley in *The Athenaeum*, he laments that the then twenty-nine-year-old Beddoes is already as good as dead for British readers. In terms of Beddoes's publications, Kelsall is right. Between the short time in which *Prometheus Unbound* was published and Shelley drowned, Beddoes completed his only two major published works in Great Britain: a collection of lyric poems, *The Improvisatore*, in 1821; and a poetic drama, *The Brides' Tragedy*, in 1822. Thus, by 1833 Kelsall is able to claim in his headnote/headstone to Beddoes's 'Lines':

> For aught, indeed, that our literature would have lost, [Beddoes] might have perished in the same fatal storm in the Gulf of Spezia. How much longer is he contented to be un-known as the author of the Bride's [sic] Tragedy—(that blossom of exquisite beauty—still but a

blossom,)—and is expectation, in the few who know his really great
and rare powers, to doze away at last into oblivion? (p. 796).

Kelsall's question is one that still haunts Beddoes's contemporary reputation. Yet, when Kelsall asks the question, Beddoes is still very much alive, and it is only by burying Beddoes prematurely that Kelsall is able to desire his resurrection. Kelsall's untimely eulogy echoes Beddoes's own strangely enabling and inexhaustible obsession with death in his texts in general, but most particularly in his sprawling, never-finished *Death's Jest-Book*. Although something of a macabre gesture, it is perfectly appropriate to imagine that Kelsall's headnote to Beddoes's poem is meant to goad Beddoes into seriously making a return to the public display of his literary efforts by finishing his revisions to *Death's Jest-Book*. However, it appears to be the case that Beddoes only sporadically looks away from his studies in anatomy to revisit a play that only became progressively longer, internally conflicted, and ever more bizarre as it accommodates the shifting views of death that preoccupy him from 1825 until 1844. During this time, the subterranean growth of Beddoes's *Death's Jest-Book* seems to have abjured the luminous, revolutionary optimism of Shelley's *Prometheus Unbound*. Both dramas present revolution as an uncanny return, but if the revolutionary force in *Prometheus Unbound* is Eros, in *Death's Jest-Book* it is Thanatos, the name Freud would later give to the death drive. *Death's Jest-Book* becomes a presentation of death as the central compulsive force common to individual desire and political revolution.

Beddoes's *Death's Jest-Book* and Freud's 'The Uncanny' come out of the same struggle to come to terms with the death drive. Ultimately, however, *Death's Jest-Book* arrives not at *Beyond the Pleasure Principle* or *Civilization and its Discontents* but, more correctly, at Lacan's rereading of the death drive in *The Ethics of Psychoanalysis*. Here, Lacan eventually identifies Freud's death drive as the un-symbolizable void of the Real. For Lacan, the Real is paradoxically that ineffable, impossible thing beyond the experiential reality of the symbolic order and the impenetrable kernel around which it is constructed.[2] In the same way, death in *Death's Jest-Book* is both beyond individual life and material history and, at the same time, functions as the centre around which the individual psyche is formed. Precisely in its paradoxical role as ineffable, non-material, outside of time, and the essential truth of the psyche, death is the basis of social-political reality as it is constructed in *Death's Jest-Book*. Rather than the life-affirming leap beyond history conveyed in *Prometheus Unbound*, revolution in *Death's Jest-Book* reveals history's essence as the compulsive return to death, understood as the ahistorical void of the Real.

---

2   Jacques Lacan, *The Seminar of Jacques Lacan, Book VII: The Ethic of Psychoanalysis*, trans. Dennis Porter (New York: Norton, 1992).

II: 'A living semiotical display': Anatomy and Tragedy

As an undergraduate at Pembroke College, Oxford, it seemed a foregone conclusion that Beddoes would be a creative writer. With the modest critical success of *The Brides' Tragedy*, Beddoes appeared poised to enter the English literary scene, and yet, one month after graduation in 1825, he leaves England to study anatomy at Göttingen University. At approximately the same time that Beddoes has resolved upon his new course of study, he starts to write *Death's Jest-Book*. The interrelationship between his study of the human body and the composition of *Death's Jest-Book* is captured in the letters Beddoes sent to his friends in England. These letters help to chart a particular shift in the place Beddoes's drama assigns death in relation to both human life and literary meaning. Seeking the principle of human life in his academic studies, Beddoes concurrently writes his *Jest-Book* as a satire on death. For Beddoes, death as a limitation that can be challenged by both science and art soon gives way to an obsession with death as a central psychic principle and an absolute condition beyond both the scope of science and language.

In the last recorded letter before he leaves for Germany, Beddoes writes to Kelsall that he has abandoned the play upon which he had been working and intends to devote himself to a new project: 'I do not intend to finish that 2nd Brother you say but am thinking of a very Gothic-styled tragedy, for w^h I have a jewel of a name—DEATH'S JESTBOOK—of course no one will ever read it' (p. 604). While it is difficult to say how much of Beddoes's fatalism about the tragedy's eventual readership stems from insecurity and bravado, and how much comes from a substantial insight into the strange text that *Death's Jest-Book* was to become, he nevertheless seems to have been well aware that *Death's Jest-Book* would represent a significant departure from English drama.

Despite Beddoes's apparent ambivalence about *Death's Jest-Book* in his letters to Kelsall, this literary effort is a part of a larger vision that Beddoes has for redefining drama in tandem with his anatomical studies. In December 1825, he writes Kelsall that *Death's Jest-Book* 'is a horrible waste of time' and that he has 'lost much, if not all of my ambition to become poetically distinguished' (p. 609). His denial of literary ambitions is not simply a rejection of his interest in literature, but rather it indicates a rejection of the Wordsworthian construction of the author as one who is solely devoted to the production of literature. Instead Beddoes appears to nurture a grand interdisciplinary vision for the merging of science and literature in the quest for an approach to both physical and mental health:

> *The studies then of the dramatist & physician are closely, almost inseparably, allied; the application alone is different; but is it impossible for the same man to combine these two professions, in some degree at least? The science of psychology, & mental varieties, has long been used by physicians, in conjunction with the corresponding corporeal knowledge, for the investigation and removal of immaterial causes of disease; it still remains for some one to exhibit the sum*

of his experience in mental pathology & therapeutics, not in a cold
technical dead description, but a living semiotical display, a series of
anthropological experiments, developed for the purpose of ascertaining
some important psychical principle—i.e., a tragedy. (p. 609)

The alliance the letter sees between 'the dramatist & physician' is grounded in a common focus on the maintenance of human life. While the physician's science can address the biological causes of death, Beddoes's letter suggests that death is equally a pathological condition. For Beddoes, drama holds the potential to perform a mental cure. As a 'psychical principle', 'tragedy' would reveal death as a 'mental pathology' that the literary text can address therapeutically. Death becomes primarily a psychical concern central to the maintenance of physical life. In his therapeutic drama, the stage becomes the site for a mimetic mental cure of the pathologies that death inspires.

A verse letter to Bryan Waller Procter, postmarked 13 March 1826, reveals Beddoes's high hopes that *Death's Jest-Book* will inspire a psychic revolution against the tyranny of death. Beddoes claims that by exposing death to observation he can render 'him' powerless: 'I've dug him up and decked him trim / And made a mock, a fool, a slave of him / Who was the planet's tyrant: dotard death' (p. 614). By casting death as a political figure, a ruling 'tyrant' who will be revealed as both 'fool' and 'slave', *Death's Jest-Book* envisions a revolutionary freedom from a universal tyrant. Yet, Beddoes's *Death's Jest-Book* recognizes that for political power to maintain itself, it must produce the conditions of its reproduction, and to do this it must generate subjects who always/already function within the ideological field that legitimates its power. Death's power over people comes from its ideological mystification as an absolute power over life. *Death's Jest-Book*'s answer to death as the point at which individuals are interpellated as subjects amounts to disrupting the ideological field that underwrites death's power with a mixture of empirical science and comedy. Beddoes writes to Procter that *Death's Jest-Book* means to 'rob [death], to un-cypress him i' the light / To unmask all his secrets' (p. 615). *Death's Jest-Book* functions as a 'living semiotical display', able to 'unmask all [Death's] secrets' leaving only a pathological remainder, 'dotard death', as the object of satire.

Beddoes's playful ambition to 'un-cypress' death in *Death's Jest-Book* and place death within 'a living semiotical display' depends in part on the success of his search for an indestructible principle of life. In the same way that *Death's Jest-Book* is intended to pioneer a new role for dramatic texts, his academic work at Göttingen attempts to effect a revolution in the understanding of human life. John Agar observes of Beddoes's medical investigations that, 'in rejecting a hypothetical 'vital principle', Beddoes presented himself with the problem of finding the real principle of life, and of finding it tangibly, on the dissection table'.[3] Beddoes, at one point, sought the principle of human life in the legend of the indestructible bone from which the living body is regenerated: the almond-shaped seed of human life,

---

3   John Agar, 'Isbrand and T.L. Beddoes' Aspiring Hero', *Studia Neophilologica* 45 (1973): 372–91 (p. 373).

called *luz*. Christopher Moylan claims that 'in the spring of 1827, Beddoes gave his late evenings to dissecting corpses in the hope of finding the bone of *luz*, associated in various Talmudic sources with the resurrection of the dead'.[4] Beddoes' interest in the *luz* is preserved in *Death's Jest-Book*.

Despite his early optimism, a letter written to Kelsall in April of 1827 suggests that Beddoes's literary and scientific attempts to establish a principle of life have failed to materialize and thus dispel the power of death. Beddoes tells Kelsall that 'I am now already so thoroughly penetrated with the conviction of the absurdity & unsatisfactory nature of human life that I search with avidity for every shadow of a proof or probability of an after-existence, both in the material and immaterial nature of man' (pp. 629–30). His search for a principle of human life has become the search for 'an after-existence'. The search for what gives life meaning, that which will somehow dispel or justify its 'absurdity & unsatisfactory nature', depends upon positing an 'after-existence' that both exceeds life itself and yet can be empirically verified and discursively articulated as life's most essential, internal component. The truly impossible dimension of Beddoes's project becomes clear, insofar as the 'after-existence' that must ground life is simultaneously the *a priori* condition of its possibility and paradoxically beyond its scope.

Despairing of achieving his goal of finding an enduring principle of life within the structure of the body, Beddoes recognizes the fantasmatic nature of the desire for a 'doctrine of immortality' as a common structural principal in religion, philosophy, and empirical science, in their attempt to repress death (p. 629). This realization allows Beddoes to reconstruct his therapeutic purpose for his play into a recognizably psychoanalytic reading of death as the central force that drives both the human subject and history. Beddoes wrote to Kelsall:

> Man appears to have found out this secret [that of the 'doctrine of immortality'] for himself, & it is certainly the best part of religion and philosophy, the only truth worth demonstrating: an anxious question full of hope & fear & promise, for w^h Nature appears to have appointed one solution—Death (pp. 629–30).

By suggesting that the 'secret' of 'immortality' is 'Death', Beddoes renders life itself an uncanny fantasm.

The disappointment Beddoes experienced in his anatomical research is also reflected in a change in what death means in *Death's Jest-Book*. Michael Bradshaw identifies the coincidence of Beddoes's inability to empirically identify a principle of life in his anatomical researches and the negative reactions to the first version of *Death's Jest-Book* by Procter and J.G.H. Bourne in early 1829 as the point at which Beddoes seeks 'to redefine the terms of his quest'.[5] Similarly, James Thompson

---

4   Christopher Moylan, '"For Luz is a Good Joke": Thomas Lovell Beddoes and Jewish Eschatology', in *British Romanticism and the Jews: History, Culture, Literature*, ed. Shelia A. Spector (London: Palgrave, 2002), pp. 93–103 (p. 93).

5   Bradshaw, *Resurrection Songs*, p. 105.

identifies the impact these personal events had on *Death's Jest-Book* by observing, 'the play is truly Death's jest book; starting as a satire destructive of death, the play has turned into death's own satire on the jest of life itself . . . Beddoes had clearly failed to achieve his original intention in the play—to make death a dotard'.[6] The text of *Death's Jest-Book* preserves a strange composite state of both of Beddoes's intentions. At the center of *Death's Jest-Book's* dramatic structure is the promise of the immortality of the body. Ziba, an African conjurer, tells Duke Melveric that it is possible to bring the dead back to life. Ziba relates the story of 'A magic scholar' who raised a flower from the tears of a woman weeping for her departed lover, and he claims that it is similarly possible to raise a deceased man. He explains that:

> . . . *even as there is a round dry grain*
> *In a plant's skeleton, which being buried*
> *Can raise the herb's green body up again;*
> *So is there such in man, a seed-shaped bone,*
> *Aldabaron, called by the Hebrews Luz,*
> *Which being laid into the ground will bear*
> *After three thousand years the grass of flesh,*
> *The bloody, soul-possessed weed called man. (γ: III, iii, 447–54)*

Even though Ziba's necromantic lore duplicates Beddoes's own anatomical research, the drama clearly does not celebrate the *luz* as a principle of life. Playing on the seed metaphor, the Duke asks Ziba, 'What tree is man the seed of?' to which the conjurer responds, 'Of a ghost' (γ: III, iii, 444–45). Life in *Death's Jest-Book* is only the preparatory stage for death, and death is privileged as the structural centre of existence and the destination of an 'after-existence'. Although the play treats the *luz* as the stuff of legend (when Ziba actually reanimates the corpse of Wolfram he uses the power of words to do so), Beddoes appends a scholarly note soberly tracing the history of the *luz* through ancient rabbinical texts. Far from dismissing the *luz*, Beddoes has clearly made it the focus of some serious research.[7] In this way, the text of *Death's Jest-Book* indicates that Beddoes's medical research had a direct impact on both the content and the hopes for the play that he originally expressed to Kelsall and Procter. That Beddoes's empirical search for the principle of life as a feature of human anatomy was unsuccessful goes without saying, but the mixed intentions of Beddoes's persistent, if intermittent, desire to treat death as a psychic principle in the form of a semiotical display opens Freudian and post-Freudian possibilities for a reading of *Death's Jest-Book*.

---

6   James R. Thompson, *Thomas Lovell Beddoes* (Boston: Twayne, 1985), p. 68.
7   He translates various Hebrew references to determine that the 'Luz is therefore the os coccyges' (p. 488).

III: 'The fictitious condition': *Death's Jest-Book* and the Uncanny

Like Sigmund Freud, Beddoes sought for connections between scientific and psychic phenomena. Beyond this general similarity, what is particularly striking is the common ground that Freud and Beddoes share with regard to the problem that death presents to the human psyche. For, as Beddoes was forced to abandon his search for a principle of life distinct from death, Freud is finally forced to concede that the life drive, Eros, is inextricably bound to Thanatos, the death drive. 'The Uncanny' presents itself as entering into a belated dispute on what creates the effect of the uncanny in E.T.A. Hoffmann's 'The Sandman'. According to Freud, Jentsch contends the uncanny involves the 'impression of automatic, mechanical processes at work behind the ordinary appearance of mental activity' and that this 'impression' gives rise to a feeling of 'intellectual uncertainty'.[8] By contrast, Freud's thesis claims that the effect of the uncanny refers 'to the castration complex of childhood' that arises from a child's initial erotic attachment to his mother, 'and that . . . intellectual uncertainty has nothing to do with the effect'.[9] Looking back on the development of Freud's thought, what is interesting about 'The Uncanny' is not the way Freud argues for his stated thesis of childhood erotic attachment but, rather, the way much of Freud's speculation about the effect of the uncanny keeps returning to the subject of death. David Ellison accurately observes that:

> Freud's writing style follows the impulse, the drive, to say again, and repeatedly, what the uncanny has already said through a multitude of texts, including, most strikingly, 'Der Sandmann'. And what the uncanny says or testifies to, ceaselessly, is death. Beyond the Pleasure Principle becomes the retroactively deferred theoretical justification for the praxis of 'Das Unheimliche'.[10]

Thus, the significance 'The Uncanny' has for thinking about *Death's Jest-Book* is two-fold, in that both texts recognize but cannot adequately theorize the place that death holds in the human psyche.

'The Uncanny' is particularly relevant to *Death's Jest-Book*, given its observation that 'many people experience the feeling [of the uncanny] in the highest degree in relation to death and dead bodies, to the return of the dead, and to spirits and ghosts'.[11] To be sure, *Death's Jest-Book* can boast all of these, and its use of doubling, reanimation of the dead, and spirit dances invite a Freudian reading of the play. Yet *Death's Jest-Book* is hardly Freud *avant la lettre*, and the play will not sit still long enough for an application of Freud's strikingly un-theorized claims in the 'The Uncanny'. The ground for a more provocative relation between the two texts

---

8 Sigmund Freud, 'The Uncanny', in *Writings on Art and Literature*, ed. and trans. James Strachey (Stanford: Stanford University Press, 1997), pp. 193–233 (pp. 201–02 and 205).

9 Freud, 'Uncanny', p. 208; p. 205.

10 David Ellison, *Ethics and Aesthetics in European Modernist Literature: From the Sublime to the Uncanny* (Cambridge: Cambridge University Press, 2001), p. 67.

11 Freud, 'Uncanny', p. 218.

lies in Freud's rationale for identifying death as the preeminent ground of the uncanny. Freud speculates that death is particularly uncanny because it continues to resist scientific inquiry: 'Biology has not yet been able to decide whether death is the inevitable fate of every living being or whether it is only a regular but yet perhaps avoidable event in life'.[12] Here, Freud's notion of the uncanniness of death is specifically the short-circuiting of an internalized scientific rationalism that also underwrites Beddoes' anatomical search for a principle of life.

The proto-Freudian uncanny of *Death's Jest-Book* lies in its generic oscillation between satire and tragedy and its epistemological oscillation between magic and science. While *Death's Jest-Book* places the story of the *luz* into the mouth of the black conjurer Ziba, both slave to the Duke and the self-proclaimed master of death, Beddoes's footnote also seeks to establish the historical existence of the *luz* and its potential importance for nineteenth-century anatomical research. If this suggests that the drama sees an empirical tradition of scientific knowledge as owing something to the necromancer, the text also undermines Ziba's claims. When Ziba endeavours to resurrect the Duke's dead wife, the effect of his effort is doubly uncertain and doubly uncanny. Ziba's incantations fail to resurrect the Duke's wife, but the results of the spell are alternately comic and then gothic.

Beddoes's satire also resists a Freudian model by providing what I will call the mock uncanny. The first figure to appear from the tomb at Ziba's call is the low comic character Mandrake. Mandrake's resurrection is only possible because he has spilled a potion of invisibility upon himself, and he has been misrecognized as the voice of his own ghost.[13] Indeed, Mandrake comes to think of himself as a ghost and addresses the audience with his conclusion:

> that death's all a take-in: as soon as gentlemen have gained some 70
> years of experience they begin to be weary of the common drudgery of
> the world, lay themselves down, hold their breath, close their eyes and
> are announced as having entered the fictitious condition by means of
> epitaphs and effigies (γ: III, iii, 4–8).

Mandrake asserts that physical death is a discursive construction, 'the fictitious condition', as if it were solely a function of language's ability to imitate reality. Mandrake's appearance and commentary satirizes both death and the uncanny. His parodic death-in-life is literally *Heimlich*: death becomes the state Mandrake mistakenly understands as his home. When Mandrake initially enters the sepulchre of the Duke's departed wife, he quips, 'here are good quarters for the like of me, there I'll sleep tonight' (γ: III, iii, 24–25). When Mandrake responds to Ziba's

---

12   Ibid., p. 218.

13   In Act II, Scene i, Mandrake's accidental invisibility, his departure from sight, is confused with his departure from the living. When Mandrake's wife hears his voice pleading, 'I'm not dead nor / gone', she assumes, in fact, that he is physically 'dead' but a ghostly presence in the symbolic order when she responds, 'Alas! that my / poor husband's ghost should not know that he is dead!' (γ: II, ii, 88–89; 99–100).

incantation, his appearance deflates the expectations of both Ziba and the Duke, primed as they are for the reanimation of the Duke's wife. Beyond his role in the plot, Mandrake offers a satire of the hopes Beddoes expresses to Kelsall and Procter for exposing death as a pathological condition. Rather than revealing 'dotard death' and affirming a life principle, *Death's Jest-Book* finds death at the centre of human activity. Before exiting the scene in humiliation, Ziba claims that 'Death is a hypocrite, a white dissembler, / Like all that doth seem good' (γ: III, iii, 610–11). For Ziba, death's power is like that of the white imperialist Duke; death produces the effect of power, because, like the Duke, death does not adhere to verbal contractual agreements that establish the rules of fair play or, by extension, scientific discourse. Ziba's incantation fails to produce a proto-empirical cause and effect relationship that allows a corpse to move between death and life. Still, the case in *Death's Jest-Book* is more complicated. Expressing a thematic repetition compulsion, a second figure emerges from the tomb: the knight Wolfram, whom the Duke has killed treacherously in the first act of the play.[14] But the reason he appears is far from clear. Neither the Duke nor Wolfram attributes this resurrection to Ziba. The Duke initially insists that Wolfram's reappearance is the result of their pact, wherein the first who dies shall return to tell the other what death is like, but the more intriguing possibility is that Wolfram is making good on his dying claim, 'I will avenge me, Duke, as never man' (γ: I, iv, 203). Even in the moment of his death, Wolfram seems to appeal to death as a realm superior to the actions of life. The first 'Song from the Waters' that immediately follows Wolfram's riddling threat of revenge specifically distinguishes Death as the superior force to living joy. The song claims that it is the uncanny presence of Death that 'Rives asunder / Men's delight' (γ: I, iv, 208–09) and becomes the very essence of living form, when 'Our ghost, our corpse and we / Rise to be' (γ: I, iv, 210–11). Rather than extolling the erotic joys of 'Men's delights' as the driving force of life, the song lyricizes being-in-death as the paradoxical core of the cycle of human existence.

It is important to note that the first 'Song from the Waters' reflects the view of death in the 1844 γ text of Act I, rather than that of the 1829 β text of the first act. Clearly, the view of γ does not represent that of the Duke's consciousness later in the play. The Duke tries to explain the presence of the uncanny, living-dead Wolfram at the end of Act III as part of a political revolution against the feudal order that includes Death among its sovereigns:

> . . . *There is rebellion*
> *Against all kings, even Death. Murder's worn out*
> *And full of holes; I'll never make it the prison,*
> *Of what I hate again . . . (γ: III, iv, 688–91)*

---

14   Wolfram is in the tomb of the Duke's wife as a result of the machinations of his brother Isbrand. Part of Isbrand's plot to overthrow the Duke involves burying the murdered Wolfram in the tomb that will eventually hold the Duke so that the Duke will have to face his victim in the hereafter. Isbrand says of Wolfram's corpse that 'he is an earthquake-seed, and will / whisper revenge to the earth' (γ: II, ii, 140–41).

The Duke's analysis is only half right. Like Ziba, the Duke has misrecognized death's failure to co-operate with his desires as death's impotence. The rebellion in the play is against his reign, as he has suspected, but the action of the play does not indicate that Death's reign has ended. Rather, death has just begun to manifest its centrality to life itself. Indeed, Wolfram, speaking for death, gets the last word in *Death's Jest-Book*, claiming that it is the Duke himself who must bear the responsibility for bringing the dead back to life. Death, rather than Wolfram himself, will be revenged 'in like manner' by taking the Duke 'still alive, into the world o' the dead' (β: V, iv, 356–57). What is at stake in the uncanny reanimation of the dead is the attempt to bring Thanatos into the symbolic order, to be able to articulate its secrets, as Wolfram says, in 'the unholy world's forbidden sunlight' (β: V, iv, 354). For *Death's Jest-Book*, life is ultimately a perverse epiphenomenon of death.

As it develops in the wake of Beddoes's frustrated anatomical investigations, the text's treatment of death anticipates what contemporary criticism has noted in the development of Freud's own work, namely that the uncanniness of death reveals itself as the effect of a central structural principle—Thanatos, or the death drive. Thus Freud's 'The Uncanny' has come to be read as a proleptic demonstration of a theory that is only articulated later in *Beyond the Pleasure Principle* and in *Civilization and Its Discontents*.[15] The 'point' of what Gilles Deleuze calls 'the turning point in Freudianism' is not so much that the feeling of the uncanny arises from a childhood experience or a disruption of rationalist assumptions, as Freud initially concluded in the 1919 essay.[16] Rather, it is the particular uncanninness of death insofar as it indicates a structural principle of repetition, the death drive, a principle that exists beyond the repressed erotic energy of the biological individual. As Neil Hertz puts it, 'the feeling of the uncanny would seem to be generated by being reminded of the repetition compulsion, not by being reminded of whatever it is that is repeated'.[17] Read through Freud's later work, the uncanny testifies to the presence of a non-biological compulsion, instinct, or drive towards death, a drive wherein an individual death is merely the visible epiphenomenon of an invisible process of destruction at the centre of the structure of human reality. The development of Beddoes's thoughts about death as he studies anatomy and intermittently works on *Death's Jest-Book* can be seen as an uncanny precursor to Freud's development

---

15   Sigmund Freud, *Beyond the Pleasure Principle*, trans. James Strachey (New York: Norton, 1961), and *Civilization and Its Discontents*, trans. James Strachey (New York: Norton, 1961). See also Neil Hertz, *The End of the Line: Essays on Psychoanalysis and the Sublime* (New York: Columbia University Press, 1985), pp. 97–121; Gilles Deleuze, *Difference and Repetition*, trans. Paul Patton (New York: Columbia University Press, 1994), pp. 11–19; Jacques Derrida, *Dissemination*, trans. Barbara Johnson (Chicago: University of Chicago Press, 1981), pp. 172–99; and most recently Teresa De Lauretis 'Becoming Inorganic', *Critical Inquiry* 29.4 (2003), 547–70.

16   Deleuze, p. 16. Freud concludes that the experience of the uncanny is produced when 'infantile complexes which have been repressed are once more revived by some impression or when primitive beliefs which have been surmounted seem once more to be confirmed', 'Uncanny', p. 226.

17   Hertz, p. 101.

of the death drive as the structural principle of existence. The April 1827 letter to Kelsall expresses a similar turn in Beddoes's thoughts about death. In writing that 'nature appears to have appointed one solution—Death', Beddoes sounds much like the Freud of *Civilization and Its Discontents* (p. 630).

The problem, then, for Freud's theoretical project and Beddoes' poetic drama, is that both concede that human experiential reality is effectuated by a principle of Thanatos. For Freud, Thanatos takes centre stage uneasily as a principle that has no material content in the reality it constitutes.[18] While Freud recognizes the death drive as a central force that drives humans to create civilization as a kind of sublimation of this instinct, he does not recognize in the death drive a structural principle that is specifically political or ideological. For Beddoes, *Thanatos* emerged as the title inclusive of *Death's Jest-Book* in the 1844 MS III title page: THE IVORY GATE / DIDASKALIA — ELEUTHERIA — ANTHESTERIA / THANATOS OR THE PRIVATE THEATRE / A Story Including / DEATH'S JEST-BOOK' (γ, p. 323).[19] Tellingly, 'Eleutheria', or the celebration of liberty, is bound together with 'Thanatos' in the impossibly ambitious text of which *Death's Jest-Book* was only a part.[20] In the expanded frame constituted by this confusing title, the very possibility of the political reality of liberty is underwritten by death. Teresa de Lauretis identifies the broader theoretical implications of Freud's problem in terms that apply equally to Beddoes' drama: 'Freud's figuration of an unconscious death drive ... conveys the sense and the force of something in human reality that resists discursive articulation as well as political diplomacy, an otherness that haunts the dream of a common world'.[21] It is precisely in the sense of the death drive as 'something ... that resists discursive articulation' that *Death's Jest-Book* takes a step beyond Freud, to find itself in accord with Jacques Lacan's rereading of the death drive and its ideological implications. *Death's Jest-Book* exceeds the false biologism of classical psychoanalysis and the naïve materialism of Beddoes's own anatomical research to posit, as does Lacan, the death drive as simultaneously the radical other and the traumatic core of reality as constituted by the symbolic order of language, a reality that is purely ideological in its nature. Beddoes's play offers a living semiotical display of Lacan's rereading of the death drive, thus conveying the play's critique of ideology as a structural principle that underwrites both the feudal order and the possibility of a post-revolutionary republic in *Death's Jest-Book*. If revolution hides its uncanniness—the structure of repetition that is the death drive—*Death's Jest-Book* compulsively adumbrates its void.

---

18   For Freud the death drive cannot be identified in and of itself 'unless', as he admits in *Civilization and Its Discontents*, 'it is tinged with eroticism'. Freud is interested in both the necessity of the death drive or 'instinct' to his theory of civilization and at the same time its elusiveness. He comments that, 'it was not easy, however, to demonstrate the activities of this supposed death instinct. The manifestations of Eros were conspicuously noisy enough. It might be assumed that the death instinct operated silently within the organism towards its dissolution, but that of course, was no proof'. Sigmund Freud, *Civilization*, p. 79; p. 78.

19   See Michael Bradshaw's reading of the 1844 MS III title page (Bradshaw, pp. 109–10).

20   Bradshaw, p. 109.

21   De Lauretis, p. 570.

IV: 'The DANCE OF DEATH': Death, the Real, and Revolution

In terms of a Lacanian paradigm, the beginning of the final scene of *Death's Jest-Book* emerges as a parable of the identity of the death drive and the Real.[22] The scene takes place in a 'ruined Cathedral . . . the cloisters painted with the DANCE OF DEATH' (γ, p. 476). The stage directions describe the following: '*The Deaths, and the figures paired with them come out of the walls, and dance fantastically to a rattling music*' (γ, p. 477). This scene is, of course, uncanny in Freud's sense of bringing to 'life' figures described as 'Deaths', but the song these Death figures sing perfectly articulates the structural paradox of the Real:

> *The emperor and empress, the king and the queen,*
> *The knight and the abbot, friar fat, friar thin,*
> *The gipsy and beggar, are met on the green;*
> *Where's Death and his sweetheart? We want to begin.* (γ: V, iv, 19–22)

Here the re-animation of the dead that so fascinated Freud is inseparable from the whole social hierarchy represented in the dance. The absence of Death-in-itself from the centre of the dance of death highlights both the dead and the social hierarchy of which they are a part as material effects of Thanatos. In this scene, Death-in-itself has the same character as the Lacanian Real, refusing to take a place in the symbolic order, and, at the same time, it is the void around which the symbolic order is structured. This scene makes a distinction between physical death and Death-in-itself. Even in its physical death, the entire feudal social hierarchy still holds a place in the symbolic order. Even though absent in the scene, Death-in-itself is the structural principle that is both radically beyond the symbolic order and simultaneously the basis of its possibility.[23] What is at stake in death is not only the physical death of the individual but also, more importantly, the death drive as the threat of the 'obliteration of the signifying network itself'.[24] *Death's Jest-Book* thus can be seen to set out the ideological implications of the problem of

---

22 Slavoj Žižek's synopsis of Lacan's seminar *The Ethic of Psychoanalysis* thus speaks with precision to *Death's Jest-Book*: here it is 'the symbolic order itself which is identified with the pleasure principle: the unconscious "structured like a language" . . . is governed by the pleasure principle; what lies beyond is . . . a real kernel, a traumatic core', Slavoj Žižek, *The Sublime Object of Ideology* (London: Verso, 1989), p. 132.

23 Žižek explicates Lacan's reading of the death-drive-as-Real as a kind of second death, which situates the death drive as 'exactly the opposite of the symbolic order' in presenting 'the possibility of the "second death"', ibid, p. 132. In this way, the second death represented by the death-drive-as-Real marks the possibility, as Žižek observes, of 'the radical annihilation of the symbolic order through which the so-called reality is constituted. The very existence of the symbolic order implies a possibility of its radical effacement, of "symbolic death"—not the death of the so-called "real-object" in its symbol, but the obliteration of the signifying network itself', ibid., p. 132.

24 Ibid., p. 132.

revolution as the anxious theoretical space between two deaths, which is to say that revolution in *Death's Jest-Book* enacts the paradox of the Real. In its threat to destroy the symbolic order, to somehow step beyond the very process of symbolization and historicization, the revolutionary moment returns to the self-destructive limit of the process of symbolization and historicization itself.

Because the symbolic order is the ontological basis of experiential or ideological reality, *Death's Jest-Book's* treatment of the dance of death as an enactment of the structural role of the death drive is crucial to a critical understanding of the way the text treats the question of political order and revolution. Michael Bradshaw identifies in the text's treatment of the dance of death both 'a submerged recollection of the muted social protest understood to be present in the motif, and [a] metaphorical dimension [that] exploits its recent decline into apolitical blandness'.[25] Insofar as the dance of death in *Death's Jest-Book* identifies a diachronic unfolding of British literature's loss of the political idealism in its representation of Death as a social leveller, an inheritance that stems from the political charge attached to Hans Holbein's sixteenth-century woodcuts, it also suggests a synchronic analysis of reality as ideological, an analysis wherein the semiotical display of the psychic principle of revolution is a return to the death drive.[26] Here, the problem of the chronological setting of *Death's Jest-Book* is instructive. If, as Northrop Frye has observed, 'the action of the play is said to take place in the thirteenth century, . . . the use of the *danse macabre* brings it closer to the fifteenth', does this mean that Beddoes was simply mistaken in the historical setting he gives the play?[27] For Frye this seems unlikely in view of the text's other 'deliberate anachronisms' that remove Beddoes's work from 'any definite historical community . . . creat[ing] the sense of something alive and dead at the same time'.[28] In view of these uncanny anachronisms, Frye concludes that the text presents 'a historical essence suspended in time'.[29] While Frye's notion of 'historical essence' correctly identifies one way the play produces the uncanny as a historical as well as a biological effect, it misses the way that the historical essence presented by *Death's Jest-Book* is a compulsive return to the ahistorical void of the Real as the absolute negative limit of history's essence.

Nowhere is revolution's return to the ahistorical void of the Real clearer than it is in the third scene of Act III, where Isbrand convenes a final meeting of his revolutionary conspirators who are attempting to supplant the reign of the feudal order of Duke Melveric with a republic. The apparent purpose of this meeting is to distribute copies of its founding principles. Isbrand calls this document '[a] quick

---

25   Bradshaw, p. 223.

26   Perhaps this very observation is what made Shelley's *Prometheus Unbound* such an exceptional text in TLB's mind. Shelley's triumph is that his play is able to maintain the idea that the return to the past is the key to the discovery of desire or Eros rather than a compulsive return to a principle of Thanatos.

27   Northrop Frye, *A Study of English Romanticism* (New York: Random House, 1968), p. 66.

28   Ibid., p. 66.

29   Ibid., p. 66.

receipt to make a new creation / In our old dukedom', and he further likens his vision of the revolt to 'the first drops of Noah's world-washing shower' (β: III, iii, 70–71; 67). The biblical inflection of Isbrand's description of revolution identifies the ideological return to the ahistorical void of the Real as both history's essence and its antithesis in its invocation of the Christian myth of the world's creation *ex nihilo* and then its destruction and re-founding after the great flood. By first likening revolution to creation, Isbrand's phrase posits it as both a pre-ontological and a pre-ideological space. For *Death's Jest-Book*, revolution is a death to the old order accomplished through a return to a moment of creation: the essence of the historical-social reality promised by the revolution depends upon presenting itself, and presumably the ideological reality of bourgeois society that would be its result, in the ghostly lineaments of the biblical time before time, a moment marking the ground zero of eschatological history. Isbrand thus figures the emergence of bourgeois ideology as prior to the originary moment of existence.

While this moment is figured as a return to a place outside of history, as a moment without ideological content, it also reveals the Real's paradoxical position as the pre-ontological and pre-ideological kernel of the history of existence and its ideological structure. Isbrand figures the annihilation of the ideological substance of society before the flood as the destructive return to a kind of social-historical symbolization that depends upon the threat of its own erasure, thus likening the process of his revolution to that of the great flood. The claims Isbrand makes for his revolution as a moment of both creation and destruction suggest the kind of uncanny sense of revolution identified by Karl Marx in *The Eighteenth Brumaire of Louis Bonaparte*, where revolution is always an 'awakening of the dead'.[30] Marx's materialist conception of history finds in revolution not so much a place outside of history but, rather, the uncanny reanimation of a prior revolutionary moment. And while Marx certainly would not have accepted the Lacanian notion of the Real as a space that is somehow pre-ontological or pre-ideological, his view of revolution as uncanny is useful for a reading of *Death's Jest-Book* in allowing for a view of the process of social-historical symbolization as a return to a dead past in the name of historical progress.[31]

In a way that is strikingly similar to *Death's Jest-Book*'s thematic enshrinement of the repetition compulsion as a force that shapes both material history and the psyche, Marx also sees the uncanny reanimation of the past in revolution in terms

---

30 Karl Marx, *The Marx-Engels Reader*, ed. Robert Tucker (New York: Norton, 1978), p. 596.

31 Ute Berns, in her essay on the politics of revolution in *DJ-B*, identifies the socio-historical dimension of the uncanny parallel between *Death's Jest-Book*'s treatment of revolution and that of Marx in his *The Eighteenth Brumaire of Louis Bonagarte*: my thoughts here are indebted to her argument and informed by her reading practice. See in particular Berns's treatment of TLB and Marx; Ute Berns, 'The Politics of Revolution in Thomas Lovell Beddoes's *Death's Jest-Book*', in *Romantic Voices, Romantic Poetics: Selected papers from the Regensburg conference of the German Society for English Romanticism*, ed. Christoph Bode and Katharina Rennhak (Trier: Wissenschaftlicher Verlag Trier, 2005), pp. 97–107 (passim).

of dramatic genre. The French Revolutions of 1789 and 1848 allowed Marx to modify Hegel's observation 'that all great, world-historical facts and personages occur, as it were twice', with the addendum: 'the first time as tragedy, the second time as farce'.[32] While the Duke's attempt to reanimate his dead wife reverses the uncanny-generic-temporal sequence Marx posits for revolution, by bringing forth Mandrake and then Wolfram, the play's treatment of Isbrand's revolution could be read in terms of Marx's account of the failure of the two French Revolutions. Marx claims that 'the parties and the masses of the old French Revolution . . . performed the task of their time in Roman costume and with Roman phrases, the task of releasing and setting up modern *bourgeois* society'.[33] In its understanding of the uncanny possibilities of revolution as both tragedy and farce, *Death's Jest-Book* also presents its revolution—like Marx's view of the French Revolution—as a return to the crucial moment of death-in-birth of the Roman Republic.

In *Death's Jest-Book*, not only does revolution rely on a past moment of greatness but also it testifies to the failure of that prior moment. The play underscores this return in the conspirators' discovery of the blind Mario, a self-described 'Roman in unroman times' (β: III, iii, 115). Mario, a witness to the crucial moment in the failure of the Roman republic, marks the uncanny return of that moment in Isbrand's revolution. Reliving the death of Caesar, Mario narrates the prior historical moment:

> Down with him to the grave! Down with the god!
> Stab, Cassius; Brutus, through him; through him all!
> Dead. — As he fell there was a tearing sigh:
> Earth stood on him; her roots were in his heart;
> They fell together. Caesar and his world
> . . . .
> The toge is cut for cowls; and falsehood dozes
> In the chair of freedom, triple-crowned beast,
> King Cerberus. Thence I have come in time
> To see one grave for foul oppression dug,
> Though I may share it. (β: III, iii, 130–34; 139–43)

Mario's example of the death of Caesar suggests that a key feature of revolution's reanimation of a prior historical moment is the way in which that prior moment obscures the content of the present moment. For Mario, the unseating of Caesar to prevent tyranny was in itself an act that opened the way for yet greater tyranny. Marx could have been writing a gloss on Mario's speech when he comments on the February Revolution that, 'instead of *society* having conquered a new content for itself, the *state* only appears to have returned to its oldest form, to the domination of

---

32   Marx, p. 594.
33   Ibid., p. 595.

the saber and the cowl'.[34] In its depiction of revolution, *Death's Jest-Book* recognizes the same distinction Marx makes between form and content in its analysis of the merger of revolution and repetition, but the analysis of revolution and repetition that *Death's Jest-Book* allows for takes a step beyond Marx's materialism. The obfuscation of content effected by the reference to a prior historical moment in *Death's Jest-Book* reveals that behind the historical movement forward promised by Isbrand's revolution lies the death drive, as made clear by Mario's description of the overthrow of Caesar. The difference is that *Death's Jest-Book* finds that the return to the crucial moment of the Roman republic is not an obfuscation of the content of Isbrand's own revolution but, rather, an admission that—as a return to the ahistorical void of the Real—revolution has no positive content at all.

The scene Mario describes of Romans calling for the death of Caesar can be read as a manifestation of the death-drive-as-Real. The implication of Mario's address is that the activities of Isbrand's conspirators are only a political mask covering a return to the death drive. As in the example of the dance of death having both a symbolic and Real component, Mario's description of Caesar's death and its ideological implications is a perfect instance of the contrast between two deaths. While the physical death of Caesar is a pivotal moment of historical possibility, a moment where society can avoid a ruler whose ideological power depends upon a claim to divine sanction, the death of Caesar also underwrites the possibility of the death of the symbolic order as the destruction of ideological reality of Roman society. Once again, however, the paradox of the Real is apparent insofar as the persistent essence of ideological reality is inextricably linked with its radical negation: the desire for destruction. In Mario's description, the revolutionary acts of Brutus and Cassius are exposed as pure expressions of Thanatos as figured as uncanny repetitions of Hercules' feat of bringing Cerberus from the world of the dead. Mario's message is not so much that Brutus and Cassius failed at a given historical moment but, rather, that their historical moment is structured by the same return to the ahistorical void of the Real that structures the present. For *Death's Jest-Book*, ideological reality does not take on a new content in revolution; rather, revolution reveals the consistency with which ideological reality depends upon terror, the secrecy of the cowl, and the hand of the assassin. Thus Mario claims that the moment of revolution places in the 'chair of freedom' the three-headed beast whose essence is the timelessness of death itself.

The irony of Mario's prophecy in Act III, 'Thence I have come in time / To see one grave for foul oppression dug' becomes clear at the end of *Death's Jest-Book*. The true inhabitant of the 'grave for foul oppression' is the revolutionary leader Isbrand, to whom Mario finally delivers a mortal blow. As soon as his republican revolution succeeds, Isbrand wants to appoint himself king. He tells his chief co-conspirator Siegfried, 'I will be no man / Unless I am a king . . . / I have a bit of FIAT in my soul' (β: V, i, 35–36; 38). The deposed Melveric identifies in Isbrand's aspirations to absolute power not the abandonment of his revolutionary plan but, rather, the reflection of his movement's adherents. As he informs them, 'Your hopes

---

34   Ibid., p. 597.

and wishes found an echo in him / As out of a sepulchral cave' (β: V, ii, 24–25). In short, revolutionary aspirations in *Death's Jest-Book* are a return to the sepulchre. Isbrand's democratic revolution reveals itself as a compulsive return to the death-drive-as-Real, and, after his hiatus from the symbolic order of feudal power, Duke Melveric is momentarily recognized as a ruler only to be taken alive to the realm of the dead by Wolfram. In an ending with as much death as the Jacobean tragedies it reanimates, *Death's Jest-Book* give a proleptic Lacanian twist to Marx's observation, 'that in order to arrive at its content, the revolution of the nineteenth century must let the dead bury their dead'.[35] Through the agency of the anachronistic Roman Mario and the reanimated corpse Wolfram, death's absence becomes the positive 'content' at which revolution arrives.

It is tempting to see the connection between the death drive and revolution in *Death's Jest-Book* as a darkly Freudian parable about the innate nature of human aggression. Of the death drive, Freud claimed that 'it constitutes the greatest impediment to civilization'.[36] For Freud, the only response to the death drive that serves the purposes of civilization is more effective repression. To simply apply this Freudian insight to *Death's Jest-Book*'s presentation of revolution would be to say that revolution does not serve the purposes of civilization. However, such a conclusion retards the possibility of practical political reform and leads only to the conclusion that Beddoes's text is unavoidably nihilistic.

By contrast, it is precisely through a Lacanian reading of revolution as an expression of the death-drive-as-Real that *Death's Jest-Book* gains its force as a sustained and pervasive engagement with a paradoxical principle of structure. What emerges from this engagement is the potential for a critique of ideology itself rather than an opposition to any particular ideological-political content. The 'living semiotical display' Beddoes sought to give to the 'psychical principle' he called 'tragedy' returns compulsively to the void of the Real as a negative limit of experiential reality. In understanding revolution in terms of the death-drive-as-Real, *Death's Jest-Book* suggests an un-locatable, unspeakable, ahistorical absence at the centre of ideological reality. Unless revolution first takes into account the essence of psychic and political reality as a negative limit rather than as an object of desire, revolution, as it is set out in *Death's Jest-Book*, is doomed to compulsively and tragically return to the void of the Real in the search for an essential substance of human desire and political power. If in a Lacanian reading of *Death's Jest-Book* revolution is a symptom of the death-drive-as-Real, then the therapeutic approach suggested by Beddoes's drama is the identification of psychic and political content with the void at its centre.

---

35   Ibid., p. 597.
36   Freud, *Civilization*, p. 81.

The *Jest-Book*, the Body, and the State

Michael Bradshaw

This essay is part of the ongoing collaborative project of developing new directions in the study of Beddoes. The contextual theme that I will discuss—the representation of the state and aspects of state security in *Death's Jest-Book*—is intended to be indicative of the many areas of Beddoes's work that still remain under-developed. There is currently much to celebrate in terms of high-profile exposure and discussion of the work—especially the dramatic work—of this neglected writer; and at long last it does not seem unrealistic that this momentum might be sustained, and Beddoes be reconstituted as the major Romantic author we have long known him to be. But it would be a shame if we were to misdirect this energy by simply feeding Beddoes's fascinating, obstinately irreducible texts into accepted idioms of Romanticism, or even perpetuate the long-established patterns by which Beddoes was interpreted throughout the twentieth century. Much of Beddoes's singularity and power derives from his unresolved contradictions: if he does find a place in the canon of Romanticism, let him not be merely subsumed into a canonical agenda, but rather continue to challenge, provoke and disturb.

Espionage

Moving away from the abiding imaginative themes of death, dying, and haunting, this discussion will centre on a material and real-world phenomenon: the state, and its representation in Beddoes's signature text. This first section will introduce a discussion of the panoptic state in *Death's Jest-Book*, based on two main premises: firstly that panopticism is sited in the textures and rhythms of the individual body; and secondly that the discourse that carries this idea is figured in terms that intimate both a linguistic formation of what Foucault refers to as the soul, and a material preoccupation with language. I will concentrate for the moment on the first phase of the great central scene of *Death's Jest-Book*, III, iii ('the resurrection scene'): here, the professional fool and disguised revenger Isbrand plays host to an alcohol-fuelled meeting of conspirators among the ruins of a Gothic cathedral. A few minutes of stage time into the scene, he extends a welcome to a new colleague, the gnomic pilgrim whom the audience recognizes as Duke Melveric himself, Isbrand's antagonist and sworn enemy. The genial presumptive host is an obsessive and cruel revenger in the mould of Vindice, who has embraced a tactical disguise under the coxcomb and licence of a fool; during the course of their revels he seems unwisely to let his guard down and to be out-manoeuvred both by the Duke and by Mario. The gracious guest is really the Machiavellian autocrat whom the conspiracy is designed to overthrow; he is moving abroad in his own birthright-state in order to spy on the conspiracy (in particular his own disloyal sons, Athulf and Adalmar). His presumed purpose is to sabotage the plot from within, and yet Melveric's melancholy and contradictory nature never allows a single clear objective, and at times he seems more intent on self-critical or -destructive reflection.

This passage, when the two heavily disguised characters sound each other out in an uneasy ritual of hospitality, is a particularly striking moment in the drama of *Death's Jest-Book*. It seems susceptible to a number of theorized and contextualized re-readings. In a contemporary idiom, we might call the Duke's strategy an example of espionage, or even of counter-insurgency. As well as seeming to dramatize a particular species of panoptic state, it also puts the contemporary reader in mind of the political disguise dramas of Shakespeare and his contemporaries — powerful and explicit influences on Beddoes — and, further, of the Foucaultian paradigm that underlies recent interpretations of these plays, the New Historicism of Greenblatt on Shakespeare's Henriad, or the Cultural Materialism of Dollimore on *Measure for Measure*. The following is a close analysis of this passage, considering some of the possibilities it raises within the changing paradigms of Beddoes criticism:

> ADALMAR   *Enough. How are the citizens?*
> *You feasted them these three days.*
>   ISBRAND   *And have them by the heart for't.*
> *'Neath Grüssau's tiles sleep none, whose deepest bosom*
> *My fathom hath not measured; none, whose thoughts*
> *I have not made a map of. In the depth*
> *And labyrinthine home of the still soul,*
> *Where the seen thing is imaged, and the whisper*
> *Joints the expecting spirit, my spies, which are*
> *Suspicion's creeping words, have stolen in,*
> *And, with their eyed feelers, touched and sounded*
> *The little hiding holes of cunning thought,*
> *And each dark crack in which a reptile purpose*
> *Hangs in its chrysalis unripe for birth.*
> *All of each heart I know.*
>   DUKE   *O perilous boast!*
> *Fathom the wavy caverns of all stars,*
> *Know every side of every sand in earth,*
> *And hold in little all the lore of man,*
> *As a dew's drop doth miniature the sun:*
> *But never hope to learn the alphabet,*
> *In which the hieroglyphic human soul*
> *More changeably is painted than the rainbow*

Upon the cloudy pages of a shower,
Whose thunderous hinges a wild wind doth turn.
Know all of each! when each doth shift his thought
More often in a minute, than the air
Dust on a summer path.
　　ISBRAND Liquors can lay them:
Grape-juice or vein-juice.
　　DUKE Yet there may be one,
Whose misty mind's perspective still lies hid. (β: III, iii, 73–100)[1]

The exchange revolves around a favourite idea of Beddoes's—the placement of an eavesdropper in the 'cracks' of our lives and perceptions, the privileged listener in secrecy, the surveillance of thought.[2]

Both of these long speeches are compellingly imaginative: Isbrand's sinister fantasy of an omniscient secret service that can betray a suppressed motive before the subject is even aware of it is countered by Melveric's assertion that it is human subjectivity itself—not the capacity of abusive power to manipulate or invade it—which is without limit, endless (appallingly so: Melveric—like his son Athulf in Act IV—is becoming trapped in his own self in such a way that he might well wish it did not go on forever). It is important to note that it is *Isbrand*, supposedly a radical opponent of autocracy, who claims the apparently amoral licence to invade the consciousness of the subject; and it is Melveric, the supposed tyrant, who reprimands him and stakes an ethical claim for inviolable subjectivity. By this point in the action, Melveric is markedly changing from the ruthless traitor of Act I into the world-weary melancholic who, from the close of Act III onwards, will be haunted by his own personal ghost. The passage is also conditioned by the fact that Melveric is in disguise as a pilgrim: Beddoes seems deliberately to engineer a degree of slippage between the ruler on the inside and the religious on the outside. The exchange at first seems to offer an intellectual deadlock of mutual incompatibility. However, the antagonists' respective positions are gradually revealed to be complementary or, at any rate, co-extensive: the organic secrecy of the human responds to the stimulus of aggressive invasion and becomes roused to continuous involution; and at the same time the ingenuity of abusive power adapts to this new challenge. And so they roll on together—the subject being formed in its response to the demands of coercive power, a complex and artistic example of individuation as post-Foucaultian subjection.

1　All references to TLB's texts are taken from *The Works of Thomas Lovell Beddoes*, ed. H.W. Donner (London: Oxford University Press, 1935; repr. New York: AMS Press, 1978); the 'β-text' is Donner's widely used terminology for the version of the drama that was prepared for the press in early 1829, the most satisfactory and complete early version of *Death's Jest-Book*.

2　See, e.g., 'Fragments of *The Last Man* and other projected plays' (the 'Adye Notebook'), XIII and XLIV.

Isbrand's image of eyed feelers suggests a slug or snail, horribly probing the chrysalis of unborn thought. But both speakers here share the use of certain linguistic tropes to convey ideas of power and resistance: 'suspicion's creeping words'/ 'the hieroglyphic human soul'. The battle for control takes place at a microscopic level, and in the very texture of language. Beddoes echoes Shakespeare's *Coriolanus* at several points in this scene and holds fast to Menenius's iconic idea of the body/ state micro-/macrocosm.[3] The body is read: the activity of reading is invasive, disruptive, wholly malignant. Beddoes actively sustains a sense of the book itself throughout his drama of political and supernatural conflicts. The scene illustrates an important feature of *Death's Jest-Book*: Beddoes's managed congruence of body, book, and state, all of which are figured as sites of reading in the play's self-conscious textuality. This might slightly amplify the familiar theme of Beddoes's horrified aversion to the practice of reading, the way he sets up aggressive and rejecting allegories of reading, in certain dramatic fragments for example.[4] In this debate on spying as reading, Beddoes provides a representation of reading as an invasive and controlling intervention into the subjectivity of the read—we all provide our own text for surveillance by the police state, materials to be taken down in evidence and used against us. It is our words that betray us, and this betrayal seems to take place inside the body of the subject.

It was in his writings for *The Last Man* and *Love's Arrow Poisoned* (1823) that Beddoes firmly established his trademark somatic textuality: several key images from the *Last Man* fragments present the body of some unfortunate being scanned and interpreted by sinister eavesdroppers, two classic instances being 'Doubt', in which onlookers read the body of the reader of an undisclosed letter, comparing him to one who discovered murdered sister while digging for treasure, and 'Anticipation of Evil Tidings', in which the speaker is convinced that another's speech contains some concealed secret, an idea that he pursues with an image of digging through the earth all the way down to the chthonic serpent. These startling passages were drafted probably in 1823, at a time when Beddoes's familiarity with Elizabethan and Jacobean drama was at its most intense and creatively volatile.

Politics

The idea of the state in *Death's Jest-Book* and other writings may be an underdeveloped theme in Beddoes criticism; but certain critics have developed explicitly political idioms for interpreting the dramas. This discussion needs some account of the

---

3   TLB alludes directly to the fable of 'The Rebellion against king Belly' in a letter to
     Procter from Cassel in September 1825 (*Works*, p. 608) and translates a quotation
     from it in his German essay, 'The English Aristocracy and the Illness of Wellington',
     published in *Bayerisches Volksblatt* in 1832 (*Works*, pp. 567 and 738).
4   See my *Resurrection Songs: The Poetry of Thomas Lovell Beddoes* (Aldershot and
     Burlington: Ashgate, 2001), pp. 105–17; and Christopher Moylan, 'T.L. Beddoes,
     Romantic Medicine and the Advent of Therapeutic Theater', *Studia Neophilologica*, 63
     (1991), 181–88.

relative neglect of Beddoes's picture of the state in *Death's Jest-Book*, and yet Geoffrey Wagner (1949) and Daniel P. Watkins (1989) provide two interesting examples of political readings, both arguing in their different styles that the apparently psychic theatre of Beddoes is actually concerned with the dramatization of anxious social change. Geoffrey Wagner stresses the bitter pessimism of much of Beddoes's writings, citing the satire on northern English industry and commerce in 'Lines Written in Switzerland' as evidence of Beddoes's hatred of capitalism:

> *Yet he deliberately erected in his plays a fantastic society, beyond bourgeois conventions and customs, an unbridled phantasmagoria [. . .] It was in this world, where bourgeois mores did not operate, and where the poet's potentialities could be fully liberated, in subject-matter as in language [. . .], that we find Beddoes's idealism'.[5]*

> *Death's* Jest-Book *satirizes a baroque, a world fetid with the bourgeois illusion, disgraced by capitalist luxury. This world yields to the world o' the dead, to a society where bourgeois conventions do not operate. But individual man is still rational, he need not lust after the mummy country, as Isbrand puts it.[6]*

In Wagner's extreme but beautifully underplayed argument, Beddoes does not share the prophetic longing for death of the corrupt, decadent, and moribund bourgeois social order; but neither does he share the absurd, puppet-like, robotic rising Marxist order with which Wagner identifies the 'world o' the dead'. Wagner reads the dream-like sameness of Beddoes's dramatic characters as a bizarre anticipation of a Marxist society. As Marxism is to bourgeois capitalism, the ghostly is a post-critical alternative to the living.

The materialist critic Daniel P. Watkins reads *The Brides' Tragedy* (1822) as an expression of historical and social change: changes in the nature of drama in the nineteenth century correspond to crises of social class. Beddoes's dramatized conflict between an aristocratic subject-matter and a bourgeois sensibility expresses a distinctively Romantic anxiety as a rising class struggles to overthrow another:

> *Not only does [The Brides' Tragedy] capture the turmoil and anxiety of a once-stable social world on the verge of historical marginalization and extinction; it painfully articulates the loneliness, fear and dread which haunt Romantic literature particularly after 1815, when both the apocalyptic hopes for a utopian society and — at the other extreme —*

---

5   Geoffrey Wagner, 'Centennial of a Suicide: Thomas Lovell Beddoes', *Horizon*, 19 (1949), 417–35 (p. 426).
6   Ibid., p. 434.

> *the nostalgic desire for a return to an aristocratic and feudal world had been irrevocably dashed'.*[7]

It is interesting to note how closely Wagner's and Watkins's readings track each other: the idioms of Marxist-influenced criticism have evolved, but Watkins—with a more scholarly and historically informed awareness of the social situation of Romantic drama—does actually seem to preserve much of Wagner's argument on class difference and change. And yet neither essay is really about the *state* as such, notwithstanding Beddoes's dramatization of issues of compromised and manipulative state government, particularly in characters such as Orlando in *The Brides' Tragedy* and Melveric in the *Jest-Book*.

The state

The completion of the first version of *Death's Jest-Book* of course predates Beddoes's political activism among the Bavarian *Burschenschaft* in Würzburg, and his series of political essays written for immediate publication in *Bayerisches Volksblatt* in 1831 and 1832. The *Jest-Book* was complete in its early form by the end of 1828. But even in his earliest writings and in his reported escapades at Charterhouse and Oxford, Beddoes had assumed a ready equivalence between the authority figure and the tyrant.[8] Already a devoted cynic on questions of authority and conservatism, Beddoes found himself in his Göttingen period studying at and owing enthusiastic allegiance to an institution that was viewed with great suspicion by the Austrian higher state.

In March 1819, the dramatist August von Kotzebue, at that time working as a paid agent and informant for the Russian Tsar, was assassinated by Karl Sand, a young German *Burschenschafter*; this was followed by an attempt on the life of a reactionary minister of Nassau. Events escalated quickly, and Metternich assembled representatives of the Federal Diet to a meeting in Carlsbad in Bohemia to discuss a series of new security laws. Metternich had his 'Carlsbad Decrees' swiftly ratified by the Federal Diet in Frankfurt. The German universities became subject to state-sanctioned intervention and surveillance as likely hotbeds of French émigré-influenced radicalism, from which Austria herself must be insulated and protected by strict limitations on the mobility of students. Visas for foreign students were restricted in the belief that a deliberate plan existed among the students of universities—including Halle, Jena, and Göttingen—to spread a Francophile radicalism to institutions within Austria. Emperor Francis gave personal instructions on the need intellectually to quarantine Austria by keeping German and Austrian

---

7   Daniel P. Watkins, 'Thomas Lovell Beddoes's *'The Brides' Tragedy* and the Situation of Romantic Drama', *Studies in English Literature 1500–1900*, 29 (1989), 699–712 (p. 700).

8   See, e.g., the *'Manus haec inimica tyrannis'* episode in Charles Dacres Bevan's memoir of TLB, quoted in Royall H. Snow, *Thomas Lovell Beddoes: Eccentric and Poet* (New York: Covici-Friede, 1928), pp. 11–15.

students apart. The Federal Diet established a Central Investigation Commission at Mainz in the Rhineland, to oversee the implementation of new security laws. Metternich himself and his commissioner Sedlnitzsky regarded student activism as a severe threat to the stability of monarchical government in the Confederation just as in the wider Empire, Metternich boasting to the emperor that he would eradicate 'the German revolution' as surely as he had defeated Napoleon.[9] Individual states were instructed to censor their own press and to place official agents in the universities, who would monitor radical political activity and report on any inflammatory rhetoric by professors or students alike.[10] The Carlsbad Decrees were renewed in 1824, the year before Beddoes's arrival in Göttingen.

Two of Beddoes's earliest Göttingen letters provide valuable evidence that on arriving to study in that city he became immediately aware of the sensitivity of the political climate, and aware also of something of the tension between the Austrian higher state and the German Confederation—and especially its many university cities. In early 1826, Beddoes wrote to Kelsall of the political limitations placed on academic study at the university, taking the case of a liberal history and philosophy professor whom he admired:

> One of the most interesting of the idler lectures given here, is by Saalfeld on the history of the French Revolution. This man is a real historian, & no bad orator; but the government people do not much patronize him, as he is extremely free, and if he does not hesitate to condemn Napoleon, he has still less remorse in laying bare the infamy of the Polish transaction: he is indeed one of those people who are dreadful to the old continental discipline for his talents and moderation; if he had less of the one, he would no longer be venerated at the university; if less of the other he would be removed from his catheder by the paw of the police; & if the latter had effected a total eclipse of the former, he might now be Hofrath & Knight of the Guelphic order.[11]

Beddoes tells the tale with his signature comic nonchalance, and yet he makes his reader understand very clearly that freedoms of thought and speech are greatly

---

9   Cited in, e.g., Arthur J. May, *The Age of Metternich, 1814–1848* (New York: Holt, Rinehart and Winston, 1966), p. 43.

10   May, pp. 39–45; Hsi-Huey Liang, *The Rise of Modern Police and the European State System from Metternich to the Second World War* (Cambridge: Cambridge University Press, 1992), pp. 18–34; Donald E. Emerson, *Metternich and the Political Police: Security and Subversion in the Hapsburg Monarchy (1815–1830)* (The Hague: Martinus Nijhoff, 1968), pp. 100–35; Robert D. Billinger, *Metternich and the German Question: States' Rights and Federal Duties, 1820–1834* (Newark: University of Delaware Press, 1991), pp. 17–36.

11   Letter to Kelsall, 'Göttingen Wintermonat 11. Sonntag' (the extant letter that immediately precedes the announcement of *DJ-B* in verse to Procter in March 1826 ('Today a truant from the odd old bones . . .'); Donner notes that Saalfeld later became a liberal member of the Hanoverian Diet (*Works*, pp. 611 and 756–57).

at issue and that, for an academic such as Saalfeld, compromise and political wholesomeness are conditions of professional advancement.

In April 1826, Beddoes described for Kelsall a public celebration of the Göttingen *Burschen*, at which Blumenbach and Eichhorn were honoured by the students in an openly politicized fashion, with strong nationalistic or even militaristic overtones:

> On the 26th Feby we had the Burschen in all their glory: Blumenbach and Eichhorn — that is to say the stream of flowers & the squirrel — celebrated the 50th anniversary of their professorships. As soon as it was dark between 5 and 600 of us, horse & foot, assembled each with a torch and formed a two & two procession thro' the town to the house where they were feasting, drew round the square, and on Blumenbach's appearance at the window a short speech was made by the leader followed by several tremendous 'vivats!' He made his speech; we departed & threw our torches on the bonfire . . . The great ceremony consisted in a long anthem during which half-a-dozen men with swords took the cap of every one present in rotation off his head and singing the solemn words thrust it on the sword — when the weapons were sheathed to the hilt in their crowns, they were again returned as solemnly to the possessor in [a] state of perforation & replaced on his head as he chaunted an oath 'bald ein wahrer Bursch zu seyn'.[12]

The viewpoint of Beddoes's narration, in this extract and in the longer passage of description from the letter, moves noticeably from documentary witness to first-person participant.

Finally, in a letter to Procter later the same year, Beddoes alludes specifically to the legal constraints on the mobility of university students that was a central feature of the state educational reforms under the Carlsbad Decrees, making clear his contempt for the reactionary suspicion of the Austrian government and those who served it: 'W.A. Schlegel is professor at Bonn, a ten years old Prussian univ^y on the Rhine. His brother Friedrich is in Austria, and writes puffs for the Holy Alliance. No Austrian is allowed to study here, Göttingen is so infamous for liberality'.[13] In his letters home to Kelsall and Procter, Beddoes was an erudite and thorough commentator on his new contiguous culture: he writes at length about language and literature; landscape, food, and hospitality; science and scholarship. He also reflects intelligently on a state structure that is still new and alien to him, and takes the opportunity to observe how his intellectual and imaginative pursuits are conditioned and hemmed in by these patterns of ideological resistance and containment.

---

12   Letter to Kelsall, 1 April 1826 (*Works*, p. 617).
13   Letter to Procter, October 1826 (*Works*, p. 626).

The view of the state that emerges particularly from Acts I and II of the *Jest-Book* is conditioned by Beddoes's multi-layered experiment in theatrical time, by his modish imagining of the late Middle Ages shot through with tactical anachronism from the specificity of his own day. Duke Melveric seems to construct the state of Grüssau in Silesia primarily in terms of birthright and primogeniture ('Your business is obedience unto him, / Who is your natal star', II, iii, 288–89); in addition to this, the tournament scene in Act II contributes to a standardized sense of chivalry—a heavily gendered feudal state held together by a Christian warrior-caste whose value-system is rooted in the crusade and the Jerusalem pilgrimage of the late Middle Ages. The *people* are mentioned at certain key moments, but tend to remain either an alluded-to off-stage idea, the citizenry who dawdle behind the relentless plot, whose absence is repeatedly complained of by conspirators (e.g., 'the twilight strollers', III, iii, 32; 'They of the town lag still', III, iii, 45) . . . or else consistently clownish—we think of Mandrake's consort Kate and the salt-of-the-earth disembarked sailors in the tavern scene (II, i), and later on the silent gravediggers. But 'the people' is cited as a key component in the father-son quarrel, when Athulf and Adalmar's treachery is said to consist in their having leapt into the people's favour, having made the people love them better than their father ('these two sons of his unfilially / Have vaulted to the saddle of the people, / And charge against him', II, iii, 263–65: a mannered echo of Shakespeare's nascent modern ruler, Henry Bolingbroke).

This composite sense of the state is further detailed and complicated by several factors. Firstly, the Duke explicitly figures the state as his own body and encourages the traditional slippage between the two bodies of the prince ('He bade me say, / His dukedom is his body', II, iii, 267–68). And for his adversaries this discourse seems to be common ground, as Isbrand briefly intimates a medical justification for his rebellion:

> *Not here? That wolf-howled, witch-prayed, owl-sung fool,*
> *Fat mother moon hath brought the cats their light*
> *A whole thief's hour, and yet they are not met.*
> *I thought the bread and milky thick-spread lies,*
> *With which I plied them, would have drawn to head*
> *The state's bad humours quickly. (III, iii, 26–31)*

It is interesting to note that Isbrand is again harping on the tardiness of the citizenry here, even as he seems to support an establishment discourse on the integrity of the state; and perhaps we are intended to pick up on hints like these. Lateness and absence clearly interest Beddoes—think of the absence of Death from the *danse macabre* in Act V: 'Where's Death and his sweetheart? We want to begin' (V, iv, 22). So we have the paradigm of an integrated state, drawing heavily on early modern discourses of micro-/macrocosm and body politic, with the occasional very explicit nod to Shakespeare. But a crucial modern component seems to be delayed: the people have not caught up—they have yet to take up their position on the imagined stage. And this may be part of an implicit articulation of Beddoes's anxiety and dissatisfaction with the contemporary politics of insurrection, his Shelleyan observation of the disengagement between bourgeois instigator and roused populace.

The other way that Beddoes complicates his picture of the state in the *Jest-Book* is to provide layers of alternative conception: notably, republican Rome, the radical intolerance of emperors and gods alike, and the Roman civic virtues, which are all trumpeted by the illusion-breaking character Mario . . . and the republic of death itself, astutely expounded by Geoffrey Wagner in 'Centennial of a Suicide'. In a famous fantastical excursion in Act III, Scene iii, Siegfried explains the decrease of haunting as the gradual overpopulation of the dead world, becoming more and more satisfied with its own company, in which great cities of the dead are being built—Memphis, Babylon, Thebes, and Troy (III, iii, 393–95). The idea of dead and reborn worlds as alternative states might be pursued further here in Beddoes's German political essays (1831–32), with their repeated tropes of national resurgence, in which (as for Shelley in 'England in 1819') the present dystopian corruption of the state is a tomb or chrysalis, from which we expect the new ideal life to break asunder.

Disguise

Death's Jest-Book has long been recognized as revenge drama, in which Beddoes rewrites the Renaissance revenge convention in terms of a nineteenth-century view of popular revolution. But there is another sub-genre of Renaissance drama (comic as well as tragic) that should be taken into account for a more complete reading of Beddoes's adapted influence—the drama of political manipulation and control that centred on a disguised prince. The disguised ruler was an important figure on the early modern stage, filled with ambiguous meanings about the theatrical nature of power in Elizabethan and Jacobean England. The undercover prince provided materials for both tragic and comic drama, with perhaps a slight shift in emphasis at the ascension of James I from the earlier tragic vision of treasonous individualism thwarted by all-seeing royal power, towards a more inclusively comic vision with an ability to take a satirical view of the power of the state: there is a whole range of available dispositions in the way this adapted influence can be interpreted. The ruler—or, in some cases, his champion or representative—goes undercover in order to spy, probe, and monitor the behaviour of his subjects. There are several versions of the convention. Sometimes this is a simple information-gathering exercise; sometimes he acts as *agent provocateur*, fomenting discontent, and simultaneously promotes and sabotages a subversive plot; sometimes the leading idea is moral regeneration, and the prince leads his people towards a deliberately engineered crisis of redemption. There are clearly uncomfortable intimations of the panoptic state in this; and yet the disguised prince can also assume a vulnerable position, either in moments of personal threat and danger, or—more interestingly?—in being exposed to satirical attack and having no recourse to discipline this without blowing his cover, so to speak (for instance, with Lucio's ribald tirades in *Measure for Measure,* in which the Duke is forced to listen to himself being described as a whore-master). The combination in this motif of masquerade and rule gives an author rich scope for dramatic and meta-dramatic experimentation.

Thomas Middleton's *The Phoenix* was probably first performed in 1602: the Duke of Ferrara has become a lax ruler, presiding over a licentious state and himself being charged with corruption; his son Prince Phoenix, to outward appearances, goes on a journey but actually goes undercover in order 'to look into the heart and bowels of this dukedom, and in disguise mark all abuses ready for reformation or punishment' (I, i).[14] Having operated as *agent provocateur* and mingled confidently with conspirators, Phoenix publicly exposes a Court plot to overthrow the Duke, nominally serving and upholding the regime of his father, but also of course reinforcing his own birthright as the heir apparent.[15] In John Marston's *The Malcontent,* probably first performed in 1603, the true Duke Altofronto is already in disguise as Malevole from the outset, although this information is at first withheld from the audience. Malevole acts as cat's paw to a series of deluded would-be villains, engineering and sometimes concealing the outcome of their plots in order to experiment on their moral and emotional responses. Malevole is a good example of the multi-layered complexity available in the convention: as well as being both Prospero-style revenger-as-healer and a prince-in-disguise, he also occupies the stock characteristics of the malcontent as his chosen disguise, dramatizing the self-conscious construction or staging of a self and giving the writer several different overlapping frames with which to investigate and diffuse the idea of subjective identity. The disguised duke confides his plans to a single confidant, Celso:

> *Hope, hope, that never forsakst the wretched'st man,*
> *Yet biddst me live, and lurk in this disguise!*
>
> . . . .
>
> *Discord to malcontents is very manna;*
> *When the ranks are burst, then scuffle Altofront (I, iv, 29–30;*
> *38–39).*[16]

Altofronto's activities as Malevole also have the side-effect of causing the usurping Duke Pietro himself to go undercover as a hermit, giving place to a third Duke, Mendoza.[17]

---

14   Thomas Middleton, *The Phoenix,* in *Thomas Middleton (1580–1627),* ed. Chris Cleary: <http://www.tech.org/~cleary/phoenix.html>.

15   Although there is no explicit mention of this play, TLB mentions Middleton's comedies twice in letters to Kelsall, in 1824 (*Works,* pp. 586, 592), and *The Witch* in a letter to Procter from Göttingen in April 1829 (p. 643).

16   John Marston, *The Malcontent,* ed. George K. Hunter (Manchester: Manchester University Press, 2000).

17   Again, there is no mention of this play in any extant letters, but TLB refers to Marston in the same two letters to Kelsall in 1824; and again in a letter to Kelsall in 1829, when

Both *The Phoenix* and *The Malcontent* have been proposed as possible sources for William Shakespeare's problem comedy *Measure for Measure*, probably first performed in 1604.[18] The action of Shakespeare's play may be read as an internalization of Middleton's and Marston's disguise dramas, in that the Duke himself is to blame for the present corruption of his state, and yet it is also he who goes undercover to explore, monitor, and manipulate a redemptive crisis:

> Sith 'twas my fault to give the people scope,
> 'Twould be my tyranny to strike and gall them
> For what I bid them do: for we bid this be done
> When evil deeds have their permissive pass
> And not the punishment. (I, iii, 36–40)[19]

A troubling and ambiguous drama that explicitly connects moral, legal, and sexual corruption, *Measure for Measure* has a long history of tantalizing and polarizing its interpreters, especially those who pursue some pre-established moral agenda. The dense and contradictory moral discourse of the play articulates either the nature of a covert political power that masquerades as divine justice, or alternatively the descent of divinely appointed justice into its compromised manifestation in the materialities of human culture.

In forming Isbrand as a knight of noble birth turned revenger in the guise of a court fool, Beddoes is not only manifestly literate in the revenge and disguise dramas of the Elizabethans and Jacobeans but also has clearly absorbed and adapted their tortuous and convoluted ways of investigating human identity, in which a performed identity (such as Altofronto's 'Malevole' in *The Malcontent*, or Edgar's 'Poor Tom' in *King Lear*) is quickly developed into the rival and usurper of its original, while both are on occasion subsumed into the meta-theatrical dispersal of illusion that leaves in their place a player capable of directly addressing the audience. In that key extract from the resurrection scene quoted above, Beddoes further complicates this process by writing an encounter between the revenger Isbrand and the undercover ruler Melveric. Disguised revenger and disguised ruler then stage a debate about the ethics and limits of political surveillance.

The disguised prince convention may be read as an allegory of the Foucaultian invisibility of state power, its propensity to dissolve into an internalized habit of self-regulation. The device does not represent the diffusion of power mimetically,

---

he describes readings in Marston, Marlowe, Shakespeare, and Webster in between bouts of writing the *Jest-Book* (*Works*, p. 645).

18 See Thomas A. Pendleton, 'Shakespeare's Disguised Duke Play: Middleton, Marston and the sources of *Measure for Measure*', in *Fanned and Winnowed Opinions: Shakespearean Essays Presented to Harold Jenkins*, ed. John W. Mahon and Thomas A. Pendleton (London: Methuen, 1987), pp. 79–97.

19 William Shakespeare, *Measure for Measure*, ed. Brian Gibbons (Cambridge: Cambridge University Press, 1991); TLB does not discuss *Meas.* in any extant writings, but admiring testimonies to Shakespeare are legion.

but stages it and aestheticizes it as an allegory of the relation between prince and subject. In the disguised ruler scenes of *Death's Jest-Book*, all parties seem at once to be held in fascinated thrall to the panoptic ideal, and repelled by it in equal measure. The fantasy of eyed feelers probing the pupating thoughts of the populace—very much in tune with Phoenix's expedition into the bowels of the dukedom—conveys a nauseating conflation of internalized self-regulation and external invasion, so that the true origin of power cannot be readily identified or sited by its victim.

One interesting contrast we can quickly observe between Beddoes's adapted use of the convention and that of his Renaissance mentors is that Beddoes does not give the fantasy of total panoptic social control only to the undercover ruler himself, but more pointedly to his principal antagonist, the rebel, revenger, or revolutionary. The obvious stage convention would surely have been to place Melveric in the prime manipulative role, gathering information incognito, possessing the power of secret knowledge. But in fact it is Isbrand who seems to imagine state power in this way most intensely and enthusiastically; and in this moment of eve-of-coup hubris, he blurts this out, only to be admonished by the man he intends to destroy and replace. What does Beddoes demonstrate with this apparent inversion? Two things, possibly: firstly in dramatic terms, Isbrand—we can all see—is being set up for a fabular downfall (c.f. Blake: 'The iron hand crushd the tyrants head / And became a tyrant in his stead')[20]: the nemesis figure Mario is already waiting in the wings (he is brought onto the stage after a struggle five lines later, not at all a coincidence), as Isbrand shows early signs of forsaking his reforming zeal for a particularly solipsistic form of overreaching. Secondly, it is possible that Beddoes is articulating a cynical equivalence between the forces of violent revolution and violent reaction as cognate manifestations of power, which will inevitably shadow each other to an extent in the ways they operate. There is a form of revolution that merely rewrites the replaced power structure and, of course, perpetuates a cycle of suppressive violence; and this is a conventionally jaundiced and disillusioned view of the French Revolution. If *Death's Jest-Book* sometimes behaves like psychomachia when it is scrutinized in this way, then Beddoes's imagining of political power loses none of its horrific visuality or experience-weary pessimism for being relocated inside a single consciousness.

Re-reading the Duke's surveillance of dissent and rebellion in Act III of the *Jest-Book*, in the context of the disguised ruler motif of early modern drama, it is clear that Beddoes's conception of espionage cannot be disposed of as modishly Gothic paranoia, but has an idiosyncratic form of political sophistication, especially in its use of the body as a textualized microcosm. At the end of Act V, Scene iv, Torwald receives the crown to rule as regent on Melveric's deportation to the 'world o' the dead' (V, iv, 357). And with this resumption of royalty ('Receive the homage / Of your revolted city', V, iv, 262–63), the appalling cycle of material power begins again, under the very nose of a misled audience or reader whose attention is focused

---

20   From the Notebook draft of 'I saw a Monk of Charlemaine': *The Notebook of William Blake: A photographic and typographic facsimile*, ed. David V. Erdman (Oxford: Clarendon Press, 1973), N8.

most strongly on images of the supernatural and metaphysical. In this deeply inflected and subversive way, *Death's Jest-Book* develops a model of the persecuting and alienating state that seems to survive the supernatural upheavals of the plot: business as usual.

The writings of Thomas Lovell Beddoes remain intensely hospitable to new readings, and it is the responsibility of future generations of critics to maintain the search for new contexts for understanding. This may entail or even necessitate a turning away from standard traditional themes such as the ghostly, the psychic, and the macabre in a quest for timely alternatives; for example, there is evidence in the present collection of a general turn to materialism in contemporary Beddoes scholarship. Beddoes can continue to serve the academy of Romanticism well as an interrogator and subversive nuisance, an undercover agent 'touching and sounding the little hiding holes of cunning thought'.

'Liberty['s] smile melts tyrants down in time':

T.L. Beddoes's *Death's Jest-Book* and German Revolutionary Discourse in Heine, Börne, and Büchner[1]

Raphael Hörmann

In the critical debate about *Death's Jest-Book*, the importance of the German literary context has been dealt with occasionally, most recently by Michael Bradshaw. He examines thoroughly the impact that German Romanticism, especially the concept of 'Romantic irony', had on Beddoes's play.[2] However, the relationship between *Death's Jest-Book* and contemporary German revolutionary literature has hardly been investigated. The fact that critics seem to have been so reluctant to contextualize the revolutionary overtones in *Death's Jest-Book* with the pro-revolutionary discourses in contemporary German political writing and literature seems surprising, especially since Beddoes's intimate engagement with both German literature and German revolutionary politics would suggest such an approach. As Beddoes boasted in a letter written to his friend Kelsall in July 1830, he 'was acquainted with everything worth reading in German belles lettres' (p. 649).

One of the few critics dealing with this relationship is Frederick Burwick. Not only has he convincingly shown how Beddoes's political articles, in both Bavarian and Swiss journals, express radical views but also he has twice argued very strongly for a possible connection between Beddoes and the revolutionary German writer

---

1   I am highly indebted to Niamh Neylon, Margaret Hiley, and Eugene de Klerk for proofreading this essay.

2   See Michael Bradshaw, *Resurrection Songs: The Poetry of Thomas Lovell Beddoes* (Aldershot and Burlington: Ashgate, 2001), especially pp. 162–75. Earlier contributions include Ken Mills, 'The Bristol Connection', in *Büchner in Britain: A Passport to Georg Büchner*, ed. Brian Keith-Smith and Ken Mills (Bristol: Bristol University, 1987), pp. 16–18; Anne Harrex, 'Death's Jest-Book and the German Contribution', *Studia Neophilologica*, 34 (1967), 15–37; and Carl August Weber, *Bristols Bedeutung für die Englische Romantik und die Deutsch-Englischen Beziehungen* (Halle: Max Niemayer, 1935; repr. Walluf: Sändig, 1973). Weber was one of the first to suggest a possible connection between TLB and Georg Büchner (pp. 240–41).

Georg Büchner.[3] Whereas, in his earlier article on Beddoes's involvement with the Bavarian opposition, Burwick sees an immediate connection between Beddoes's 'literary works and political writings' and furthermore detects a revolutionary optimism in both, he completely contradicts this view in later essays on Beddoes and Büchner.[4] Comparing their literary works, he argues that *Dantons Tod*, *Woyzeck*, and *Death's Jest-Book* poignantly express a shared disillusionment with revolutionary change. Clearly concerned to de-politicize their plays, he maintains that both writers effectively abandoned their revolutionary ideas and political struggle and replaced them with a concept of a solely philosophical revolution. As he phrases it, their concern was increasingly 'the larger revolution of man against the dehumanizing factors of all political strife'; a claim that is untenable at least in respect to Büchner, as critics have conclusively shown.[5]

In stark contrast to Burwick's view that Beddoes abandoned his belief in revolutionary change, Ute Berns suggests in a recent essay that *Death's Jest-Book* affirms contemporary revolutionary discourses.[6] Not only does the play anticipate Marx's critique of the bourgeois revolution in *Der achtzehnte Brumaire des Louis Bonarparte* (1852) but also it refers to contemporary revolutionary discourses reflected in works of German political writers such as Heine, Grabbe, and Büchner.

Taking up Berns's cues, this essay seeks to illustrate that *Death's Jest-Book* is very closely related to contemporary revolutionary discourses voiced in German political literature. Choosing Heine, Börne, and Büchner as paradigmatic authors, I will show that Beddoes refers specifically to them, at times even engaging intertextually with their texts. On a more general level, it will also be argued that the revisions of *Death's Jest-Book* that Beddoes undertook between 1828 and the mid-1840s reflect the overall trend from a political to a socio-political revolutionary concept.[7] This change took place between the 1820s and the 1840s, with the 1830s—

---

3   Frederick Burwick, 'Beddoes, Bayern und die Burschenschaften', *Comparative Literature*, 21 (1969), 289–306; 'Beddoes and the *Schweizerischer Republikaner*', *Studia Neophilologica*, 44 (1972), 91–112; 'The Anatomy of Revolution: Beddoes and Büchner', *Pacific Coast Philology*, 6 (1971), 5–12; and 'Death's Fool: Beddoes and Büchner', in *The Haunted Eye: Perception and the Grotesque in English and German Romanticism* (Heidelberg: Winter, 1987), pp. 274–300.

4   'Beddoes, Bayern und die Burschenschaften', pp. 305–06; my translation.

5   'Death's Fool', p. 300. Key contributions that argue against Büchner's retreat from revolutionary politics are Georg Lukács, 'Der faschisierte und der wirkliche Büchner' (1937), in *Büchner im 'Dritten Reich': Mystifikation—Gleichschaltung—Exil: Eine Dokumentation*, ed. Dietmar Goltschigg (Bielefeld: Aisthesis, 1990), pp. 185–203; Jan-Christoph Hauschild, 'Neudatierung und Neubewertung von Georg Büchners 'Fatalismusbrief'', *ZfdPh*, 108 (1989), 511–29; and Terence Michael Holmes, *The Rehearsal of Revolution* (Bern: Peter Lang, 1995).

6   Ute Berns, 'The Politics of Revolution in Thomas Lovell Beddoes' *Death's Jest-Book*', in *Romantic Voices, Romantic Poetics*, ed. Christoph Bode and Katharina Rennhak (Trier: Wissenschaftlicher Verlag Trier, 2005), pp. 97–107.

7   See for example Eric Hobsbawm, *The Age of Revolution: Europe 1789–1848* (1962; London: Abacus, 1977), especially the chapter on 'Revolutions', pp. 138–63. For an account of the contemporary German socio-historical development, see e.g.: Wolfgang

and in particular the July Revolution of 1830 in France—marking the watershed for the 'emergence of the new social-revolutionary trend'.[8] Not only did the German egalitarian-revolutionary movement and the developing German working-class movement crucially contribute to the formation of the concept of a 'social revolution', but this very concept is also prominently mirrored in German political literature of this period.[9] In the final part of this essay, it will be argued that in the revisions made to *Death's Jest-Book* after 1829, in the γ version of the play, the social question and socio-revolutionary discourses play a key role.

However, in the late 1820s when the α and β versions of the play were written, the main revolutionary concern in the neo-absolutist German states was still the achievement of civil liberties. Socio-economic concerns were secondary in German revolutionary literature. As Walter Grab and Uwe Friesel point out, even in the 1830s, most democratic authors were still more concerned with political liberty and freedom of thought than the social question.[10] Symptomatic of this is Heine's complaint in his preface to a liberal anti-nobility essay by Robert Wesselhöft, *Kahldorf über den Adel in Briefen an den Grafen M. von Moltke* (1831), which Heine published. In this text, the last he wrote before emigrating to Paris, Heine argues that in contrast to neighbouring France where the liberal July Revolution had achieved the emancipation of the bourgeoisie and the establishment of civil liberty and equality,

---

Hardtwig, *Vormärz: Der monarchische Staat und das Bürgertum*, 4th edn (Munich: DTV, 1998); and Hans-Ulrich Wehler, *Deutsche Gesellschaftsgeschichte II: Von der Reformära bis zur industriellen und politischen 'Deutschen Doppelrevolution', 1815–1848/49*, 2nd edn (Munich: Beck, 1989).

8   Hobsbawm, *The Age of Revolution*, p. 149. For the impact of the July Revolution on democratic movements in Europe, see, e.g., Kurt Holzapfel, 'Der Einfluß der Julirevolution von 1830–1832 auf Mitteleuropa', in *Die demokratische Bewegung in Mitteleuropa von der Spätaufklärung bis zur Revolution 1848/49: Ein Tagungsbericht*, ed. Helmut Reinalter (Innsbruck: Inn-Verlag, 1988), pp. 177–83. He points out that the July Revolution marked the beginning of 'the epoch of the social mass struggles and the rise of the international workers' movement' (p. 177; my translation).

9   See, e.g., Walter Grab and Uwe Friesel, *'Noch ist Deutschland nicht verloren': Eine historisch-politische Analyse unterdrückter Lyrik von der Französischen Revolution bis zur Reichsgründung* (Munich: DTV, 1973), pp. 133–220, and *Der deutsche Vormärz*, ed. Jost Hermand (Stuttgart: Reclam, 1967). As Hermand writes in the epilogue to his anthology of German texts of the 1830s and 1840s, 'hardly any other epoch was as strongly preoccupied with the social question' as the German literary 'Vormärz' (p. 382, my translation). For the influence the exiled German working-class community had on the emerging concept of a social revolution, see, e.g., Waltraud Seidel-Höppner, 'Die "Soziale Republik" in der frühproletarischen Verfassungsdebatte: Kontinuität und Brüche vor und während der Revolution', in *Demokratie und Arbeiterbewegung in der deutschen Revolution von 1848/49: Beiträge des Kolloquiums zum 150. Jahrestag der Revolution von 1848/49 am 6. und 7. Juni 1998 in Berlin*, ed. Helmut Bleiber et al. (Berlin: Trafo-Verlag, 2000), pp. 13–25; and Hans-Joachim Ruckhäberle, *Frühproletarische Literatur: Die Flugschriften der deutschen Handwerksgesellenvereine in Paris 1832–1839* (Kronberg, Ts.: Scriptor-Verlag, 1977), especially pp. 40–60.

10   See *'Noch ist Deutschland nicht verloren'*, p. 146.

in Germany '"bürgerliche Gleichheit"' has still to be 'das erste Losungswort der Revolution'.[11] For in Germany, he pointedly states, the anti-liberal forces have taken refuge in 'entlegene Klöster, Schlösser [. . .] und dergleichen letzte Schlupfwinkel des Mittelalters'.[12] It is these places that they haunt as 'unheimlich[e] Schatten und Gespenster'. Although endangered by the approaching 'Sonnenstrahlen' (B II, 655) of freedom, the relative safety of their strongholds will enable them to resist the advancing liberal revolutionary ideology for some time.[13]

This is exactly the revolutionary situation that we find in Beddoes's Gothic play *Death's Jest-Book*. Reflecting contemporary German late absolutism that still retained strong feudal elements, the play is set 'at the end of thirteenth century' (β, p. 326), predominantly in castles and ruined cathedrals plagued by despotic dukes. Comparable to Heine's preface, Beddoes's play leaves little doubt that the days of the absolutist rulers are numbered. As the tyrant-slaying Mario—a staunch republican revolutionary—points out, their fate is sealed, although they might still be able to resist the force of bourgeois revolutionary force for some time. Employing similar imagery to Heine, Mario claims that the radiance of Liberty's smile will eventually melt those shades of tyranny:

> Liberty, whose shade
> Attends, smiles still in patience, and that smile
> Melts tyrants down in time [. . .] (β: V, ii, 37–39)

Significantly, at the end of the play, Mario not only assassinates the usurping tyrant Isbrand; the legitimate ruler Duke Melveric is also taken to the world of the dead as a living ghost. The latter, who had been instrumental in turning a republican revolution into a petty court intrigue, has to shrink away from the 'unholy world's forbidden sunlight' (β: V, iv, 354). From a nineteenth-century republican viewpoint, the monarch Melveric is the ghost of a dark political past and thus a living anachronism. The monarch is one of the living-dead. Although 'still alive', he actually belongs more to 'the world o' th' dead', as Wolfram emphasizes in the last line of the play. So when the latter snatches the '*DUKE* [away] *into the sepulchre*' (SD, β: V, iv), the aristocratic ruler has indeed found his rightful place.

Since the ending of the play exposes monarchy as a doomed political system, *Death's Jest-Book* offers a hopeful scenario for the bourgeois revolution. The restoration of monarchic power in the drama fails spectacularly, thus foreshadowing the eventual failure of the European Restoration. In a moment of revolutionary subversion, Wolfram presents a 'masque and dance' to Duke Melveric, supposedly

---

11   'Civil equality' should be 'the first watchword of the revolution'. Heinrich Heine, *Sämtliche Schriften*, ed. Klaus Briegleb (Munich: DTV, 1997), II, 660. All further quotations from Heine's writings will be taken from this edition, which will subsequently be referred to as B.

12   'Isolated monastries, castles . . . other such last hiding places of the middle ages' (my translation).

13   'Uncanny shades and ghosts', 'the rays of the sun' (my translation).

'in honour of [his] restoration'. The masque, however, turns out *not* to be an apotheosis of restored monarchy but, on the contrary, exposes its decay and even prophesies its doom. What is enacted in the drama is a '*dance of Deaths*', a grotesque 'antimasque' that is 'satirical' (c.f. β: V, iv, 299–300) when the slain successor to the throne, Melveric's son Adalmar, is borne onto the stage. In this light, Burwick's apodictic verdict that *Death's Jest-Book* shows that the 'revolution could not be won' and 'the futility of that battle' is doubly problematic, since it neither does justice to the text nor to the revolutionary discourses that lie behind it.[14] The entire political system as depicted in *Death's Jest-Book* is so unstable and inherently anachronistic that the eventual restoration of monarchy in the person of the Governor Thorwald rings as hollow as the historical attempt to restore the pre-revolutionary order after 1815. The restored monarchic order is already doomed even before the July Revolution of 1830 sees the aristocracy suffering a major 'Hirnschlag' ('stroke') and makes this 'bittere Schule der Vergangenheit' vanish like a light dream, as Beddoes writes in a political article in November 1831 (c.f. p. 561).[15] Neither was it possible to reverse the socio-political changes that the French Revolution had achieved, nor could the revolutionary momentum that it had triggered be stopped. Reflecting these socio-historical facts, the political scenario in the play decisively changes at the end. The Duke and all his kin are dead, as well as the usurper Isbrand and his brother, the knight Wolfram, who are both murdered; the latter having been a faithful defender of the monarchy. The fact that the new duke, Thorwald, had previously been overthrown in a rebellion does not bode well for the future stability of the monarchy. Rather than expressing a pessimistic view of revolutionary change as Burwick claims, it could be argued that, on the contrary, *Death's Jest-Book* suggests that the bourgeois revolution is inevitable. I would argue that in its medieval setting it exposes the decadence and pettiness of German court-politics. Therefore it passes a damning verdict on the future of its aristocratic governments, which beneath their modern bureaucratic structures retained strong feudal elements. Similar to Heine's *Deutschland: Ein Wintermärchen* (1844), Beddoes's play presents the German political stage as a grotesque anachronism: a 'Kamaschenrittertum', a disgusting mixture 'Von gothischem Wahn und modernem Lug, / Das weder Fleisch noch Fisch ist' (Caput XVII, ll. 41–44; *B* IV, 617).[16]

In *Death's Jest-Book*, Beddoes anticipates the impending demise of this outmoded system, which Heine will emphatically prophesy in his epic poem. However, I would argue that Beddoes's revolutionary play is in turn influenced by an early revolutionary poem by Heine: the Gothic ballad 'Belsazar', which transforms the biblical story of the fall of the tyrannical King Belshazzar into a prophecy of doom for German neo-absolutist despotism. Since its first publication in 1822 it had become one of Heine's most popular poems, not least because it was also included in his extremely successful collection of poems *Buch der Lieder* (1827). This cycle

---

14   'The Anatomy of Revolution', p. 8.
15   'Bitter school of the past' (my translation).
16   'Galoshes-knighthood', 'Of gothic madness and modern lies / Which is neither fish nor fowl' (my translation).

of poems marked Heine's breakthrough as a poet, thus making 'Belsazar' widely known among the contemporary German reading public. These facts suggest that it is very likely that Beddoes, with his extensive knowledge of 'German belles lettres' and his professed aim to be acquainted with 'everything worth reading in German literature' (p. 649), knew Heine's poem when he was working on the α and β versions of *Death's Jest-Book*.

Harking back to the biblical story of the fall of the Mesopotamian King Belshazzar (Daniel 5), and probably also to Byron's poems 'To Belshazzar' (1814) and 'Vision of Belshazzar' (1815) that both denounce tyrannical rule, Heine details in 'Belsazar' how the king's subordinates assassinate the absolutist monarch during a drunken midnight feast.[17] Thus the plot of Heine's ballad forms a striking parallel to the plot of the fifth act of *Death's Jest-Book*, in which the absolutist tyrant Isbrand is also slain by his fellow conspirator Mario during a drunken midnight feast. But the similarities go beyond the conspiracy thus enacted and extend to an ideological level. In both texts the hubris of the monarch consists in his claim that he is as omnipotent as the Judaeo-Christian God. In an important departure from the biblical source, where Belshazzar merely desecrates holy vessels stolen from the Temple of Jerusalem, Heine adds a speech, in which Belsazar posits his rule as absolute:

> *Jehovah! dir künd ich auf ewig Hohn—*
> *Ich bin der König von Babylon! (ll. 25–26; B I, 55)[18]*

His sacrilege consists in his claim that as an absolute monarch he is not bound by any will other than his own, neither the will of God nor that of his subjects.

Death's Jest-Book places even more emphasis on the fact that the absolutist monarch is a tyrant to his people, who claims divine power for himself. Indeed the speech in which Isbrand reveals his claim to the throne clearly expresses his contempt for the people as well as for any superior agency:

> SIEGFRIED *They wait still for you in their council chamber*
> *And clamorously demand . . . your intentions*
> *Towards the new republic.*
> ISBRAND *They demand!*
> *A phrase politer would have pleased me more.*
> *The puppets, whose heart-strings I hold and play*
> *Between my thumb and fingers, this way, that way;*

---

17   See Winfried Freund, *Die deutsche Ballade* (Paderborn: Schönigh, 1973), p. 73; Katharina Mommsen, 'Heines lyrische Anfänge im Schatten der Karlsbader Beschlüsse', in *Wissen aus Erfahrungen: Werkbegriff und Interpretation heute: Festschrift für Herman Meyer zum 65. Geburtstag*, ed. Alexander von Bormann (Tübingen: Niemeyer, 1976), pp. 451–73 (p. 456); and Margaret Anne Rose, 'A Political Referent and Secular Source for Heine's "Belsatzar"', *Heine-Jahrbuch*, 21 (1982), 186–90 (p. 188).

18   'Jehovah! Thee I will hold in contempt forever/ I am the King of Babylon!' (my translation).

. . . .
SIEGFRIED *Mean you*
Openly to assume a kingly power . . . ?
ISBRAND . . . *In one word hear, what soon they all shall hear:*
A king's a man, I will be no man
Unless I am a king . . . *(β: V, i, 1–36; my emphases)*

With Winfried Freund, one could claim that both Belsazar and Isbrand form 'a cipher for the absolute potentate in the age of Restoration'.[19] However if one looks closely at both declarations of royal hubris, it is evident that Beddoes clearly sees the monarch's crime from a republican perspective, whereas Heine holds a liberal view.[20] Isbrand's spite is specifically directed at the ideal of a democratic 'republic', whereas Belsazar's claim for absolute power merely violates the liberal ideal of a constitutional monarchy in which the ruler is bound by the will of his people.

Despite these ideological differences, both texts equally affirm revolutionary action against those rulers who violate the natural rights of their subjects. They also share a strong anti-aristocratic tendency. In 'Belsazar', the king's followers are portrayed as a group of sycophantic drunkards. In *Death's Jest-Book*, most noble male characters are implicated in the insidious scheming that turns a potential revolution into a mere court intrigue. The only two who do not take part in these selfish power struggles are the fool figure Mandrake and the freedom fighter Mario. Modelled on the lowly comic servant figure from the *commedia dell'arte*—'zany to a mountebank', as he is called in the *dramatis personae* (β, p. 324)—Mandrake is most definitely not part of the nobility, nor is the usurper's nemesis Mario, being a revolutionary ghost from the Roman Republic. Thus it could be claimed that what Freund regards as the socio-political implications of 'Belsazar' also apply to *Death's Jest-Book*. Both Heine's poem and Beddoes's play reflect the revolutionary struggle of the bourgeoisie against the nobility.

Taking this point further, Freund argues that Heine established with 'Belsazar' a tradition of political gothic ballads in which the fantastic serves both as a disguise for an implicit revolutionary call and 'as a signal for impending socio-political change'.[21] In fact, in 'Belsazar', the poet fashions himself as the prophet of this revolutionary upheaval. When he depicts in great length how the fiery letters are being written on the wall during the tyrant's lavish banquet—the description takes up two whole stanzas—this is clearly a meta-textual hint that the poem itself forms a call to revolution. As Mommsen has argued, Heine's ballad aims to rouse

---

19   Die Deutsche Ballade, p. 74; my translation.
20   For Heine as a liberal, see, e.g., Hans Bold, 'Heine im Zusammenhang der politischen Ideen seiner Zeit', in *Heinrich Heine im Spannungsfeld von Literatur und Wissenschaft: Symposium anläßlich der Benennung der Universität Düsseldorf nach Heinrich Heine*, ed. Wilhelm Gössmann and Manfred Windfuhr (Düsseldorf: Hobbing, 1990), pp. 65–80.
21   Winfried Freund, '"Allnächtlich zur Zeit der Gespenster": Zur Rezeption der Gespensterballade bei Heinrich Heine', *Heine-Jahrbuch*, 21 (1981), 53–71 (p. 58); my translation.

revolutionary feelings among its readers, similar to the way in which the writing on the wall does among the king's subordinates within the poem.[22] Through a direct address to the reader to pay special attention to it, the meta-textual dimension of this event is highlighted: 'Und sieh! und sieh!' (l. 31).[23] Furthermore, the act of writing on the white wall is depicted as if it were the poet writing letters on white sheets of paper, with a particular emphasis on the process of writing itself through the three-fold repetition of the verb 'to write':

> Und schrieb, und schrieb an weißer Wand
> Buchstaben von Feuer, und schrieb und schwand. (ll. 33–34)[24]

In *Death's Jest-Book* we find comparable meta-textual hints that highlight the function of the play as a text advocating revolutionary change. In particular, the play contains a fragmentary 'new ballad called "The Median Supper"' (β: IV, iv, 57) that strongly stresses this aspect. Isbrand recites it during a midnight banquet in front of Governor Thorwald. Similar to Heine's ballad about King Belshazzar's ill-fated midnight feast, it also deals with the overthrow of a Mesopotamian tyrant. Not only does Isbrand's ballad allude to the coup against Thorwald that is already underway, but, ironically, it also foretells his own downfall, which will take place during the next dinner banquet. However, the ballad's political importance within the play is even greater than being a mere *prophecy* of revolution. Comparable to the revolutionary writing on the wall in 'Belsazar', it serves as a direct *signal* for it:

> All kingdomless is thy old head,
> In which began the tyrannous fun;
> Thou'rt slave to him, who should be dead:
> . . . .
> Now let the clock strike, let the clock strike now,
> And world be altered!

> The clock strikes one, and the hour is repeated from the steeples
> of the city. . . . A trumpet is heard, followed by a peal of cannon
> . . . The stage is lined with soldiery. (β: IV, iv, 116–29)

In its meta-textual function, the ballad is not only crucial to the revolutionary events within the play but also comments on the play's relationship to contemporary politics, in particular the issue of revolutionary change. Thus the ballad constitutes a strong meta-textual hint that *Death's Jest-Book* is supposed to work both as a prophecy of and a call for a *political* revolution.

---

22   Mommsen, 'Heines literarische Anfänge', pp. 459–62.
23   'And look! And look!' (my translation).
24   'And wrote, and wrote on the white wall / letters of fire, and wrote and vanished' (my translation).

However, the developing socio-historical situation (which I have outlined earlier) increasingly raised the question of whether a purely political revolution—a type of revolution that the α and β versions deal with—would be enough to create a more just system and society. In particular, the emergence of liberal regimes dominated by the rich bourgeoisie in France, Belgium, and Switzerland soon made it obvious that liberalism did *not* mean the end of repressive social policies towards the poorer majority. Indeed, when the German revolutionary author Ludwig Börne, in the 14th letter of the *Briefe aus Paris* (1832), paradigmatically calls the rich bourgeoisie a 'Geldaristokratie, einen Glücksritterstand'—thus stressing its affinity with the old aristocracy—he is only one of several German voices that indict continuing social injustice under the new liberal systems.[25] Beddoes also dismisses the French bourgeois regime for being as tyrannical in a socio-political respect as the monarchy that it had replaced. His article on the political changes in France (1831)—on the rule of its liberal government, which came to power through the July Revolution (1830)—strikingly demonstrates this: 'dass das nackte Unrecht der Menschheit sich nicht mit den Lumpen der Restauration zu bedecken und erwärmen braucht' (p. 562).[26] This quotation clearly suggests that in the early 1830s Beddoes had already abandoned his former belief that a mere political revolution against a monarchic system of government would secure a more just society. When he affirms the idea

---

25   'Moneyed aristocracy, an order of knight-adventurers' (my translation). Ludwig Börne, *Sämtliche Schriften*, ed. Inge and Peter Rippmann (Düsseldorf: Melzer, 1964), III, 67 (hereafter abbreviated as R). Wolfgang Strähl, a Swiss joiner and piano-maker, also ranks France among the 'Geldaristokratien' ('moneyed aristocracies'). For him, liberal states necessarily constitute 'unfreien Staaten', since they are governed solely by the wealthy bourgeoisie and their class interests: 'um die Reichen zu begünstigen und die Wenigerhabenden zu unterdrücken' ('to favour the rich and to oppress the ones who own less'). Strähl, *Briefe eines Schweizers aus Paris 1835–1836: Neue Dokumente zur Geschichte der frühproletarischen Kultur und Bewegung*, ed. Jacques Grandjonc, Waltraud Seidel-Höppner and Michael Werner (Vaduz: Topos Verlag, 1988), p. 215. A pamphlet 'Glaubensbekenntnis eines Geächteten' (1834) published by the eponymous German exile association in Paris even distinguishes between an *'aristokratische Republik'* and a genuinely free state, a *'demokratische Republik'*, which will safeguard political and social equality. Quoted in Hans-Joachim Ruckhäberle, *Frühproletarische Literatur: Die Flugschriften der deutschen Handwerkergesellenvereine in Paris 1832–1839* (Kronberg: Scriptor Verlag), p. 132. Georg Büchner in a letter to August Stöber (9 December 1833) indicts the implication of the liberal bourgeoisie in the exploitation of the poor: 'Das arme Volk schleppt geduldig den Karren, worauf die Fürsten und Liberalen ihre Affenkomödie spielen' ('The poor people patiently draw the cart upon which the princes and the liberals play their comedy of apes). Georg Büchner, *Complete Works and Letters*, ed. Walter Hinderer, ed. and trans. Henry J. Schmidt (New York: Continuum, 1986), p. 256; Georg Büchner, *Sämtliche Werke, Briefe und Dokumente*, 2 vols, ed. Henri Poschmann (Frankfurt a. Main: Insel Verlag, 2002), II, 400; hereafter abbreviated as P and H respectively.)
26   'That the naked injustice of humankind does not need to be covered and kept warm by the rags of Restoration' (my translation).

of 'allgemeiner Gütergemeinschaft',[27] he clearly moves towards a concept of social revolution, which 'does not stop with the change of ... political structures, but fundamentally changes all areas of social life' including 'the modes of production and distribution', as Waltraud Seidel-Höppner defines it.[28]

This ideological shift from a political to a social revolution is also reflected in the revisions that Beddoes undertook in the γ version of *Death's Jest-Book*. The radical socio-revolutionary tendency of Beddoes's revisions only becomes fully evident when they are compared to the extreme leftist voices among contemporary German political authors, for instance, to the aforementioned Ludwig Börne. After the July Revolution, the latter moved to Paris, where—as a result of his disillusionment with French liberalism—he changed very rapidly from a liberal to a radical activist with socio-revolutionary leanings.[29] Becoming increasingly hostile towards the liberal regime, he accused the bourgeoisie of recklessly exploiting the poor and in the 70th letter of the *Briefe aus Paris* (1833) even compared their capitalist practices to the crimes of medieval *'Raubritter'* ('robber barons'; *R*, p. 473; Börne's emphasis). When, in 1831, a rising by the Lyon silk weavers, which conjured up the spectre of a proletarian revolution, was brutally crushed, Börne subsequently lost his belief in a political revolution altogether and moved towards the concept of a social revolution. Expounding in the 60th letter of the *Briefe aus Paris* (1833) on the stupidity of the then French Prime Minister Casimir Périer, who saw in the—mainly economically motivated—rebellion in Lyon 'gar nichts von Politik ... nichts als Mord, Raub und Brand' (*R*, p. 371), Börne clearly no longer regards political, but rather socio-economic reasons as the main driving force of revolution.[30] Viewing the whole of human history as a struggle between oppressed and oppressors—according to him 'schon die Staaten des Altertums kränkelten an diesem Übel der Menschheit' (*R*, p. 372)—he claims that now this smouldering conflict is erupting in the open 'Krieg der Armen gegen die Reichen, derjenigen, die nichts zu verlieren hätten, gegen diejenigen, die etwas besitzen!' (*R*, p. 371).[31] Juxtaposing the allegations of contemporary liberals (for instance, Saint-Marc Girardin notoriously called the

---

27   'Community of goods' (my translation).

28   My translation; 'Die "Soziale Republik" in der frühproletarischen Verfassungsdebatte', p. 19. TLB, 'Die Gespenster', *Bayerisches Volksblatt* (suppl.) (27 April 1831), quoted in Burwick, 'Beddoes, Bayern und die Burschenschaften', p. 297. When TLB advocates the egalitarian concept of a community of goods, he in fact adopts an avant-garde position among the German revolutionaries. According to Ruckhäberle, this concept did not become widespread in German revolutionary pamphlets until the mid- and late 1830s, in *Flugschriftenliteratur im historischen Umkreis Georg Büchners* (Kronberg: Scriptor-Verlag, 1975), pp. 225–31.

29   See Inge Rippmann, 'Börne und Heine', in *Heinrich Heine 1797–1856: Internationaler Veranstaltungszyklus zum 125. Todestag 1981 bei Eröffnung des Studienzentrums Karl-Marx-Haus Trier* (Trier: Karl-Marx-Haus, 1981), pp. 120–33 (p. 107).

30   'Nothing of politics, ... nothing but murder, robbery and arson' (my translation).

31   'War of the poor against the rich, of those who had nothing to lose against those who own something'. The previous quotation translates as 'already the states of antiquity were afflicted with this ill of humankind' (my translations).

urban poor 'barbarians' who wage war on civilized society), Börne argues that it is not the proletariat who are the aggressors but, instead, the rich bourgeoisie and their system of exploitation.[32] Consequently, Börne in this letter regards socio-revolutionary action as the only option for the lower classes to resist and to end the sustained socio-economic attacks by the bourgeoisie; an ideological stance he shares with the most radical early socialist factions in contemporary France.[33]

In the revised first act of Beddoes's play we find a passage in Scene i that mirrors—on an ideological level—this view of a war between the rich and the poor. Like Börne, Beddoes also reflects both growing socio-economic injustice and resistance against it by the exploited.[34] Seemingly only referring to the play's pseudo-medieval world of robber-barons, Isbrand cynically exposes the underlying system of socio-economic exploitation that guarantees the perpetuation of the feudal system. Importantly, however, he stresses, like Börne, that this practice is not limited to this particular period. It is but one stage in the 'real history of the World' (γ: I, i, 123–24) that is fundamentally based on exploiting the majority of humankind.[35] In fact—as Isbrand sarcastically makes clear—for the poor, the sole purpose of living is to ensure the material well-being of the rich; with the consequence that the former are driven literally to the brink of starvation, while the latter grow fatter and fatter:

> *A whole people is stout and surly, being mostly certain steaks and Barons of beef gone human: another, after a century of amphibious diet, owes to the frog's legs in its wooden shoes the agility with which it jumps over gentle King Log, and devotes itself patriotically to the appetite of Emperor Stork, his follower: aye, it would even blow itself up to be bull itself.* (γ: I, i, 123–29)

---

32 Saint-Marc Girardin, 'La révolution prolétaire', *Le Journal des Débats* (8 December 1831). Quoted in Hobsbawm, *The Age of Revolution*, p. 245.

33 See Hans-Joachim Ruckhäberle, 'Der Krieg der Armen gegen die Reichen: Ludwig Börne und die deutschen Handwerker und Arbeiter in Paris', in *'Die Kunst—eine Tochter der Zeit': Neue Studien zu Ludwig Börne*, ed. Inge Rippmann and Wolfgang Labuhn (Bielefeld: Aisthesis, 1988), pp. 99–110 (p. 107).

34 Titmouse's nonsensical social ballad about the starving tailor who steals eggs from a witch in order to survive and is transformed into a human hen that lays eggs clearly shows TLB's heightened awareness of socio-economic oppression (γ: I, iv, 74–121). The increasing industrialization of the traditional artisan professions led to an enormous rise in unemployment, deprivation, and proletarianization among the craftsmen and women, both in Germany and Britain. For two contemporary social realist ballads that indict this development with particular regard to the tailoring sector, see, e.g., Thomas Hood's 'Song of the Shirt' (1843) and Georg Weerth's 'Es war ein armer Schneider' (1845).

35 For instance, in German towns the lower classes formed 65–90% of the population, with more than half of them existing below the poverty line. See Peter Stein, 'Sozialgeschichtliche Signatur 1815–1848', in *Hansers Sozialgeschichte der Deutschen Literatur: Vol. V: Zwischen Restauration und Revolution 1815–1848* (Munich: Hanser, 1998), pp. 16–37 (p. 28).

What Isbrand allegorically pictures here—'in Æsop's fable-book in masquerade' (γ: I, i, 123)—is an extremely polarized society of idle consumers and slaving producers.[36] The rich are fat, complacent, lethargic, and bad-tempered ('stout and surly'), while the poor are lean and supple, due to their active lifestyle, which their struggle for subsistence necessarily entails. While the former are metaphorically linked to fattened cattle ('Barons of beef gone human'), the latter are described as amphibious animals, in particular bullfrogs. Since those—in contrast to the stuffed 'bull[s]'—are able to move very quickly, both on land and water, they could theoretically overcome their degenerate rulers. To use Isbrand's image, they can easily jump over their 'gentle King Log'.[37] The socio-revolutionary potential of the poor is high. However a major ideological delusion prevents them from staging a social revolution against the complacent middle classes, the fat bulls. Rather than revolting against the latter, they try to emulate them, as Isbrand expresses in a pun on bulls and bullfrog. The frogs would do anything; they 'would even blow [themselves] up to be bull'. Yet, by imitating them, they are not being transformed into proper well-nourished bulls, but still remain starving bullfrogs. If instead the poor used their superior agility and their strength in numbers to attack the bourgeoisie, they would easily manage to overthrow them. However, being caught up in a system of severe repression and extensive state propaganda, they have been able neither to develop the means to revolt effectively nor to become fully conscious yet of the extent to which they are being exploited, two key pre-conditions for a successful social revolution. For the moment, the poor are still in the grip of the ideology of the ruling class, when they devote themselves 'patriotically to the appetite of the Emperor Stork', their natural archenemy. When the poor are feeding the rich, they are tragically caught up in the delusion that they are performing this sacrifice for a greater good, such as the fatherland. Yet, in fact, the only ones to benefit from their sufferings are the rich.

Such a grim outlook on a society that is characterized by stark social divisions and an impending class war is reminiscent of the socio-revolutionary views of the German writer Georg Büchner (1813–37). In his farcical comedy *Leonce und Lena* (written 1836–37), which is a bitter satire of a fictitious German mini-kingdom, he puts forward a comparable socio-revolutionary ideology through similar imagery. As in the passage from *Death's Jest-Book* quoted above, the latter is taken from

---

36   For a brief overview of the heightening socio-economic confrontation between the labouring poor and the bourgeoisie across Europe in 1830s and 1840s and the connected rise of the working class movement, see, e.g., Hobsbawm, *The Age of Revolution*, pp. 245–65 (chapter 'The Labouring Poor'). The image of the poor as amphibians might be inspired by a passage from *The Constitution of a Perfect Commonwealth* (1798, 2nd edn) by the radical Thomas Spence. In an ideal state, he maintains, there would be 'no lords, no gentlemen . . . no amphibious class between the government and his people', quoted in Olive D. Rudkin, *Thomas Spence and His Connections* (London: Allen and Unwin, 1927), p. 37.

37   In my opinion, the attribute 'gentle' must be understood as highly ironic in the context of *Death's Jest-Book*'s anti-monarchic ideology.

the semantic fields of food and animals. For example, when, in a draft version of Büchner's play, the fool Valerio stresses the 'Fleiß' of the ants and paradoxically regards them as 'ein sehr nützliches Ungeziefer', he is in fact talking about the labouring poor with the voice of the rich.[38] Like Beddoes's fool Isbrand, Büchner's fool mocks the contempt of the rich for the poor. Both are employing—grotesquely exaggerated—the cynical discourse the rich use to talk about the poor. On another occasion, Valerio even sarcastically comments on this ideological-rhetorical strategy. As he expresses it with a paradoxical neologism, the rich talk very 'philobestialisch' of the poor.[39] Not only do they speak contemptuously of the poor, but they are at the same time misguided in their patronizing and belittling attitude towards the poor that consists in reducing them to animals. As both fools reveal, regarding the poor as harmless and useful slaves is as wrong as it is dangerous. Isbrand warns in his allegorical language that the bullfrogs might eventually triumph over the bulls. Valerio points out that even the seemingly harmless and useful ants are 'wieder nicht so nützlich, als wenn sie gar keinen Schaden thäten'.[40] In the same vein, but even more explicitly, he exclaims shortly afterwards: 'Seht, was man nicht mit einem Floh ausrichten kann!'[41] With this comment, he emphasizes the potential power of the poor to overthrow the present system if they unite against it. Despite all the efforts of the ruling class to vilify, to contain and belittle them, even to the state of fleas, the power of the unified masses constitutes the basis for any potential social revolution.

The harsh confrontation between the rich and the poor is enacted very vividly in the final two scenes of Büchner's play. In Act III, Scene ii, we see a schoolmaster who has to drill a group of starving peasants to applaud the royal couple during their sumptuous wedding celebrations.[42] In the next scene we hear the master of ceremonies complaining that the mass of food prepared for the wedding is perishing, since the rich people are too caught up in self-indulgent ennui to eat it:

> Es ist ein Jammer. Alles geht zu Grund. Die Braten schnurren ein ... Alle Vatermörder legen sich um, wie melancholische Schweinsohren ... und der Hofpoet grunzt ..., wie ein bekümmertes Meerschweinchen.[43]

---

38   *P* I, 137–38; 'diligence' (*H*, p. 193).

39   *P* I, 120; 'philobestial' (*H*, p. 185).

40   *P* I, 138; 'again not as useful as if they did no damage at all' (my translation).

41   *P* I, 139; 'Look what one can accomplish with a flea' (*H*, p. 194).

42   In fact Büchner, in this scene, sarcastically parodies an actual royal wedding between the successor to the dukedom of Hesse and Princess Mathilde of Bavaria, which took place on 5 and 6 January 1834. The wedding celebrations are depicted in a chronicle, on which Büchner's social satire is mainly based (for excerpts from the chronicle, see *P*, I, 652–57).

43   *P*, I, 122. 'What a shame! Everything's going to pot. The roasts are drying up ... Stand-up collars are all bending over like melancholy pigs' ears ... and the Court Poet grunts ... like a distressed guinea pig' (*H*, p. 186–87).

By contrast the peasants, who are nearly collapsing from hunger, are mercifully granted that they 'einmal in [ihrem] Leben einen Braten riech[en]'.[44] In the passage above, Büchner indicts both this inhuman behaviour towards the poor as well as the related inhumane discourse. Subverting it, he turns it against the rich. When they treat the poor worse than animals, the rich in fact become 'pigs' themselves, in the figurative sense of the word, as the reference to pigs in the words 'Schweinsohren' and 'Meerschweinchen' implies.

This inhuman treatment naturally breeds strong social resentment among the oppressed for their oppressors. However—comparable to the passage above from *Death's Jest-Book*—the poor are not yet ready to overthrow their oppressor. In fact, their revolutionary power is also still misdirected and auto-aggressive. In mockery of the festivities of the rich, they will perform a proto-revolutionary 'transparenten Ball mittelst der Löcher in [ihren] Jacken und Hosen, und schlagen [sich] mit [ihren] Fäusten Kokarden an die Köpfe', the schoolmaster announces.[45] The cockades— prominent revolutionary insignia—are bruises inflicted on each other's heads and not on the heads of their oppressors. However, there can be no doubt either of the immense socio-revolutionary potential that manifests itself in this scene or of the fact that Büchner believed that the poor would eventually overthrow the equally degenerate classes: the aristocracy and bourgeoisie, which together make up 'die abgelebte moderne Gesellschaft', as Büchner expressed it in a letter to Gutzkow in June 1836.[46]

In short, as the intertextual reading of these passages from the γ version of *Death's Jest-Book* and *Leonce and Lena* suggests, Beddoes was as far from abandoning his belief in revolutionary change as was Büchner. It is *not* an abstract and de-politicized 'larger revolution of man against the dehumanizing factors of all political strife', as Burwick maintains, that increasingly preoccupied Beddoes and Büchner.[47] This argument is not supported by either *Death's Jest-Book* or by Büchner's works. On the contrary, what we find in the γ version of Beddoes's play is a clear move away from a purely political towards a social revolution, a change that the younger Büchner had already undergone before writing his first play, *Dantons Tod*, in 1835.[48] Thus, far from abandoning politics for philosophy, Büchner and Beddoes were actually among the avant-garde of revolutionary writers of their time. As the γ version of Act I of the *Jest-Book* and his continued political writings and poetry all suggest, it was no longer a bourgeois political revolution that Beddoes put his hope

---

44   *P*, I, 121; 'for once in [their] life [they'll] smell a roast' (*H*, p. 186).
45   *P*, I, 122; 'a transparent ball thanks to the holes in our jackets and [trousers], and we'll beat [cockades] onto our heads with our fists' (*H*, p. 186; my alterations to the translation in brackets).
46   *P*, II, 440; 'effete modern society' (*H*, p. 286).
47   Burwick, 'Death's Fool', p. 300.
48   Büchner's school essays and speeches still revolve about the concept of political freedom. For instance the essay 'Helden-Tod der vierhundert Pforzheimer' (1829 or 1830) is a patriotic apotheosis of the concepts of political freedom and freedom of thought. To achieve these aims, Büchner advocates revolutionary change in the German neo-absolutist states (see *P*, II, 18–28).

in but an eventual proletarian social revolution. For both Beddoes and Büchner, the degenerate bourgeoisie had lost all the revolutionary spirit it once possessed. As Büchner writes in a letter to Gutzkow in 1835—again employing the imagery of food and eating in a revolutionary context—the bourgeois revolution 'muß von der ungebildeten und armen Klasse aufgefressen werden; das Verhältnis zwischen Armen und Reichen ist das einzige revolutionäre Element in der Welt'.[49]

Most strongly and poignantly, Beddoes voices a comparable view, not in *Death's Jest-Book* but in one of his last poems that Donner entitled 'Lines written in Switzerland'. In Geoffrey Wagner's opinion, this fragmentary poem shows how much 'Beddoes loathed capitalism'.[50] At the very least, it is strongly critical of British capitalism, since it accuses the latter of being based on 'slave-raised' (l. 32) profits. With exploitation abounding both at home and abroad in the colonies, the poem depicts a doubly explosive social situation. Even the patriotic myth of the British Empire—traditionally a potent ideological tool to pacify the discontented masses—is shown to be crumbling. This is epitomized in the decline of the sublime Goddess Britannia to a mundane bourgeois figure minted 'on a copper coin'. Her fierce companion, the Lion, has turned into a harmless 'toothless cat', and instead of the deadly trident she holds a 'toasting fork' in her hand.

Under these circumstances, it is highly doubtful that the British bourgeoisie will be able to stem the rising socio-revolutionary tide for much longer. If not in the countryside, at least in the industrial cities of Britain such as 'Manchester', social unrest among the proletariat is brewing. In an allusion to the Italian volcano Avernus, whose crater in antiquity was thought to be an entrance to the underworld, Liverpool, one of the foremost seaports of the British Empire, is termed 'Ocean-Avernus'. Thus it is allegorized not only as the entrance to the hell of industrial capitalism and colonial exploitation, but also suggests—through the revolutionary connotations of the volcano image—violent resistance by the oppressed both at home and abroad. The modern proletariat will not devote her/himself much longer 'patriotically to the appetite' of the ruling class as the lower orders in the neo-feudal world of *Death's Jest-Book*. As soon as the proletariat manages to overcome the remaining ideological illusions and the conditioned fear of the ruling class and its system of control, then the latter's days are numbered, the poem prophesies. A faint but clear socio-revolutionary voice is already audible in its revolutionary-apocalyptic scenario, which is strongly reminiscent of Percy Bysshe Shelley's *The Mask of Anarchy*. Like the voice of the allegorical Phantom figure in Shelley's poem, it will also increase in volume and intensity. Depending on the listener's political attitude, it might either be interpreted as triumphantly proclaiming the doom of bourgeois rule through impending proletarian social revolution or warning starkly of such a disquieting scenario:

---

49   *P*, II, 400; 'will have to be devoured by the uneducated and poor classes; the relationship between the poor and the rich is the only revolutionary element in the world' (*H*, p. 274; my alteration).

50   Geoffrey Wagner, 'Centennial of a Suicide', *Horizon*, 109 (1949), 417–35 (p. 423).

> Be proud of Manchester
> Pestiferous Liverpool, Ocean-Avernus,
> Where bullying blasphemy, like a slimy lie,
> Creeps to the highest church's pinnacle,
> . . . .
> O flattering likeness on a copper coin!
> Sit still on your slave-raised cotton ball,
> With upright toasting fork and toothless cat:
> The country clown still holds her for a lion.
> The voice, the voice! when the affrighted herds
> Dash heedless to the edge of craggy abysses,
> . . . .
> But clearer, though not loud, a voice is heard
> Of proclamation or of warning stern. (ll. 26–41)

Death's Jest-Book and the Pathological Imagination[1]

Frederick Burwick

Death's Jest-Book is the literary product of Thomas Lovell Beddoes's four years at Göttingen, from July 1825 to February 1829, when he sent a completed copy to London. In June 1825, just prior to his departure from Oxford, he already had the title of his new play.[2] It was at Göttingen, however, that he delved into the current animal morphology and studies of cell growth that challenged traditional notions about the boundaries of life and death and provided significant motifs in the play.[3] The copy of the play was sent to Thomas Forbes Kelsall with the request that their mutual friends, Bryan Waller Procter and John Bourne, determine whether it should be submitted for publication.[4] In his own appraisal of the play's shortcomings, Beddoes thought his readers might object to the long speeches and the irreverent German sentiments. 'My cursed fellows in the jest would palaver immeasurably, & I could not prevent them'. Because he had become 'so accustomed to German

---

1   Due to the highly specialized nature of many of the author's sources, not all works cited in this essay have been logged in the General Bibliography, but detailed notes and references accompany the text below.

2   To Thomas Forbes Kelsall, n.d. [early April? 1825]; *Works*, p. 598: 'I wrote in the coach w^h brought me from Southampton to London 5 months since [Oct. 1824], a famous one beginning—Ho! Adam the carrion crow / The old crow of Cairo &c. w^h is sung with much applause by one of my dramatis personae in the unfinished drama No. 3 in my possession'. The song is sung by Wolfram in *DJ-B* V, iv. To Thomas Forbes Kelsall, Pembroke College, Oxford, 8 June 1825; *Works*, p. 604, TLB announced his plan for 'a very Gothic-styled tragedy, for w^h I have a jewel of a name—DEATH'S JESTBOOK'.

3   On TLB's studies at Göttingen, see especially: Christopher Moylan, 'T.L. Beddoes, Romantic Medicine, and the Advent of Therapeutic Theater', *Studia Neophilologica*, 69 (1991), 181–88; and Jon Lundin, 'T.L. Beddoes at Göttingen', *Studia Neophilologica*, 43 (1971), 484–99. For a historical overview, see *Göttingen and the Development of the Natural Sciences*, ed. Nicolaas Rupke (Göttingen: Wallstein, 2002). An annual account of the professors, lectures, and academic events is Johann Stephan Pütter (1725–1807), *Versuch einer academischen Gelehrten-Geschichte von der Georg-August-Universität zu Göttingen* (Göttingen: Vandenhoek, 1765–1838); the annual records in this series were continued posthumously by Friedrich Saalfeld and Georg Heinrich Oesterley for thirty-one years following Pütter's death.

4   To Thomas Forbes Kelsall, Göttingen, 27 February 1829; *Works*, p. 639.

professors, & rationalist Theologians', he wrote 'too irreligiously' for prevailing British tastes.[5]

These were not the faults, however, to which Procter objected. The major defects, according to Procter, were the play's 'obscurity, conceits, and mysticism'. In the way of revision, Beddoes might have been able to abbreviate some of the long speeches and tone down some of the more blatant blasphemies. But he was at a loss how to correct the 'obscurity, conceits, and mysticism'. He defended his partiality for 'conceits', his penchant for Elizabethan and Jacobean locutions, the poetic style he admired in Abraham Cowley, and he claimed to be utterly blind to 'obscurity' and 'mysticism'. 'I may be supposed to have associated a certain train of ideas to a certain mode of expressing them', he told Procter, 'and my four German years may have a little impaired my English style'.[6] He assured Procter that he would attend to revisions during summer, but his drunken carousing that summer resulted in his expulsion from the university. He continued to tinker with the play through his subsequent years at Würzburg, where he took his doctoral degree in medicine, and at Zürich, where he lectured in anatomy.[7] During those latter years, the play soon split its seams as he added new scenes and songs, yet made no attempt to expurgate any ideas responsible for 'obscurity ... and mysticism'.

Procter's objections to 'obscurity ... and mysticism' were possibly motivated by a concern with a public response to the play's homoeroticism.[8] The male characters—Melveric and Wolfram, Adalmar and Athulf—are presented as rivals, but their rivalry derives from an inability to cope with desire. The female characters—Sibylla and Amala—function simply as foils for male relationships. The curse of the living is that their very material being gives rise to jealousy, greed, a lust for power and possession, and a means to manipulate and exploit others. Impossible in a material world, love is liberated when the 'flesh-concealed soul' (*DJ-B*, III, iii, 102) is freed from material restraints.[9] All moral hypocrisy arises from

---

5   To Thomas Forbes Kelsall, Göttingen, 27 February 1829; *Works*, p. 639.

6   To Thomas Forbes Kelsall, Göttingen, 19 April 1829; *Works*, p. 642.

7   In August 1829, TLB was dismissed from Göttingen for drunken and disorderly conduct. He then attended the University of Würzburg, where in September 1831 he completed his medical degree under Dr Lucas Schönlein. In July 1832 he was forced to leave the university because of his involvement in the protests against the Bavarian monarch for suppressing freedom of the press. He fled to Strasburg and subsequently joined his professor at the new University of Zürich in 1833 as lecturer in anatomy. His tenure at Zürich was terminated in 1840 because of his pamphleteering for academic freedom. Burwick, 'Beddoes, Bayern und die Burschenschaften', *Comparative Literature*, 21 (1969), 289–306; and 'Beddoes and the *Schweizerischer Republikaner*', *Studia Neophilologica* 44.1 (1972), 90–112.

8   This possibility seems to be born out by the endeavour of Kelsall and Procter to arrange for the posthumous publication of TLB's works. From the trunk of unpublished manuscripts, many were lost or destroyed, apparently because they revealed political or sexual indiscretions.

9   Cited parenthetically in the text by act, scene, and lines, quotations from *Death's Jest-Book* are from H.W. Donner, *Works of Thomas Lovell Beddoes* (1935). As noted in the parenthetical reference, I have quoted on two occasions from the edition of 1851, and

ignorance of basic anatomy and the nature of the flesh. The spiritual afterlife, as Beddoes depicts it, is utterly godless, untroubled by any material scheme of right or wrong, reward, or punishment. There is neither heaven nor hell.[10] Beddoes's characters refer frequently to hell, but hell is defined by the material conditions necessary for propagating torment and pain. The only 'wicked' are those 'who have not yet died' (*DJ-B*, V, iv, 38). If 'obscurity . . . and mysticism' referred to necromantic conjuring and occult speculations, Procter might well have thought of the tales of sodomy with the devil historically associated with the witchcraft trials. Necromancers, blasphemers, heretics were deviants, and deviants of any sort undermine the community by opposing its most cherished values. Within the university environment of Göttingen, Beddoes found a degree of tolerance. But even that tolerance had perimeters set by the religious guardians of public morality.[11]

Death's Jest-Book (1829) may be seen to extend certain patterns of theme and style already evident in his earlier plays.[12] His interest in German literature is also evident during his Oxford years. In October 1824, he said of his study of German, that he had 'just tasted the nouns, but not touched the verbs'.[13] One month later, he confessed that German 'has flooded my brain no higher than der die das'.[14]

---

on another from Donner's transcription of the γ mss. See *Works*, pp. xxxi–xliii, for Donner's account of the MSS and the chronology of their composition, and *Works*, pp. 788–91, for his list of the autographs and transcripts.

10   Jean Paul [Richter], 'Rede des toten Christus' (1796) presented a vision of a godless afterlife, with neither heaven nor hell, that gained a pan-European audience when it was subsequently translated in Germaine de Staël, *De l'Allemagne* (1810). For a fuller exposition of TLB's obsession with the afterlife, see Michael Bradshaw, *Resurrection Songs: The Poetry of Thomas Lovell Beddoes* (Aldershot and Burlington: Ashgate, 2001).

11   As an indication of the homophobia at the time of TLB's arrival in Germany, see the following moral caveats on homosexual behavior: Johann Philipp Bauer, *Der Mensch in Bezug auf sein Geschlecht, Oder Aufsätze über Zeugung, Befruchtung, Fruchtbarkeit, Enthaltsamkeit, Beischlaf, Empfängniß, Ehe u. a. ähnliche Gegenstände* (1820); and Wilhelm Martin Leberecht de Wette. *Vorlesungen über die Sittenlehre* (1823–24). On homosexual desire as mental aberration, moral and legal deviance, see François Emmanuel Fodéré. *Traité du Délire appliqué à la médecine, à la morale et à la législation* (1817). On TLB's homosexuality, see: Gregory Ross, 'The Cherub and the Bacchanal: The Poetry of Thomas Lovell Beddoes' (unpublished doctoral dissertation, UCLA, 1983); Christopher Moylan, '"For Luz Is a Good Joke": Thomas Lovell Beddoes and Jewish Eschatology', *British Romanticism and the Jews: History, Culture, Literature*, ed. Sheila Spector (New York: Palgrave, 2002), pp. 93–103; Shelley Rees, 'Gender and Desire in Thomas Lovell Beddoes' *The Brides' Tragedy* and *Death's Jest-Book*' (unpublished doctoral dissertation, University of North Texas, 2002); Shelley Rees, 'Melveric and Wolfram: A love story', *Journal of the Thomas Lovell Beddoes Society* 8 (2000), 14–25; and Virginia Blain, 'Browning's Men: Childe Roland, Homophobia and Thomas Lovell Beddoes', *Australasian Victorian Studies Journal*, 7 (2001), 1–11.

12   See the review of TLB's work in the Introduction to this volume.

13   To Thomas Forbes Kelsall, 6 Devereux Court, London, 4 October 1824; *Works*, p. 591.

14   To Thomas Forbes Kelsall, Clifton, 8 November 1824; *Works*, p. 592.

In December, he visited John King, a 'demi-uncle' married to his mother's sister, Emmeline Edgeworth. John King was actually Johann König, one-time student of mathematics, theology, and the natural sciences at Berne, subsequently assistant to the senior Thomas Beddoes at the Pneumatic Institute in Bristol.[15] By the following March, 1825, he announces, 'lo! I am expert in reading German'. As evidence he declares his familiarity with Goethe and Schiller.[16] At the close of his final year at Oxford, he published a translation of Friedrich Schiller's 'Philosophic Letters' in the *Oxford Quarterly Magazine* (June 1825). He is now frequenting Johann Heinrich Bohte's German bookshop in London and translating lines from the Middle High German epic, the *Niebelungenlied*. His plan is to 'sell & pay & impoverish myself to the bone, & then set off for Germany'.[17]

Although he mentioned that he attended the lectures on Comparative Anatomy, that he had been denounced 'as one of a "villanous school"' by the Professor of Poetry, Henry Hart Milman, and that he was 'absolutely unfit' for the examinations, Beddoes had little to say in his letters to Kelsall about his studies at Oxford.[18] His letters from Göttingen, by contrast, are filled with details about his studies and his professors. 'There is an appetite for learning, a spirit of diligence, and withal a good-natured fellow-feeling unparalleled in our old apoplectic & paralytic Almae Matres'.[19] The university, founded by the House of Hanover one hundred years earlier, had enjoyed a century of British royal munificence and had achieved a status at that period as one of the greatest universities of Europe. To be sure, many of its most prominent professors were in the final years of their careers. On 26 February 1826, at the close of his first semester, Beddoes describes participating in the celebration offered to Professors Johann Friedrich Blumenbach, Johann Friedrich Stromeyer, and J.G. Eichhorn on their fifty years at the university.[20]

---

15   To Thomas Forbes Kelsall, Clifton, 6 December 1824; *Works*, p. 593; see also Donner's note on John King, p. 750.

16   To Thomas Forbes Kelsall, Southampton, 25 March 1825; *Works*, p. 597.

17   Johann Heinrich Bohte died on 2 September 1824; the bookshop was then run by the widow, Sarah Lloyd Bohte. It was Sarah who attended to the posthumous publication, mentioned by TLB, of Bohte's *Handbibliothek zu Deutschen Litteratur mit einer Vorrede von A. W. Schlegel* (London: G. Schulze, 1825); to Thomas Forbes Kelsall, Southampton, 25 March 1825; *Works*, p. 598. During his stay in London while writing for the *London Magazine*, Thomas De Quincey rented a room from Bohte and made use of the German books for his articles; c.f. n. 39 below.

18   To Thomas Forbes Kelsall, Pembroke College, Oxford, 8 June 1825; *Works*, p. 604.

19   To Thomas Forbes Kelsall, Göttingen, 4 December 1825; *Works*, p. 611.

20   Two celebratory pamphlets were published to commemorate the event: *Den preiswürdigen Jubelgreisen Blumenbach, Stromeyer und Eichhorn bei dem Jubelfeste ihres 50jährigen öffentlichen Lehramts den 26. Februar 1826*, by Georgia's Zöglinge (Göttingen, 1826); and Conrad Johann Martin Langenbeck, *Academiae Georgiae Augustae Prorector Conr. Jo. M. Langenbeck D. Cum Senatu Successorem In Magistratu Academico Bernh. Frid. Thibaut D. Civibus Suis Honoris Et Officii Caussa Commendat Simulque Collegis Suis De Academia Meritissimis Joanni Frid. Blumenbach Et Joanni Frid. Stromeyer Sacrum Semisaeculare Muneris Professorii Per L Annos Continuati Gratulatur. Illustratur versus Horatii Solventur Risu Tabulae Tu Missus Abibis* (Göttingen: Dieterich, 1826).

> *As soon as it was dark between 5 and 600 of us, horse & foot, assembled*
> *each with a torch & formed a two & two process thro' the town to*
> *the house where they were feasting, drew around the square, and on*
> *Blumenbach's appearance at the window a short speech was made*
> *by the leader followed by several tremendous 'vivats!' He made his*
> *speech; we departed & threw our torches into the bonfire.[21]*

Beddoes goes on to describe a *Commerz* and his carousing with the *Burschenschaftler*.[22] 'Blumenbach', Beddoes had already declared at the beginning of the semester, 'is my best friend among the Professors', ranking him among 'the first rate as mineralogist, phisiologian, geologist, natural historian & physician, over and above which he possesses an exuberant fancy, & a flow of wit w^h is anything but German'.[23] Twenty-six years earlier, Samuel Taylor Coleridge, who had taken quarters in Blumenbach's household and formed a close friendship with Blumenbach's son Friedrich, recorded similar praise for the professor's cleverness.[24] Unlike Coleridge, however, Beddoes was seriously involved in the lectures:

> *Blumenbach is one of the cleverest men in Germany; his works are*
> *distinguished for nicely, acuteness, and the minutest acquaintance*
> *with the in- and outside of Nature: but in his lecture-room he would*
> *be a capital subject for Mathews: he lectures on Natural History, that*
> *is, his auditors bring his very capital manual in their hands & sit*
> *out: in an instant one hears a noise as of Punch on the stairs & the*
> *old powdered professor pushes in grunting amid as much laughter*
> *as Liston. He then begins a lecture composed of jokes, good stories,*
> *imitations, inarticulate sounds, & this being ended goes as he came—*
> *a good clever merry old man.[25]*

A crucial detail in this account of the lecture hall is that the substance of the lecture is already in the hands of the students, published as a *Lehrbuch* or *Handbuch* or *Grundriß* specifically intended as a text *zum Gebrauche bei seinen Vorlesungen* ('for use in his lectures'). Conrad Johann Martin Langenbeck, the professor of Anatomy who led the ceremonial festivities for his senior colleagues, is compared to Blumenbach as 'the Kemble of this Munden: during his lecture he throws himself into a thousand attitudes—starts, points and declaims and paces loftily up and down his

---

21   To Thomas Forbes Kelsall, Göttingen, 1 April 1826; *Works*, pp. 617.

22   TLB later joined the fraternity movement as a student at Würzburg; see Burwick, 'Beddoes, Bayern und die Burschenschaften', *Comparative Literature*, 21 (1969), 289–306.

23   To Thomas Forbes Kelsall, Göttingen, 29 September 1825; *Works*, pp. 606.

24   Letter to Mrs S.T. Coleridge, 17 May 1799, in *The Collected Letters of Samuel Taylor Coleridge*, ed. Earl L. Griggs (Oxford: Clarendon Press, 1956–71), I, 497.

25   To Thomas Forbes Kelsall, Göttingen, 1 April 1826; *Works*, pp. 617–18.

little stage—he too is a man of first rate merit as anatomist and surgeon'. Although one cannot miss the cross-references to the stage and the actors (Charles Mathews, John Liston, John Philip Kemble, Joseph Shepherd Munden—and Punch), Beddoes insists that he has put off his role as playwright and donned a new disguise: 'no human being w^d imagine that I was anything but the most stoical, prosaic, dull anatomist: I almost outwork the laborious Sauerkrauts—and to tell you truly I begin to prefer Anatomy &^{c} to poetry, I mean to my own, & practically'. The revelation, here, is that his study of anatomy has merged with, and transformed, his writing of the play: 'Ask me about poets? &c, talk of Anatomists & I'll tell you something: I have left off reading Parnassian foolery: I can bear a satire tho' and write one, as Jest-book shall show'.[26]

For Stromeyer's lecture, Beddoes was reading the *Grundriß der theoretischen Chemie*, and for Blumenbach's course, he read first the *Handbuch der Naturgeschichte* and then, in his second semester, *Handbuch der vergleichenden Anatomie*. Among the professors with whom he was studying, Beddoes also lists: 'Langenbeck & Hempel, Anatomists, & Surgeons; Krauss, Conradi, and Himly, medical professors'.[27] He attended Conradi's lectures on mania and delirium, Himly's on opthamology, and Benecke's on mental pathology. For zootomy he had the young lecturer, Arnold Adolf Berthhold. His fellow students at Göttingen typically 'rise at 5 or 6, study the whole day & night'.[28] Beddoes's daily studies were no less rigorous:

> Up at 5, Anatomical reading until 6—translation from English into German till 7—Prepare for Blumenbach's lecture on comp. Anat^y & breakfast till 8—Blumenbach's lecture till 9—Stomeyer's lecture on Chemistry till 10. 10 to ½ p. 12, Practical Zootomy—½ p. 12 to 1 English into German or German literary reading with a pipe—1 to 2 Anatomical lecture. 2 to 3 anatomical reading. 3 to 4 Osteology. 4 to 5 Lecture in German language. 5 to 6 dinner and light reading in Zootomy, Chem. Or Anat^y. 6 to 7, this hour is very often wasted in a visit, sometimes Anatomical reading until 8. Then coffee and read Greek till 10. 10 to 11, write a little Death's Jest Book w^h is a horrible waste of time, but one must now & then throw away the dregs of the day.[29]

Rigorous, yes, but also rewarding: 'I was never better employed, never so happy, never so well self-satisfied'.[30] The reward was substantiated in the way his readings of the day were absorbed into his literary composition at night:

---

26   To Thomas Forbes Kelsall, Göttingen, 1 April 1826; *Works*, pp. 618–19.
27   To Thomas Forbes Kelsall, Göttingen, 11 December 1825; *Works*, p. 612.
28   To Thomas Forbes Kelsall, Göttingen, 11 December 1825; *Works*, p. 612.
29   To Thomas Forbes Kelsall, Göttingen, 4 December 1825; *Works*, p. 608–09.
30   To Thomas Forbes Kelsall, Göttingen, 4 December 1825; *Works*, p. 610.

even as a dramatist, I cannot help thinking that the study of anat^y,
phisiol-, psycho-, & anthropo-ology applied to and illustrated by
history, biography and works of the imagination is that w^h is most
likely to assist one in producing correct and accurate delineations
of the passions: great light w^d be thrown on Shakespeare by the
commentaries of a person educated. The studies then of the dramatist
& physician are closely, almost inseparably allied; the application alone
is different; but is it impossible for the same man to combine these
two professions, in some degree at least? The science of psychology,
& mental varieties, has long been used by physicians, in conjunction
with the corresponding corporeal knowledge, for the investigation &
removal of immaterial causes of disease; it still remains for some one to
exhibit the sum of his experience in mental pathology & therapeutics,
not in a cold technical dead description, but a living semiotical display,
a series of anthropological experiments developed for the purpose of
ascertaining some important psychical principle—i.e., a tragedy.[31]

The poet learns from the scientist, and no philosopher is capable of astute insight into the human condition without being fully trained as a scientist. 'I am determined', Beddoes writes 'never to listen to any metaphysician who is not both an anatomist & physiologist of first rank'.[32]

Throughout the first decade of the century, the union of philosophy and science was ambitiously promulgated by F.W.J. Schelling in his *Zeitschrift für spekulative Physik* (1802–03) and his *Jahrbücher der Medicin als Wissenschaft* (1805–08). Schelling held that all physical and biological nature, indeed the nervous system and consciousness itself, were an electro-dynamic construct. Although the fascination with *Naturphilosophie* had just about run its course by the end of the 1820s, a tension between speculative and empirical approaches still persisted in the sciences. In spite of the rise of empirical medicine in the latter eighteenth century, much of the teaching of medicine as a branch of natural philosophy was still under the sway of an older metaphysical tradition. Even after the advent of the nineteenth century, the older theories of Albrecht von Haller, Thomas Brown,[33] Johann Caspar Lavater,

---

31   To Thomas Forbes Kelsall, Göttingen, 4 December 1825; *Works*, p. 609.
32   To Thomas Forbes Kelsall, Göttingen, 11 December 1825; *Works*, p. 612.
33   Albrecht von Haller (1708–77), Professor of Anatomy, Chirurgy, and Botany at Göttingen, introduced the theory of 'sensibility and irritability' into medical practice, in *De partibus corporis humani sensilibus et irritabilibus* (1732) and *Primae lineae physiologiae* (1747). Haller's theory was elaborated by John Brown (1735–88), whose *Elementa medicinae* (1780) classified diseases as over- or under-stimulating and held that internal and external 'exciting powers', or stimuli, operate on living tissues. Brown argued that physical life consists in a peculiar excitability, the normal excitement produced by all the agents that affect the body constituting the healthy condition, while all diseases arise either from deficiency or from excess of excitement and must be treated with stimulants or sedatives. The Brunonian system basically

Franz Anton Mesmer, Franz Joseph Gall, and Johann Caspar Spurzheim continued to prevail over the new physiological and anatomical investigations of Johann Christian Reil, Charles Bell, Thomas Young, and Johannes Müller. Not surprisingly, the composition of *Death's Jest-Book* is marked not just by a predilection for metaphors of the diseased nervous system and the conditions of morbid anatomy but also by a fascination with the speculative, the occult, the hoaxing, and the quackery. In the dialogue given to Isbrand, Mandrake, Wolfram, the Duke, and Ziba, Beddoes repeatedly inquires into the nature of decay and dissolution, engaging both the science and the lore of death.

Several of Beddoes's professors had adapted the methods of the *Naturphilosophen*. In Benecke's lectures on psychology, for example, Beddoes was instructed on the interaction of mind and body affecting physical well-being and on the interdependency of experience and speculation in thought processes.[34] In Barthold's lectures in zootomy and comparative anatomy, Beddoes was informed of Goethe's signal contribution to the morphological analysis of the parallel structure and development of all animals.[35] Among the questions raised by the scientist raised and pondered by the playwright, none were more dominant in *Death's Jest-Book* than those relating to the pathologies of mind and body. The advent of experimentation with the Voltaic pile, which Blumenbach had introduced into his laboratory at the turn of the century,[36] had opened up research into the effects of electricity on the vital processes. In his readings on morbid anatomy for Conradi, Beddoes studied the continuous death and replacement of individual cells in healthy tissue, the persistence of cell division in a dead body.

---

favoured supporting and stimulating rather than the old practices of 'lowering', bleeding, etc. on the argument that diseases are owing more to debility than to excess of vital needs. TLB's father adopted Brunonian medicine in his practice and provided a biographical preface to the English translation, *Elements of Medicine* (1795); see Neil Vickers, 'Coleridge, Thomas Beddoes, and Brunonian Medicine', *European Romantic Review*, 8.1 (1997), 47–94.

34   The texts that Benecke used in his lectures during TLB's first years at Göttingen were *Beiträge zu einer reinseelenwissenschaftlichen Bearbeitung der Seelenkrankheitkunden* (1824), *Das Verhältniss von Seele und Leib* (1826), and *Psychologische Skizzen* (1827). Benecke's philosophical commitment is evident in his *Kant und die philosophische Aufgabe unserer Zeit* (1832), a commentary written for the fiftieth anniversary of the publication of the *Kritik der reinen Vernunft* (1781).

35   Later in his career, Berthold presented a retrospective, *Über Goethe's Anatome comparata* (1849), but even his earlier work demonstrates his reliance of Goethe's morphology; see especially his *Lehrbuch der Physiologie des Menschen und der Thiere* (1829) and *Beiträge zur Anatomie, Zootamie und Physiologie* (1831). The influence of Goethe's morphology is documented in Adolf Meyer-Abich, *Die Vollendung der Morphologie Goethes durch Alexander von Humboldt: Ein Beitrag zur Naturwissenschaft der Goethezeit* (1970). See also Rudolf Beneke, 'Goethe als pathologischer Anatom', *Die medizinische Welt*, 12 (1932).

36   Achim von Arnim, in 'Bermerkungen über Volta's Säule' (1801), describes his experiments with the large voltaic battery (sixty silver and zinc layers) constructed by Blumenbach; *Achim von Arnim Werke*, VI, 73–114; see esp. pp. 78, 112, and 1109n., 1215n.

The boundaries between life and death are repeatedly challenged in his play, not simply in the comic mockery of Mandrake wandering in the tombs, nor in the pretences of supernatural conjuring practised by the necromancer Ziba, but in the more complicated philosophical challenge posed by the resurrected Wolfram when he addresses the Duke:

> But dead and living, which are which? A question
> Not easy to be solved. Are you alone,
> Men, as you're called, monopolists of life?
> Or is all being, living? and what is,
> With less of toil and trouble, more alive,
> Than they, who cannot, half a day, exist
> Without repairing their flesh mechanism?
> Or do you owe your life, not to this body,
> But to the sparks of spirit that fly off,
> Each instant disengaged and hurrying
> From little particles of flesh that die?
> If so, perhaps you are the dead yourselves:
> And these ridiculous figures on the wall
> Laugh, in their safe existence, at the prejudice,
> That you are anything like living beings. (V, iii, 206–20)

If it is true, as Wolfram poses the problem, that an organism is maintained by a constant process of cellular replacement, as cells die and new cells are generated, the 'flesh mechanism' is indeed made up of 'little particles of flesh that die'. Because the vital 'sparks of spirit ... fly off', the body is simply a receptacle for cellular exchange, nor does the process immediately cease when the heart stops. Nor is it just that hair and nails continue to grow. A myriad of organisms to which the body was host continue to thrive. To underscore the irony, Wolfram points to the depiction of the 'Dance of Death' on the cloister wall and poses the possibility that 'their safe existence' is far more secure, so that 'these ridiculous figures' may indeed laugh at the prejudice of the other characters that they are not already being transformed to suit their sepulchral surroundings.

Living is a paradoxical process of ceaselessly dying away. Death has variable boundaries, for the body does not disintegrate all at once like Oliver Wendell Holmes's 'Wonderful One-Hoss Shay', rather the different parts decay and cease to function at different times. Physicians and psychologists, then as now, collected accounts of 'near death experiences' and studied 'Scheintod' in order to arrive at a better understanding of death and dying.[37] Mandrake, duped into thinking that his potions have rendered him invisible, wanders among the tombs and begins

---

37   C.f. n. 42 below; recent studies include Evelyn Elsaesser Valarino, *Erfahrungen an der Schwelle des Todes: Wissenschaftler äussern sich zur Nahtodeserfahrung* (1995), and Christian Kupatt, *An der Schwelle des Todes: Zur Kontroverse um den Hirntod* (1994).

to consider death as a 'ridiculous game of hide-and-seek', a hoax perpetrated by 'doctors and undertakers':

> *I begin shrewdly to suspect that death's all a take-in: as soon as gentlemen have gained some 70 years of experience they begin to be weary of the common drudgery of the world, lay themselves down, hold their breath, close their eyes and are announced as having entered into the fictitious condition by means of epitaphs and effigies . . . That is my conviction, and I am quite impartial being in the secret, but I will only keep away from the living till I have met with a few of these gentle would-be dead, who are shy enough, and am become initiated into their secrets. (III, iii, 3–18)*

Like Wolfram, he readily grants the vague boundaries between life and death, and he makes the same point about the need for the living constantly to repair 'their flesh mechanism':

> *And how came I to this pass? Merry, I must either have been very sound asleep when I died, or else I died by mistake for I am sure I never intended it: or else this being dead is a quite insignificant habit when one's used to it: 'tis much easier than being alive, now I think on it once more: only imagine of the trouble one has to keep up life! One must breathe, and pass round the blood and digest and let hair and nails, and bone and flesh grow. (II, ii, 73–79)*

In the very opening lines of the play, Beddoes reveals that Mandrake is eager to quit his role as 'zany to a mountebank' and become a dedicated 'student in the black arts' by joining Wolfram's expedition to Egypt. In that 'Sphinx land', where the roads are paved with 'philosopher's stone', he hopes to discover the old secrets of the cult of Isis. Wolfram has no sooner rescued the Duke and the maiden Sibylla from captivity than the two men begin their quarrel over the woman. Mandrake, meanwhile, prowls the woods for roots and toadstools, bones and minerals, eager to compound a salve of invisibility with a pound of crocodile's fat (I, iv, 1–9). When he rubs himself down with this concoction, Kate and Isbrand pretend that he has indeed rendered himself invisible, which gives rise to a farcical scene of cudgeling in which the blows, so Isbrand claims, are invisible bolts from an air charged with electricity (II, ii, 128).

But the air really is charged with invisible deadliness. Mandrake's mock invisibility, as well as his mock ghosthood, provides Beddoes with ironic leverage in setting forth the real terrors of the unknown and unseen. Every plague and pestilence that ever moved through cities, destroying entire populations, did so invisibly. As the Duke observes:

The look of the world's a lie, a face made up
O'er graves and fiery depths; and nothing's true
But what is horrible. If man could see
The perils and diseases that he elbows,
Each day he walks a mile; which catch at him,
Which fall behind and graze him as he passes;
Then would he know that Life's a single pilgrim,
Fighting unarmed amongst a thousand soldiers.
It is this infinite invisible
Which we must learn to know, and yet to scorn,
And, from the scorn of that, regard the world
As from the edge of a far star. (1851: IV, i, 7–18)

The lethal stirrings of 'this infinite invisible' are to be feared less as unseen 'perils and diseases' that float in the breeze than as hidden intrigue plotted by one's visible and palpable fellows. The first version of this passage emphasizes that the invisible threat is a 'windless pestilence, / Transparent as a glass of poisoned water / Through which the drinker sees his murderer smiling' (IV, i, 14–16).

Death's Jest-Book contrasts real ghosts with fake ghosts, real invisibility and fake invisibility. The real invisibility resides in the complex passions, concealed from others, often concealed even from the very person who harbours them. A case in point is the love triangle between Adalmar, Athulf, and Amala. Amala is not sure which of the two brothers she loves: 'one brave, honourable is my bridegroom, / But somewhat cold perhaps'; the other 'wild' and passionate, if only he had a little more constancy and a little less insolence, 'were a man much to my heart' (II, ii, 16–19). Pained by Amala's rejection, Athulf commits suicide with a vial procured from the necromancer Ziba. He then changes his minds and sends his brother off to obtain an antidote. Ziba, whose primary functions in the play are to expound on the mysteries of raising the dead and to dispense potions and poisons, scoffs at Athulf's suicidal posturing:

Let him rise.
Why, think you that I'd deal a benefit,
So precious to the noble as is death,
To such a pampered darling of delight
As he that shivers there? (IV, iii, 317–21)

Ziba thinks too much of his precious brews and their high purpose to waste such plants as nightshade or hemlock, such metals as arsenic or mercury, on a love-sick prince. He tells Adalmar simply to let his brother sleep it off:

> *He may live,*
> *As long as 'tis the Gout and Dropsy's pleasure.*
> *He wished to play at suicide, and swallowed*
> *A draught, that may depress and shake his powers*
> *Until he sleeps awhile; then all is o'er. (IV, iii, 325–29)*

Athulf, delighted that he is merely drugged and not poisoned, that he may still have a chance for Amala's love, decides that he made the wrong choice about which brother ought to die, so he stabs Adalmar and then, as Ziba's soporific draught numbs his mind and body, lies down to slumber alongside his brother's corpse:

> *Precious cup,*
> *A few drops more of thy somniferous balm,*
> *To keep out spectres from my dreams to-night:*
> *My eyelids thirst for slumber. (IV, iii, 364–67)*

Anticipating only drowsiness and sleep, Athulf expects the drug to stifle the guilty images that haunt his dreams. He is surprised, then, that the drug wreaks other changes in his blood, his brain, his very bones. Bulging and distending, he feels himself transformed into a grotesque Bakhtinian body,[38] with caves and lairs penetrated by beasts, a body inhabited by perverse and criminal men:

> *But what's this,*
> *That chills my blood and darkens so my eyes?*
> *What's going on in my heart and in my brain,*
> *My bones, my life, all over me, all through me?*
> *It cannot last. No longer shall I be*
> *What I am now. O I am changing, changing,*
> *Dreadfully changing! Even here and now*
> *A transformation will o'ertake me. Hark!*
> *It is God's sentence muttered over me.*
> *I am unsouled, dishumanized, uncreated;*
> *My passions swell and grow like brutes conceived;*
> *My feet are fixing roots, and every limb*
> *Is billowy and gigantic, till I seem*
> *A wild, old, wicked mountain in the air:*
> *And the abhorred conscience of this murder,*
> *It will grow up a lion, all alone,*
> *A mighty-maned, grave-mouthed prodigy,*
> *And lair him in my caves: and other thoughts,*

---

38 See Mikhail Bakhtin, *Rabelais and His World*, trans. Hélène Iswolsky (Cambridge, Mass.: MIT Press, 1968), pp. 18–20, 26–27.

Some will be snakes, and bears, and savage wolves:
And when I lie tremendous in the desart,
Or abandoned sea, murderers and idiot men
Will come to live upon my rugged sides,
Die, and be buried in me. Now it comes;
I break, and magnify, and lose my form.
And yet I shall be taken for a man,
And never be discovered till I die.
Terrible, terrible: damned before my time,
In secret!' Tis a dread, o'erpowering phantom. (1851: IV, iii, 367–96)

Thomas De Quincey, or as Beddoes called him, 'that thrice double demoniac . . . oeconomical opium-eater', first introduced this sort of narrative into the pages of the *London Magazine* in 1821.[39] Like De Quincey, Beddoes gives detailed attention to the effects of the drug on the body and the mind. At first, his body swells into a vast shape of degradation and debasement occupied by wicked beasts and men. Then his body seems to undergo further changes, as if Ziba's sorcery were altering his inner being into some sort of were-creature with only the outward appearance of a man. Before he loses consciousness, he realizes that his terrible transformation will remain secret and invisible to others.

The principles of comparative anatomy and animal morphology seem to run amok in Beddoes's imagination as he returns again and again to images of shape-shifting and were-like transformation. Nor does it take opium to arouse the awareness that the body harbours secret instincts, a concealed otherness. Although brothers, Athulf and Adalmar become creatures of different species. So stark is the difference he sees in Wolfram, Isbrand asks whether his brother had not had a blood transfusion:

> *Say when hast thou undergone transfusion, and whose hostile blood*
> *now turns thy life's wheels? Who has poured Lethe into thy veins, and*
> *washed thy father out of heart and brains? (I, i, 151–53)*

Isbrand's mocking accusation that a transfusion has caused strange blood to course through Wolfram's veins is echoed when Melveric reminds Wolfram of their blood bond:

> *At parting each of us did tear a leaf*
> *Out of a magic book, and, robbing life*

---

39   To Thomas Forbes Kelsall, 6 Devereux Court, London, 17 April 1824; *Works*, p. 586; see n. 17 above. While he was still at Oxford, TLB watched the pages of the *London Magazine* because Procter was also submitting to it regularly. *The Confessions of an English-Opium Eater* appeared in two instalments in 1821; De Quincey's essays on economic theory appeared in 1823 and '24.

> Of the red juice with which she feeds our limbs,
> We wrote a mutual bond. (I, ii, 217–20)

Wolfram recalls the bond and also the oath he swore:

> And if a promise reaches o'er the grave
> My ghost shall not forget it. There I swore
> That, if I died before thee, I would come
> With the first weeds that shoot out of my grave,
> And bring thee tidings of our real home. (I, ii, 221–25)

The mixing of blood, in occult terms, formed an inviolable bond. With the belief that taking in the blood of some other being would alter one's identity, Beddoes combines medical practice with the lore of were-wolves and vampires. Again, in the song 'Squats on a Toadstool', Isbrand imagines the plight of an aborted fetus, exuded from the 'wicked womb' of its mother and discarded in the wild, striving to survive in some animal shape, some host body, be it crocodile, or hedgehog, or snake, or some compounded creature, a new dodo.[40] 'Anatomy, anatomy, anatomy, of man, & dog, & bird, occupy so much of my time, that you must forgive me for being very dull'. This dull routine of memorizing the characteristics of each phylum and species, Beddoes went on to assure Kelsall, was but the 'the worst part of the science, which after all is a most important and most interesting one'.[41] So many physical attributes are shared, so many more attributes subtly altered and transformed from one species to the next, that it was easy to imagine the basic kinship between man and the other animals.

With drugs and potions, the characters in this play frequently find themselves meandering a borderless realm of delusion, trance, and death—*Schein, Scheintod, und Tod*. Many medical accounts, among them two by Beddoes's professors Benecke and Conradi, had been written on the problem of *Scheintod*,[42] which was

---

40   It may not be irrelevant to the lyrics of 'The New Dodo', that one of the professors under whom TLB studied comparative anatomy and opthamology, Karl Gustav Himly, had compared muscular reflex of the iris to his account of why the hedgehog would 'roll up like an apple'; Himley, *Über das Zusammenkugeln des Igels: Eine anatomische Untersuchung* (1801). For the lectures in opthamology, TLB was assigned Himly's *Ophthalmologische Beobachtungen und Untersuchungen* (1801).

41   To Thomas Forbes Kelsall, Göttingen, 11 December 1825; *Works*, p. 612.

42   Benecke, *Beiträge zu einer reinseelenwissenschaftlichen Bearbeitung der Seelenkrankheitkunden* (1824); Conradi, *Commentatio de mania sine delirio* (1827). Many medical books in this period address what must have been a widespread fear of a deathlike trance and premature burial: Ackermann, *Der Scheintod und das Rettungsverfahren: Ein chimiatrischer Versuch* (1804); Hufeland, *Der Scheintod oder Sammlung der wichtigsten Thatsachen und Bemerkungen darüber in alphabetischer Ordnung* (1808); Müller, *Über den Scheintod* (1815); Orfila, *Rettungsverfahren bei Vergiftung und dem Scheintode; Nebst Mitteln zur Erkennung der Gifte, und der verfälschten Weine, und zur Unterscheidung des wirklichen Todes vom Scheintode* (1818), Bernt, *Vorlesungen über die Rettungsmittel*

recognized to occupy a dangerous midway position between *Schein* and *Tod*. The causes could be physical or mental, external or internal. Drugs or poisons were the usual physical, external cause. An internal cause might be diagnosed as epilepsy or apoplexy, but even these, it was argued, could be brought on by severe emotional duress. The detrimental effects of opium and other widely dispensed medicines, as well as the equally detrimental practices of bleeding and purgation, were denounced by Christoph Wilhelm Hufeland, professor of Medicine in Berlin, who became a leading advocate of natural medicine. He opposed the stimulants and depressives used in Brunonian medicine. He was also outspoken in his opposition to the practice of animal magnetism or mesmerism, introduced sixty years earlier by Franz Anton Mesmer.[43] Hufeland's objections were not that mesmerism was a fraudulent hoax but, rather, that its application was neither controlled nor even adequately understood. The magnetic trance he held to be an intrusive manipulation of natural sleep.[44]

Beddoes's characters, wary of invisible powers at work on physical beings, are also leery of the magnetic gaze. Wolfram warns Sibylla that she may fall victim to his unintended spell:

> Listen not to me, look not on me more.
> I have a fascination in my words,
> A magnet in my look, which drags you downwards,

---

beym Scheintode und in plötzlichen Lebensgefahren (1819); Rudtorffer, *Abhandlung über die Verbesserung der zur Wiederbelebung der Scheintodten erforderlichen Instrumente, Geräthe und Nebenerfordernisse* (1821); Kaiser, *Über Tod und Scheintod oder die Gefahren des frühen Begrabens* (1822); Donndorf, *Über Tod, Scheintod, und zu frühe Beerdigung: ein Buch zur Verhütung des Lebendigbegrabens* (1823); and Taberger, *Der Scheintod in seinen Beziehungen auf das Erwachen im Grabe und die verschiedenen Vorschläge zu einer wirksamen und schleunigen Rettung in Fällen dieser Art* (1829). C.f. n. 37 above.

43 Franz Anton Mesmer (1734–1815) first presented his concept of Animal Magnetism in his doctoral thesis, *De influxu planetarum in corpus humanum* (1766), reviving the ancient idea that the planets exude invisible rays, a Magnetic Fluid, that affect our bodies. Mesmer founded a school in Vienna, where he practised healing through Animal Magnetism, harnessing the Magnetic Fluid through pieces of iron and conductive metals placed on the diseased spot of the patient's body. He soon found, however, that he could achieve the same 'magnetic' effect through the laying of hands and producing the trance merely by speaking with the patient. Published just prior to Mesmer's death, Karl Christian Wolfart edited the full exposition of his 'magnetic' practice: *Mesmerisumus. Oder System der Wechselwirkungen. Theorie und Anwendung des thierischen Magnetismus als die allgemeine Heiljunde zue Erhaltung des Menschen von Dr. Friedrich Anton Mesmer* (1814), to which Wolfart added his own *Erläuterungen zum Mesmerismus* (1815).

44 Hufeland, *Makrobiotik oder die Kunst, das menschliche Leben zu verlängern* (1796); *Bemerkungen über die Brownsche Praxis* (1799), and *Über den Schlaf und die verschiedenen Zustände desselben* (1821). For a positive appraisal of the medical applications of magnetism, see Loewe, *Treatise on the Phenomena of Animal Magnetism; in which the same are systematically explained, according to the laws of nature* (1822).

> *From hope and life. You set your eyes upon me,*
> *And think I stand upon this earth beside you (IV, ii, 63–67)*

Duke Melveric, of course, is convinced that Wolfram has made deliberate use of his magnetic power to seduce her:

> *For thou hast even subdued her to thy arms,*
> *Against her will and reason, wickedly*
> *Torturing her soul with spells and adjurations, —*
> *Unless thou giv'st her the free will again*
> *To take her natural course of being on,*
> *Which flowed towards me with gentle love (I, ii, 287–92)*

In his inquiry into the demarcations of life and death, the visible and the invisible, Beddoes's implication of drugs and mesmerism swirl together in a dramatic brew mixed of lore and science, magic and medicine.

In *Paradise Lost* (Book II, 649–73), Death is begotten from Satan's incestuous coupling with Sin. In *Death's Jest-Book*, Ziba declares his necromantic power as a descendent of Death:

> *Thus passing through a grassy burial-ground,*
> *Wherein a new-dug grave gaped wide for food,*
> *"Who was she?" cried he, and the earthy mouth*
> *Did move its nettle-bearded lips together,*
> *And said "'Twas I—I, Death: behold our child!"*
> *The wanderer looked, and on the lap of the pit*
> *A young child slept as at a mother's breast.*
> *He raised it and he reared it. From that infant*
> *My race, the death-begotten, draw their blood:*
> *Our prayer for the diseased works more than medicine. (γ: III, iii,*
> *489–98)*

As a member of the race of 'death-begotten' Ziba claims more power over life and death than can be wrought by medicine. Like Victor Frankenstein, he too practises the art of propagation without the intervention of the female body:

> *The dead and gone are re-begotten by us,*
> *And motherlessly born to second life. (γ: III, iii, 499–500)*[45]

---

45   H.W. Donner, Preface, *Works*, pp. xxxi–xliii, describes the MSS and his construction of the text. The γ MSS Donner dates from the Würzburg period, 1829–32. I resort to the γ text here because it casts Ziba in the role of male midwife assisting in the 'motherless'

Ziba compares the raising of the dead to the rebirth of a plant from seed:

> The mould was cracked and shouldered up; there came
> A curved stalk, and then two leaves unfurled,
> And slow and straight between them there arose,
> Ghostily still, again the crowned flower.
> Is it not easier to raise a man,
> Whose soul strives upward ever, than a plant,
> Whose very life stands halfway on death's road,
> Asleep and buried half? (III, iii, 435–42)

Duke Melveric is sceptical:

> This was a cheat:
> The herb was born anew out of a seed,
> Not raised out of a bony skeleton.
> What tree is man the seed of? (III, iii, 442–45)

When his analogy between plant and animal reproduction (an analogy that Beddoes may well have heard in Barthold's lectures) is challenged, Ziba replies that there is indeed a seed, a bone in the human body in which the regenerative power resides:

> Of a ghost;
> Of his night-coming, tempest-waved phantom:
> And even as there is a round dry grain
> In a plant's skeleton, which being buried
> Can raise the herb's green body up again;
> So is there such in man, a seed-shaped bone,
> Aldabaron, called by the Hebrews Luz,
> Which, being laid into the ground, will bear
> After three thousand years the grass of flesh,
> The bloody, soul-possessed weed called man. (III, iii, 445–54)

Commenting to Kelsall that 'Luz is an excellent joke', Beddoes also expressed his worry that he might 'write to irreligiously for Cantland'.[46] His note to the text indicates the basis of the joke, for he identifies the bone as the *os coccyges*, the 'tail bone'.[47] In a careful elucidation of this passage, Christopher Moylan observes that

---

birth. In the earlier text, Ziba states that his mother was dead and that his birth was assisted by the sexton who lifted him from the corpse (III, iii, 489–500).

46   To Thomas Forbes Kelsall, Göttingen, 27 February 1829; *Works*, p. 640.
47   *Works*, pp. 487–88.

the joke is layered, and he proceeds to explicate those layers, specifically in relation to the motifs of resurrection and eschatology in *Death's Jest-Book*. As Moylan points out, Beddoes acquired his knowledge of Jewish theology through his companion, Benjamin Bernard Reich.[48] There are more layers to the joke than Moylan has glossed. For one thing, contemporary books on anatomy and osteology did indeed present a class of 'seed-shaped bones' (*kernförmige Knochen*), but these were the patella (*Kniescheibe*) and the sesamoid (also called *patellae*), small flattened and convex bones, which develop in tendons near the joints in hands and feet. Part of the joke, then, is that Beddoes has altered the standard classification of bones by locating a seed-shape bone in a very different part of the anatomy. The seat of male regeneration is in the tail bone. But there are even more homoerotic implications to Beddoes's joke: the Latin noun *patella* referred to a shallow pan used by the Romans, or to the natural formation of the form: in animals, a cup-like *cotyle*; in plants, a pod, flat seed, or husk. In the *Philosophical Transactions*, one early report (1671; VI. 2165) describes the appearance 'on Plumb trees and Cherry trees; also on the Vine and Cherry-Laurel certain patellae or flat Husks containing worms'. The seed-shaped bone is thus a vessel of corruption already present on the living organism. In addition to the etymology that Beddoes gives in his note, the Hebrew word has other cognate forms: a verb meaning (literally) to turn aside or depart, (figuratively) to be perverse, forward, deviant, corrupt; a noun for an almond or other nut; a place-name for locations in Palestine, presumably where the nut was grown.[49] Neither Beddoes nor Moylan offer a clue for naming the bone *Aldabaron*. The obvious reference is to the magical properties of Aldabaron in alchemy. The word derives from the Persian: *Na'ir al Dabaran*, the Bright One of the Follower, referring to the bright red star that follows the Pleiades; the star Aldabaron is the eye of Taurus.[50] In terms of Beddoes 'joke', it follows the vertebrae of the spinal column and is nestled just above the anus.

A major topic in early nineteenth-century pathology of mental aberration concerned the possibility of a person hallucinating with conscious awareness, knowing that the perception is only a hallucination. At the Royal Society of Berlin in 1799, Friedrich Nicolai, a prominent critic and publisher, reported a period of illness in which he experienced a series of hallucinations.[51] The case was referred to

---

48 Moylan, '"For Luz Is a Good Joke"', pp. 93–103.
49 *Strong's Exhaustive Concordance of the Bible With Hebrew Chaldee and Greek Dictionaries* (1890), entries 3868, 3869, 3870: *luwz/looz*: to turn aside (compare *lavah*), *luwt* and *luwn*, i.e., (literally) to depart, (figuratively) to be perverse, forward, deviant, corrupt; *luwz/looz*: a nut, perhaps the almond or hazel; *Luwz/Looz*: probably because of the nut growing there, the name of two places in Palestine.
50 Julie Gillentine, 'Persia's Royal Stars', *Atlantis Rising Magazine*, 27 (2001), 8–12.
51 Friedrich Nicolai, 'A Memoir on the Appearances of Spectres or Phantoms occasioned by Disease, with Psychological Remarks'. Read by Nicolai to the Royal Society of Berlin, on the 28th of February, 1799', *Journal of Natural Philosophy, Chemistry, and the Arts*, 6 (1803), 161–79.

repeatedly in the subsequent medical inquiries into the nature of apparitions.[52] At Göttingen, Conradi had lectured on the occurrence of mania without delirium.[53] The problem of seeing an apparition, however, might not be solved with the conviction that it can be, indeed must be, only an hallucination. What if ghostly apparitions are real?—or, What if one has mistakenly supposed that one is still in possession of one's rational faculties?

When Wolfram arises from the dead to confront his murderer, Duke Melveric vacillates between these two possibilities. His shout, 'Lie of my eyes, begone!' seems to affirm that he regards the apparition only as visual aberration. Yet why then ask 'Art thou not dead?' His objection that 'Thou art not truer than a mirror's image' suggests that he sees the image as a reflection of his own guilt. Yet, again, why then attempt to exorcize the spirit, 'Back again to coffin' (III, iii, 653–58)? Melveric is not frightened but, rather, angered and confounded that he should be having this experience:

> *Darest thou stand there,*
> *Thou shameless vapour, and assert thyself,*
> *While I defy, and question, and deride thee?*
> *The stars, I see them dying: clearly all*
> *The passage of this night remembrance gives me,*
> *And I think coolly: but my brain is mad,*
> *Else why behold I that? (III, iii, 673–79)*

Caught between the two possibilities, he struggles with a paradox. Either there is a projection of his own guilt, or there is a ghost. 'I think coolly: but my brain is mad'. Once he has reconciled himself to the fact that Wolfram has returned from the dead, he must accept that the boundaries between life and death are not intact.

> *Come with me, spectre;*
> *If thou wilt live against the body's laws,*
> *Thou murderer of Nature, it shall be*
> *A question, which haunts which, while thou dost last. (III, iii, 691 94)*

---

52   For example: Ferriar, *An essay towards a theory of apparitions* (1813); Hibbert, *Sketches of the Philosophy of Apparitions* (1824); Dendy, *On the phenomena of dreams and other transient illusions* (1832); also such German works as Suabedissen, *Über die innere Wahrnehmung* (1808), and Schwab, *Von den dunkeln Vorstellungen* (1813).

53   Conradi, *Commentatio de mania sine delirio* (1827); among the texts assigned for his lectures in mental pathology, see Conradi, *Handbuch der allgemeinen Pathologie*, 4th edn (1826); *Handbuch der speciellen Pathologie und Therapie zum Gebrauche bei seinen Vorlesungen. Teil 2. Von d. abnormen Ausleerungen, Kachexien, Nervenkrankheiten, Seelenkrankheiten etc.* 3rd edn (1828); and *Beytrag zur Geschichte der Manie ohne Delirium* (1835).

Because there is rebellion against the finality of death, against the presumed materiality, Melveric recognizes that the supernatural has intruded upon the natural world. The question remains whether Wolfram haunts Nature, or murdered Nature haunts Wolfram.

At the close of Act III, Duke Melveric accepts that Wolfram has returned from the dead as his ghostly accuser. He thinks, however, that the retribution is manifest to his troubled senses only. He is not prepared for the fact that Wolfram might appear to others as well. As he awakens next morning, he is cheered that his sleep has been dreamless, yet he has qualms about confronting a new day. He now suspects that 'The look of the world's a lie, a face made up / O'er graves and fiery depths; and nothing's true / But what is horrible' (IV, i, 7–9). To his dismay, he discovers that Thorwald also sees the presence that he thought had stepped through the threshold of his own troubled mind. When his attempts to banish the spirit fail, he resorts to the counter-measure of denying his perception. Since delusion consists in seeing what is not there, he shall pretend not to see what is there:

> Impudent goblin!
> Darest thou the day-light? Dar'st be seen of more
>
> Than me, the guilty? Vanish! Though thou'rt there,
> I'll not believe I see thee. (IV, i, 32–45)

If it is madness to see a ghost, what is to pretend not to see what is visible to others? Modifying this pretence, the following lines are added in Kelsall's text:

> Or is this
> The work of necromantic Conscience? Ha!
> 'Tis nothing but a picture: curtain it.
> Strange visions, my good Thorwald, are begotten,
> When Sleep o'ershadows waking. (1851: IV, i, 40–44)

These lines step back from the supernaturalism and return to psychological ground. The phantom is the product of the guilty conscience, not of the sort of magic with which Ziba seeks to conjure. The phantom is a mental image, Melveric wants to believe, that can be obliterated by a clear mind. Yet in the very address to Thorwald, Melveric undermines his argument. While it is possible that sleep had intruded on his own mind and engendered 'Strange visions' in his waking conscience, how could Melveric's sleep possibly effect Thorwald's perceptions?

The nature of the resurrected dead in *Death's Jest-Book* is as ambiguously variable as the doctrine of life in death and death in life that informs the science of cell replacement. The plot, of course, calls for something more comprehensive than replacement of individual cells. Although Melveric sneers sceptically at the necromancer's boasts, he nevertheless enlists Ziba to find a gap in the boundary. Infestations of life's passions might perforate the walls of death. Because 'Death is old and half worn out', Melveric asks, 'Are there no chinks in't?' (III, iii, 244–45). When Wolfram steps across from the realm of death, the question is answered: 'Murder's worn out / And full of holes' (IV, iii, 689–90). Wolfram shifts from being a ghost or spirit, to being a reanimated cadaver. Now you see him, now you don't. As disintegrating corpse, Wolfram seems to be a part of the material world. Thus the Duke claims Wolfram as his ghastly jester, asserting the same material authority that he is accustomed impose over his vassals:

> So thou'rt yet visible,
> Thou grave-breaker! If thou wilt haunt me thus,
> I'll make thee my fool, ghost, my jest and zany.
> 'Tis his officious gratitude that pains me:
> The carcase owes to me its ruinous life,
> (Between whose broken walls and hideous arches
> You see the other world's grey spectral light). (IV, i, 40–46)

Scorning subservience and the claim to his carcass, Wolfram shifts from the apparent physical to a spiritual form, from visible to invisible:

> I vanish: now a short farewell. I fade;
> The air doth melt me, and, my form being gone,
> I'm all thou see'st not. (IV, i, 57–59)

Wolfram becomes ubiquitous, present in all that is invisible, all that surrounds Melveric, all that flows through his mind and body. Although he acknowledges this interpenetration, he seems more relieved that Wolfram is 'viewless' than he is concerned that the haunting is now relentlessly omnipresent:

> Dissolved like snow in water! Be my cloud,
> My breath, and fellow soul, I can bear all,
> As long as thou art viewless to these others. (IV, i, 60–62)

That Wolfram has now entered into him as his 'breath', his 'fellow soul', means that the Duke no longer exercises any aristocratic authority at all. There is another cohort on the throne of his own consciousness, governing his own being. Esquirol and other writers on mental aberration presented case studies of those who heard interior voices or felt possessed by an alien spirit.[54] This paranoiac delusion becomes the Duke's reality.

---

54   Esquirol, 'Délire', *Dictionanaire des Sciences Médicales* (Paris: Panckoucke, 1814). Esquirol used the term 'monomania' (rather than 'paranoia') to describe the delusional disorder, departing from logical reasoning and including obsessive fears. As defined by R. Hooper, *Lexicon Medicum* (1811) 596/2, paranoia resulted from an 'alienation of

Wolfram has bridged that gap, which, earlier in the play, Melveric scoffingly pronounced 'a perilous boast'. Isbrand claimed a power to know the minds of others, to probe the 'deepest bosom', map the thoughts, penetrate the 'still soul / Where the seen thing is imaged'—and coveted (III, iii, 75–80). His methods are scurrilous rather magical. He preys on people's fears and desires:

> my spies, which are
> Suspicion's creeping words, have stolen in,
> And, with their eyed feelers, touched and sounded
> The little hiding holes of cunning thought,
> And each dark crack in which a reptile purpose
> Hangs in its chrysalis unripe for birth.
> All of each heart I know. (III, iii, 80–86)

The Duke rejects Isbrand's pretension as grossly exaggerated. The human mind is far too complex to be subjected to such an inventory:

> O perilous boast!
> Fathom the wavy caverns of all stars,
> Know every side of every sand in earth,
> And hold in little all the lore of man,
> As a dew's drop doth miniature the sun:
> But never hope to learn the alphabet,
> In which the hieroglyphic human soul
> More changeably is painted, than the rainbow
> Upon the cloudy pages of a shower,
> Whose thunderous hinges a wild wind doth turn.
> Know all of each! when each doth shift his thought
> More often in a minute, than the air
> Dust on a summer path. (III, iii, 86–98)

Isbrand and the Duke, of course, are talking about very different modes of 'knowing the minds of others'. The Duke imagines the deep spelunking into the consciousness, and deeper yet into the recesses of the unconsciousness, where not even the mesmerist can penetrate. Isbrand is concerned with expediency, knowing enough of a person's secrets that whispered insinuations can prompt them to respond as he wishes. In response to the Duke's assertion that the wild wind stirs a person's more than the 'Dust on a summer path', Isbrand observes that the dust can be laid with 'Liquours . . . / Grape-juice or vein-juice', alcohol or threats (III, iii, 98–99).

---

the mind' or a 'defect of judgment'. Not until the mid-century did the term begin to refer specifically to delusions of persecution.

The fundamental lesson, however, is that mental coercion is more effective than physical coercion. Isbrand, as experienced practitioner in manipulation and exploitation, knows, too, that mental torment is more effective than physical torment. Standing aloof from the moral laws that govern the behaviour of others, he sees their utility only as they might enable him to inflict the mental wounds of guilt. He laughs at the fact that incest 'should count so doubly wicked'. What is important about a secret sin or a virulent hate is that they become piercing weapons in the hand of a foe.

> Sire and mother
> And sister I had never, and so feel not
> Why sin 'gainst them should count so doubly wicked,
> This side o' th' sun. If you would wound your foe,
> Get swords that pierce the mind: a bodily slice
> Is cured by surgeon's butter: let true hate
> Leap the flesh wall, or fling his fiery deeds
> Into the soul. (II, iv, 186–93)

While Beddoes certainly derived much of his knowledge of aberrational psychology from Benecke, Conradi, and other contemporary expositions, he clearly took an assertive and independent stance on issues of morality and sexual relations. His representation of women, of Sibylla and Amala in *Death's Jest-Book*, often seems misogynist. In fact, both sexes are subject to indictment. Society constructs sexual behaviour, not the other way around. Athulf, tormented by his jealous rivalry with his brother, realizes that rivalry is inherent in the roles that they have adopted and has little to do with the woman both claim to love:

> Curse the word!
> And trebly curse the deed that made us brothers!
> O that I had been born the man I hate!
> Any, at least, but one. Then—sleep my soul;
> And walk not in thy sleep to do the act,
> Which thou must ever dream of. My fair lady,
> I would not be the reason of one tear
> Upon thy bosom, if the times were other;
> If women were not women. When the world
> Turns round the other way, and doing Cain-like
> Passes as merrily as doing Eve-like,
> Then I'll be pitiful. Let go my hand;
> It is a mischievous limb, and may run wild,
> Doing the thing its master would not. (IV, ii, 10–23)

Much of morality would indeed be turned topsy-turvy 'If women were not women' and the world, and the sexes, turned 'round the other way'. Heterosexual love, if it is love, lapses quickly into misogyny. Athulf tells Sibylla what is wrong with all of her sex:

> From me no comfort. O you specious creatures,
> So poisonous to the eye! Go! You sow madness. (IV, ii, 1–2)

No less than Athulf in his rivalry with Adalmar, Melveric in his rivalry with Wolfram is left in the aftermath wondering why he allowed a woman to come between them.

> It was a fascination, near to madness,
> Which held me subjugated to that maiden.
> Why do I now so coldly speak of her,
> When there is nought between us? (III, i, 53–56)

There was no love, only 'a fascination, near to madness'. Whether fascination, obsession, or madness, the woman was not the object of desire but, simply, a convenient surrogate for the passion that had been hidden in secrecy.

Substituting a practical sense of what makes people tick for any allegiance to moral principles, Isbrand places the blame for human folly on the sexual roles people are forced to play. 'As I live I grow ashamed of the duality of my legs, for they and the apparel, forked or furbelowed, upon them constitute humanity; the brain no longer'. The shame is not due to sexual identity but to the behaviour demanded once one has donned breeches or skirt. It is not the brain that defines humanity, it is the gendered role-playing. Folly enough, Isbrand says, to 'wish I were an honest fellow of four shins' (II, iii, 86–90), a horse or a dog who might run around unclothed, yet not be coerced into adhering to arbitrary codes for sexual behaviour.

Death's Jest-Book is not a play that explores the fate of the 'effete king' in the tradition Marlowe's *Edward II*, or Shakespeare's *Richard II*, or Byron's *Sardanapalus*. Beddoes has a very different agenda as playwright. His exploration of homoerotic desire draws not from the foregone conclusions of moral arbiters, but turns to contemporary psychology, anatomy, and physiology. He locates the human condition in a context in which life is caught up in death, the flesh in the process of decay, sanity in the welter of insanity. None of the boundaries—social, moral, religious—hold. 'As a dramatist', he stated during his first semester at Göttingen, 'I cannot help thinking that the study of anat^y, phisiol-, psycho-, & anthropo-ology applied to and illustrated by history, biography and works of the imagination is that w^h is most likely to assist one in producing correct and accurate delineations of the passions'. His goal was to transform 'his experience in mental pathology

& therapeutics', into 'a living semiotical display, a series of anthropological experiments'. Those experiments would produce an "important psychical principle—i.e., a tragedy."[55] When Procter called for revisions of a play fraught with 'obscurity, conceits, and mysticism', Beddoes must have despaired of ever realizing that 'psychical principle', yet he was possessed by it until his suicide twenty years later. His last wish was for Kelsall 'to look at my MSS—and print or not as *he* thinks fit'.[56]

---

55   To Thomas Forbes Kelsall, Göttingen, 4 December 1825; *Works*, p. 609.
56   To Revell Phillips, Basel, 26 January 1849; *Works*, p. 683.

Between the 'Hostile Body' and the 'Hieroglyphic Human Soul':

The Ethics of Beddoes's 'Mental Theatre'

Nat Leach

Death's Jest-Book has long been read in the context of Romantic 'closet drama', as a boldly expressive (if not excessive) poetic work whose pretensions to theatricality were nevertheless laughable. Recent criticism of Romantic drama, however, has debunked the myth of Romantic anti-theatricality and has sought to explore the significance of the concrete theatrical contexts of Romantic plays. Beddoes's play perhaps exceeds all other Romantic works in insisting on the problematic nature of the physical body and, thus, disrupting any simple delineation of an idealized, 'closet' space. The particular challenge posed by the play is that, rather than seeking to withdraw from the world of performance into a transcendent mental space, as many Romantic plays have been accused of doing, it performs the very limitations of performance. Beddoes's rather obsessive fixation on the corporeal body and its susceptibility to death not only demonstrates his resistance to an abstract idealizing view of human nature but also suggests the theatrical body's inability to perform any supposedly essential identity. Like many other Romantic plays, *Death's Jest-Book* invites consideration as a form of 'mental theatre', not in the rather simplistic sense of positing a transcendent mental space wholly distinct from the actual stage but in a more complex sense of its recognition of the inextricable connection between the mind and the theatrical body. The term, 'mental theatre', coined by Byron, has long been read as indicative of a typically Romantic desire to privilege the mind as the site and origin of a dramatic encounter with that which is foreign to it and has, thus, been aligned with the privacy of the closet and opposed to the actual space of the stage. Nevertheless, the juxtaposition of the words 'mental' and 'theatre' also invites a reading that troubles the supposedly clear distinction between closet and stage; the conjunction of the two words suggests a chiasmatic crossing of properties that may be taken as a symptom of the troubled relations between mind and body, self and other, ideal and real, at work in much Romantic drama. To posit a space that is both mental *and* theatrical is not simply to challenge the adequacy of the stage but, further, to acknowledge that the workings of the mind are in some ways theatrical and that the theatre necessarily entails a relation between the minds of author, actor and audience. Many Romantic plays thus suggest that neither the closeted mind nor the public stage may be posited as a pure space of representation, but that each is haunted by the implications of the other in a way that destabilizes any attempt to impose any absolute distinction between the two.

In keeping with the recent critical consensus that the Romantic imagination is not to be understood as inherently anti-theatrical, I argue that the difference between Beddoes's form of 'mental theatre' and those of his Romantic predecessors is not one of kind but one of degree. Beddoes's anxiety about the body and its representation is typical of Romantic drama, while, as Northrop Frye has suggested, he also has links to a much more modern sensibility. While Frye suggests that Beddoes anticipates the 'theatre of the absurd', with death and with the absurdity of life that I would like to pursue here.[1] My attempt to situate 'mental theatre' in a space beyond the limited conception of mind as self and as ego owes much to the versions of subjectivity theorized by Emmanuel Lévinas, Maurice Blanchot, and Jacques Derrida. For Lévinas, the mind is not the closeted site of its own truth but an opening towards the radically Other that disturbs the idea of the mind's transparency to itself. Moreover, the mind is inextricably linked to the body, which can neither be subordinated to the mind nor simply opposed to it. Lévinas speaks of the body as 'neither an obstacle opposed to the soul nor a tomb that imprisons it, but that by which the self is susceptibility itself'.[2] This susceptibility necessitates an openness to the Other that Lévinas describes in terms of the face-to-face encounter, which is the fundamental relation to the Other, as it is the face of the Other that disrupts all attempts to reduce the Other to a language of the same; 'the face, still a thing among things, breaks through the form that nevertheless delimits it'.[3] For Lévinas, the face is thus both a physical phenomenon and that which disrupts the reduction of the world to the merely physical; it is a 'trace' of the infinite that is irreducible to the totality of representation.[4] Moreover, the face of the Other is fundamentally linked to the alterity of death; death is precisely that which is beyond experience, and it therefore can only be experienced as the death of the Other, a phenomenon irreducible to the self's conception of it. It is here that this radical ethics intersects with my reading of 'mental theatre'; Beddoes's play works to signify the resistance of alterity and death to representation, exposing the gaps in its own dramatic construction. What Frye calls 'the feeling that the moment of

1   Northrop Frye, 'Yorick: The Romantic Macabre', in *A Study of English Romanticism* (New York: Random House, 1968) pp. 51–85. Frye concludes this essay with the claim that 'it is Beddoes, as far as English literature is concerned, who brings us most directly into contact with the conception of the absurd in a way that permits of compassion but excludes self-pity', p. 85.

2   Emmanuel Lévinas, *Otherwise than Being or Beyond Essence*, trans. Alphonso Lingis (Pittsburgh: Duquesne University Press, repr. 1998) (1974), p. 195, n. 1.

3   Lévinas, *Totality and Infinity: An Essay on Exteriority* trans. Alphonso Lingis (1961; Pittsburgh: Duquesne University Press, repr. 1996), p. 198.

4   For Lévinas, the trace is a sign that registers alterity without making it present, and, as a result, the trace itself has only a liminal presence; it is 'the presence of that which properly speaking has never been there', 'The Trace of the Other', in *Deconstruction in Context*, ed. Mark C. Taylor (Chicago: University of Chicago Press, 1986), p. 358.

death is also a crisis of identity' is, for Lévinas, an ethical moment in which alterity breaks through the totalizing representations of the self.[5] It is Beddoes's recognition of the irreducibility of this alterity to theatrical representation that constitutes the ethical tendency of his play.

Beddoes's obsession with this moment of bodily death and openness to alterity radicalizes the work of other Romantic dramatists whose 'mental theatre' is similarly concerned with the question of how to represent a self that consists not only of a mind, but a susceptible body. Joanna Baillie's project of 'mental theatre', the *Plays on the Passions*, were, like Beddoes's play, intended for the stage, but in a way that seeks to bring the private truth of character from the secret 'closet' to the public stage. She expresses her intention to write a comedy and a tragedy to delineate each 'passion', beginning in the first volume with love and hate. In her 'Introductory Discourse' to this volume, she posits a closet space in which the expressive power of tragedy can harness 'the language of the agitated soul' in order make the passions legible.[6] By positing the soul as fundamentally readable through the medium of the body, Baillie's theory seeks to make the theatrical body into a transparent signifier that can unproblematically reproduce the truth of the closet on the stage. Her project is based on the idea that character may be 'anatomized' by the gaze of the spectator, a popular metaphor in the late eighteenth century, and aims to reduce the human soul to its fundamental constituent parts and thus make it understood. For Beddoes, however, anatomy was not a metaphor but a science, quite literally bound up with drama insofar as both are concerned with the act of making visible the nature of the human being. He expressed the desire to connect the two through a 'living semiotical display' rather than a 'cold technical dead description', but while his letters often claim that anatomy is the source of his play, critics have long noted that his stated aims are refuted by the work he produced (p. 609). For example, in a verse letter to B. W. Procter, he expresses the desire to make 'a mock, a fool, a slave' of death (l. 56) and says of his knowledge of death, 'I owe this wisdom to anatomy' (l. 75). Nevertheless, the end result of *Death's Jest-Book* seems to be quite the opposite, or at least it insists on the ambiguity of the title and brings together its two possible meanings; death is not only shown to be a fool, but death's jest is also a terrifying one, a joke at the expense of humanity and beyond the control of the author's attempt to anatomize human nature.

A similar contradiction exists between Baillie's theory and her practice; if the 'Introductory Discourse' offers a 'cold technical dead description' of the passions, her plays form a 'living semiotical display' that exceeds the limits of the anatomizing gaze. Where Baillie claims to desire to reduce the passions to a totalizing knowledge of human nature by representing 'those passions to which all are liable', her dramatic representations are, in fact, of strange, pathological, and excessive passions.[7] For example, in *De Montfort*, her tragedy on hatred, Baillie can

---

5   Frye, p. 85.
6   Joanna Baillie, 'Introductory Discourse', in *Plays on the Passions* (1798 edition), ed. Peter Duthie (Peterborough, Ontario: Broadview, 2001) p. 73.
7   Baillie, pp. 93–94.

only succeed in producing sympathy for the main character by showing that his hatred for his enemy is pathologically beyond his control and therefore outside of the audience's own experience. Baillie's plays exceed and, in fact, exclude the sameness of the passions from the field of representation and instead suggest that the mind is theatrical only insofar as it is Other to this homogenous idea of human nature.

Baillie's practice is also indicative of the way in which many Romantic plays vacillate between directing themselves towards an Other whose gaze holds the promise of a completion of their meaning, and retracting this possibility of full completion and understanding. Baillie, Byron, and Beddoes, among others, not only represent subjects haunted by an alterity that thwarts the sentimental ideal of the sameness of human nature but also acknowledge the impossibility of reducing this theatrical relation to the Other to a totalizing sameness. These writers vacillate between the stage and the closet in ways that are not simply anti-theatrical but also attest to a tension between the language of the self and a movement towards the Other that recognizes the impossibility of fully remaining in the closet. Such 'mental theatre' is anti-theatrical only insofar as it rejects the idea of a necessary correlation between closet and stage, but it may be described as ethical insofar as it acknowledges a human alterity that is irreducible to either.

Byron, whose usage of the term 'mental theatre' has been taken as a typical expression of Romantic anti-theatricality, is explicitly concerned with the theatrical relation to the Other implied by dramatic writing. His historical tragedies (about which he was writing when he coined the term 'mental theatre')[8] in particular show the marks of both a fervent desire for actual communication with an audience and an anxiety-ridden resignation to his plays remaining in the closet, which David Erdman calls his 'stage fright'.[9] These historical tragedies are explicitly concerned with the susceptibility of the body and its resistance to totalizing historical narratives. His two Venetian tragedies in particular represent characters who are bound to the limitations of their bodies and to their social, historical, and ideological positions, and forced to acknowledge the fact that, as Jacopo Foscari says in his prison cell in *The Two Foscari*, 'the mind is much but is not all' (III, i, 85). This could be the motto of Byron's historical 'mental theatre' as a whole; just as the bodies of the protagonists are imprisoned by historical and ideological forces, so is the performance of the plays constrained by a strict neo-classical regularity that calls into question the power of the mind to transcend physical representation. As Thomas Crochunis has recently argued, Byron's 'mental theatre' renders theatrical and ideological action as a potentiality located within the un-transcendable

---

8   Byron explains that his primary objective in his historical tragedies is to 'make a *regular* English drama no matter whether for the stage or not, which is not my object—but a *mental theatre*', *The Works of Lord Byron with his Letters and Journals and his Life By Thomas Moore*, 14 vols (London, 1832), 5, 347.

9   David V. Erdman, 'Byron's Stage Fright: The History of his Ambition and Fear of Writing for the Stage', *English Literary History*, 6 (1939), 219–43.

horizon of the body, and directed outwards towards an audience or reader.[10] This potentiality, of course, entails the possibility that its movement towards the Other may be a missed encounter, as in the dramatically innovative end of *Marino Faliero*. After the Doge's failed revolution, the audience sees his final speech and the preparations for his execution; this scene is then supplemented by what is excluded from it, the people whom the Doge has been told cannot hear his speech because the palace gates are barred against them. The people are shown straining to hear the Doge's final speech, but they can neither hear a word nor prevent his execution, rushing through the gates after he has been killed. This final scene is powerful in that it both represents the people as a force of alterity, excluded from historical representation, and shows that this alterity cannot be fully represented within a dramatic form. The play ends on a note of potential revolution in a way that only exacerbates an awareness of the gap between representation and effective political action, drawing attention to the fact that the relation to the Other at the heart of the play remains fundamentally unrepresentable. Byron's play invites a completion in the mind of a reader/audience but also signals that this movement towards an Other must be excluded from representation, and can remain only the trace of an ethical demand.[11]

Byron's theatre is in many ways opposite to that of Beddoes; Byron uses a strictly regular dramatic form in order to produce a claustrophobic sense of the body's subjection to history, while Beddoes's highly irregular pastiche overtly challenges these normalizing codes of representation that seek to reduce the human body to the status of a signifier. The unrepresentable hope for a revolutionary communication in *Marino Faliero* becomes, in *Death's Jest-Book*, an emptying out of the signifiers of revolution into a schematic narrative filled with stock characters that attests more radically to the irreducibility of lived experience to political discourse. Both writers signal the irreducibility of the theatrical body to an idealized political narrative and use the body to expose the limits of the Romantic mind. In the examples of Baillie and Byron, the theatrical body is exposed as a problem insofar as it cannot be reduced to the sameness of the audience's gaze. The theatrical body cannot simply 'perform' the passions, just as it cannot unite the two halves of Byron's scene. The audience is invited to fill out these representations and, theoretically, to connect the theatrical body with the experiencing mind, but this invitation is always fraught with its own impossibility; there remains an alterity at the heart of these representations that cannot be reduced to the sameness of either the body or the mind.

With Beddoes, this gap between mind and body is all the more insistent; his play places a great deal of emphasis on the physical body, but at the same time, it is a body that is marked by its artificiality and literariness. Indeed, critics have long noted that Beddoes's characters are 'not intended to be human, except indeed

---

10   Thomas C. Crochunis, 'Byronic Heroes and Acting: The Embodiment of Mental Theater', in *Contemporary Studies on Lord Byron*, ed. William D. Brewer (Lewiston: Edwin Mellen, 2001), pp. 73–94.

11   I develop this argument more fully in my essay 'Historical Bodies in a Mental Theatre: Byron's Ethics of History', *Studies in Romanticism* (forthcoming).

in the wizard humanity of death'[12] and 'are not acting out what they are but are being made to do things'.[13] The body in Beddoes, for all its grotesque physicality, is an abstract literary signifier that does not perform the fullness of its presence but remains a ghostly signifier of absence. Beddoes explicitly invokes this sense of literary history as a spectral scene in a letter to his friend Thomas Forbes Kelsall: 'Such ghosts as Marloe, [sic] Webster &c are better dramatists, better poets, I dare say, than any contemporary of ours—but they are ghosts—the worm is in their pages—& we want to see something that our great grand-sires did not know' (p. 595). He advocates originality over imitation of past models, even as his own play is a highly self-conscious pastiche of these models, suggesting that literary work is always already inhabited by its ghosts.[14] This relationship between the ghost and the body is theorized by Derrida, who says, 'For there to be ghost, there must be a return to the body, but to a body that is more abstract than ever' and the ghostly nature of Beddoes's work bears this out.[15] Beddoes's 'return to the body', does not seek to identify the body as the site of concrete meaningfulness, but exposes the abstract and ghostly quality of this meaning. In Derrida's terms again, this may be seen in terms of what he calls the *différance* that lies between 'spirit' and 'specter'; 'specter' introduces corporeality and deferral into the structure of 'spirit', preventing 'spirit' from simply expressing the sameness of the mind and thus always representing a promise of something Other. If the influence of Renaissance tragedy persists in Beddoes, it is not simply that he reproduces the 'spirit' of that age; rather, he conjures its 'specter', dwelling on the bare physicality of the tragic body. The idealizing and totalizing impulse of spirit is disrupted by the carnal haunting of the spectre, which prevents the body from being subsumed by the mind. Beddoes's work thus suggests that the originality he craves may only be obtained through a ghostly encounter with tradition, which necessarily exposes the artificiality of its form and can thus only signify the corporeality of the body by representing it in a way that is 'more abstract than ever'.

Beddoes thus goes beyond the ways in which Baillie and Byron trouble the relations between the 'mental' and the 'theatrical' in the more radical 'spectral' structure of his play that exposes the trace of alterity that haunts both concepts. The ethical dimension of Beddoes's work can be seen in the way this spectral structure insists that neither mind nor body can be understood as an isolated and

---

12   Arthur Symons, 'From *The Academy*, 15 August 1891', in *Plays and Poems of Thomas Lovell Beddoes*, ed. with an introduction H.W. Donner (London: Routledge and Kegan Paul, 1950), lxxviii–lxxx (p. lxxx).

13   Frye, p. 64.

14   Greg Kucich reads this letter as representative of the feelings of Romantic dramatists as a whole, who were ambivalently 'enthralled by a specter they could neither embrace nor dismiss', in a way that contributed to their conflicted relationship towards the theatre, '"A Haunted Ruin": Romantic Drama, Renaissance Tradition, and the Critical Establishment', *The Wordsworth Circle* 23.2 (1992) 64–75 (p. 68).

15   Jacques Derrida, *Specters of Marx: The State of the Debt, the Work of Mourning, and the New International*, trans. Peggy Kamuf, intro. by Bernd Magnus and Stephen Cullenberg (New York: Routledge, 1994), p. 126.

autonomous entity but that both stand in relation to something that is Other to their representations. It may seem perverse to attribute this ethical quality to a writer whose critics have most often attacked his failure to speak from any point of view other than his own. I would, however, argue that Beddoes's 'mental theatre' functions to demonstrate the inescapable alterity that inhabits even this language of the self. Most of Beddoes's early critics commented on the excessive literariness of *Death's Jest-Book*, its lack of individuated characters, its exhaustive procession of geographical settings, and its grandiose speeches. While these may seem to be the conventional hallmarks of Romantic closet drama, Beddoes often claimed that he did intend the play for the stage, suggesting not so much that he thought his characters could be given life on the stage as that its literariness is not a strategy to elide the troublesome embodiment of the mind but to point to the problematic nature of the physical and theatrical body. Even Beddoes's admirers have called his poetic language solipsistic, but like Byron and many other proponents of a Romantic 'mental theatre', the language of the self is not simply asserted but subjected to an intense scrutiny. Christopher Ricks has defended Beddoes from this charge by arguing that for Beddoes there is 'no such thing as a thing that is alone'.[16] Ricks shows that Beddoes's language is haunted by the response that it knows it cannot receive; it is not that Beddoes locates truth in selfhood but that his language bears an ethically anguished relation to the Other it cannot reach. In *Death's Jest-Book*, Sibylla seems to speak for Beddoes when she rejects the poetic notion that flowers are 'symbols of humanity' and therefore 'the sacred source of poetry' (β: V, iii, 23, 28). The language of symbol is not based on an idealized sameness but is inhabited by the radically Other space of death, of which Sibylla argues that flowers bear the trace. The alterity of death is both inescapable and irreducible to the language of life, and, for Beddoes, language is necessarily fraught with this paradoxical relation, able neither to capture the Other, nor to avoid the disintegration of autonomous selfhood caused by this relation to alterity.

Moreover, the scene's literary debt to *Hamlet* for Sibylla's Ophelia-like welcoming of death itself suggests that there is no 'sacred source' of poetry, only a corpus of ghostly texts to be cannibalized for their signifiers. Beddoes frequently makes a pointedly mechanical use of such repetition, again challenging the idea of originality, both by utilizing precedents in Jacobean tragedy and Gothic literature and by repeating events within the play itself. For example, Isbrand turns into another version of the tyrannical Duke, while Adalmar and Athulf repeat the pattern of forgiveness, betrayal, and murder found in the Duke's earlier murder of Wolfram, which itself repeats the Duke's earlier attempted murder. Beddoes thus represents a limited range of theatrical possibilities, drawing attention to the artifice of the stage and depicting the surfaces of human life as, essentially, repetition without difference, a dance of life no more meaningful than the dance of death he stages in the final act.

---

16   Christopher Ricks, 'Thomas Lovell Beddoes: A Dying Start', in *The Force of Poetry* (Oxford: Clarendon, 1984), 135–62 (p. 159).

This 'dance of death' is also a self-consciously artificial representation of death and points to the way that death itself exceeds representation. Beddoes's stage directions call for the figures of death to emerge from a painting of the dance of death on the wall of a sepulchre, producing an obviously artificial effect, while also blurring the boundary between the flat representation of the painted figures and the apparent physical reality given to stage performers. While the rather vague stage directions suggest that the effect is more to be imagined than performed, the play also constructs death as, precisely, a performance. This performance of death points to the gap between the painted representations and the living figures but, in so doing, implicates itself in the artificiality of representation insofar as the figures of death are self-reflexively identified as performers. At the conclusion of one of the dances of death, Wolfram observes that it is 'the anti-masque ... 'tis satirical', and this sums up the general tone of the play's representation of death (β: V, iv, 293). In fact, death is both an un-transcendable horizon and a performance; when Isbrand is stabbed, he claims, 'I but pretend to die', a statement that is both exposed as hubris (he later concedes 'Now Death doth make indeed a fool of me') and also shown to be quite true, as the actor who speaks these lines is doing exactly that (β: V, iv, 278). Death constitutes both an absolute limit and the impossibility of limit; death always wins, but there are nevertheless 'chinks' in death that somehow allow Wolfram to come back, and thus attest to the radical impossibility of knowing death (β: III, iii, 246). Thus, while Beddoes's desire to stage what he called a 'living semiotical display' of death seems paradoxical, it in fact produces an awareness of the distance between death and signs. By refusing to attempt verisimilitude in his representations, Beddoes insists forcefully on the irreducibility of the physical world to literary representation. By denying that the signifying surface can be used to read a deeper truth, Beddoes suggests that neither the theatrical body nor the closeted mind can be claimed as the pure site of the play's meaning. For Beddoes, the mental *is* the theatrical, insofar as consciousness is by definition a consciousness of a performance of signifiers that conceal the radical alterity of the body and its death.

Beddoes depicts a version of subjectivity that is incoherent and unreadable precisely because it can never be anything more than a signifier disconnected from the alterity of death that lies at its root. His depthless characters play out a series of roles unrelated to any essential identity as Beddoes parodies the kind of attempt to reduce character to a knowable essence typified by Baillie's 'Introductory Discourse'. Isbrand makes the anatomizing claim that there are none 'whose deepest bosom / My fathom hath not measured; none, whose thoughts I have not made a map of ... All of each heart I know' (β: III, iii, 77–88). Beddoes exposes the hubris of Isbrand's belief that he can reduce the encounter with the Other to the status of knowledge in the Duke's retort: 'never hope to learn the alphabet, / In which the hieroglyphic human soul / More changeably is painted than the rainbow' (β: III, iii, 91–93). The Duke insists on the alterity of character, using 'hieroglyphic' as an adjective to suggest that the 'soul' is not a transcendent essence but an unreadable materiality resistant to the anatomizing gaze. Isbrand's revolutionary plot succeeds because he convinces the conspirators that he is 'open', but as the Duke points out, they could only see their desires reflected in him because 'his soul was in a deep, dark well' (β: V, ii, 16, 22). They misread the emptiness of Isbrand's self-representation as mental transparency. But while the Duke points out the unreadability of Isbrand's soul, he too seeks to master the unknown; he attempts to conjure his wife back from the dead but succeeds only in resurrecting his victim, Wolfram. Each of the characters in turn gives in to the hubris of believing in the mastering power of the mind, while the play itself reasserts the alterity inherent within the mind by showing that it is itself constituted by an unstable set of material signifiers.

Recent critics, such as Alan Richardson[17] and Frances Wilson,[18] have noted that language for Beddoes is above all defined as failure, an inability to communicate with the Other. Where Baillie's and Byron's plays contain within themselves the possibility of a missed encounter with the audience, Beddoes's insistence on the artificiality of language more radically points to the impossibility of attributing to language any stable significative or communicative function. Rather, its raw materiality suggests the state of neutral, irremissible being that Lévinas and Blanchot call the 'there is'. The play's horror stems less from its Gothic trappings than from the horror that Lévinas defines as 'a movement which will strip consciousness of its very "subjectivity"' and which 'returns in the heart of every negation . . . the impossibility of death, the universality of existence even in its annihilation'.[19] The characters in the play are confronted with the horror of the fact that representation is nothing but a veneer covering over the bare fact of existence. The Lévinasian horror of irremissible being is conveyed through a realization of the interpenetration of language and being with death. The Duke's encounter with the resurrected Wolfram makes him feel that 'The look of the world's a lie, a face made up / O'er graves and fiery depths; and nothing's true/ but what is horrible' (β: IV, i, 7–9). His relation to death unsettles his sense of identity, as he is made to feel like 'a ghost among the men' and claims that the fact 'that I am is but the obstinate will / Of this my hostile body' (β: IV, i, 70–71). The Duke begins to experience himself as a Gothic phenomenon, as his encounter with Wolfram leaves him feeling trapped in the unmasterable materiality of his body. This Lévinasian sense of the impossibility of death is dramatized at the end of the play, as the Duke is not killed but brought by Wolfram 'still alive, into the world o' th' dead' (β: V, iv, 357). By showing the fruitlessness of his characters' efforts to master death, Beddoes, like Lévinas, insists on the tenuous embodiment of human subjectivity that can neither master being nor escape its horror.

The ethical implications of this version of subjectivity that is always inhabited by death and thus irreducible to representation, come from the way in which the

---

17   Alan Richardson, 'Death's Jest-Book: "Shadows of Words"', in A Mental Theater: Poetic Drama and Consciousness in the Romantic Age (University Park, Penn. and London: Pennsylvania State University Press, 1988), pp. 154–73.

18   Frances Wilson, '"Strange Sun": Melancholia in the Writings of Thomas Lovell Beddoes', in Untrodden Regions of the Mind: Romanticism and Psychoanalysis, ed. Ghislaine McDayter (Lewisburg: Bucknell University Press, 2002), pp. 127–43.

19   Emmanuel Lévinas, Existence and Existents, trans. Alphonso Lingis (Pittsburgh: Duquesne University Press, repr. 2001), pp. 55–56.

subject is shown to be necessarily structured in relation to an alterity that signs can never be sure of reaching but which they can also never escape. The Duke, for example, explains his melancholic fixation on his wife's death by the fact that thoughts, 'fleeting, unsubstantial things ... formless, viewless, and unsettled memory' nevertheless 'survive that gracious image, sculptured about the essence whence ye rose' (β: III, iii, 207–10). On the one hand, words have a life of their own, but on the other, it is an inessential life that remains determined by mortality, as the Duke's desire to resurrect his wife comes from his agonized inability to respond to the alterity that nevertheless inhabits him in the form of 'words of hers' that 'dwell in [him]' (β: III, iii, 218). Transcendence is impossible precisely because the spiritual can only be mediated through its material form. The Duke refuses the comfort of a heavenly reunion with his wife's soul because:

> I loved no desolate soul, she was a woman,
> Whose spirit I knew only through those limbs,
> Those tender members thou dost dare despise;
> By whose exhaustless beauty, infinite love,
> Trackless expression only, I did learn
> That there was aught yet viewless and eternal;
> Since they could come from such alone (β: III, iii, 227–33)

Transcendence is not simply impossible but it is, in fact, undesirable, as the very possibility of meaning is dependent on its physical incarnation. The body here replaces the 'hieroglyphic' soul as the point of contact with the infinite.

At the same time, however, the Duke's obsession with the corporeal leads only to the resurrection of Wolfram. Wolfram's unapologetic return to embodiment in the play and on the stage dramatizes the hostility rather than the divinity of the body. Neither a rational phenomenon nor a proper ghost in the Gothic tradition, Wolfram demonstrates how uncontrollable the body's meaning can be, in that he appears instead of the Duke's wife, but also in that his body becomes a profoundly indeterminate signifier, no longer a sign of either life or death. In returning Wolfram from the dead, Beddoes flouts both theatrical and Gothic conventions, choosing neither to provide rational explanations for the supernatural nor to treat the supernatural as pure fantasy, as the possibility is held out that death and therefore haunting are explicable phenomena, as Ziba claims they are, but these explanations are not adequately supplied. Moreover, Wolfram is a ghost with very little ghostliness about him; he takes a remarkably corporeal form and appears as baffled about the line between life and death as the other characters. He is not simply another ghostly figure in a poetic drama but, rather, a theatrical signifier who blurs the boundaries between presence and absence by calling attention to the degree of performance involved in theatrical presence. Wolfram's body, inhabited by death, disrupts the totalizing systems that seek to enclose it, both the exclusion of death by life and the exclusion of absence by theatrical presence. The body, for Beddoes, is thus at once a 'hostile' entity that condemns the subject to the horror of being and also the source of any potential human meaning or access to the infinite. The body and the soul engage in a chiasmatic exchange of properties, as Beddoes insists on the soul's materiality and on the body's relation to the divine. The body is at once inaccessibly Other and irremissibly present, and the play insists on the impossibility of reducing the subject to a representation. This concern with the body also attests to the impossibility of locating the play either in the closet or on the stage. Beddoes's artifice makes him neither a closet writer nor a failed dramatist but a proponent of a spectral form of 'mental theatre' that rejects the totalizing claims of the mind. Whether staged or read, Beddoes's play points to a deathly absence inherent within representation and develops the preoccupation with the body found in the 'mental theatres' of Baillie and Byron into a more radical problematization of the space of the mind. Like them, his representations vacillate between a language of the self and a movement towards the Other, but Beddoes stages the body in a way that more explicitly calls attention to both the inadequacy and the inescapability of the body's representation, whether on stage or in a text. Beddoes stages bodies that perform a haunting not only of the Romantic mind but also of literature itself; his play stands on the cusp of a modernism that Beddoes invokes not as a hope for the future but as an emptiness that resurrects the textual past, only to expose it as a naked set of material signifiers. Body and word thus become co-extensive in Beddoes's theatre, one that can be located neither in the ideal mind nor in the illusory presence of the body but that functions ethically to signal the unreadably Other space of the 'hieroglyphic human soul'.

Performing Genres in
Death's Jest-Book:
Tragedy as Harlequinade

Ute Berns

If Thomas Lovell Beddoes's *Death's Jest-Book; or, The Fool's Tragedy* is generally perceived to be one of the strangest of late Romantic dramas, this perception is due not least to the riddle of the text's poetic form or genre. The title of the play involves the notions of tragedy and foolery simultaneously, and it is followed by a succession of dramatic dialogues in brilliantly versatile blank verse and comic prose, drawing on Classical and Medieval, Early Modern and Romantic *topoi* alike. Spiced with satirical and lyrical songs, this mixture presents an example of genre hybridity virtually unparalleled in the British canon of 'high' Romantic drama. Although this is especially true for the later version of *Death's Jest-Book* with its looser structure, additional songs, and extended comic passages, the genre ambiguities are germane also to the early text.

Beddoes's lifelong interest in Early Modern drama obviously influenced his own use of genre and recalls the frequent blurring of generic boundaries we encounter in Shakespeare's plays, most importantly in the so-called 'tragicomedies'. With few exceptions, modern readers have tended to discuss *Death's Jest-Book* as a 'closet drama'. This category reifies into a genre description of its own, and, thus, is prone to suppress the more specific concern with the generic conventions deployed in the text. Perhaps the most rewarding studies of the generic question of *Death's Jest-Book* are those that deal with Beddoes's indebtedness to the theory of Romantic Irony. Beddoes is likely to have read its foremost German proponent, Friedrich Schlegel, and in addition Beddoes would have absorbed Schlegel's ideas through the drama of Ludwig Tieck, whose comic inversions and metadramatic sophistication he greatly admired. Hence Anne Harrex, Frederick Burwick, and Michael Bradshaw all argue for the impact of German aesthetic theory on Beddoes's work, reading the ironic reversals and severe clashes of mood, the generic ambiguities and obsessive revisions of *Death's Jest-Book* as potent forms of Romantic Irony.[1]

---

[1]   Anne Harrex, '*Death's Jest-Book* and the German Contribution: Part I—Literary and Philosophical Influences in *Death's Jest-Book*', *Studia Neophilologica*, 39 (1967), 15–17; and '*Death's Jest-Book* and the German Contribution: Part II—Romantic Irony and *Death's Jest-Book*', *Studia Neophilologica*, 39 (1967), 302–18; Frederick Burwick, *The Haunted Eye: Perception and the Grotesque in English and German Romanticism* (Heidelberg: Winter,

Rather than further exploring the implications of Beddoes's use of genre on a purely aesthetic plane, I will here take a less text-centred approach and draw on recent historicist and cultural studies that situate Romantic drama in contemporary theatre culture. My focus will be on 'tragedy' and 'harlequinade' as two distinct purveyors of generic conventions deployed in *Death's Jest-Book*—conventions that do, of course, qualify as ironic opposites. But instead of tracing how they are played out against each other in the text, I will investigate how they are appropriated, adapted to current political issues, and made to signify or 'perform' in a culture characterized by the opposition of legitimate and illegitimate drama.

When Beddoes was still living in Britain, he was already highly aware of the Romantic debate about drama in which the Early Modern models loomed large. It is against this backdrop that he argues, in 1825, for the need to find a dramatic form appropriate to his own time:

> I am convinced the man who is to awaken the drama must be a bold
> trampling fellow—no creeper into worm-holes—no reviser even—
> however good ... Such ghosts as Marloe—Webster &c are better
> dramatists, better poets, I dare say, than any contemporary of ours—
> but they are ghosts—the worm is in their pages—& we want to see
> something that our great-grandsires did not know. With the greatest
> reverence for all the antiquities of the drama I still think that we had
> better beget than revive—attempt to give the literature of this age an
> idiosyncrasy & spirit of its own, & only raise a ghost to gaze on, not
> to live with—just now the drama is a haunted ruin (p. 595).

Reverently calling up 'all the antiquities of the drama' for inspiration and issuing, simultaneously, the urgent warning that one must not fall prey to their ghostly lure when writing for one's own age, Beddoes concisely summarizes a pervasive strand of the cultural debate about the state of the drama. Whether he himself actually followed the policy he advocated is a subject of critical controversy. I will argue that as far as his use of genre is concerned, Beddoes does indeed thoroughly transform the Renaissance revenge tragedy, first by politically reconceptualizing its protagonist and his relation to the body politic, and second by making both the avenger and the body politic signify in the contemporary theatrical culture.

Relating *Death's Jest-Book* to the stage is, however, not an evident thing to do. Let me recall that the contemporary debate on drama and theatre covered not only the Early Modern precursors but also the emerging concept of interiorized drama. Especially with a view to the perceived abysmal state of the stage, the discussion revolved around the question as to whether dramatic writing, both contemporary or of earlier periods, should be staged or whether it ought rather to be submitted to the liberating experience of reading. Critics have been well-nigh unanimous

---

1987), pp. 274–300; Michael Bradshaw, *Resurrection Songs: The Poetry of Thomas Lovell Beddoes* (Aldershot and Burlington: Ashgate, 2001), pp. 160–90.

in their opinion that *Death's Jest-Book* is meant to be read and belongs to the so-called 'mental theatre'. Alan Richardson can be called exemplary when he claims, 'working from Shelley's dramatic poems of 1819, Beddoes extended the tradition of mental theatre and pushed it to extremes that have left its handful of readers intrigued but ... bewildered'.[2] We must, however, remind ourselves that this scholarly perception of *Death's Jest-Book* is diametrically opposed to Beddoes's own declared stance. To his friend Kelsall he writes:

> You are, I think, disinclined to the stage: now I confess that I think this is the highest aim of the dramatist, & I should be very desirous to get on it. To look down on it is a piece of impertinence as long as one chooses to write in the form of a play, and is generally the result of a consciousness of one's own inability to produce anything striking & affecting in that way. (p. 640)

According to Beddoes, to get on the stage is the highest aim of the dramatist, and the very choice of the dramatic form ought to commit an author to the goal of theatrical performance. In view of this unequivocal statement, the perception of *Death's Jest-Book* as 'mental theatre' has to be reconsidered—especially as this perception has effectively removed the text from any connection with the contemporary stage.

Greg Kucich's article '"A Haunted Ruin": Romantic Drama, Renaissance Tradition and the Critical Establishment', which draws on Beddoes's letter for its title and motto, provides a new entry into the discussion of the author's relation to the stage. Kucich claims that the contemporary critical debate on drama and theatre has been seriously distorted by twentieth-century scholars foregrounding a handful of sensational theoretical statements, often taken out of context, about the non-representational essence of dramatic writing. Redressing this misrepresentation in a nuanced analysis of, amongst other sources, a wide selection of periodicals, Kucich concludes that rather than denouncing the stage, 'it appeared more in keeping with the critical spirit of the age for someone like Beddoes to declare that writing for the stage should be "the highest aim of the dramatist, & I should be very desirous to get on it"'.[3] In this reading, Beddoes's explicit desire to get on the stage is perceived no longer as an eccentric whim voiced in opposition to the drift of the times but as representing, again, a major strand of the early nineteenth-century state of the debate. Beddoes's declaration, thus endowed with new plausibility, could not be more straightforward. Not only does it tie in perfectly with his own eager interest in what was happening on the stage but also, written in February 1829, the statement coincides with the completion of the first manuscript of *Death's Jest-Book*.

---

2   Alan Richardson, *A Mental Theatre: Poetic Drama and Consciousness in the Romantic Age* (University Park: Pennsylvania State University Press, 1988), p. 155.

3   Greg Kucich, '"A Haunted Ruin": Romantic Drama, Renaissance Tradition, and the Critical Establishment', *The Wordsworth Circle*, 23 (1992), 64–76 (p. 67).

Thus, the following observations are based on the assumption that Beddoes did in fact write 'with the stage in mind'. In its weak sense, this is to say that all dramatic texts are implicitly furnished with a stage, even an imagined one, and that this stage is necessarily impregnated with the theatrical realities of its time and culture. In its strong sense, it maintains that Beddoes, up to the completion of the first manuscript version of *Death's Jest-Book*, did intend the play for the stage, and that this is reflected in the way in which the text engages with contemporary theatrical conventions, exploiting the way in which they signify in the cultural arena. And, finally, this approach is meant to leave room also for the position of Lytton Strachey, one of the few critics seriously contemplating *Death's Jest-Book* as a stage play before it was first performed in 2003. Strachey seems to suggest that Beddoes may have written for a utopian stage of the future.[4]

Beddoes's excellent knowledge of Renaissance drama and his wide acquaintance with contemporary plays, both British and German, hardly need recapitulating. Yet Beddoes did not only read plays—he also was an avid theatre-goer. While still in London, his letters are interlarded with references to individual theatres and actors. During his tour to Italy, his correspondence tells us more about the state of the opera in the countries he visited than about their natural beauties.[5] And when in Germany, he refers to London actors in order to characterize his German professors for his friend.[6] His moving to Göttingen, however, would have largely deprived Beddoes of the lively theatre scene he was so familiar with—the theatre at Göttingen was, literally, nothing to write home about.[7] And his association with the theatre in Basel, where he had later staged a private theatrical, or his friendship with Degen, an actor working in Frankfurt, date in the late 1830s and '40s. Hence, although *Death's Jest-Book* is steeped in German literary, political, and scientific discourse, the culture of performance it negotiates remains essentially determined by Beddoes's experience of the London stage.

As is well known, the theatrical scene in London was divided between 'legitimate' and 'illegitimate' performances. Monarchical patronage had bestowed on the patent theatres Covent Garden and Drury Lane the cultural monopoly to stage tragedies and comedies, and the Licensing Act specified that they had first to be submitted to the textual censorship of the Lord Chamberlain. As a corollary, the term 'illegitimate' originally referred to performances in those theatres where

---

4   Lytton Strachey, 'The Last Elizabethan' (1907), in Lytton Strachey, *Literary Essays* (New York: Harcourt Brace, 1969), pp. 171–94 (pp. 187 ff.).

5   *Works*, pp. 587–88.

6   *Works*, pp. 617–18.

7   Up into the 1830s, there were no regular performances. Touring companies had to apply, they could be refused permission to play, and they were censored. In 1825 a newly completed concert house was aptly named 'Restauration'—it housed a theatre room as well. C.f. Sigrid Fährmann, 'Musik, Theater, Kunst und Vereine', in *Göttingen: Geschichte einer Universitätsstadt*, ed. Dietrich Denecke and Helga Maria Kühn, 3 vols (Göttingen: Vandenhoeck & Ruprecht, 2002), II: *Vom Dreißigjährigen Krieg bis zum Anschluss an Preußen: der Wiederaufstieg als Universitätsstadt (1648–1866)*, pp. 905–30 (pp. 922–30).

legitimate drama, i.e., tragedy and comedy, was prohibited. And while the interdiction of the spoken word exempted these performances from censorship, it also accounted for their visual spectacle and musical ingenuity, their hyperbolic acting style and foregrounded corporeality, and for their predilection for the supernatural. To this the cannibalistic appropriation of widely diverging sources added a pervasive pastiche effect. This applied not only to texts but also to the combining of parlour songs with airs from *Don Giovanni*, or the realizations of famous paintings in melodramas through the momentary stillness of the bodies in tableaux. As Jane Moody argues, all of these features, together with the common marginalized status of the performances, jointly forged the conventions and iconography of illegitimacy.[8] And its characteristics remained legible even after the boundaries began to dissolve—with the daring illegitimate productions reinserting the spoken word or using 'legitimate' sources such as Shakespeare, and patent theatres importing illegitimate productions to keep afloat financially.

Could it not be that with a view to the contemporary distinction between legitimate and illegitimate theatre, the 1829 title of Beddoes's *Death's Jest-Book; or, The Fool's Tragedy* advertises a text that straddles the fence? Its credentials as a tragedy need hardly be stressed; its aristocratic personnel is precipitated towards a tragic end in death or 'limbo', and furnished with a dialogue largely cast in neo-Elizabethan blank verse. At the same time, however, the *Fool's Tragedy*, though staunchly word-based, also possesses definite affinities with the illegitimate theatre. The taste for the spectacular is well catered for in the settings of the play, be it the orientalism of the African coast or the gothic graveyard scenes. And the dance of death, the performance of magic, and the subsequent appearance of a ghost form strong supernatural ingredients. Furthermore, the contemporary frenzy for 'realizing' paintings on stage, which then become alive in action, provides a plausible model for Beddoes's apparently singular device of having the Deaths step into and out of a mural. The widely differing moods of the songs and the switches from comic registers to lyrical pathos help to enhance the resulting reckless pastiche effect. It could even be argued that Beddoes's *Fool's Tragedy*—with its references to 'puppets' and 'mummery' (β: V, i, 7; V, iv, 299), 'masque' and 'anti-masque' (β: V, iv, 282, 300), and later to 'Harlequin' (γ: I, i, 63)—boldly flaunts allusions to its own generic ambiguities. I will now investigate more closely how Beddoes raises conventions of Renaissance tragedy and turns them into something his 'grandsires did not know', something that, moreover, draws whole layers of significance from contemporary theatrical culture.

---

8   My description of the British theatrical culture is indebted to Jane Moody's study *Illegitimate Theatre in London, 1770–1840* (Cambridge: Cambridge University Press, 2000). She makes this specific argument on pp. 79–80.

II

It has become commonplace to observe that the so-called neo-Elizabethan *Death's Jest-Book*, like much other Romantic and Gothic drama, is modelled on the Elizabethan or Jacobean revenge tragedy, being full of references to Shakespeare in particular. This indebtedness notwithstanding, Beddoes's plot is made to support a complex and surprisingly well-developed allegory about the hopes and failures of the French Revolution, the 'master-narrative' of Romantic drama. The structural core of the text, the all-male triangle consisting of Isbrand, Wolfram, and Duke Melveric, is loaded with rivalry and desire. Isbrand and the Duke participate in a full-blown revenge plot, while the revenge plot involving Wolfram and the Duke covers up a highly ambivalent friendship plot. The strategic uses of the discourse of revenge for the representation of revolutionary ideas in Romantic drama, especially under the conditions of censorship, have been so well established by Julie Carlson, John Kerrigan, and Michael Simpson among others that there is no need to labour this point.[9] In the case of *Death's Jest-Book*, however, the revenge plot also refers through allusions and displacements to a variety of more contemporary discourses in British and German political culture.[10] I will concentrate here on only one strand of the twofold tragic plot line—the one centring on Isbrand and the Duke—and I will begin by looking at how Beddoes fashions the role of the avenger.[11]

Isbrand's self-styling as an avenger explicitly evokes tradition and pedigree when he exclaims 'Brutus, though saint of the avenger's order; / Refresh me with thy spirit, or pour in / Thy whole great ghost' (β: I, i, 176). Yet Isbrand not only draws on the passion of his precursors; he is also intent on rivalling their political mastery. Casting himself as a puppet-player, he refers to his accomplices as 'The puppets, whose heart strings I hold and play / Between my thumb and fingers, this way, that way' (β: V, i, 7). Thus he establishes himself in the position of the would-be playwright or stage-director already familiar from the self-conscious theatricality of his Jacobean forebears. And like, for instance, Vindice in Middleton/Tourneur's *The Revenger's Tragedy*, Isbrand's scheming scripts much—though by no means all—of the play's action. Ultimately, his thirst for revenge that is mantled

---

9   Julie Carlson, *In the Theatre of Romanticism: Coleridge, Nationalism, Women* (Cambridge; New York: Cambridge University Press, 1994), 100–101; John Kerrigan, 'Revolution, Revenge and Romantic Tragedy', in *Revenge Tragedy: Aeschylus to Armageddon* (Oxford: Clarendon Press, 1997), pp. 242–67; Michael Simpson, *Closet Performances: Political Exhibition and Prohibition in the Dramas of Byron and Shelley* (Stanford: Stanford University Press, 1998), p. 46.

10   C.f. Burwick, *The Haunted Eye*, pp. 274–300; Raphael Hörmann, in this volume; and my article 'The Politics of Revolution in Thomas Lovell Beddoes's *Death's Jest-Book'*, in *Romantic Voices, Romantic Poetics: Selected papers from the Regensburg conference of the German Society for English Romanticism*, ed. Christoph Bode and Katharina Rennhak (Trier: Wissenschaftlicher Verlag Trier, 2005), pp. 97–107.

11   For this reason my analysis will not comment on the performance in 2003. Concentrating on the 'Gothic' Melveric-Wolfram plot, it completely deleted the plot-line I am investigating here.

by the rhetoric of Classical republicanism displays more than its own inherent destructiveness as it turns into an overreacher's will to power. Picturing himself as 'One of the drivers of this racing earth / With Grüssau's reins between my fingers' (β: II, iv, 14), Isbrand's rhetoric evokes Marlowe's *Tamburlaine* in his war chariot rather than any republican cause.

On a political or social plane, Isbrand is, indeed, portrayed as, in Athulf's words, 'a plotter, / A politician' (β: II, iv, 143). Suggesting to Burwick the critical comparison with Shakespeare's Iago, Isbrand nevertheless remains difficult to place.[12] Though an impoverished aristocrat, his contempt for military prowess and his delight in the unrefined pleasures of the senses are a far cry from chivalric codes of honour and polished forms of nobility. This is emphasized on the night of the overthrow, when he does not make any effort to re-assume his purported old rights. Instead he refers to royal consumption—'wine, and women, and the sceptre'—as the means to make him 'heavenly in my clay' (β: IV, iv, 194, 195). His aristocratic origin seems almost obliterated, moreover, first by his disguise and performance as a court jester who is paired, over and again, with Mandrake, the play's clown and quack, and second—'What Isbrand, thou a soldier?' (β: II, iii, 69)—by his outfit of a military man and his commanding actions. In the course of the play, the portrait of Isbrand thus amalgamates features of the overreaching general and the court fool. The macabre result is evoked in his gruesome vision of 'a war chariot in which I shall triumph like Jupiter in my fool's cap, to fetch the Duke and his sons to Hell, and then my bells will ring merrily, and I shall jest more merrily than now: for I shall be Death the Court-fool' (β: II, ii, 143–46).

In this perspective, Isbrand conforms to John Moore's observation that the Gothic villain is a versatile construct, easily transformed from the aristocrat of the old order 'into the great upstart of the new order—Napoleon'.[13] As this historical figure turns into the pervasive challenge to British Romantic drama, the social origins of his career elicit both admiration, as for instance in Hazlitt applauding the self-made man, and disdain, as in Coleridge's reference to the 'Corsican upstart'.[14] Isbrand's ruthless 'social mobility', his moving through various disguises and projecting himself beyond mankind, seems to reflect this mixture of anxiety and fascination. On the Continent, moreover, the attraction of Napoleon reached way into the next generation. Especially in Germany, the anti-Napoleonic sentiments of the *Befreiungskriege* (wars of liberation) gave way, in the face of the apparently unshakable structures of the reactionary governments, to an explosive blend of the Napoleonic legend or 'Bonapartism', which, in the late 1820s and early 1830s, influenced a considerable faction of the liberal spectrum as well as radical politics.[15]

---

12   Burwick's comparison has a different focus, though (*The Haunted Eye*, p. 296).
13   John David Moore, 'Coleridge and the "Modern Jacobinical Drama": *Osorio, Remorse,* and the Development of Coleridge's Critique of the Stage, 1797–1816', *Bulletin of Research in the Humanities*, 85 (1982), 443–65 (p. 449).
14   Quoted by Carlson, p. 60.
15   Sergio Luzatto, 'European Visions of the French Revolution', in *Revolution and the Meaning of Freedom in the Nineteenth Century*, ed. Isser Woloch (Stanford: Stanford

Situated in the contemporary culture of performance, this portrait of the avenger accumulates further layers of meaning. One of them, I suggest, derives from the illegitimate genre of the harlequinade. In a letter from 1824, Beddoes asks his friend Procter (Barry Cornwall) about a tragedy he had mentioned—'What is this Covent Garden tragedy? And whose? L.E. Landon's, Sheil's, or Grimaldi's?'[16] In yoking all of these names to the genre of tragedy, Beddoes's bantering betrays an awareness not only of the contemporary fluidity of genre boundaries but also of the transgressive potential of Joseph Grimaldi's harlequinade in particular.

By the early nineteenth century, the plot of the pantomime or harlequinade had become a mere peg, holding together a loose series of scenes exploited predominantly for satire and social criticism. They remained largely uncensored, because they were written off as irrational or absurd. Their central characters were Harlequin and Clown, the former shaped by John Rich in the 18th, the latter by Joseph Grimaldi in the first decades of the 19th century. Their joint British transformation of the Italian pantomime turned Harlequin into a symbol of retributive energy. With the help of 'real' magic, he drove the action forward in bouts of episodic violence, often turning into a Lord of Misrule. The Clown, as perfected by Grimaldi, became an emblem of gross sensuality—crafty, witty and shameless—who relied on quack magic or trickery and, as Moody puts it, transformed 'moral delinquency into a form of hedonism'.[17]

This duo of Harlequin and Clown and the two distinct kinds of magic make their transposed reappearance in *Death's Jest-Book*. In the later version a reference to this genre opens Mandrake's first song, describing 'Mankind and Fate' as 'Jove's Harlequin and Clown' in a rather philosophical vein (γ: I, i, 63–64). Yet we also know that the Isbrand-narrative is inspired by a source collected in Karl Friedrich Flögels *Geschichte der Hofnarren*.[18] There a court fool is said to have killed his Duke and usurped his place, a story with a similar trajectory to that of the harlequinade. And although Isbrand is the son of the rightful Duke, I have already indicated how he obscures all signs of aristocratic nobility by energetically fashioning his 'plebeian' nature (β: IV, iv, 201). To be sure, the serious magic is largely displaced on the magician Ziba. Nevertheless Isbrand's cunning boldness does work magic on the political situation, and it could be argued that he satirically transforms the court in the scene where he distributes his fool's garb among the courtiers and ministers—over whom he later presides as Lord of Misrule (β: II, iii, 67 ff.). Mandrake, the clown, pursues his quack magic as fervently as beer and beef, objectives that counterbalance the heroic code displayed in the second act. Apart from this general affinity with the contemporary clown, his name Mandrake (a man-plant) seems to come straight out of the stock tales of strange origins—tellurgic, botanical, oceanic etc.—with which the pantomime clown used to explain his own existence. Finally,

---

University Press, 1996), pp. 31–65 (pp. 34–35).
16   *Works*, p. 580.
17   *Illegitimate Theatre*, p. 215. I have also drawn on pp. 209–28 and on David Mayer III, *Harlequin in his Element: The English Pantomime, 1806–1836* (Cambridge, Mass.: Harvard University Press, 1969).
18   *Works*, p. 712, n. for p. 487.

Mandrake's *laissez-faire* attitude towards death ties in with the conventions of the harlequinade, in which chopped off limbs are glued on again just as death does not hinder the characters from getting up again and pursuing their business.[19]

This association with the figures of Harlequin and Clown strengthens the plebeian features of Isbrand and Mandrake, thus further loosening the hold of the tragic conventions. In evoking the popular harlequinade and its audience, the text—not to speak of its envisioned contemporary performance—gives virtual presence to a social segment of society that remains conspicuously absent from the stage. Or, to put it differently, in linking an aristocratic character's vengeful indignation about the feudal abuse of power to the retributive materialist force of the harlequinade and its supportive audience, *The Fool's Tragedy* is invested with a social energy that would easily have fallen victim to censorship if it had been embodied on stage.[20] A closer look at the way in which the text moulds the relation between this avenger and the body politic will elucidate further implications of these two genres performing side by side in Beddoes's play.

III

With his adversary, the Duke, believed absent, Isbrand redirects his hatred to surrogate objects, most notably the Duke's 'body politic' or realm. Tried and tested in Early Modern drama, this plot and trope here skilfully rework tragic revenge patterns in a post-Waterloo context. Referring to himself, the disguised Duke Melveric states 'his dukedom is his body that may be sleeping' (β: II, iii, 269). Once established, this trope later adds collateral meaning to Isbrand's bloody military conquest, which he describes as a marital union with his 'paramour', the 'spirit' of the 'sleeping city['s] ... rocky body' (β: IV, iv, 4–6). After all, the identical trope of the sleeping body earlier refers to the Duke's body politic with himself as its dreaming spirit. Thus, as Isbrand appropriates the trope of the wedding for his 'paramour', implying love without legal recognition, this connotes both an unlawful appropriation of the Duke's political prerogatives and—despite this spirit's female gender—an illicit homosexual consummation.

Yet the true challenge to the concept of the body politic as the eternal political body of the sovereign resides in the speech with which Isbrand fends off the demands of his republican collaborators. He declares that he used them only as 'tools':

---

19   Burwick gives a historical survey of the contexts and traditions on which Beddoes's version of death's fool may have drawn, and he also mentions the harlequinade (*The Haunted Eye*, p. 280).

20   Simpson argues that it was essential for the reader/spectator to be cast as 'solitary and polite rather than massed and vulgar' for political plots and agency to pass censorship (*Closet Performances*, p. 4). Of course, there were plays that presented mass scenes on stage, as in e.g., James Sheridan Knowles's *Virginius* (1820) or Mary Russel Mitford's *Rienzi* (1828), but these masses are swayed rather than initiating.

> The tools I've used
> To chisel an old heap of stony laws,
> The abandoned sepulchre of a dead dukedom,
> Into the form my spirit loved and longed for;
> Now that I've perfected her beauteous shape,
> And animated it with half my ghost,
> Now that I lead her to our bridal bed,
> Dare the mean instruments to lay their plea,
> Or their demand, forsooth, between us? (β: V, i, 13)

In this passage, Isbrand's phrase of 'a dead dukedom' questions the very eternity of the monarch's body. Moreover, the image of the ruler as a sculptor reshaping the 'laws' of this political body undermines the notion of its natural form, which identifies political laws with natural laws. Actually, the 'stony laws' might even allude to the Ten Commandments and, thus, to the divine foundation of the political laws themselves. In Isbrand's conceit, however, none of these laws remains sacred. The revolutionary usurper enacts his possessive and exclusive desire for power by sculpting an apparently malleable material into 'the form my spirit loved and longed for'.

Vandalizing and reassembling the stony laws, Beddoes's protagonist re-enacts the unravelling and recycling of metaphors and images of the body politic that characterized the revolutionary period in France. Referring to this context, Dorinda Outram speaks of a tendency to 'disarticulate and use in different ways elements which in fact had their roots deep in the office of the absolutist king' in order to valorize the revolutionary actors.[21] And if the violence of Isbrand's will takes any guidance in this, his language—'perfect', 'beauteous'—implies that this guidance is aesthetic. Beddoes's important long poem 'Pygmalion', in which the sculptor's chisel 'thrust, and gashed, and swept', actually suggests that Isbrand's political conquest and his restructuring of society to suit his one-man rule is itself rendered as a Pygmalion narrative.[22] Both Isbrand and the sculptor in the poem create the object of their desire as a work of art, and both experience or fantasize its animation in an autoerotic encounter associated with death. The protagonist thus disarticulates the feudal body politic and transforms it into an aesthetic construct and object of eroticized desire.

More particularly, Beddoes's text should be seen to engage with a highly sensitive and specifically British discourse. Michael Simpson has convincingly argued that second-generation Romantic dramatists were prone to return, in coded form, to the radical debates in Britain during the 1790s, especially as these debates impinged on the legal discourse.[23] With its trope of the 'stony laws', *Death's Jest-Book* can

---

21   Dorinda Outram, *The Body and the French Revolution: Sex, Class and Political Culture* (New Haven and London: Yale University Press, 1989), p. 22.
22   *Works*, pp. 80, 111.
23   *Closet Performances* p. 3; c.f. also pp. 74–111.

be seen to participate in this tradition. John Barrell points out that, in Britain, the charge of high treason was spelt out in legal terms as 'imagining the king's death', and he claims that this wording and its figurative implications shaped the debate during the revolutionary decade.[24] The problem seems to have been that for many of the charges the authorities wished to bring against British revolutionaries and reformers, the literal sense of the phrase—killing the king in person—did not strictly apply. The law did not seem to take into account what came to be known as 'modern treasons', namely, attempts on what may be loosely termed 'constitutional laws'.[25] As Barrell demonstrates, the way to make the law applicable in such cases was to revive the trope of the King's Two Bodies. With its help, it could be reasoned that 'any challenge to the king's authority, or majesty, was a threat to the existence of his "political body", and so amounted to imagining his death', even when there was no design to kill him in person.[26] So this argument conceptualizes treason in Britain as a 'figurative treason' in conjunction with a 'figurative death'.

Before the backdrop of Barrell's findings, the accusation that Beddoes does not get his revenge plot right, because Isbrand never kills the Duke, appears in a different light. After all, Isbrand does kill the Duke, though it is a figurative murder, a killing in the modern, constitutional sense. When Isbrand, the politician/ artist, dismisses the shape of the 'old heap of stony laws' and cuts out his own, this actually amounts to the figurative killing of the king in modern treason. Hence Donner's verdict that 'the details of his [Beddoes's] plot became as traditional as ever' needs to be revised.[27] The modern treason featured in Death's Jest-Book effectively modernizes the notion of revenge by directing its political force away from the actual body of the feudal sovereign and towards the constitutional laws of feudalism. In the specific conditions detailed in Beddoes's play, however, this revenge is presented as a force that, in pretending political re-form, ultimately effects its dis-figurement.

Beyond this legal frame of reference, the tropological negotiations of the 'stony laws' may anticipate the gradually emerging British debate on the number of laws to be called the Reform Bill, which Beddoes staunchly supported, and they forcefully evoke the principal topic dominating the political discourse in Germany, namely, the question of constitutional laws.[28] As the 'stony laws' in Beddoes's play are embedded in a plot triangulating feudal structures, radical Bonapartism, and constitutional laws, the German debate may be the more relevant here. After the German *Befreiungskriege*, and with the new constitutions passed in America and France, members of virtually all classes felt that their sacrifices had earned them a constitution, which, at that stage, was identified less with democratic representation than with some form of separation of powers and basic political liberties. During the

24   John Barrell, *Imagining the King's Death: Figurative Treason, Fantasies of Regicide 1593–1796* (Oxford: Oxford University Press, 2000).
25   Barrell, p. 40.
26   Barrell, p. 40; cf. also pp. 127–402.
27   Henry Wolfgang Donner, *Thomas Lovell Beddoes: The Making of a Poet* (Oxford: Blackwell, 1935), p. 214.
28   'The Struggle for Parliamentary Reform', *Works*, pp. 263–66.

German *Vormärz*, the constitution in fact became the vanishing point for the struggle for liberty itself.[29] Read as an implicit comment on revolutionary Bonapartism, *Death's Jest-Book* challenges the assumption that this prevailing political strategy would result in any kind of progressive constitution—a point Christian Dietrich Grabbe makes just as forcefully in his play *Napoleon oder die Hundert Tage* (1831).[30] Turning the constitution into a touchstone, Beddoes's *Fool's Tragedy* insists on the abysmal affinity of ducal absolutism and a new form of Bonapartist dictatorship. Yet instead of dousing the stage in the gore accompanying the Jacobean abuses of monarchical power, the text identifies the—temporary?—defeat of the republican struggle with a complex conceit of the body politic that signals to the rebels their leader's abuse of his constitutional powers.

Beddoes's ingenious adaptation of the Elizabethan/Jacobean revenge plot to topical political issues presents an achievement in itself. And to the extent that this re-fashioned revenge plot and its protagonist resonate with the plot and central figure of the contemporary harlequinade, the agent and plot of *The Fool's Tragedy* appear not only richer but also more ambiguous. To be sure, Isbrand's revolutionary power is invested, via the conventions of illegitimacy, with a social force that remains absent in the play itself. By blending the roles of dictatorial 'liberator' and Harlequin in the figure of Isbrand, however, Beddoes simultaneously exploits and questions the cultural dynamics and ultimate political vision of the contemporary harlequinade. Confronted with this powerful evocation of illegitimacy, the readers/ spectators are left to make their own choices as far as a political interpretation of the text is concerned—and if the play had been performed in contemporary London, the venue and its audience would have played a large role in determining these choices.

Apart from this, Beddoes's deployment of such widely differing generic conventions also possesses a meta-theatrical dimension with aesthetic and political implications that may even be more important in this context. After all, the opposition between legitimate and illegitimate theatre also formed a more fundamental distinction in the debate of the period's drama. In fact, categories of genre became part of a major ideological dispute over cultural merits and hierarchies in an increasingly heterogeneous entertainment culture. The discourse of illegitimacy opposed supposedly authentic English genres with spurious forms drawing on German drama or the Italian pantomime, and it was haunted by Edmund Burke's discussion of political legitimacy in generic terms. Notoriously, Burke's concept of political legitimacy—hereditary, monarchical, and Anglican—corresponded to

---

29   Dieter Grimm, 'Verfassung (II)', in *Geschichtliche Grundbegriffe: Historisches Lexikon zur politisch-sozialen Sprache in Deutschland*, ed. Otto Brunner, Werner Conze, and Reinhart Koselleck, 8 vols, VI: *St—Vert* (Stuttgart: Klett-Cotta, 1990), pp. 868–99, esp. pp. 876–87 and 878–79.

30   In Grabbe's play, Napoleon himself is given the words, 'Aber glauben Sie mir, meine Herren, Charten und Konstitutionen sind zerreißbarer als das Papier auf welches man sie druckt' ('Believe me, Gentlemen, charters and constitutions are more easily torn up than the paper they are printed on', my trans.). Christian Dietrich Grabbe, *Napoleon oder die Hundert Tage* (Stuttgart: Reclam, 2002), p. 77.

the tragic genre. Hence his description of the French Revolution as a 'monstrous tragic-comic scene' aptly translated revolutionary action into a mixed genre.[31] Yet precisely this meaning of the word 'legitimate' was itself inverted as it came to be identified with the merely formal legitimacy of the arbitrary and oppressive Regency rule. In this context, the 'legitimate' theatres, propped up by censorship and police, were perceived as mere extensions of state corruption or, as Hazlitt put it, as an *imperium in imperio*.[32]

In this discourse, the body politic is reflected in the 'body theatrical'. The gagged 'legitimate' theatres turn into mirror images of the sham legitimacy of the repressive government. Hence it could be argued that just as Isbrand, the avenger-director within the play, uses his tools to dismantle the 'stony laws of the sepulchre of a dead dukedom' or body politic, so the play's author deploys his own tools to raze the generic laws of a 'patent theatre' or body theatrical that is designed to keep the obsolete feudal structures of society in place. Here, however, the analogy ends. Whereas Isbrand rearranges the remnants of the feudal state to shape his dictatorial one-man-rule, Beddoes undermines the homogeneity and monarchical position of tragedy by opening it up to oppositional codes and conventions. Formally oscillating between the grotesque and the dialogic, his text allies itself with the *pasticcio* constructions of illegitimate theatre and their attack on the hierarchies within the bodies theatrical and politic.

Finally, it could be claimed that Beddoes's *Fool's Tragedy*, displaying its 'neo-Elizabethanism' spiced with illegitimate features and codes, does more than approximate a way of dramatic construction familiar from illegitimate theatre. Arguably, the play also picks up a subject explicitly sported there, namely, the rivalry between Harlequin and Shakespeare. In a symbolic sense, their rivalry characterized the theatrical culture as a whole, but their battle also featured explicitly in David Garrick's successful harlequinade *Harlequin's Invasion* (1750) — unusually furnished with a text and based on an earlier pantomime by the title *Harlequin Student, or the Fall of Pantomime with the Restoration of the Drama* (1741). The latest revival of *Harlequin's Invasion* is recorded in 1820 under the title *Shakespeare versus Harlequin*.[33] In its frame narrative, heralds and choir announce a frenchified invasion by a fleet carrying harlequin and his associates, and the speakers/singers call upon the 'light Troops of Comedy' and 'Tragedy[['s] . . . Daggers' to defend 'King Shakespeare'.[34] When the frame narrative is finally picked up again, it provides for the play's spectacular ending and full deployment of stage machinery:

31   Edmund Burke, *Reflections on the Revolution in France* [1790]: *A Critical Edition*, ed. Jonathan C.D. Clark (Stanford: Stanford University Press, 2001), p. 155.

32   Quoted in Moody, *Illegitimate Theatre*, p. 76.

33   Elisabeth Paula Stein, Introduction to *Three Plays by David Garrick*, ed. with introduction and notes by Elisabeth Paula Stein (1926; New York: Bloom, 1967), pp. 3–5.

34   David Garrick, *Harlequin's Invasion*, in *Three Plays by David Garrick* (see Stein, above), pp. 11–53 (p. 13).

The Second Transparency appear [sic] Representing the powers
of Pantomime going to Attack Mount Parnassus. A Storm comes
on, destroys the Fleet . . .

     MERCURY *Hear Earthly Proteus, hear great Jove's decree*
His Thunder Sleeps, and thus he speaks by me
Descend to Earth be Sportive as before
Wait on the Muses Train, like Fools of Yore
Beware encroachment and invade no more.

. . . Temple of the Gods

Now let immortal Shakespeare rise
Ye Sons of Taste Adore him
As from the Sun each Vapour flies
Let Folly sink before him.

. . . Shakespeare Rises: Harlequin Sinks
Song . . . , Dance . . .
Finis.[35]

As the earthly Harlequin is admonished to stay in his place ('beware encroachment
and invade no more'), the elect are invited to admire the divine Shakespeare
('Sons of Taste Adore him'). Apparently, the script for the performance in 1820 was
much altered, and in any case it is difficult to determine with what authority, if
any, this voice of Jove and his messenger were actually endowed.[36] Yet considering
such popular spectacles and their—possibly deeply satirical—closing messages,
Beddoes's *Fool's Tragedy* is thrown into relief as a tragedy that urgently invites
Harlequin to encroach, hoping to join forces with him in an invasion that will upset
the distinction between divine and earthly aesthetics, legitimate and illegitimate
culture, and even national and foreign cultural traditions.

    Beddoes would have found powerful allies for this target in the contemporary
theatre, and it seems most likely that the theatrical *gestus* scripted into his text is
inspired not only by the art of Joseph Grimaldi but also by yet another brilliant
player on the London stage. This actor, who virtually embodied and performed
the deconstruction of the conventions of legitimacy, though from within the
patent theatres, is, of course, Edmund Kean. Isbrand's renunciation of decorum,
together with his passionately hyperbolic language, point to a performance style
that was then indissolubly linked with the name of Kean in the patent theatres. In
iconoclastic opposition to the classicism of John Kemble, Kean's savage renderings
stripped Shakespeare's protagonists of all gentility and thus fiercely demolished the

---

35   Garrick, pp. 46–47.
36   Stein, 'Introduction', p. 5.

ruling stage image of the aristocracy—which made him, in the words of William Hazlitt, a truly 'radical performer'.[37] As critics point out, Kean, closely allied with the aesthetics of the Cockney School, became an inspiration for a whole generation of playwrights, including Shelley, Byron, and Keats, who created individual characters for Kean or modelled them on him.[38] I believe that Beddoes's Isbrand may also be counted among them. But it seems that Beddoes was interested in a trait of Kean's acting which none of the other playwrights dared to pick up, namely, his years of apprenticeship in the role of Harlequin which, as his enemies pointed out, had deeply impregnated Kean's performance style.

Drawing on and adapting the Elizabethan/Jacobean revenge tragedy, *Death's Jest-Book; or, The Fool's Tragedy* grapples with major questions of political change familiar from earlier high Romantic drama, such as the potential and limit of retributive action and the failure to overcome the desire for vengeance through love, here in friendship. In doing so, however, it thoroughly refashions the role of the avenger and his relation to the body politic. Beddoes's revenge plot not only revisits the disarticulation of the monarchical body politic during the French Revolution but also evokes the British legal discourse on high treason and constitutional change in which this monarchical body looms large. In addition, the revenge plot is made to signify in the German discourse of the later 1820s, balancing, against a feudal backdrop, the desire for revolutionary change in the guise of a radical Bonapartism, and the vision of a republican government and constitution.

Thus gazing on the 'old ghosts', Beddoes has indeed provided the literature of his own age with an idiosyncrasy and spirit of its own. It is a spirit vehemently sharpened by the form and tone of the drama, tapping into codes and conventions of a variety of other genres, and infusing the behaviour of the aristocratic protagonist, in particular, with the retributive violence and greed familiar from the popular hero of the harlequinade. In this way, Beddoes's play becomes a 'bold trampling' intervention in the contemporary theatrical debate and practice. It presents a well-aimed coup against the atrophied cultural hierarchies that were firmly bound up with a politicized view of generic boundaries, both stabilized and subverted through censorship and institutional monopolies. In fact, the transgressive and irreverent chiselling of the stony laws of the body theatrical in *Death's Jest-Book* appears much more daring than the playwright's anecdotal attempt to set fire to Drury Lane theatre with a five-pound note.[39] Against the foil of a radical critical discourse attacking the patent theatres and keepers of the tragic genre as representatives of a repressive state, we find Beddoes, like his creation—Isbrand, committing high treason.

---

37   Jane Moody, 'Romantic Shakespeare', in *The Cambridge Companion to Shakespeare on Stage* (Cambridge: Cambridge University Press, 2002), pp. 37–58; Hazlitt is quoted on p. 50.

38   Moody, *Illegitimate Theatre*, pp. 228–41; Jonathan Mulrooney, 'Keats in the Company of Kean', *Studies in Romanticism*, 42 (2003), 227–50.

39   Donner, *Thomas Lovell Beddoes: The Making of a Poet* (1935), pp. 375 ff.

IV

I have argued that Beddoes's generic transformation of the Elizabethan revenge tragedy can be shown to intersect not only with contemporary political discourse but also with the British debate on the theatre and with British theatrical practice. Let me restate, however, that the British theatrical context offers only one perspective on the multiple performance of genre in Beddoes play. By way of conclusion, I will re-situate my argument—and Beddoes's generic experiments—in a slightly wider context.

Regarding Romantic concepts of genre, Tilottama Rajan loosely distinguishes between a British and a German discussion. She sees the British debate shaped by 'criticism' in reviews and amateur essays, and oriented towards the public sphere.[40] There, genre remains part of the endeavour to constitute public taste and judgement, and is largely considered in judgemental terms. In Germany, by contrast, Rajan singles out a developed and distinct sphere of aesthetics in treatises, academic lectures, and even the fragment. There, theories of genre shift from a formalist to a phenomenological concept, stressing the individuality of the work of art and extending the term 'genre' itself to forms of consciousness, modes and moods, all of which are approached with a great methodological variety. Though unduly schematized in my summary, this comparative grid may yield a useful perspective for reconsidering genre in Beddoes's work.

As the quotations from his letters have documented, Beddoes was well aware of the ideologically charged 'criticism' that was closely linked to British theatrical practice and oriented towards the public sphere. Moreover, while still in England, Beddoes would have gleaned more specific inspiration from the generic debates and experiments of the Hunt circle, on the periphery of which he moved through his adoration of Shelley, his friendship with Barry Cornwall, and his contacts to John Hunt and Mary Shelley. If we follow Jeffrey Cox's study of this group, their debates on drama and theatre are not to be seen as an attack on the stage as such. On the contrary, 'they are in fact a kind of canon reformation, ... a struggle to derive new cultural power by turning from the "great tradition"—not to the artistic limbo of the closet—but to alternative sources of cultural authority'.[41]

Incidentally, one of the forms that attracted attention in this circle was the masque or anti-masque, which Hunt himself deployed in *The Descent of Liberty*. These two genres were linked both to aristocratic culture and the harlequinade, and the group's attraction to masques and anti-masques lay precisely in their subversive heterogeneity. As I have already pointed out, *Death's Jest-Book; or, The Fool's Tragedy* explicitly and self-reflexively refers to both these genres. It is possible, of course, to describe these references as further instances of the play's ostensible neo-Elizabethan character, but they may just as well be read as flagging the text's

---

40   Tilottama Rajan, 'Theories of Genre', in *The Cambridge History of Literary Criticism*, vol. 5: *Romanticism*, ed. Marshall Brown (Cambridge: Cambridge University Press, 2000), pp. 226–49 (p. 228).

41   Jeffrey N. Cox, *Poetry and Politics in the Cockney School: Keats, Shelley, Hunt and their Circle* (Cambridge: Cambridge University Press, 1998), p. 124.

affinities to the just mentioned contemporary debate and aesthetic projects. Cox even argues that echoes of the harlequinade may be traced in Shelley's *Prometheus Unbound*, though he admits that 'they are not likely to be heard in the play's complex orchestration of dramatic variations'.[42] If Beddoes heard these echoes, he amplified them, unmistakably, in this own play. As may be expected, Cox's analysis of the aesthetic and ideological tension bound up with the group's experiments seems to bear also on *The Fool's Tragedy*. He points out that the desire to find generic forms and a political agenda that engages a wider audience on the one hand did not easily square with the embrace of cultural values that entailed a potentially exclusive literary style on the other.[43]

As Beddoes turned his attention to the German context, his interest in generic multiplicity—sharpened, as it was, by British criticism, literary experiments, and theatrical practice—would have found additional theoretical nourishment in the work of Schlegel and others. Whether Beddoes read and consciously appropriated aspects of these theories—which we do not know for sure—or alternatively, as Rajan claims, British literary experiments and their 'unwritten poetics' call for the German innovative theory of genre, the critical approaches to *Death's Jest-Book* already mentioned, which draw on contemporary theory such as Romantic Irony or the grotesque, have proved illuminating.[44] It is by no means clear, however, that Beddoes, who was highly conscious of how genre signifies socially, would have limited his understanding of Romantic Irony to the individual work of art in an autonomous sphere, whether on the level of theory or in his appreciation of Tieck, whose work he devoured.

Take, for instance, Tieck's play *Verkehrte Welt* (1799), a work that to my knowledge has not yet been mentioned in connection with Beddoes. It is a perfect piece of meta-theatrical anarchism, featuring Parnassus as a mountain that is shoved onto the stage and financially evaluated, only to be turned into a side show as the stage becomes crowded by masquerades, Harlequin in a sea-battle, a playlet in a private theatre on stage, a poet and a reader in court, and so on. In a final battle, Apollo successfully defends Parnassus against a force of characters from a wild mix of genres, only to find that the audience climbs the mountain to reclaim it for the actor desiring another role. Even today the liberating force of this text seems enormous as it overturns, in epic style, aesthetic and social hierarchies alike. A British contemporary writing a play in English with the British stage in mind, could hardly have missed the deconstructive power of Tieck's text for the distinctions characterizing the London theatre culture. And in deploying the concept of Romantic Irony in the way he does, Beddoes joins the tendency in German literature in the 1820s and '30s to revisit earlier theorems and strategies

---

42   Cox, p. 143.
43   Cox, p. 127.
44   With a view to the grotesque that features in Bakhtin's theory, Rajan's comment is worth noting: 'Bakhtin's metamorphoric phenomenology of genre develops directly from his Romantic forefathers, but since they had no encompassing name for their practice, the Romantic contribution, though profoundly influential, has remained unrecognized'. 'Theories of Genre', pp. 242–43.

developed for the realm of autonomous art and to relate them to issues of 'real life' and especially social issues.[45] For Johann Jokl, for instance, the achievement of Heinrich Heine consists precisely in his removing the notion of Romantic Irony from its transcendental context and turning it into a means of artistic and political confrontation.[46]

Unsurprisingly, the two 'modernizers' of the German stage, Georg Büchner und Christian Dietrich Grabbe, also drew on Tieck, and the relation of *Death's Jest-Book* to their work has already been approached from different angles. Let me merely point out here that these German dramatists who innovated the dramatic genre in Germany and later became important models for Bertold Brecht were not only indebted to Shakespeare, Tieck, and a developing aesthetic discourse. Like the generic features on which I concentrated in Beddoes's *Fool's Tragedy*, the forms of Büchner's and Grabbe's work can also be related to popular dramatic and cultural traditions, testifying to a 'counter-cultural' affinity that, though revitalizing the drama, severely antagonized the critics and hindered the reception of those works.[47] Thus it seems that the performing genres in *Death's Jest-Book* can be made to signify not only across the unstable divide of the legitimate and illegitimate theatre in Britain but also, and just as importantly, across the no less permeable British and German theatrical cultures.

---

45   Peter Stein, 'Operative Literatur', in *Zwischen Revolution und Restauration 1815–1848*, ed. Gerd Sautermeister und Ulrich Schmid (Munich: Deutscher Taschenbuch Verlag, 1998), pp. 485–505; c.f. also Wolfgang Bunzel, Peter Stein, and Florian Vaßen, '"Romantik" und "Vormärz" als rivalisierende Diskursformationen der ersten Hälfte des 19. Jahrhunderts', in *Romantik und Vormärz: Zur Archäologie literarischer Kommunikation in der ersten Hälfte des 19. Jahrhunderts*, ed. Wolfgang Bunzel, Peter Stein, and Florian Vaßen (Bielefeld: Aisthesis, 2003), pp. 9–49.

46   Johann Jokl, 'Heinrich Heine', in *Zwischen Revolution und Restauration 1815–1848* (see Peter Stein, above), pp. 526–78 (pp. 534–35).

47   The obvious example in Büchner are the scenes taking place on a fairground in *Woyzeck*; for Grabbe, see Jürgen Hein, 'Grabbe und das zeitgenössische Volkstheater', in *Grabbe und die Dramatiker seiner Zeit*, ed. Detlev Kopp and Michael Vogt (Tübingen: Niemeyer, 1990), pp. 117–35.

Beddoes and the Theatre of Cruelty; or, the Problem of Isbrand's Sister:

Some thoughts arising while re-editing *Death's Jest-Book*

Alan Halsey

Has there been a reader who has felt more than the vaguest understanding of *Death's Jest-Book* at first acquaintance?—a grasp, even, of what is going on in the main action?—or, indeed, what the 'main action' is? I remember something of my own first sense of it, more than twenty years ago—certainly I remember Mandrake, the quickfire puns and fantastical allusions, and passages of blank verse as wild and startling as long. Death, who will receive 'the crown of folly', and of course the songs. I gathered little else except a great excitement: a text all electric charge, and it has never bothered me that I do not understand electricity.

Something similar may be said of other literary works, and yet *Death's Jest-Book* has some uncommon features. One is the fact that a new reader will almost certainly read it as if it had been written two hundred years before its actual composition, even if the reader knows very well that Romantic poets had a liking for writing plays in the Jacobean mode—the 'ventriloquism' of *Death's Jest-Book* is all too convincing, even in its advanced obscurities; it was only after many readings that I began to see its assembled ghosts inhabiting a time nearer our own. A second feature is quite other: even a seasoned reader of the play is liable to be foxed by its narrative peculiarities.

Over the last ten years I have written several essays on Beddoes, all of which have demanded a simple synopsis of *Death Jest-Book*'s plot. In each case I have struggled to present such a synopsis, and in some I have certainly made mistakes. I would be willing to concede that I am a careless reader where stories are concerned, a hedonist who just wants that electric charge, and yet I notice that others have also been deceived. A notable example is H.W. Donner's account of the Mandrake subplot: 'on the way back [from Egypt] his own pot of balsam falls down and kills him. He is now dead and invisible, and wherever he goes he is taken for a spook until cudgelling brings him to his senses and he takes his place among the living'.[1]

---

1   H.W. Donner, *Thomas Lovell Beddoes: The Making of a Poet* (Oxford: Basil Blackwell, 1935), p. 216.

We might object that even Beddoes in his quirkiest moments would not suppose that a spook could be cudgelled back to life; more critically, however, the entire subplot would be in large part pointless and humourless *if* the pot of balsam had indeed killed Mandrake, since both the cudgelling scene and the 'resurrection' at Grüssau depend upon the fact that although alive Mandrake *believes* he is dead.

Perhaps we should not be surprised that the play welcomes even careful readers aboard the ship of fools—it does so, we may think, by its very nature. It is nevertheless a peculiarity, and I have begun to think of it as 'the problem of Isbrand's sister'. This factor specifically concerns so significant a matter as Isbrand's motive for revenge, of singular importance in a 'revenge tragedy'. In the earlier drafts, Beddoes is perfectly clear about this: Isbrand's revenge is for a parricide, 'A father slain and plundered'; he asks Wolfram for his 'fraternal bond against the assassin' (β: I, i, 108–09). It is in a later draft that Beddoes expands this to 'A father slain and plundered; a sister's love first worn in the bosom, then trampled in the dust . . . ' (γ: I, i, 195–96). What should we make of this addition? It is, perhaps, no more than a (somewhat clichéd) rhetorical flourish. And yet: *if* the Duke's dead wife is the sister of Wolfram and Isbrand, then it is she whom the Duke attempts to resurrect in Act III, and an entirely different complexion is cast on this central aspect of the plot. Was Beddoes contemplating such a novel twist to his story? We have no later draft of Act III that bears such a mark. And of course we must bear other possibilities in mind. The Duke may not have *married* Isbrand's sister, or he may have had more than one wife and he is not attempting to resurrect the one who was Isbrand's sister—yet this would need to be made clear to the reader, which is not the case in any surviving draft. It is noteworthy, however, that in a list of 'Persons Represented' Beddoes compiled in the 1830s we find 'ATROPA, *a widow of rank and possessions, sister of Isbrand*'.[2] 'Atropa' is deadly nightshade, a very likely character for Beddoes to imagine in a humorous mood: how did he envisage her, if at all, in the play itself?—as a living character?—or resurrected ghost?—*also* raised from the tomb by Ziba?—and widow of whom (for it is the Duke who is a widower)?—or was she a whim, jotted down in a similar vein as the dramatis personae of *A Comic Legend on Three Legs*?

It will be reasonably objected that this 'problem' only arises because we are looking at drafts of the play made at different times. There are, however, peculiarities that appear in all surviving versions. In the resurrection scene, for example, Ziba always refers to the corpse to be raised as 'he' or 'him', although the Duke is specific in his desire to raise his wife, however uncertain we may feel about his reasons. And we must not overlook the abiding failure to tie the Adalmar and Athulf subplot into the main action: it stands as its own playlet, an absurd sideshow whose verse nevertheless vies on occasions with that of the major characters. Why is one of the play's most astonishing lines, one of the several interstices in which Beddoes's overriding obsession with death unfolds, most tellingly, as an interrogation of *origin*—'The spell of my creation is read backwards'—given to *Athulf*?

2   *Works*, p. 325.

I see 'the problem of Isbrand's sister' as an instance of all such unresolved aspects of the play, in its several versions and revisions, and specifically an instance of Beddoes's apparently fatal drive towards excess.

We are all too familiar with the history of the composition of the play, and yet it continues to invite re-examination. A version was written between 1825 and 1829, in which year Beddoes sent a completed manuscript to his friends Procter, Kelsall, and Bourne in London, looking forward to its 'furtherance to the press'. This is the version Donner denotes β, and it is the only full version of *Death's Jest-Book* that we have. Discouraged from publication by his friends' (and in particular Procter's) criticism, he at once proposed to rewrite it. He seems to have made additions at various times, and there appear to have been a few periods of intensive rewriting: the early 1830s, 1837–38 when he was again thinking of publication alongside a new work entitled *The Ivory Gate*, and again when he drafted a complete new manuscript of Act I, which Donner suggests was in 1843. The later text was established by Donner and designated γ.

In the introduction to his edition of the 1829 text, Michael Bradshaw elucidates the differences between the β and γ versions: '*Death's Jest-Book; or the Fool's Tragedy* (1829)', he writes, 'is a satirical tragedy, essentially obedient to the conventional five-act structure, centred on a revenge plot, and predominantly written in blank verse and prose. *Death's Jest-Book; or, The Day Will Come* (post-1829, but principally 1838–44) has developed far away from this origin, the tragic structure fading to the point of dissolution with the incorporation of nine new lyrics in the first act; the material stage play element has also waned in favour of a psychic "theatre" of disembodied voices'.[3] Bradshaw states his preference for the play as it 'would have been published in Beddoes' lifetime', when it was 'still a tragedy in form'. There is much to be said for this preference, and Bradshaw's account of the differences between the two versions is admirable. I feel less convinced, however, that we should see the γ version as, in Bradshaw's words, 'the creature of Procter's rejection'.

In a joint consideration of the β and γ texts, we must in any case be wary of treating them as *entirely* comparable. β is a completed work, and its author saw it as such, at least in 1829. γ is an editorial construction, a fusion of several strands of text and occasional revisions written over a long period; taken as a whole, γ is no more than a series of drafts for a projected work we may designate δ, which as far as we know was never completed and perhaps never attempted. β and δ would be directly comparable, and utterly different. We cannot know, however, what relation γ would have to this notional δ. Considered in itself, γ is certainly 'a strange conglomerate'; if we regarded it too uncritically as a 'finished' work, it would seem in its odd protrusions and unresolved byways an ur-text of postmodernism, in the most misleading way possible.

It seems worth questioning the significance of 'Procter's rejection' for Beddoes personally — why, precisely, did he find it so devastating? Although Procter was considerably his senior and Beddoes is generally polite about his poetry in letters,

---

3   *Death's Jest-Book: The 1829 Text*, ed. Michael Bradshaw (Manchester: Carcanet/ Routledge, 2003), p. xx.

it is unlikely that he held Procter's work in any great regard. In the final lines of his verse-letter of March 1826, Beddoes compares Procter's poems favourably with his own:

> Your call
> Is higher and more human: I . . .
> . . . e'er admire you
> And own that you have nature's kindest trust
> Her weak and dear to nourish as I must.
> Then fare, as you deserve it, well, and live
> In the calm feelings you to others give.[4]

A less flattering view of Procter has however been revealed earlier in the poem:

> I dare write to thee,
> Fearing that still, as you were wont to do
> You feed and fear some asinine Review [5]

—a well-judged foresight of Procter's timidity about *Death's Jest-Book* three years later. Yet Beddoes himself was by no means an unknown poet, and despite his public silence since the appearance of *The Brides' Tragedy* and his residence abroad there would have been other routes to publication open to him. At worst he could have had the play printed himself and arranged a London imprint, as Shelley had done with *The Cenci* after its rejection by Covent Garden.[6] Ian Jack sets out the grounds for a widely received view of Beddoes's later career in his remark, 'If Beddoes had published this "strange conglomerate" he would certainly have been attacked by the reviewers; yet publication is the only way in which a poet can escape from a poem and as it turned out Beddoes was never to escape from *Death's Jest-Book*'.[7] Jack does not tell us what it would be for a poet to 'escape' from a poem and offers no support for his assertion that 'publication is the only way' this can be done. Did Coleridge 'escape' from *Christabel*? There are sufficient examples of

---

4   Verse letter to Procter, March 1826, *Works*, p. 615.
5   *Works*, p. 614.
6   Writing to Kelsall in 1837 (*Works* p. 662), TLB mentions this possibility but remarks that 'no Ollier exists at present'. Ollier had been Shelley's London publisher. Shelley had *The Cenci* printed at Livorno, and the imprint reads 'Italy. Printed for C. and J. Ollier'.
7   Ian Jack, *English Literature 1815–1832: Oxford History of English Literature Vol. X* (Oxford: Oxford University Press, 1963), p. 141. Although Jack's discussion is generally perceptive, it regards *Death's Jest-Book* as a single work rather than one that exists in distinct versions. The consequence of such a view is that TLB's later work on the play must be regarded as mere revision and akin to tinkering; we must assume that Jack considers the revisions deleterious, since he regards TLB's prose as 'laboured' and argues that 'As a lyric poet Beddoes is seldom at his best'.

poets haunted by published texts and sometimes obsessively revising them, just as there are examples of poets laying one work aside to begin another. Whatever the case, we should not underestimate the strength of the spell *Death's Jest-Book* had cast on Beddoes from the first. ('Spell' is, I think, the exact word for this and for the effect the work has on certain readers, myself included, without regard to sundry and often sound reservations.) Must we suppose that publication would have broken the spell? Isn't it quite probable that *Death's Jest-Book* would have nevertheless provided the ground for practically all Beddoes's later compositions, including the one apparently separate project of the 1830s, *The Ivory Gate*, whose surviving fragments show an attempt to break away from the formal restraints of the five-act play but whose content is clearly an outgrowth, a mixed crop of aconite and hellebore planted somewhere in the ruins of *Death's Jest-Book*'s cathedral? How can we be confident that Beddoes would have written anything different (or better) if he had left *Death's Jest-Book* safely behind?

The conspicuous fact about Procter's rejection is that, in his revisions, Beddoes seems to have taken a precisely opposite course from whatever Procter proposed. Procter's letter has not survived, but we know the tenor of his remarks and some of his specific suggestions from Beddoes's reply of 19 April 1829:[8] 'erasure' of some or many of the 'larger passages', rewriting (or possibly, again, erasure) of 'all the prose scenes and passages', and presumably clarification of whatever 'obscurity, conceits and mysticism' escaped the blue pencil. The aim was a lighter, more concise version, and as late as 1838 Beddoes was promising Kelsall that the play 'will be very much cut down'.[9] There is no evidence that Beddoes did any such thing. His revisions are in large part additions, expansions of the prose passages, further conceits and wordplay, deepening obscurities—and of course the several songs, which increasingly tip the balance from tragedy toward lyric drama. It seems then that Beddoes was willing to follow Procter's advice against publication but not his suggestions for revision.

The conclusion must be that Beddoes himself felt severe doubt about publishing *Death's Jest-Book* as it stood in 1829, but of a different kind than Procter's. To understand his dissatisfaction, we may consider again one of his most memorable statements, in a letter to Kelsall on December 4 1825, in his first flush of excitement about the new play: 'it still remains for some one to exhibit the sum of his experience in mental pathology & therapeutics, not in a cold technical dead description, but a living semiotical display, a series of anthropological experiments, developed for the purpose of ascertaining some important psychical principle—i.e., a tragedy'.[10] After the flourish of 'a living semiotical display' the final words of this sentence, 'i.e., a tragedy', strike a somewhat bathetic note. Not because tragedies do not display 'important psychical principles' but because the thrust of the preceding passage has a hint of the visionary about it, as if Beddoes were looking beyond the established forms of drama and had glimpsed a hitherto unknown theatre.

---

8   *Works*, pp. 642–44.
9   *Works*, p. 659.
10   *Works*, p. 609.

There is a similar spirit in an earlier remark (to Kelsall, January 11 1825): 'Such ghosts as Marloe, Webster &ᶜ are better dramatists, better poets, I dare say, than any contemporary of ours—but they are ghosts—the worm is in their pages—& we want to see something that our great-grandsires did not know'.[11] And yet the *Death's Jest-Book* of 1829 is a satirical tragedy, if not the ghost of one, in a form with which Beddoes's great-grandsires were perfectly familiar. Whatever its merits, it is not 'a living semiotical display', and it has not moved one degree nearer a new theatre.

It seems possible that considerations like these weighed more heavily with Beddoes in 1829 than Procter's cautious criticalities. His 'very Gothic-styled tragedy' had 'a jewel of a name', and it was also a jewel of an idea. Its riches pushed at the formal limits of a resurrected 'old English Play', and perhaps Beddoes believed that he might still find a form in which the excess could be harnessed. It would not be a form compatible with the contemporary theatre, and Beddoes almost certainly had no workable notion of what territory lay beyond the traditional five acts. It would seem a dim place, largely void, but it's probably where Isbrand's sister lives and certainly where deadly nightshade grows.[12]

'All the characters in *Death's Jest-Book* are, except for Isbrand, automatons in love with death', writes Geoffrey Wagner,[13] by way of supporting the widely held view that Beddoes was no good at all at making plays; as a 'practical playwright', remarked Arthur Symons, Beddoes is 'beneath contempt'. Northrop Frye seems to have been the first critic to see Beddoes the dramatist in a different light; Frye suggests that Beddoes's acute sense of alienation makes him the forerunner of the later drama, which reaches from Chekhov and Strindberg to Sartre and Beckett:

---

11   *Works*, p. 595.
12   The argument of TLB's 'Preface to *Death's Jest-Book*', first drafted in 1828, drives to the conclusion 'that the Shakespearian form of the Drama . . . is the best, nay, the only English one', suggesting that TLB's confidence in the five-act tragedy remained intact. There is, however, a marked change of tone in the final paragraph of the 'Preface', beginning 'These remarks it is hoped the favourable reader will apply with the greatest modification to the judgement of the poem before him. This is undoubtedly a very faulty one, nor is it intended to be otherwise; it is offered as a specimen of what might be called the florid Gothic in poetry, which the author desires to leave alone and hopes therefore, probably quite superfluously, that it will meet with no imitators'. Beneath the characteristic irony and sheer offhandedness, is TLB not marking out an area of doubt and difference here, and taking care to flag it with the expression 'the florid Gothic'? In an earlier passage he develops 'the analogy between an old English Play and one of our ancient Cathedrals' so vividly that the reader begins to wonder whether the analogy of the cathedral has more to do with *Death Jest-Book* itself, at least in TLB's conception, than with the 'old English Play'. The 'Preface' appears in *Works*, pp. 530–35.
13   Geoffrey Wagner, 'Centennial of a Suicide: Thomas Lovell Beddoes', *Horizon*, 19 (1949), 417–35 (p. 426).

'He anticipates later preoccupations with the relation of being and nothingness more directly than most Romantics'.[14]

In fact, the modernist we are most likely to think of in relation to Beddoes is Antonin Artaud — 'some one to exhibit the sum of his experience in mental pathology & therapeutics . . . in . . . a living semiotical display' might easily have been said of, if not by, Artaud. Not the least of the resemblance is that although they were both passionate about the theatre, their estrangement from their contemporary theatres means that they have left little in the way of actable texts. Artaud did attempt to create his new theatre and wrote a body of work that has considerably influenced theatre since his death; Beddoes did not, and yet their situations are similar — neither had a ready-made theatre in which to realize his ideas. Artaud tends toward more extreme expression, but surely we hear something of the 'living semiotical display' in 'If fundamental theatre is like the plague, this is . . . because . . . it is a revelation, urging forward the exteriorisation of a latent undercurrent of cruelty through which all the perversity of which the mind is capable, whether in a person or nation, becomes localised'.[15] Artaud stresses that his 'theatre of cruelty' has 'nothing to do with the cruelty we practise on each other . . . but the far more terrible, essential cruelty objects can practise on us. We are not free and the sky can still fall on our heads. And above all else, theatre is made to teach us this'.[16] We find this 'far more terrible, essential cruelty' embedded in the heart of *Death's Jest-Book*, in that act of necromancy whose consequences, in spite of the 'satiric pathos', are a most awful demonstration that in the face of death we are indeed not free and the sky will certainly 'fall on our heads' — a lesson the more potent in that both Beddoes and his dramatis personae had initially sought to prove the opposite. It is simple enough to be amused or appalled by the 'grotesque' and 'macabre' aspect of Beddoes's work, but neither reaction should obscure the fact that he was convinced that death can be confronted and even 'conquered' and that this could be achieved by poetry in a manner analogous to the methods of scientific anatomy. He would feel an immediate affinity with Artaud's statement that 'I cling to the idea that death is not outside the realm of the mind, that it is within certain limits knowable and approachable by a certain sensibility'.[17] *Death's Jest-Book* does not appear among the plays Artaud proposed for his theatre, and he probably knew nothing of it, but he might have enjoyed directing Mandrake: '. . . to have a fabricated being appear, made of wood and cloth, resembling nothing, yet disturbing in nature, able to reproduce on stage the slightest intimation of the great metaphysical fear

---

14   Northrop Frye, *A Study of English Romanticism* (New York: Random House, 1968), p. 85.

15   Antonin Artaud, *The Theatre and its Double*, trans. Victor Corti (repr. London: Calder, 1995), p. 21.

16   *The Theatre and its Double*, p. 60.

17   Antonin Artaud, *Art and Death*, extracted in *Selected Writings*, trans. Helen Weaver, ed. Susan Sontag (repr. Berkeley and Los Angeles: University of California Press, 1988), p. 123 n.

underlying all ancient theatre'.[18] The easy notion of Mandrake as a mere clown would have undergone some such transformation in the Theatre of Cruelty.

They speak for themselves and we can listen to the dialogue:

> ARTAUD *This whole active, poetic way of visualizing stage expression leads us to turn away from present-day theatre's human, psychological meaning and to rediscover a religious, mystical meaning our theatre has forgotten.*
>
> BEDDOES *Many things are quite absurd, and destructive of all poetry, in arrangements which appear not of the slightest consequence. I am convinced that playbills for instance are very pernicious; one should never know the actors' names and private circumstances.*
>
> ARTAUD *There is something about a spectacle like the Balinese Theatre which does away with entertainment, that aspect of useless artificiality, an evening's amusement so typical of our theatre. Its productions are hewn out of matter itself before our eyes, in real life itself. There is something of a religious ritual ceremony about them, in the sense that they eradicate any idea of pretence, a ridiculous imitation of real life, from the spectator's mind. This involved gesticulation we see has a goal towards which it aims by effective means, and we are able to experience its direct effectiveness. The thought it aims at, the states of mind it attempts to create, the mystical discoveries it offers are motivated and reached without delay or periphrasis. It all seems like an exorcism to make our devils FLOW.*
>
> BEDDOES *The Greeks (from whom we can learn much if we understand their motives —) were in possession of this secret, and this is the real meaning of their masks, which have so much bothered the critics; and these were doubly useful, they deceived to a certain degree, not only the spectator, but also the actor, with the semblance of an heroic and unknown person, and prevented the annoying familiarity of the people on the stage. Of course I do not wish to see their sort of masks on our stage . . . it is only to be lamented that we have no other means of completely disguising our actors and making Richard, Hamlet, Macbeth, as absolutely distinct and independent individuals, as Œdipus & Orestes must have been.*[19]

---

18   *The Theatre and its Double*, p. 32.

19   Artaud's words from *The Theatre and its Double*, pp. 35 and 42; TLB's from his letter to Kelsall, 10 January 1831, *Works* pp. 651–54. *The Theatre and its Double* is generally and justifiably regarded as Artaud's most cohesive extended essay on his proposed theatre. TLB's letter is of particular interest in that it begins with an excited account of his latest plans for rewriting *Death's Jest-Book*, including for the third act 'some bold and unexpected invention; a new event, the development of a character, hitherto

We may be curious enough to look beyond or behind these scruples and struggles with what the theatre is and what it might become for some deeper resonance between the two poets. This must be done with caution, for Artaud was a remorseless chronicler of his own turmoil, constantly probing his sense of being unable to write but leaving so graphic an account of his madness. We find nothing comparable in Beddoes, although we may suppose that the defensive ironies of his letters, the long silences and the hearsay tales of his sometimes riotous behaviour, reveal some considerable turmoil and that this may have to do, as cause or effect, with feeling that he 'ought to have been a good poet',[20] that he *could* not write as he would. What can be clearly identified is a fundamental shared sense between Beddoes and Artaud of the discontinuities of thought and the self, and the voids between, with the resultant failures of (among other things) our common language. The sense of discontinuity is arguably the source of the notion of the 'double' which was obsessional with Artaud; in Beddoes it appears in his ubiquitous pairing of characters and mirroring of plot, becoming particularly conspicuous in his use of the 'two brothers' theme, which Frye sees as a life-death identity/antithesis, the one brother representing 'ordinary life driving toward, the other death seeping back into life'.[21] 'The real pain is to feel one's thought shift within oneself', writes Artaud in 'The Nerve Meter',[22] and that same 'thought shift' appears throughout *Death's Jest-Book*, being most memorably expressed by the Duke (who is surely no automaton) in his answer to Isbrand's claim that 'All of each heart I know':

> *O perilous boast!*
> *Fathom the wavy caverns of all stars,*
> *Know every side of every sand in earth,*

---

obscure, a new resolve &ᶜ gives a new turn to the aspect of the future'. He offers no clue what the 'new event' might be, and it is probably gratuitous to wonder if it involves Isbrand's sister, but his excitement leads him on via the playbills to the remarks about Greek drama (an unusual enthusiasm—he was more apt to regret the influence of Greek drama on Shelley) and a theatre different in kind from the contemporary. He anathematizes theatre as 'entertainment', as Artaud would do a century later. The flow of ideas is too agitated to be entirely coherent, but the metaphysical thrust is sufficiently clear: 'the change is grounded on the law of oscillation wʰ pervades all physical and moral nature—sleeping and waking—merriment & tears—sin & repentance—life & death—wʰ all depend & are consequent on one another'.

20   See his deathbed letter, *Works* p. 683. TLB certainly began writing with a great *belief* in 'Literature', whereas Artaud expressed his antipathy to it at the earliest opportunity. It seems as if TLB developed a distrust in poetry and drama, perhaps in the recognition that 'Literature' as he understood it would not serve as the vehicle for a consciousness at odds with itself, ridden by the desire to witness its own death but entrapped within conventional notions of ghostliness and the pleasures of the grave. The result of such distrust—or antipathy—was inevitable in either case: the drive towards a work that cannot be accomplished, the accumulation of often astonishing fragments.
21   *A Study of English Romanticism*, p. 53.
22   *Selected Writings*, p. 84.

> And hold in little all the lore of man,
> As a dew's drop doth miniature the sun:
> But never hope to learn the alphabet,
> In which the hieroglyphic human soul
> More changeably is painted than the rainbow
> Upon the cloudy pages of a shower,
> Whose thunderous hinges a wild wind doth turn.
> Know all of each! when each doth shift his thought
> More often in a minute, than the air
> Dust on a summer path. (γ: III, iii, 86–98)

Such an awareness is a dubious asset for a playwright if a playwright is expected to present the interaction of distinct characters with recognizable continuity. Beddoes was conscious of his failure to do so within the confines of a five-act tragedy; if his hesitant push beyond those confines resulted in a 'psychic "theatre" of disembodied voices', is the 'strange conglomerate' the worse for that? Certainly we go on hearing the voices, and perhaps more clearly as they echo in the void.

All which may be entirely unhelpful to the reader grappling with *Death's Jest-Book* for the first or fiftieth time. After initial bafflement, there is presumably for most readers a growing sense of certainty, and this disturbingly complex text does offer various paths to understanding. But one's grasp can easily be shaken, particularly perhaps if one is foolhardy enough to edit a new edition; unforeseen mutabilities may appear at any turn. During my own recent readings, I have felt increasingly unsure about the temper of the verse. I think that I originally read it as I might the verse of Webster or Marston, accepting what I would in another context regard as unduly Gothic or at least overwritten as par for the course. Perhaps the doubt arises with Beddoes because the verse is so evenly disposed. Adalmar and Athulf speak in pentameter as readily and grandly as Isbrand and the Duke, and can sing as good a song as Siegfried; yet they are minor characters, weak, silly, and somewhat comic — surely we are to regard these speeches of theirs as pastiche? And yet perhaps by the same token we should say the same of Isbrand and the Duke. Is the Duke's 'Fathom the wavy caverns of all stars' the grandiloquent phrase of a pompous old fellow who also has a penchant for mimicking metaphysical poets: 'As a dew's drop doth miniature the sun'? Beddoes had arguably set himself an impossible task from the start in that, although death offers fertile ground for the grimmest of jokes, it (or he) presents as invulnerable a target for satire as one could ask. Medical science *might* but satirical poetry *cannot* 'un-cypress him i' the light / To unmask all his secrets';[23] poetry's occasional triumphs are of a different order, and Artaud's search for a cognizable death did end in the asylum at Rodez. Satire as such must glance off and hit the nearest available target, which in *Death's Jest-Book*'s case was evidently the Jacobean five-act tragedy itself, with the result that Beddoes was undermining his own model and its language. If this is so then his dissatisfaction with the

---

23   *Works*, p. 615.

version of 1829 was inevitable and, failing a radically new approach to his subject, the longer term consequence would predictably be that he came to see his satire as an unalloyed comedy in which the characters speak in pentameters most foolishly. ('A fool's tragedy', indeed, but by this time the subtitle had mutated into 'The Day Will Come'.) How are we to judge such a matter? Beddoes's letters are of limited help. He has too crafty a line in self-deprecation and wears the most inscrutable masks when his poetry is the subject. He appears to have had no correspondent he could regard as his equal, poetically or intellectually. He acts up when addressing Kelsall, ranging wittily over all manner of topics, but we never feel that he wants or expects a reply in kind. This renders his apparent humility toward Procter in 1829 the more striking and questionable. His elusiveness has encouraged some to identify him with Isbrand, taking the 'Isbrand and I say . . .' of a letter quite literally and as if Isbrand were Beddoes himself speaking in and through his labyrinthine text, but this is simply no help at all. For one thing, Isbrand is an inveterate liar, willing to say anything if it helps his case; he is the embodiment and cause of the play's instabilities. Beddoes could not have chosen a more unreliable antihero, and would not have wanted to. Nothing Isbrand says can be trusted. When it suits him he goes so far as to say that 'Sire and mother / And sister I had never' (β, γ: II, iv, 186–87).

Thomas Lovell Beddoes and the Vampires of History:

Reading the Poet's German Prose

Andrew James Johnston

By the time Thomas Lovell Beddoes left Göttingen for Würzburg in 1829, he had already published a volume of poetry, completed his drama *The Brides' Tragedy*, and finished the first version of *Death's Jest-Book*, in addition to working on other plays that remained fragmentary. Thus, when the poet moved to Bavaria, the bulk of his surviving oeuvre had already come into being. By comparison, the few pages of his German prose, the most substantial part of which appeared in Würzburg's radical democratic newspaper *Bayerisches Volksblatt* in 1831 and 1832, seem of minor significance. Yet the events that motivated Beddoes to contribute that handful of articles shook the whole of Europe and may well have affected the late Romantic in a way not too dissimilar from the impact the French Revolution of 1789 had on the first generation of English Romantics. After all, Beddoes's journalism of 1831–32 marks an important turning point in the author's life, since it coincides with his being active in the democratic student movement of the *Burschenschaften*. Hence the political commentaries written for *Bayerisches Volksblatt* are part of a biographical development that would turn him into a haunted martyr of democratic radicalism and determine the increasingly restless course of his self-imposed exile, right up to his suicide a decade and a half later. With the journalism of the early thirties he adds the mantle of the political activist to those of the writer and the scientist.[1]

The French Revolution of July 1830 triggered a succession of revolutionary uprisings all over Europe, and also accelerated a reform process in England that had made its first tentative steps with Catholic emancipation in 1829. Given the very different political and social conditions prevailing in the countries affected by the dramatic spirit of change, the revolutions varied considerably as to the forms they took, the aims they pursued, and the successes they enjoyed. In France, the arch-legitimist government of the Bourbon king, Charles X, was supplanted by that of

---

1   For an account of TLB's journalistic and political activities in Würzburg between 1829 and 1832, see Carl August Weber, *Bristol's Bedeutung für die englische Romantik und die deutsch-englischen Beziehungen* (Halle: Niemeyer, 1935), pp. 208–36, and Frederick Burwick, 'Beddoes, Bayern und die Burschenschaften', *Comparative Literature*, 21 (1969), 289–306; for a more detailed and critical discussion of TLB's German prose, see Michael Bradshaw, *Resurrection Songs: The Poetry of Thomas Lovell Beddoes* (Aldershot and Burlington: Ashgate, 2001), pp. 197–204.

the *Roi Bourgeois*, Louis Philippe, who was backed by the nation's financial interest rather than its land-owning magnates. If the situation had initially appeared to promise an upheaval on the scale of the 1790s, it soon became clear that this was a revolution of a *grande bourgeoisie* desiring no more than minimal changes in the system. Under the leadership of the financier Casimir Périer, the *'juste milieu'* took over. In the Netherlands, the Revolution appeared in the guise of the secession of the Catholic South, which ultimately became Belgium. In Poland, Italy, and Germany the revolutionary thrust combined liberal, democratic, and nationalist impulses. In some of the German states—Saxony, Hanover, Brunswick, and Hesse-Cassel—constitutions were introduced as a consequence of revolutionary unrest, but no steps were taken towards national unification. The Polish uprising failed completely. Poland's unsuccessful bid for independence from Czarist autocracy excited considerable sympathy all over Europe, as the Polish army was defeated in a series of pitched battles against superior Russian forces.

In his German prose, Beddoes deals with events in Britain, Poland, and France, but his central concern is with the struggle for the English Reform Bill (1830–32) and its leading protagonists, to whom he devotes three out of the seven texts. The revolution in Paris and the death of King George IV provoked a widespread call for parliamentary reform in England—for a redistribution of the seats according to the demographic and economic realities of the country. The boundaries of England's parliamentary constituencies had not been redrawn since the Middle Ages, which meant that the vast majority of seats represented boroughs inhabited by a scandalously small number of voters, the most famous example being, of course, Old Sarum, a borough entirely depopulated since medieval times. In effect, such 'rotten boroughs' were in the hands of great landowners or controlled by the government. Only a small minority of seats were ever contested during elections. The demographic and economic changes in the wake of the industrial revolution made the system look increasingly anachronistic, and when the prime minister in 1830, the Duke of Wellington, declared that he had no intention of permitting even a mild redistribution of seats, an outcry of public opinion, accompanied by riots in many parts of the country, led the new king, William IV, to call in a Whig ministry committed to parliamentary reform. The new cabinet introduced a bill that contained not only a large-scale redistribution of seats but also extended the franchise. The Tory majority defeated the bill in the House of Commons, but the king dissolved Parliament, and subsequent elections returned an overwhelming majority of candidates in favour of the reform. Consequently, a newly introduced and slightly modified Reform Bill passed the lower House. Notwithstanding this significant reformist triumph, the Tory-dominated House of Lords rejected the bill. At this point, the king proved instrumental in saving the bill, since he threatened to flood the Upper House with a sufficiently large group of new lords so as to ensure a majority for the Reform Bill, thus breaking the Lords' resistance. Although the changes were not revolutionary—even after 1832, scions of the aristocracy and gentry still filled the vast majority of the seats and the franchise was extended to no more than eighteen per cent of the male population instead of the previous fourteen—the reform irrevocably placed political power in the Lower House.

Besides, the reform demonstrated that it was possible to change the political system.[2]

Beddoes views these events from the perspective of a radical, and his characterizations of Grey, the Whig Prime Minister, and Brougham, the radical Lord Chancellor, imply that he understood the different aims of the traditional Whig magnates and their allies, the more democratic radicals. The poet's German prose leaves no doubt about his being an acute observer of contemporary politics, whether in Britain, France, or elsewhere. Yet what makes his texts so intriguing is not their level of political analysis but, rather, the typically Beddoesian language and imagery they deploy, for even when elucidating English or French politics to German readers, Beddoes applies what is an essentially poetic approach. It is precisely this conflation of political narrative and poetic interpretation that provides, I argue, illuminating insights into the dramatic fashion in which Beddoes conceptualizes history.

At this point, a caveat seems necessary, however, since, as one critic has remarked a little condescendingly, 'Neither in his scientific empiricism nor in his poetic vision is Beddoes . . . a philosopher'.[3] Although an extremely alert and quite obviously well-informed commentator who does, once in a while, employ terms like *Weltgeist*, which to twenty-first century readers have acquired a distinctly Hegelian savour, Beddoes claims no allegiance to any specific school of thought in his German journalism, radical though he undoubtedly is. Consequently, we must not expect a consistent theory of history to be uncovered by scraping away the layers of his poetic diction. What we will find, instead, is a set of more or less coherent notions of how history influences the present, a set of notions not hidden behind the poetic language but, rather, evolving from it. Because the poet's ideas come into being through the idiosyncratic play of his images, metaphors, and allusions it would be wrong to argue that they are in some way 'expressed' in his journalistic work, as this would imply a conceptual stability that Beddoes seems at pains to avoid. On the contrary, in his political writings Beddoes's ideas gain shape in a processual, performative manner, thereby defying the Procrustean bed of a fixed philosophy of history. For all its perspicacity, satirical incisiveness, and indisputable radicalism, Beddoes's journalistic prose tends constantly to revisit its problems through metaphorically recasting them as it proceeds, thereby dispensing itself from the excessive drive for closure traditionally inherent in partisan political journalism. And since quite a number of Beddoes's passages and phrases border

---

2   For a recent assessment of the extent to which England's political system was modernized by the Reform Bill, see John A. Phillips and Charles Wetherell, 'The Great Reform Act of 1832 and the Political Modernization of England', *The American Historical Review*, 100 (1995), 411–36.

3   James R. Thompson, *Thomas Lovell Beddoes* (Boston: Twayne, 1985), p. 84. In her inquiry into the German philosophical influence on *Death's Jest-Book*, Anne Harrex comes to the conclusion that TLB does not adhere to any specific contemporary philosophical system, but that he prefers 'an unsystematic borrowing of the right idea for a particular scene or situation'; Anne Harrex, '*Death's Jest-Book* and the German Contribution', *Studia Neophilologica*, 39 (1967), 15–37 (p. 37).

on the enigmatic or obscure, no single reading of his political prose can hope to reconstruct an exhaustive map of the poet's ideas on politics and history.

Two themes have a particular hold on Beddoes's imagination and recur throughout his political prose: the aristocracy and—not unsurprisingly—death.[4] Of his three articles on the Reform Bill, two take their cue from the illnesses of two major players, the leader of the Tories, the Duke of Wellington, and his radical opponent Henry, Lord Brougham. Within the terrifying context of the cholera epidemic raging in Europe in 1831–32, Beddoes was not being overly dramatic in expecting those illnesses to be fatal. (As a matter of fact, Wellington lived for another twenty years and Brougham for thirty-six.) In both articles, the themes of death and the aristocracy are interwoven, as Wellington's illness is made to stand for the death-throes of a caste that has become obsolete. The Duke is described as having long been spiritually dead already, even though he is still alive physically: 'One deceased, whose spirit has long deserted him, the ex-minister, the ex-man Wellington is lying on his death-bed'.[5] The trope according to which a decadent and decaying aristocracy is deprived of its humanity—'ex-man Wellington'—may sound fairly conventional, but Beddoes's predilection for the macabre and the paradoxical place it in a more complex context.

One of the ways Beddoes pours scorn on the victor of Waterloo is by ridiculing the conservative tradition of organicist political tropes. Citing a classical commonplace of aristocratic ideology, Menenius Agrippa's political fable of the stomach and the other bodily organs, Beddoes identifies Wellington not with the aristocratic stomach but, rather, quoting Shakespeare's *Coriolanus*, with the big toe, the least dignified of all the extremities (p. 738).

More fascinating still is the way Beddoes accuses Wellington of having attempted to conjure up the spectres of by-gone centuries but of having been too weak for such a task. Consequently, it is the past centuries that are pulling the Tory leader down with them rather than the other way around: 'He wanted to exorcise the old centuries back into his own, but they were too strong for him and drag him down to themselves' (pp. 738–39). Wellington is likened to a sorcerer haunted by the very spirits he sought to control. Thus the past possesses a power over those who attempt to rekindle it, a power that is deadly. Yet that power ascribed to the past renders doubtful its very pastness. After all, according to Beddoes, Wellington is defeated not so much by the might of the present, by democracy, progress, or any such thing, as by his inability to cope with the ghosts he tried to invoke.

---

4   Weber even suggests that TLB'S views on death are nowhere more clearly expressed than in his political prose; Weber, p. 211.

5   'The English Aristocracy and the Illness of Wellington', *Works*, pp. 737–38 (Donner's notes and translation to pp. 566–68) (p. 738). The English translation 'one deceased' is not entirely accurate for German 'der abgestorbene'. The German verb *absterben* does not have an English equivalent, as far as I know. It refers not to entire organisms but to individual limbs, branches, or organs of a greater living whole. TLB's use of the word is not entirely logical, since he describes a human being and not a body part, yet the term nevertheless seems to fit the context aptly, since it suggests that the Duke existed in a state of semi-death long before he actually fell ill.

Indeed, English aristocrats in general, Beddoes implies, are characterized by a ghostly quality:

> There is nothing more frivolous than the English aristocracy. They live by candle light and everywhere shun the light of day, for they feel that their humanity lacks more than their second creator, their tailor, could supply. They spend their day with dogs, horses, games, mistresses, and ambassadors of the great powers; then comes the most important business of the day — the visit to the opera, and only after the last ballet, at midnight or at one in the morning, do they turn up mostly drunk at the House of Lords to vote against the upstart Brougham. (p. 738)

At first glance, this appears to be no more than another conventional attack on the aristocratic way of life with its frivolity, conspicuous consumption, and endless succession of entertainments. Yet there is also a distinctly Gothic atmosphere to these scenes, with a vampire-like nobility living by candlelight and convening in the House of Lords at midnight. Indeed, as we shall see, references to vampires or notions related to them reappear throughout Beddoes's political prose.

Even the satirically comic idea of the tailor being a lord's true creator plugs into the theme of the living dead. Ultimately, this image turns the nobleman into a mere husk of humanity, an idea that Beddoes expands at the beginning of his article on Brougham's illness, written two and a half months after the article on Wellington (26 January 1832). Here, Beddoes adds a further twist to this theme, linking it even more closely to the subject of death:

> Civilized man, however, and especially the aristocrat, has turned dying into a totally different sort of jest. If, for instance, the hour arrives of the Hero of Waterloo, only the very least important part of the great man departs with death: he himself flutters away like a moth out of the belly of a stuffed camel, but the field marshal's tunic, the stiff boots, the pantaloons, and the whole zodiac of orders, the English and the Spanish title, in short the hollow dukedom remains standing, like the stiff and ghostly slough cast by the boa in the forest. He alone cannot die who has nothing immortal in him that might return to the great source of spiritual life, out of which the human souls spring like clear or troubled brooks.[6]

The Duke's soul escapes from his body like a moth from a stuffed camel. What remains is the ghostly exterior of the great hero — his military paraphernalia such as his boots, medals etc. — whereas his soul has shrunk to the size of a moth, a moth

---

6   'Brougham', *Works*, pp. 739–41 (notes to pp. 568–70) (p. 739).

living in a carcass artificially kept in a state supposed to resemble the living animal. The Duke, Beddoes implies, belongs to a soulless species unable to die because it has already lost its capacity for immortality and is, therefore, barred from re-entering the stream of souls from whence it ultimately derives.[7]

What is most fascinating about this passage, however, is the way dead and living matter are juxtaposed in such a rapid linking and merging of images that it becomes impossible to distinguish which is which. For instance, we are shown the soul of an already half-dead Wellington escaping from a dead camel's body in the form of a moth that would surely have been feeding on the stuffed animal it inhabited. This would amount to Wellington's minuscule soul—a soul deemed unfit for immortality—actually devouring the already dead body it resided in, thus engaging in a surreal act of self-cannibalism. Conversely, the boa, leaving behind the dead skin it has shed like some ghostly memento, is still very much alive as a violent predator of the jungle, fully capable of strangling its victims. Thus the image of death, or even of the living dead, is substituted by one of metamorphosis according to which living matter is transformed into dead without, however, destroying the organism as a whole. Closely linked by theme, albeit contradictory, this succession of ideas defies a clear-cut political analysis. What Beddoes appears to create here is an intermediate space where the spheres of life and death lose their distinctiveness.

Not only aristocrats but also bankers are drawn into the orbit of Beddoes's political imagery of the living dead. He attacks Louis Philippe's prime minister, Casimir Périer, for wasting time on drawing up his list of new candidates for the French chamber of peers while he should be pursuing a vigorous foreign policy in aid of the Polish insurgents. The creation of new peers is a move that signals the continuance of aristocratic forms of politics even under a régime serving the interests of the *grande bourgeoisie*. In a passage full of bitter irony, Beddoes declares that the throne and the ministries are like an Elysium to their incumbents—that is, an ancient form of paradise sometimes depicted as being entirely distinct from Hades, sometimes seen as a specially privileged precinct within the underworld. He appears to favour the latter version, since he depicts Périer as Charon, the ferryman who ships the dead across the river Styx into the underworld—except that in this case the dead he is shipping are the Polish casualties and the payment he receives is the sacrifices they made for the liberty of their nation. It is from their bloody mouths that Périer receives the coin traditionally given to Charon by those crossing into Hades.[8] Again we witness Beddoes's typical blending of images and allusions, as Elysium, with its largely positive associations, is supplanted by the horrific image of Charon. In strictly logical terms, Périer cannot be both, a minister comfortably ensconced in Elysium with the happy dead and the ferryman who guides the souls into the underworld. At the same time, by casting Périer as Charon, Beddoes classes him with the living dead as he did Wellington. The Styx represents

---

7   As Michael Bradshaw so succinctly puts it, the Duke is 'not immortal enough to be mortal' (Bradshaw, p. 202).
8   'Changing France', *Works*, pp. 734–35 (notes to pp. 561–63) (p. 735).

a zone between life and death, and the ferryman who rows back and forth between its banks himself never actually enters the underworld he helps to guard.

In a short piece devoted to Périer exclusively, Beddoes produces what he describes as a political allegory, an image he wishes to have visualized by a painter. The French politician is presented as a bat, a creature Beddoes describes as a zoological hybrid—'hybrid flitter-mouse'.[9] Hiding in a rock's crevice, the bat is threatened both from above and below, by birds of prey and by four-footed wild animals:

> *There he sits, the four-footed bird and winged quadruped, now pressing*
> *anxiously into the chink, now angrily uttering an impotent wail; he*
> *can neither fly nor creep, neither win nor lose. (p. 741)*

The bat's hybridity—to Beddoes it is neither truly avian nor truly terrestrial— renders it incapable of action, so that it can neither triumph nor be defeated.[10] The space thus circumscribed makes meaningful political action impossible and effectively mirrors the conditions characterizing the existence of the living dead. And this should not surprise us, since the bat is closely associated with vampire folklore. Needless to say, Beddoes's image of the bat is not entirely fair, since bats are extremely efficient fliers, but what seems to count here is the bat's connection to the concept of the living dead, on the one hand, and the way it symbolizes hybridity in general, on the other.

This consistent habit of linking related yet contradictory allusions and images does not necessarily increase the usefulness of Beddoes texts as political propaganda, let alone analysis, but there is no doubt that this is part of a deliberate rhetorical strategy introduced into political journalism from the realm of poetry. Beddoes is not simply being carried away by his propensity for poetic language; he is consciously aestheticizing politics in a particularly macabre way. Two arguments, at the very least, can be adduced in favour of this claim. First, Beddoes is quite capable of being both lucid and informative if he chooses, for instance in his description of Henry Brougham's career and merits. Thus his poetic passages alternate with others, aptly fulfilling journalistic purposes of the more conventional kind. Second, some of his most richly allusive passages can be shown to mirror the political confusion presenting itself in the wake of the revolutions: to a certain extent they recreate on the textual level the political confusion they seek to describe. Beddoes's view of Chateaubriand's political stance in the aftermath of the French revolution of July 1830 is a case in point. François-René, vicomte de Chateaubriand (1768–1848),

---

9   'Périer. An Allegory', *Works*, p. 741 (notes to p. 571) (p. 741).
10   The image of the bat seems to have been very much on TLB's mind at various stages during his lifetime. Frederick Burwick suggests that TLB may have inspired an image that appeared on the title page of the political journal *Schweizerischer Republikaner* in 1836, which features bat-winged creatures arranged in a grotesque circular procession; Frederick Burwick, 'Beddoes and the *Schweizerischer Republikaner*', *Studia Neophilologica*, 44 (1972), 90–112 (p. 109).

was the leading poet of early French Romanticism. He was also an ardent royalist and upholder of the Catholic religion, which he eulogized in much of his writing. Chateaubriand was bitterly opposed to Napoleon and played an important role in the diplomatic service of the restored Bourbon monarchy. When, in the article dealing with events in France, Beddoes's vituperations against Périer have run their course, he turns to Chateaubriand, whose plight as a supporter of the defunct regime he describes with a remarkable sensitivity bordering on sympathy. Beddoes ends his discussion with a passage presented as a long quote from Chateaubriand in which the French poet elaborates on the futility of his own plans to topple the newly established Orléanist regime and proclaim Emperor Napoleon II, that is to make Napoleon's Austrian-educated son, the Duke of Reichstadt, emperor of France based on a coalition of old-style royalists, Bonapartists, and republicans. Beddoes clearly observes the absurdity of these plans and argues:

> *If actually brought about, this coalition must necessarily stumble on the choice of Either-Or and become dislocated (perhaps it will even stumble on a totally different conditional); and this is as plain as the truth that the naked injustice of humanity needs not the rags of the Restoration in which to clothe itself in order to keep warm. Hence we must remain sceptical concerning the offensive alliance between Lamarque [i.e., a Bonapartist general] and the Knight of the Order of Jerusalem [i.e., Chateaubriand].[11]*

Beddoes's preoccupation with this subject is highly significant, since it illustrates his obsession with political paradox and confusion. Chateaubriand, the former arch-reactionary is making common cause with his one-time revolutionary enemies in order to undo a 'revolution' radical only in its perpetrators' desire for power but not in the grandeur of their vision. The playwright seems to empathize with two elements of the Frenchman's stance in particular. First, he savours the paradoxical reversal inherent in Chateaubriand's position, as a part of the convulsions that France's traditional political parties have been plunged into by the events of July 1830. Second, he seems to sense an affinity with Chateaubriand's essentially aesthetic style of politics, which prefers an alliance with the enemy to the perceived mediocrity of the *juste milieu*. It is this specifically aesthetic perspective that makes Beddoes train his gaze on the absurd, grotesque, and macabre in politics and history.

Though Beddoes does seem to feel a certain degree of sympathy for Chateaubriand, his overall position vis-à-vis the French poet's politics is at best ambivalent, as is proven by Beddoes's telling remark that it is unnecessary for human injustice to clothe itself in the rags of restoration. The basic idea, as well as the language used to express it, foreshadows Karl Marx's perspective on the

---

11   'Changing France', *Works*, p. 735.

French revolution of 1848.[12] In Beddoes's eyes, there seems to be no fundamental difference between a Bourbon restoration and a Napoleonic one. Both would serve merely as propaganda ploys meant to hide the basic corruption of the system. Although Beddoes does not say it in so many words, the very fact that a legitimist like Chateaubriand feels capable of planning an alliance with his former arch-enemies shows that the forces at work are factions clinging to distinctions which may enable them to squabble amongst themselves but not to effect real political change. The very concept of restoration, Beddoes seems to say, leads to injustice, since by definition restoration equals political and ideological rags barely covering the immoral drive for power they are meant to conceal. Restoration, however, is the most conspicuous type of political action or programme that derives its legitimacy from the past, from a desire to return to a bygone era. Consequently, it is the desire to return to the past that is in and of itself part of the political evil.

Karl Marx expressed a similar view in 1852:

> The social revolution of the nineteenth century cannot create its poetry from the past but only from the future. It cannot begin till it has stripped off all superstition from the past. Previous revolutions required recollections of past world history in order to dull themselves to their own content. The revolution of the nineteenth century must let the dead bury the dead in order to realize its own content.[13]

Marx's argument is that the bourgeois revolutions of the seventeenth and eighteenth centuries—Cromwell's revolution and the French Revolution of 1789—were justified in taking their language and images, their 'poetry', from the past. The Puritan revolutionaries derived their models from the Old Testament while the French revolutionaries took theirs from classical Rome. But, according to Marx, the nineteenth century faces an entirely different situation. Since the bourgeoisie have achieved their goals and the industrial revolution has produced a new class, the proletariat, the period of bourgeois revolutions is, in effect, over and what must follow is the 'social revolution of the nineteenth century', that of the proletariat. Thus the bourgeois tendency to shroud political activity in images of the past has lost its legitimacy, the language of the past has ceased to be a force in the service of the future and has degenerated into a veil designed to dignify the bourgeoisie's attempts to deny the proletariat its rightful role in politics. The Napoleonic posturing of Prince Louis Napoleon amounts to no more than a ridiculous charade. By contrast, the proletariat, with whom the future lies, must not imitate the bourgeois

---

12   Ute Berns points out similar parallels between *Death's Jest-Book* and Karl Marx's *Eighteenth Brumaire* in 'The Politics of Revolution in Thomas Lovell Beddoes's *Death's Jest-Book*', in *Romantic Voices, Romantic Poetics*, ed. Christoph Bode and Katharina Rennhak (Trier: Wissenschaftlicher Verlag Trier, 2005), pp. 97–107.

13   Karl Marx, 'The Eighteenth Brumaire of Louis Bonaparte', in *Marx's 'Eighteenth Brumaire': (Post)modern Interpretations*, ed. Mark Cowling and James Martin, trans. Terrell Carver (London: Pluto, 2002), pp. 19–109 (p. 22).

penchant for enacting its political rituals in historical drag but must seek a mode for symbolically representing its programme and actions in a fashion uncontaminated by the spectres of the past.

To be sure, Beddoes's view of the nineteenth-century political stage is not nearly as heavily theorized as Marx's, nor does the English poet conceive of the proletariat as a political force in its own right. Set beside Marx's hard-nosed socialist insistence on economic conditions, the English radical's description of Brougham's efforts to raise the working classes' level of education betrays a charming Enlightenment naiveté. Most importantly, while Beddoes, the democratic radical, sees the aristocracy as the main enemy, for Marx the aristocracy has long become the land-owning segment of the ruling bourgeoisie in a society whose economy has shed all feudal features and cannot, therefore, harbour an 'aristocracy' in any analytical sense of the word.

Where Marx's and Beddoes's views do, however, display parallels is in the way they critique the histrionic invocations of history that accompany contemporary political struggles. And if Marx enigmatically suggests that the dead should now be permitted or even made to bury their dead, then he draws on an imagery that resembles Beddoes's own obsession with the living dead such as vampires. Yet for Marx, the metaphor of the dead burying their dead holds much less power than Beddoes's similar concepts do. Because, ultimately, Marx does not take seriously the first French Revolution's theatrical re-enactment of ancient Roman glory, he judges these cultural forms merely by their capacity for facilitating revolutionary action. Beddoes, who is looking backward rather than forward, at the reactionaries rather than at the revolutionaries, accords the spectres of the past a power of their own that goes beyond their function as theatrical props or even mere ideological window-dressing. As we have seen, the Duke of Wellington's failure to resuscitate the centuries of the past is due not so much to the ideological transparency of his reactionary propaganda but more to his inability to control the spectres he has summoned. Hence, Beddoes grants those historical shadows a degree of independence that Marx must, of necessity, deny them. If, in Marx's view, the past seems always already to be dead, then Beddoes appears to believe that it is possible to revive the past like a world of the living dead, but that that past possesses an uncanny dynamic of its own, one that is certain to triumph over the victor of Waterloo.

Marx's relationship to the past thus betrays traces of what Bruno Latour would consider typically modern, since Latour argues:

> *The moderns have a peculiar propensity for understanding time that passes as if it really were abolishing the past behind it. They all take themselves for Attila, in whose footsteps no grass grows back.*[14]

---

14   Bruno Latour, *We Have Never Been Modern*, trans. Catherine Porter (Cambridge, Mass.: Harvard University Press, 1993), p. 68.

Whereas for Marx, a revival of the past must always be merely histrionic, Beddoes's position acknowledges a constant intermingling of past and present in a temporal hybridity that logically follows from that other hybridity which the playwright establishes between the realms of life and death. According to Bruno Latour, the denial of hybridity—for example, the hybridity between the social and the natural spheres, between human and animal existence, between culture and technology— is a hallmark of the modern. Beddoes, himself an odd historical hybrid between a 'modern' scientist and a (neo-)Elizabethan playwright and natural philosopher,[15] refuses to indulge in modernity's rejection of the hybrid. To be sure, his attacks on Wellington and Périer could be read as denunciations of hybridity, but the very language Beddoes deploys betrays such a fascination with hybridity as to render ineffectual his own denunciations. It is to the hybridity of life and death that Beddoes's imagery is inexorably drawn, thereby poetically invoking the very spectres that supposedly turned out to be so intractable for the Duke of Wellington. In Beddoes's universe, the dead are never quite dead, and the discarded skin of a boa constrictor testifies to the vigour (and violence) of life just as much as to the constant presence of death within life. Consequently, Beddoes's notion of history consists in a co-presence of the past and the present in which historical revenants continually prey on the living, not least because the living themselves are prone to summon them. Such a stance may help to explain some of the oddly sympathetic undertone in Beddoes's critique of Chateaubriand's attempt to forge an alliance between royalist hard-liners and Bonapartists. Reactionary though the French poet may be, he knowingly chooses the impossible, the paradoxical and hybrid, thereby displaying sensibilities not too different from that of his radical critic.

In the final analysis, Beddoes is torn between a revolutionary desire to lay the past to rest and a morbid acknowledgement of the impossibility of ridding oneself of history,[16] an impossibility that parallels the poet's implicit insistence that life and death are always intertwined and cannot be unravelled. Beddoes's political prose thus engenders the spectre of history as the realm of the living dead, a world of vampires constantly transgressing the borders of the present.

---

15   TLB was particularly interested in the Elizabethan alchemist John Dee, but also in the alchemical tradition in general. For TLB's research into the hermetic tradition, see Jon W. Lundin, 'T.L. Beddoes at Göttingen', *Studia Neophilologica*, 43 (1971), 484–99, esp. pp. 494–97.

16   As critics have long noted, TLB's attitude towards death is highly ambivalent; to quote only one of the most recent statements on the issue: 'Beddoes's seemingly contradictory yearning for resurrection and for death are united by a common desire to remove the body from the dialectic of natural process as he saw it'; Christopher Moylan, 'In the Air: T.L. Beddoes and Pneumatic Medicine', *Studia Neophilologica*, 73 (2001), 48–54 (p. 54).

Three of
Thomas Lovell Beddoes's
Dramatic Fragments:
Fractured Techno-Gothic Appendages
and Thomas Beddoes's *Hygëia*

Marjean D. Purinton

Romantic drama that took on fantastical and spectacular forms was variously informed by science, and this interconnectedness between theatre and science may explain the popularity of the gothic and melodrama in the theatre of the day. As I have argued elsewhere, drama achieved this gothic-science linkage through two primary performance manifestations, grotesques and ghosts, resulting in what I have termed the 'Techno-Gothic'.[1] The Techno-Gothic is an ideologically charged and melodramatic structure in which disturbing issues and forbidden topics are recontextualized by the intersecting fields of the supernatural and science—or gothic and technology. Science was a technology during the late eighteenth and early nineteenth centuries in the sense that it was a system of thought and representations, a set of practices and services that fostered power and control, a body of methods and materials used to achieve cultural objectives.[2] Romantic-period science and medicine constituted a technology of cultural transformations, a process being played out in gothic dramas. The Techno-Gothic relies upon a set of readily available and easily recognizable dramatic (gothic) conventions that function as interpretations of scientific/medical discourses (technology) at a time when various social critiques, cultural changes, and paradigm shifts were reflected in the theatre and in drama. The Techno-Gothic is, in fact, a product of the Romantic revolution in science, as its forms mediate post-Enlightenment dualisms such as

---

1   See, for example, 'Theatricalised Bodies and Spirits: Techno-Gothic as Performance in Romantic Drama', *Gothic Studies*, 3.2 (2001) 134–55, and 'Science Fiction and Techno-Gothic Drama: Romantic Playwrights Joanna Baillie and Jane Scott', *Romanticism on the Net* 21 (2001) <http://www.ron.umontreal.ca>.
2   The Greek root of *technology* is *techne*, meaning to make, to craft, to build, which Margrit Shildrick maintains 'plays a part in the construction of all monsters, indeed of all bodies'. Margrit Shildrick, *Embodying the Monster: Encounters with the Vulnerable Self* (London: Sage, 2002), p. 10.

biochemistry and magic, romance and gothic, medicine and quackery, bodies and spirits.

It is in this context that I will examine three dramatic fragments written by Thomas Lovell Beddoes as significant contributions to the Techno-Gothic, in which medical science and theatrical performance are woven intertextually and comment on each other. Because *Love's Arrow Poisoned* (1822–25), *Torrismond: An Unfinished Drama* (1824), and *The Second Brother: A Tragedy* (1824–25) are incomplete, fragmentary dramas, they are particularly well-suited to demonstrate the Techno-Gothic dramatic mode, for, like dissected and fractured appendages of completed dramas, they reflect and challenge the clinical and conceptual changes occurring in Romantic medicine during the 1820s. In this essay, I wish to argue two ways of seeing these T.L. Beddoes's dramatic fragments as Techno-Gothic, and I suggest that these two ways occur in tandem rather than sequentially. First, the intertextuality of Thomas Beddoes's treatise *Hygëia; or, Essays Moral and Medical on the Causes Affecting the Personal State of Our Middling and Affluent Classes* (1802–03) constitutes a particularized science/literature linkage between father and son, both trained physicians and accomplished writers. T.L. Beddoes transforms the preventative medical precepts of *Hygëia* into Techno-Gothic grotesques and ghosts. Second, T.L. Beddoes's dramatic fragments parallel reforms in medical methodology at the beginning of the nineteenth century so as to engage readers to simulate the anatomical gaze at the centre of medical training and advice literature, including *Hygëia*. The Techno-Gothic grotesques and ghosts in T.L. Beddoes's fragmentary dramas invite readers to engage in the anatomical gaze that characterized the new technology of medical diagnoses and treatments, to examine the dramatic text in much the same way that a physician would examine a living or morbid body, so as to expose changes and conflicts in the period's medical thinking. Like Romantic-period medical students, readers are invited to learn how to cultivate their anatomical gazes by working with an appendage of a drama, an amputated arm or leg of a whole body, and thus to replicate the skill-acquiring process by which physicians and surgeons became qualified experts. In a sense then, these fractured appendages are the materials of T.L. Beddoes's operating theatre, staged as dramatic limbs so that their pedagogical function might be realized.

Like his politically radical father, T.L. Beddoes believed that medicine was the key to the survival and betterment of humankind, and his dramatic fragments engage critically with issues raised by *Hygëia*. But T.L. Beddoes struggled with his own personal demons. An alcoholic, often depressed, T.L. Beddoes attempted suicide in 1848 by using a scalpel to open an artery in his leg. Although doctors saved him, T.L. Beddoes repeatedly reopened the wound, causing it to become infected and leading eventually to its being amputated. His body was rendered fragmentary and, like his dramatic fragments, partial and fractured. A year later, T.L. Beddoes amputated more than an appendage when he committed suicide by imbibing poison—a poisoned arrow marked with self-loathing rather than love. Even in death, T.L. Beddoes evoked the interconnectedness of drama and science, his final performance a lived Techno-Gothic that his dramatic fragments enacted, another reason, this one personally relevant to T.L. Beddoes, that the fragmentary dramas are well-suited to the Techno-Gothic.

T.L. Beddoes's crippled body, like his dramatic appendages, offers us material and textual forms of the Techno-Gothic grotesque. As monster or aberration, Techno-Gothic grotesques embodied and performed cultural fascination with the body, its anatomy, its physiology, its potential for disease and deformity, its propensity for physical disabilities and socio-sexual transgressions, and self-mutilation. The Techno-Gothic grotesque gave T.L. Beddoes a performance mode, a staging strategy for representing on a fictive body what science attempted to explain and to produce. It is here that the grotesque makes visible the threatening 'other', now technologically constructed and anatomized, simultaneously disturbing and appealing.[3] While the malformed, hybrid, and at times carnivalesque, monstrous, and sick body of the grotesque excited contradictory responses of sympathy and abomination, it also destabilized cultural values and norms as it invited theatre-goers or readers to participate in the culture's scientific interpretations and medical diagnoses by trying to read its aberrant body as a politicized and medicalized text. Science and stage engendered new perceptions of physicality, transforming the body into a text that could be read and interpreted by curious readers in an experience that approximated medical practices of the day. The Techno-Gothic grotesque was a spectacular body put on display in the anatomical 'clinic' of the theatre, where the 'anatomical gaze' registered a safe distance for its spectators. Reading a performing grotesque body, however, was especially exacting, as it was legitimately fictive and artificial, disguised and costumed as an element of gothic drama.[4]

If the Techno-Gothic grotesque created a performing body that could not be easily read, the Techno-Gothic ghost challenged legibility in its performance

---

3   Marina Warner has shown how the grotesque paradoxically presents terror and mockery in its 'parodic harshness, sick humour, shivery manipulation of fear and pleasure in the monstrous'. Marina Warner, No Go the Bogeyman: Scaring, Lulling and Making Mock (New York: Farrar, Strauss and Giroux, 1999), p. 67. Julia Kristeva addresses the 'other' as abjection, that which is reabsorbed in the grotesque, a structure or monster within the body that persists as exclusion or taboo. Julia Kristeva, Powers of Horror: An Essay on Abjection, trans. Leon S. Roudiez (New York: Columbia University Press, 1982), pp. 10–17.

4   Deirdre Lynch points out that a performer's face provided spectacular evidence of how passions 'stamped' the muscles of the face. Spectators were expected to look at the sentiment written across the performer's body. Deirdre Lynch, 'Overloaded Portraits: The Excess of Character and Countenance', in Body and Text in the Eighteenth Century, ed. Veronica Kelly and Dorothea von Mücke (Stanford: Stanford University Press, 1994), p. 137. In his discussion of the sympathetic body, Steven Bruhm emphasizes that the corporeal feeling was rendered visible by the physician's gaze. Steven Bruhm, Gothic Bodies: The Politics of Pain in Romantic Fiction (Philadelphia: University of Pennsylvania Press, 1994), pp. 10–12. According to E.J. Clery, David Garrick's technique of acting was dependent on the audience's knowledge of the body, a taxonomy of the passions registered by facial expressions and bodily gestures. E.J. Clery, The Rise of Supernatural Fiction, 1762–1800 (Cambridge: Cambridge University Press, 1995), pp. 42–49.

of disembodiment. Gothic conventions, ghosts were dramatic figurations for scientific scrutiny and speculation of mental disorders—hallucination, hysteria, hypochondria, mania, and madness. The physiology of excessive emotions had become, by the end of the eighteenth century, a significant subject of inquiry by scientists and dramatists, like T.L. Beddoes. Ghosts from the gothic tradition were, like monsters, forms upon which science could write new meanings. Medical discourses during the early nineteenth century demonstrate ambiguities and contradictions expressed about ghosts at a time when explanations of what these spectres *mean* were newly infused with scientific explanations, at a time when explanations about the supernatural by religion and superstition were giving way to explanations by science and medicine. In *Hygëia*, Thomas Beddoes asks, 'And will not those terrific phantoms, which once for all croud [*sic*] before the student and disappear, be flitting in view or others continually through life?'[5] *Hygëia* distinguishes reasoning dreams from waking dreams, the former engendering 'strangely wrought up scenes'[6] in which 'impressions, ideas, pleasure and pain mix and alternate in an endless diversity of ways . . . though the order that presides over these phaenomena, has not been, by any means, completely investigated.'[7] Thomas Beddoes sceptically alleges that the belief in things unseen often functions as a symptom for subsequent mental disease.[8]

The Techno-Gothic and the Anatomical Gaze

The movement of medical reform in the early nineteenth century was not unilateral; the inchoate profession struggled to define what it was to be, but it staged this metamorphosis publicly in several forms. William Buchan, James Parkinson, Thomas Trotter, and the elder Beddoes, among others, contributed to the growing number of medical advice books available to the public as well as various medical practitioners. Ironically, this commercialization of health-consciousness fostered the need for more medical publications and doctors that, in turn, contributed to the phenomena of an increasingly sick society through the (mis)education they pandered. Nonetheless, Thomas Beddoes saw medicine as a promising technology if ethically and professionally applied. Perhaps the most important of the reforms at the beginning of the nineteenth century, medical science was undergoing a paradigm shift in which nosological prognosis was being replaced by pathological anatomy, a methodology that required the anatomist to acquire skill in reading the body beyond its surface and into its organic density. This methodological reform shaped the ways in which physicians were being trained, the curriculum they

---

5   Thomas Beddoes, *Hygëia; or, Essays More and Medical, on the Causes Affecting the Personal State of Our Middling and Affluent Classes*, 3 vols (Bristol: J. Mills, 1802–03), I: 1, 56. All quotations are from this edition.
6   *Hygëia*, III: 9, 64.
7   *Hygëia*, III: 9, 71.
8   *Hygëia*, III: 10, 69.

studied, and the laboratory where they gained 'hands-on' experiences. Anatomy was becoming central to medical education and practice.

Hygëia acknowledges the importance of the anatomical gaze in diagnosis, and so it is particularly significant in our gaze at the methodological shift in medical practice reflected in the figures of grotesques and ghosts in T.L. Beddoes's dramatic fragments. 'A body of information on health', as it advertisement claims, *Hygëia* seeks a responsible educating of the public in physiology and health while simultaneously defining the appropriate purview of a medical profession properly trained and credentialed. Thomas Beddoes urges physicians to '*look-more-than-skin-deep*'[9] and recommends 'the study of anatomy, which hitherto [was] . . . considered as a ridiculous whim'. Anatomical dissection, Beddoes proclaims, enables the physician to 'read the state of the interior as plainly as if the body were a book, and the alternation in organs accessible to sense and the patient's account of his feeling, serving him for letters.'[10] The reform Beddoes brings to medicine seeks to cultivate physicians as medical spectators who see both manifest and latent signs of disease.[11] The method by which doctors were being trained to read the human body corresponds to the anatomical gaze required to read T.L. Beddoes's dramatic fragments, for like anatomists, we must explore the 'deep layers' of the subtext, the latent content of the dramatic fragments in order to perceive their embedded meanings.

As the methods and curriculum for physicians' training were undergoing changes during the early nineteenth century, so were the ways in which the general public was being educated about health, disease, and hygiene. Although preventative medicine was generally not viewed as 'medicine' proper, enthusiasm for the regimen of the 'non-naturals', air, diet, sleep, exercise, evacuations, and passions of the mind became increasingly popular, connecting lay audiences, professional practitioners, and surgical anatomists. William Buchan's *Domestic Medicine* (1769), for example, was one of the first advice books that exposed the mysteries and magic of medicine to the general public, advocating that most illnesses and disorders could be self-treated.[12] *Hygëia*, in contrast, advocates for a professionalized medicine and admonishes the advice penned by those untrained as contrary to the progress of medical care. Thomas Beddoes found most health

---

9   *Hygëia*, II: 6, 16 and 47.

10   *Hygëia*, III: 9, 13.

11   Hermione de Almeida asserts that Romantic medicine was concerned with 'the domain of the careful gaze'. Hermione de Almeida, *Romantic Medicine and John Keats* (New York: Oxford University Press, 1991), p. 47. Medical instruction prepared the Romantic physician, explains de Almeida, to 'invoke his trained eye and penetrating vision' and to master a medical semiotics that 'sought to look beneath the manifest symptoms of a body to those more interpretable, universal signs of health or diseased life', p. 127.

12   C.J. Lawrence asserts that *Domestic Medicine* made a contribution to education as an instalment in the rise of popular scientific education, in the rebirth of the health movement, and in the tradition of domestic handbooks of all kinds. C.J. Lawrence, 'William Buchan: Medicine Laid Open', *Medical History*, 19 (1975), 20–35, passim.

publications woefully inadequate and dangerously inaccurate. By 1770, Thomas Beddoes, among others, had come to recognize, as Ginnie Smith reports, that few sections of the population would have been untouched by notions of the 'cool regimen', the staple of preventative medicine in the advice books.[13] Thomas Beddoes contributed to this locus of public education in his proposal for 'lectures for a *mixed* audience, on select subjects of ANATOMY' to be delivered by active members of the medical profession or travelling professors of science and accompanied by models, drawings, exhibitions.[14]

T.L. Beddoes was writing the fragmentary dramas at a time when his father's ideas about the roles of the public and the professional in the nation's health were still to be realized and occasionally outright rejected. The elder Beddoes's contributions to medical reform were, like his son's fragmentary dramas, fractured appendages from his corpus, unevenly acknowledged and implemented by lay and professional practitioners. In *Love's Arrow Poisoned*, for example, Erminia has been abandoned by her lover Leonigild, who has spurned her to maintain:

> a poisonous strumpet in his arms
> On whom he gets confusion, war, disease,
> Prodigies, earthquakes, blights: she's in his blood
> The hell-wombed witch, hagged and hideous nature! (X, 120–23)[15]

Erminia here relies on conventional gothic language to depict the Techno-Gothic grotesque/ghost that her anatomical gaze of Leonigild's girlfriend would reveal to others. Erminia implies that the witch-like, unnatural monster has given Leonigild some infectious disease, syphilis, the 'pox' or gonorrhoea, the 'clap', perhaps, that has driven him to pathological dementia or madness. Late Georgians believed that one might easily become 'poxed' or 'clapped' if one's partner were unfaithful, and it seems furthermore that Leonigild and his 'poisonous strumpet' have produced offspring tainted with the diseased blood of their incestuous intercourse, one likely to have monstrous birth defects from the venereal disease. Moral indignation here is expressed in medical and scientific terms, a dramatic rhetoric that resonates with the elder Beddoes's belief that physiology and lifestyles were the foundations of morality.[16]

Erminia of *Love's Arrow Poisoned* and the title character from *Torrismond* evoke grotesques that result from confounding codified bodies under the two-sex model

---

13 Ginnie Smith, 'Prescribing the Rules of Health: Self-Help and Advice in the Late Eighteenth Century', in *Patients and Practitioners: Lay Perceptions of Medicine in Pre-Industrial Society*, ed. Roy Porter (Cambridge: Cambridge University Press, 1985), pp. 249–82 (p. 254).

14 *Hygëia*, I: 1, 37–38.

15 All quotations from TLB's dramatic fragments are taken from *Plays and Poems of Thomas Lovell Beddoes*, ed. H.W. Donner (London: Routledge and Kegan Paul, 1950).

16 Roy Porter, *Doctor of Society: Thomas Beddoes and the Sick Trade in Late-Enlightenment England* (London: Routlege, 1992), pp. 189–90.

of biology championed by late eighteenth-century anatomists.[17] When Erminia vows that she too will pluck a heart of the devil's side, becoming a 'new-made, / Fiend-hearted, woman-corpsed, but man-arrayed' (X, 172–73), she turns into the Techno-Gothic grotesque that she beholds. Because Erminia has been robbed of her child, her natural maternal role, and her brother has been poisoned, she believes that Nature has brought these miseries upon her, and she implores nature to 'resex or uncreate' her (X, 157). Erminia claims that as transsexual or transvestite, 'I'll be the father of world of ghosts' (X, 163). To make her transformation visible, she will wear her brother's garments. Erminia's dramatic proclamation and costume bring the taxonomical category of sex into question as well as blur the boundaries between the procreation of spirit and flesh. She embodies the grotesque even as she promises the progeny that will haunt future generations. After Torrismond overhears Veronica reflect upon her dream, Torrismond extols in an aside that he is no man if her dream is not about love and that 'she is not a woman, / If this same secret, buried in her breast, / Haunt not her tongue—and hark! here comes its ghost' (I, iii, 73–76). Like Erminia, Torrismond dislodges categorical lines between male and female and between body and spirit, both grappling with grotesques and ghosts that express their physical and mental agitations.

In *Torrismond*, the title character as Techno-Gothic grotesque/ghost represents early nineteenth-century understandings of the physiological effects of excessive drinking. Thomas Beddoes rails in *Hygëia* against the injuries caused by the abuse of stimulating liquors. He suggests that if the public knew about the physiological and pathological consequences of alcohol use, many would control their appetites. Wine and spirits, exclaims Beddoes, impede digestion and 'impair the circulating power of the stomach'.[18] Alcohol results in 'the most monstrous deformity' as the testimonies of anatomists reveal,[19] and 'the drinker of too much wine commonly finds himself what in medical phraseology is called *cachetic*'.[20] While *Hygëia* provides the template for the characterization of T.L. Beddoes's lush Torrismond, the dramatist would have been familiar with the period's discursive anatomical gaze at alcoholism. Thomas Trotter contributes to the medical discourse on intoxication in 1804 with *An Essay, Medical, Philosophical, and Chemical, on Drunkenness, and Its Effects on the Human Body*: 'But a long train of the most dangerous diseases are the certain consequence of habitual intoxication; the mind and body equally suffer. Sudden death, apoplexy, palsy, dropsy, madness, and a hideous list of mental disquietudes and nervous failing, prey upon the shattered frame of the inebriate, and prove fatal in the end.'[21] It was Trotter who recommended the treating of the mind and the body in tandem, a combined methodology of physiology and

---

17   See Thomas Laqueur, *Making Sex: Body and Gender from the Greeks to Freud* (Cambridge, Mass.: Harvard University Press, 1990), pp. 154–81.
18   *Hygëia*, II: 8, 29.
19   *Hygëia*, II: 8, 34.
20   *Hygëia*, II: 8, 47.
21   Thomas Trotter, *An Essay, Medical, Philosophical, and Chemical, on Drunkenness, and Its Effects on the Human Body* (London: T. N. Longman and O. Rees, 1804), p. 2.

psychology, for alcoholism, and we see this methodology being played out in T.L. Beddoes's fragmentary dramas.

Readers of *Torrismond* are invited to perform the anatomical gaze through the reports of characters' observations of Torrismond's unhealthy habits. Referring to Torrismond's irresponsible drinking and rioting, Garcia reports that the young lord's 'veins are stretched by passion's hottest wine' (I, i, 70). The Duke of Ferrara accuses Torrismond of rebelling against him and of robbing the public treasury. Nature's corruption, poison and monstrous offspring, which we have seen in *Love's Arrow Poisoned*, similarly occurs in this fragmentary drama as the Duke alleges that Torrismond is an unnatural son and diagnoses some genetic calamity responsible for such a human defect growing from his body. Perplexed that Torrismond could be a product of his body but determined to preserve the body politic, the Duke concludes that the alcoholic body of Torrismond needs to be removed,

> Like thorns or poison on a wholesome tree,
> The rank excrescence of my tumid sins, —
> And so I tear thee off; for, Heaven doth know,
> All gentler remedies I have applied;
> But to this head they rankling vice has swelled,
> That if thou dwellest in my bosom longer,
> Thou wilt infect my blood, corrode my heart,
> And blight my being. (I, iv, 97–104)

Just as the scalpel of the anatomical surgeon removes a diseased lesion, so Torrismond is to be excised from the body politic and to be disowned by his father's body, lest he infect the stability and health of Ferrara. The 'spirit' of alcohol haunts Torrismond, turning him, at least in the eyes of this father, into a grotesque. T.L. Beddoes knew well the ways that alcoholism transformed actual doctors and surgeons into Techno-Gothic grotesques, as it was estimated that one in 68 of London's medical practitioners were alcoholics, the substance abuse constituting one way to block out memories of suffering and nightmarish operating room scenes.[22] Some sceptics of new medicine held training responsible for students' addictions to alcohol as its was believed that drinking, smoking, and brawling were encouraged by the shocking indecencies of the dissecting rooms.[23]

T.L. Beddoes actually began his medical studies at the same time that he initiated writing of *The Second Brother*. As in *Torrismond*, alcohol takes centre stage, the primary medical issue of the fragmentary drama. Lord Orazio is cast as a Techno-Gothic grotesque; he proclaims himself the son of Bacchus, figuratively an unnatural father. At a banquet, Orazio is so drunk that he believes 'there were more shadows . . . than men', his ghosts the effects of his inebriation, symptoms

---

22   Peter Stanley, *For Fear of Pain: British Surgery, 1750–1850* (Amsterdam: Rodopi, 2003), pp. 233–34.
23   Stanley, p. 167.

delineated by Trotter: 'vigour of body and mind, pleasurable sensation, and power of intellect', followed by 'loss of voluntary motion, and delirium'.[24] Orazio's brother, Lord Marcello, refers to him as 'brother skeleton' (I, i, 138), whose flesh is of the 'common plaister / That wraps up bones' (I, i, 132–33). The emaciated body could be the result of alcoholism, or any variety of consumptive diseases afflicting the public during the early nineteenth century. Marcello, likewise, claims unnatural birth and linkage to deity, and when he inherits the Duke's title, he believes that he can rule the kingdom invisibly as spirit. His grotesqueness becomes manifest when he directs a stage trick for his brother: the conjuring of the spirit and the resurrecting of the body of Valeria, Orazio's wife, whom he believes to be dead. Superstitious Orazio argues that such a transformation would be dangerous and only result in pain, but Marcello taunts his brother: 'Be happily incredulous. Perchance / It were a cursed and unhallowed rite: / Let's think it all a fiction' (III, ii, 115–17).

The fiction exposed here and in the other two fragmentary dramas is a methodology that fails to look beneath the surface for pathological symptoms for what seem to be purely psychological infirmities or character deficiencies. T.L. Beddoes manipulates these grotesques and ghosts to demonstrate the connections of mind and body and to suggest the limitations of a medical profession that was improperly trained to execute the anatomical gaze in diagnosing illness and disorders. The grotesques and ghosts in T.L. Beddoes's fragmentary dramas illuminate in Gothic terms medical reform in which clinical diagnosis was emerging but not realized as the method of modern medicine. The methodological critique is made possible by the intertextual connections between drama and medicine specific to *Hygëia* and the fragments.

The Techno-Gothic and Hypochondria-Hysteria

Many practitioners and patients of the early nineteenth century remained sceptical about the role of anatomy in understanding illness, especially mental disorders. *Hygëia* notes the frequency of lunacy in British society and literature, suggesting 'the belief that insanity is a more common affliction here than in other countries'.[25] The conceptual and epistemological bases for explanations of mental disturbances seemed reductive, and during this period of paradigmatic shifts in medicine, T.L. Beddoes would have known the discourses that called them into question. Alexander Crichton is the mad-doctor who identifies unrestrained passions' capabilities of turning humans into monsters, a transformation that T.L. Beddoes seemed interested in developing in the fragmentary dramas. It is Erminia's attendant who foresees the consequences of uncontrollable passions in *Love's Arrow Poisoned*. She tries to console her charge by telling her, 'For grief and laughter, mingled in the skull, / Oft boil to madness' (X, 48–49). Erminia denies any mental infirmity and quips: 'If my brain were capable / Of this dear madness, should it not be now

---

24   Trotter, *Drunkenness*, p. 31.
25   *Hygëia*, III: 10, 4.

/ All in a bubble with't?' (X, 60–62). Despite her exhortation of good mental health, Erminia has good reasons for psychological disorders, for her brother has been poisoned and her child abducted. Grief and anxiety would certainly explain her distress, but Erminia asks, 'If I could be so, / Should I not be tempestuous mad?'(X, 66–67). If it is life's circumstances or Nature that causes her to go mad, then, asserts Erminia, she will simply 'defy, / Curse, and abandon Nature henceforth ever' (X, 153–54). For Erminia, the grotesqueness of madness is indeed like a stage costume that she can wear or discard at will.

Torrismond renders a more fully developed Techno-Gothic character possessed by unrestrained passions and situated in a carnivalesque setting conducive to its enactments. The imbibing Torrismond tells his guests that they should 'shiver the air with laughter and rough songs, / And be most jovial madmen' (I, ii, 50–51). Torrismond's sleep is punctuated by dreams, his part that of a 'shadow-catcher' (I, ii, 100), and by day, he is haunted by his belief that Veronica has not been faithful to him. Torrismond might have been the subject of a case study upon which Crichton commented: 'The corporeal pleasure of pain which accompanies our passions, always tends to disengage attention from objects of abstract thought, and they consequently tend to destroy the restraint which the mind must be in while exercising the operation of judgment . . . The voluntary actions of a person, therefore, who is under the influence of a strong passion, is, in this respect, like those of a maniac.'[26] *Hygëia* repeatedly refers to imaginary maladies and distresses of the mind as fancy monsters,[27] and Veronica's sleep is also dream-filled. Torrismond tries to interpret her dream visions by watching her corporeal responses to what she sees in her mind's eye:

> *O that this gaze could be eternity!*
> *And yet a moment of her love were more*
> *Were there infection in the mind's disease,*
> *Inoculation of a thought, even now*
> *Should she, from all the winding of her dream,*
> *Drink my impetuous passion, and become*
> *All that I ask. (I, iii, 46–52)*

Torrismond seeks to render meaning through the anatomical gaze, articulating the medical diction of disease shared by the emergent field of psychology in the early nineteenth century.

T.L. Beddoes's mentally disturbed characters from his fragmentary dramas reflect changing medical thinking about gendered associations of madness. During the eighteenth century, hypochondria afflicted men, and women experienced hysteria.

26   Alexander Crichton, *An Inquiry into the Nature and Origin of Mental Derangement: Comprehending a Concise System of the Physiology and Pathology of the Human Mind, and a History of the Passions and Their Effects* (London: T. Caddell and W. Davies, 1798), II, 138–39.

27   For example, *Hygëia*, I: 1, 57.

Throughout most of the eighteenth century, 'hysteria' was used to identify volatile physical symptoms associated with hyper-sensitivity and derived primarily from women, but in a culture blamed for making men 'effeminate', not exclusively so.[28] Thus, hysteria emerged, however, by the beginning of the nineteenth century, as a separate disorder as the medical terminology acquired nomenclature to describe psychogenic disorders. Gendered connections remained but were applied in new ways. By the 1820s, madmen were seen less as physically threatening but more effeminate, a possible explanation for the psychologically disturbed men in the fragmentary dramas as weak, pathetic, ineffectual, passive, enervated, and feminized, in other words, Techno-Gothic grotesques. Torrismond, for example, worries about being seen by his friends as 'weak, unintelligible, fanciful' (I, ii, 99), for to be effeminate risks being considered mad or hypochondriac. T.L. Beddoes would have recognized his father's allusions to Sardanapalus and Moliere's *Malade imaginaire* as effeminate and susceptible to nervous disorders.[29] Thomas Beddoes asserts the period's misogyny that reduced female inferiority to her biological functions and therefore more subject to mental alienation: 'It is well known that . . . nervous disorders are very frequent consequences of the exercise of functions peculiar to the female constitution',[30] a condition that was being associated pejoratively with unmanly men.

T.L. Beddoes's grotesques and ghosts invite readers of these fragmentary dramas to participate in the medical diagnosis of madness that had become a complex process by the 1820s. Erminia's attendant of *Love's Arrow Poisoned*, for instance, makes fun of her charge's lovesickness, an infirmity associated with the antiquated system of humouralist medicine, when she argues that humans with sudden pluckings of the heart, such as Erminia has experienced, 'people the madhouses, and cram up the grave!' (X, 107). The briefly delineated character Erminia nonetheless enacts a Romantic consciousness that, as Roy Porter explains, 'encouraged to look inwards, introspecting upon the painful perturbations of the self'.[31] Torrismond is a hypochondriac who dreads the night, and in the words of *Hygëia*, 'a season of peculiar agony, and its horrors are often deeply imprinted on [the sufferer's] morning countenance'.[32] Erminia is one of the women *Hygëia* describes as especially vulnerable to nervous disorders, who for 'the slightest moral or physical impulse gives a shock, which is felt with equal violence throughout the system'.[33] Erminia and Torrismond are fragmentary, fractured representations of a society that encouraged and extolled self-dramatizing hypochondriacs/hysterics.

T.L. Beddoes's depictions of mental instability were personally pertinent, as he would have known how his father's innovative Pneumatic Institute in Bristol and his experiments with nitrous oxide, his 'air machine', were represented in the press

---

28   Porter, *Doctor of Society*, p. 108.
29   *Hygëia*, III: 9, 173–74.
30   *Hygëia*, III: 10, 23.
31   Roy Porter, *Health for Sale: Quackery in England, 1660–1850* (Manchester: Manchester University Press, 1989), p. 42.
32   *Hygëia*, II: 8, 81.
33   *Hygëia*, II: 8, 96.

and in literature as sheer madness.[34] Some public opinion cast the elder Beddoes as a madman and one who failed, one who was no better than the quacks he had admonished, ridiculed, and had hoped could be disenfranchised by law. Doctors introducing new diagnostic technology in the early nineteenth century, explains Roy Porter, ran the risk of being accused of practising quackery, a strategy the elder Beddoes astutely observed for diverting attention from those physicians who were, in fact, quacks in masquerade.[35] Although the Pneumatic Institute's experiments and clinical work resulted in no actual cures, it did generate public attention and made manifest the theatrical nature of experimental science. Some patients who took breathing treatments reacted in histrionic spectacles. According to Dorothy Stansfield and Ronald G. Stansfield, the uncontrolled and bizarre behaviour of some experimental subjects attracted greater attention than all other research conducted at the Bristol Institute, including developments in the understanding of respiration.[36] Ironically, as Jan Golinski demonstrates, the elder Beddoes's nitrous oxide became the material of public entertainment rather than serious medical use.[37] During the 1820s and 1830s, it was employed in music hall stage acts, where volunteers would be intoxicated for the amusement of the audience.[38] T.L. Beddoes's fragmentary dramas embed the theatrics of pneumatic medicine from his father's experiments, making medicine, in both content and in methodology, an integral part of his dramatic experiments.

The Techno-Gothic and Death

T.L. Beddoes's fragmentary dramas invite audiences to perform metaphoric anatomy through their use of the medical language of disease and drugs. The very title of *Love's Arrow Poisoned* suggests that the chemistry of love could be deadly. The poisoned arrow may be an allusion to inoculations, a medical innovation of considerable controversy as treatment for smallpox, especially, as contagion and infection were only beginning to be understood. The inoculation required a patient being given a small portion of the very poison against which the body would struggle as it created antibodies to discharge the disease/poison. The elder Beddoes testifies in *Hygëia* how the public could be confused and frightened by this preventative

34   Trevor H. Levere's 'Dr. Thomas Beddoes: The Interaction of Pneumatic and Preventive Medicine and Chemistry', *Interdisciplinary Science Reviews*, 7 (1982), 137–47, points to the failure of pneumatic medicine.
35   Porter, *Health for Sale*, pp. 199–200.
36   Dorothy Stansfield and Ronald G. Stansfield, 'Dr. Thomas Beddoes and James Watt: Preparatory Work 1794–96 for the Bristol Pneumatic Institute', *Medical History*, 30 (1986), 276–302 (p. 279).
37   Stansfield and Stansfield claim that the novel experience of breathing laughing gas led to a cult of breathing the 'heavenly air' so to stimulate 'heightened sensibility'. Beddoes's hospital was ridiculed by lay and medical publications.
38   See Jan Golinski's insightful discussion of Thomas Beddoes's Pneumatic Institute in *Science as Public Culture: Chemistry and Enlightenment in Britain, 1760–1820* (Cambridge: Cambridge University Press, 1992), 153–87 (p. 175) .

process: 'Between what are called poisons and what are called medicines, there exists no fundamental difference . . .'[39] Humphry Davy optimistically points to the curious discovery of the inoculation for cow-pox throughout Britain and Europe, 'taking circumstances as they now stand, it promises gradually to annihilate small-pox'.[40] As we have seen, drinking as disease shadows the fragments *Torrismond* and *The Second Brother*. Medical questions about the potential effects of analgesics and sedatives, painkillers such as alcohol, opium, laudanum, and other nostrums were only beginning to surface in the 1820s after Georgian England had become a medicated society, as Roy Porter terms it, 'drunk on self-drugging'.[41] By the early nineteenth century, the sick has unprecedented access to potent drugs, marketed so to foster an indulgence in medicines, many of which were habit-forming and therefore generating a greater demand for doctors and apothecaries.[42] Substances such as opium in alcohol, argues Thomas Trotter in *An Essay, Medical, Philosophical, and Chemical, on Drunkenness, and Its Effects on the Human Body*, 'in a large dose . . . brings on delirium, stupor, and other phaenomena of ebriety'.[43] But a generation earlier, the elder Beddoes had recommend substituting opium for alcohol to relieve pain so to mitigate the harmful effects of alcohol on the mucous membranes of the stomach.[44]

Despite these efforts to deter the public's love of drugs, opiates were widely recommended, almost as a panacea, and there was increasingly heavy consumption of opium during the early nineteenth century, when it was openly on sale and part of the self-medicating person's repertoire to stimulate as well as to calm. As we have seen, access to nostrums fostered and fuelled the nation's epidemic of hypochonria-hysteria. In *A View of the Nervous Temperament* (1807), Thomas Trotter reported: 'All nervous persons are uncommonly fond of drugs; and they are the chief consumers of advertised remedies, which they conceal from their medical friends. Among some well-meaning people, this inordinate desire for medicine has frequently become of itself a disease.'[45] Quacks often advertised nostrums on bills with great gothic letters to stimulate consumers' attention.[46] The Apothecaries Act of 1815 attempted to regulate the purveying of drugs, but it was largely not enforced and was therefore ineffective.[47] In the competitive London medical market where, by

---

39   *Hygëia*, I: 2, 43.

40   Humphry Davy, *Memoirs of the Life of Sir Humphry Davy in The Collected Works of Sir Humphry Davy*, ed. John Davy (London: Smith, Elder, 1839), I, 80.

41   Porter, *Health for Sale*, p. 43.

42   Porter, *Health for Sale*, pp. 24–42.

43   Trotter, *Drunkenness*, p. 35.

44   Frederick Fox Cartwright, *The English Pioneers of Anaesthesia: Beddoes, Davy, and Hickman* (Bristol: J. Wright, 1952), p. 137.

45   Thomas Trotter, *A View of the Nervous Temperament; Being a Practical Enquiry into the Increasing Prevalence, Prevention, and Treatment of those Diseases Commonly Called Nervous, Bilious, Stomach and Liver Complaints; Indigestion, Low Spirits, Gout, &c.* (London: Longman, Hurst, Rees, and Orme, 1807), p. 104.

46   Porter, *Health for Sale*, p. 112.

47   Joan Lane, *A Social History of Medicine: Health, Healing and Disease in England, 1750–1950* (London: Routledge, 2001), p. 29.

the mid-1820s, there were nearly four thousand physicians, surgeon, apothecaries, and druggists, it seems unlikely that legislation would curb addiction.[48] Despite experiences and reports to the contrary, most doctors withheld any claim that opium would prove addictive.[49]

T.L. Beddoes stages early nineteenth century preoccupations with disease and addictions to medicines in his fragmentary dramas. In *Torrismond*, the title character confesses that he experiences an 'unfathomable fever' (I, ii, 107), which might describe the effects of alcohol and opium. According to the Duke, his son Torrismond has 'poisoned my age' (I, iv, 67) with his partying, rioting, and rebelling. In *The Second Brother*, Orazio recoils from a beggar—in reality his brother Marcello—who asks, 'Doest fear the plague?' (I, i, 124). Epidemic language occurs again when Marcello refers to his solitude as that like 'the last survivor of a city's plague' (I, i, 205). His brother Orazio quips: 'I'm somewhat dull; / But let me not infect you' (I, ii. 45–46), as if mental conditions were infectious. The Duke sustains an injury during a hunting trip, and the Jewish doctor Ezril is called, who reports, 'I went to his bedside, and there made trial / Of my best skill in physic' (I, i, 257–58). After the Duke admonishes his efforts, the doctor confesses inefficacy in treating the unresponsive patient: 'He lay in a red fever's quenchless flames, / Burning to dust: despairing of my skill' (I, i, 264–65). Orazio casts the unsuccessful doctor as Techno-Gothic grotesque, calling Ezril an 'age-hidden monster' (II, ii, 53), a wise, elderly physician on the surface but a monster underneath.

Other family politics in the fragmentary drama are depicted in terms of disease and medicine. Varini refers to Valeria, his daughter, as 'the very fool and sickness of my blood' (I, ii, 179), suggesting the possibility that Valeria is illegitimate. Melodramatically, Valeria complains to her attendant: 'I am not well: / My body and my mind are ill-agreed, / And comfortless strange' (II, ii, 23–25). Valeria here points to the entwined mind/body pathology that both the anatomical gaze and the theatrical ogling sought to decipher. *Hygëia* estimates that 100,000 died from consumption annually in Great Britain,[50] as professional and lay practitioners sought to decipher this ailment that was in the blood of Romantic culture.

It is not so strange for T.L. Beddoes's characters to die, even in these fragmentary dramas, given the public fascination and abhorrence with the grave-robbing activities of resurrection men. Mary G. Winkler points out that anatomical books made the results of dissection increasingly public, with dissections themselves often ceremonial or theatrical events and punitive spectacles. Anatomists had to sever connections between dissection and criminality, as only hanged criminals could, by law, be subjected to dissection, and to realign themselves with the new science in which the cadavers' roles were to assist in the revelation of disease and death.[51] Anatomical knowledge and surgical skills could by improved only

---

48   Stanley, p. 23.

49   Dorothy Porter and Roy Porter, *Patient's Progress: Doctors and Doctoring in Eighteenth-Century England* (Stanford: Stanford University Press, 1989), pp. 150–64.

50   *Hygëia*, III: 11, 7.

51   Mary G. Winkler, 'The Anatomical Theatre', *Literature and Medicine*, 12 (1993), 65–80 (pp. 66–68).

if physicians and students were allowed to practise on corpses. Even viewing a dissection had educational merit, and as Ruth Richardson explains, as many as 100 students could observe a demonstration of dissection in the operating theatres of major London teaching hospitals.[52] In the operating theatre, anatomy was a dramatic event, in Richardson's words, 'the element of theatricality implicit in the naming of operating theatres signifies their potential to provide the locus for an action to be performed, a spectacle displayed.'[53] James Thompson speculates that T.L. Beddoes probably witnessed his father's dissections of animals, even though he was less than six years old when his father died.[54] T.L. Beddoes's training may well have involved his viewing or participation in European operating theatres, a site that he incorporates into his fragmentary dramas where his 'students' watch the transformations of grotesques and ghosts into anatomized corpses and spirits for dissections, theatricalized and medicalized.

The Second Brother reflects scientific disputes about anatomical dissections, reanimation, and resurrection experiments accompanying anatomical attention to the body. At the beginning of the drama, Battista characterizes Marcello, a poor man, in terms of a Techno-Gothic grotesque raised from the dead:

> What is this?
> Methinks that a prae-adamite skeleton,
> Burst from the grave in a stolen cloak of flesh,
> Ragged and threadbare, from a witch's back
> Who live an hundred years . . . (I, i, 64–68)

Battista's friends ignore his efforts to perceive resurrected death. Following the Duke's death, Marcello sends the nobles home, and interpreting the supernatural that haunts their evening festivities, proclaims, 'let the churchyard's sleep / Whisper our goblins' (III, i, 55–56). Disguised as a nun, Valeria reports on her own willingness to die rather than to be abandoned by Orazio. Apparently, Orazio is tricked into believing that Valeria is dead when, in fact, she has been taken to the Campo Santo, to Death's 'Cabinet' (IV, i, 8), where she, resurrected from the dead, will meet her husband. The play's final speech by Valeria reflects her intensity in convincing others that she is her physical self and not a reanimated corpse:

> I have a plea,
> As dewy-piteous as the gentle ghost's
> That sits alone upon a forest-grave
> Thinking of no revenge: I have a mandate,
> As magical and potent as e'er ran
> Silently through a battle's myriad veins,

---

52   Ruth Richardson, *Death, Dissection and the Destitute*, 2nd edn (Chicago: University of Chicago Press, 2000), pp. 15–50.

53   Richardson, p. 48.

54   James R. Thompson, *Thomas Lovell Beddoes* (Boston: Twayne, 1985), p. 2.

> Undid their fingers from the hanging steel,
> And drew them up in prayer: I AM A WOMAN. (IV, i, 22–29)

Valeria cites her physicality as evidence of life; it is her physical and sexed body that marks her as alive. Her body has no need of the dissecting scalpel, 'the hanging steel', to expose its hidden essence. She refuses to play the part of the grotesque laid out on the dissecting table of the anatomical theatre to receive its penetrating gaze.

Conclusion

T.L. Beddoes's three fragmentary plays are dramatic amputations, much like his self-inflicted wounded and infected leg, partially dissected, fractured bodies of drama. T.L. Beddoes's grotesques and ghosts ominously foreshadow the transformations of his own physicality, becoming as he did, an actual grotesque haunted by the ghost of his father. T.L. Beddoes's three fragmentary dramas as fractured appendages represent another paradigm in medical practice at the beginning of the nineteenth century in which unbridled amputation of injured or infected limbs was giving way to more conservative treatment directed at saving life and limb. Late Georgian surgeons, explains Peter Stanley, learned new methods of double and triple incisions so to effect a more clean amputation and to resort to this severe and often fatal operation only for dire cases.[55] Just as many amputees of the period reported suffering pain from a 'phantom' limb that had been amputated, critics of T.L. Beddoes have generally seen his fragmentary dramas as mere shadows of his completed dramas *The Brides' Tragedy* and *Death's Jest-Book*, painful limbs of his literary corpus that fail to function fully as tragedies.

It is another irony that the elder Beddoes saw *Hygëia's* precepts as preventions of suicide, a prescription that T.L. Beddoes did not take: 'I believe, too, that this study would be the best preservative against that weariness of living, which is among the most hopeless of our miseries, and the surest forerunner of suicide.'[56] While his father's study might have provided material for his drama, T.L. Beddoes could not find in it a way to resolve his mental and physical pain. His dramatic, fractured appendages are emblematic of his own life, prematurely finished but important in ways newly explored by literary critics and students. Beyond the textual reconfigurations of *Hygëia* in three of T.L. Beddoes's dramatic fragments, we have seen that by applying the methodology of the anatomical gaze to these three dramas, the methodology by which medical training and practice was being conducted in the 1820s, the methodology advocated by *Hygëia*, we have discovered that these fractured appendages yield significant medical semiotics and insights. Teaching materials upon which readers can practise literary/medico dissection, these three fragmentary dramas cast readers as anatomists/physicians and engage their participation in the clinical methodology initiated by the medical reform movements of the 1820s.

---

55   Stanley, pp. 79–84.
56   *Hygëia*, I: 1, 59.

The Brides' Tragedy
and the Myth of
Cupid and Psyche

Shelley Rees

In his introduction to *The Brides' Tragedy* (1822), Thomas Lovell Beddoes offers the following history as source material for the play:

> *The Manciple of one of the Colleges early in the last century had a very beautiful daughter, who was privately married to a student without the knowledge of the parents on either side. During the long vacation subsequent to this union the husband was introduced to a young lady, who was at the same time proposed as his bride: absence, the fear of his father's displeasure, the presence of a lovely object, and, most likely, a natural fickleness of disposition overcame any regard he might have cherished for his ill-fated wife, and finally he became deeply enamoured of her unconscious rival. In the contest of duties and desires, which was the consequence of this passion, the worse part of man prevailed, and he formed and executed a design almost unparalleled in the annals of crime. His second nuptials were at hand when he returned to Oxford, and to her who was now an obstacle to his happiness. Late at night he prevailed upon his victim to accompany him to a lone spot in the Divinity Walk, and there murdered and buried her. The wretch escaped detection, and the horrid deed remained unknown till he confessed it on his deathbed.[1]*

This narrative, even as related by Beddoes, bears only a slight resemblance to the play he claims it inspired. Most notably, the husband's motive for murdering his first wife is more selfish ambition than anything else, and the motives of Hesperus, the wife-killer of *The Brides' Tragedy*, defy such simplistic explanation. As James R. Thompson observes:

---

1   Donner, *Works*, pp. 172–73.

> Beddoes rejects that motive [of ambition], overtly at least, for three
> others: Hesperus must escape his first marriage in order to save his
> father; he is jealous of Floribel after seeing her kiss a page; and he suffers
> periodic madness. One of the conventional dramatic weaknesses of the
> play is the confusion these three motives produce. But the murder is
> actually symbolic; its significance is not to be found in plot.[2]

One thing is clear: the Oxford story does nothing to illuminate the symbolic
significance of Floribel's murder. For that we must look to Beddoes's unnamed
source, the story of Cupid and Psyche, a classical dramatization of the perfect
union between masculine and feminine.[3]

In brief, the story tells of the beautiful Psyche, a human woman with divine beauty.
Her two sisters find husbands quickly, but Psyche is worshipped as a manifestation
of the goddess Venus, and thus potential suitors remain too intimidated to court
her. Psyche's parents take their frustration to an oracle, which tells them to leave
Psyche on a high mountain where her husband, a being so fierce that even the
gods fear him, will collect her. Meanwhile, Venus hears of this human woman to
whom her own celebrated beauty is ascribed and, overcome with jealously and
hatred, commands her son Cupid to ruin Psyche by causing her to fall in love with
a penniless ugly man. Cupid flies to do his mother's bidding but pricks himself
with his own arrow and falls in love with Psyche himself. When Psyche's terrified
parents leave her at the crag, Cupid sends the west wind to carry her to a divine
hideaway, where invisible hands tend to her every want and Cupid makes love to
her in the dark. Cupid tells his wife that she must never attempt to discover his
identity or he will be forced to abandon her, and Psyche promises to stay content in
ignorance. Psyche's sisters, jealous of her obviously divine marriage, visit Psyche
and tell her that her husband is really a monstrous snake who will devour her and
the child she is by this time carrying. They advise her to wait until he sleeps that
night and hold a lamp over him, ready to kill him with a knife when she sees the
monster he is. Terrified, Psyche follows her sisters' advice and lights a lamp while
her husband sleeps. Holding it over him, she sees the beautiful young god and,
overwhelmed by love, leans forward to kiss him, causing a drop of oil from the
lamp to fall and burn his shoulder. Cupid wakes, sees what Psyche has done, and
flies away to his mother's palace to nurse his wound. The pregnant Psyche wanders
in search of Cupid, tries unsuccessfully to kill herself, and finally arrives at Venus's
palace. Venus beats her cruelly and assigns her two impossible tasks, but other
gods are so anxious to see Cupid's antics forestalled by a wife and family that they
assist Psyche in completing them. Finally, Venus sends Psyche to the underworld
to collect some of Persephone's beauty. With more help, Psyche secures the beauty,

---

2   James R. Thompson, *Thomas Lovell Beddoes* (Boston: Twayne, 1985), p. 34.
3   I am indebted to Eleanor Wilner for alerting me to this connection; I am grateful for
        her help and encouragement. TLB's attraction to the Cupid/Psyche myth also appears
        in a prose piece drafted for inclusion in *The Ivory Gate*, 'The Tale of the Lover to His
        Mistress'; see *Works*, p. 129.

but on the way back she cannot resist opening the case, thinking divine beauty will bring Cupid back to her, and she falls into a death-like sleep. The myth ends with Cupid finding Psyche on the ground, wiping the sleep from her and escorting her back to the palace. The gods decide to make Psyche immortal so that she and Cupid may stay married, Venus accepts the marriage, and Psyche gives birth to the girl child called Pleasure.[4]

In *The Brides' Tragedy*, Beddoes adapts and alters the story of Cupid and Psyche to reflect his own agenda, in particular his denial of the androgynous ideal the myth embodies, a concept celebrated by the Romantic poets of Beddoes's youth. The Cupid and Psyche myth presents a Jungian integration of body (coded masculine in the young god of love) and soul (coded feminine through Psyche). Scholars identify a desire for similar male-female integration in male Romantic poetry, giving gender a crucial position in the literature. For example, in his discussion of Romantic gender, Marlon Ross argues that, 'As self possession and influence become crucial determinants within the discourse of Romanticism, categories of gender take on an intensified role, a role that can be examined through the basic permutations of gender relations'.[5] Ross goes on to explain that male Romantics attempted to adopt a feminine value system as a vehicle for more intuitive and emotive verse.

The inevitable destruction of the feminine in this dynamic is well documented in recent studies of Romantic literature. For example, according to Diane Long Hoeveler:

> The ideology of androgyny required not only the subjugation of women, but the (de)humanization and eradication of the female representation as well. The Romantics cannibalistically consumed these female characters, shaped them into alter egos, and most of the time destroyed them by the conclusion of the poem. That cycle—idealization of women followed by fear, loathing, and destruction—corresponds also to the poets' growing realization that androgyny was only an alluring siren song of escape from the body. In the end, both women and androgynes become the subject of scorn, anger, and ridicule.[6]

In addition, Anne K. Mellor argues that sexual love in Romantic literature embodies the masculine desire for androgyny, also with erasure of the feminine as the result:

---

4   This paraphrase and all subsequent references to the myth are taken from Apuleius, 'The Myth of Cupid and Psyche', in *The Transformations of Lucius; Otherwise Known as The Golden Ass; a New Translation by Robert Graves from Apuleius* (New York: Noonday, 1951).

5   Marlon Ross, *The Contours of Masculine Desire: Romanticism and the Rise of Women's Poetry* (New York: Oxford University Press, 1989), p. 93.

6   Diane Long Hoeveler, *Romantic Androgyny: The Women Within* (University Park: Pennsylvania State University Press, 1990), p. 9.

> *Since the object of romantic or erotic love is not the recognition and*
> *appreciation of the beloved woman as an independent other but rather*
> *the assimilation of the female into the male (or the annihilation of any*
> *Other that threatens masculine selfhood), the woman must finally be*
> *enslaved or destroyed, must disappear or die.*[7]

Beddoes rejects the androgyne fantasy outright in *The Brides' Tragedy* by establishing Floribel as a Romantic version of Psyche and Hesperus as her lover/destroyer. The opening scene establishes the masculine/feminine dichotomy the characters represent. Floribel is surrounded by—is, in fact, the embodiment of—Romantic ideals. Her home is a cottage in a beautiful wood; she enters the play with flowers for her husband hanging around her neck.[8] She is the 'beautiful flower' of her name, as well as the Romantic noble savage, cultivated by nature and referred to in the play as a 'wood-nymph' (II, i, 78) and 'the Dian of our forests' (I, ii, 19). As Daniel P. Watkins points out, 'her constructed significance for Hesperus is that she inhabits and even constitutes a private and innocent realm more meaningful than the world of daily life that he inhabits'.[9] In essence, the ultra-feminine Floribel provides Hesperus a haven from the politics of his own patriarchal aristocratic environment.

Of course, Hesperus cannot truly escape those politics. He keeps his marriage secret because Floribel is a commoner, and Hesperus fears the disapproval of his father, Lord Ernest. Hesperus's reluctance to confess his imprudent marriage to his father partly reflects a lack of maturity and independence, but it also underscores the significance of isolation for Hesperus's marital happiness. He must be aware that if Lord Ernest acknowledges their marriage, the blissful secrecy of the woods will no longer shelter them; they will take their places as young members of the upper class, and Hesperus will be back where he began. As Thompson points out, 'the play's first scene indicates that love, the single redemptive force the work offers, can succeed only when hidden outside life'.[10]

Cupid faces similar problems in his own marriage. His mother would disapprove of his wedding any common mortal, but she particularly loathes Psyche. In addition, Cupid has a reputation to uphold among the gods; as the oracle reveals, 'Even Jove fears him'. (In fact, at the end of the tale Jove blesses the marriage and makes Psyche immortal because all the gods agree that domestication might keep Cupid from his usual mischief.) Thus, if he were to reveal his marriage, Cupid would forfeit some

---

7   Anne K. Mellor, *Romanticism and Gender* (New York: Routledge, 1993), p. 26.

8   The image of a woman with flowers around her neck appears in *Death's Jest-Book* to associate her with a sacrificial animal: 'I would say / She's sleek, and sacrificial flowers would look well / On her white front' (II, iii, 128–30). Floribel's necklace of flowers may be a less overt use of the same image, foreshadowing her sacrifice at the hands of Hesperus.

9   Daniel P. Watkins, 'Thomas Lovell Beddoes's *The Brides' Tragedy* and the Situation of Romantic Drama', *Studies in English Literature 1500–1900*, 29 (1989), 699–712 (p. 706).

10   Thompson, p. 36.

of his mystique among the other gods, along with the freedom of visiting Psyche for sex at his convenience without any of the hassle of a 24-hour wife. After all, while Venus's hatred comprises a believable reason for keeping Psyche hidden, it hardly explains why Psyche herself cannot know who her husband is. Cupid clearly relishes the power over his bride that his anonymity grants him.

Indeed, both husbands strive to integrate the feminine but lack the requisite emotional maturity. Their childishness is never more obvious than in their respective break-up scenes, in which disempowerment, expressed as castration fear, sends each husband into a panic. Thompson argues that Hesperus is 'an essentially passive character' who 'can only react',[11] and indeed Act I follows Hesperus's embarrassing vacillation between his father and his wife, swayed and re-swayed by whichever is near him at the moment. For example, in the opening scene Floribel pleads with Hesperus to make their marriage public:

> *Yet surely mine's a sad and lonely fate*
> *Thus to be wed to secrecy; I doubt,*
> *E'en while I know my doubts are causeless torments.*
> *Yet I conjure thee, if indeed I hold*
> *Some share in thy affections, cast away*
> *The blank and ugly vizor of concealment,*
> *And if mine homely breeding do not shame thee,*
> *Let thy bride share her noble father's blessing. (I, i, 72–79)*

Hesperus replies to this tearful speech as an indulgent lover: 'In truth I will; nay, prithee let me kiss / That naughty tear away; I will, by heaven' (I, i, 80–81), and at this point appears at last to have chosen his wife over his father's will. But Floribel represents not just adulthood and independence from parental control but a specifically female influence, and immediately upon leaving Floribel's idealized feminine environment Hesperus again confronts the patriarchal world of politics and money in the form of his father's imprisonment for debt. Hesperus learns that Orlando, the nobleman to whom the debt is owed, will forgive the debt if Hesperus agrees to marry Orlando's sister Olivia. Thus, Act I ends with a scene of emotional appeal strikingly like the one with which it begins, as Lord Ernest begs Hesperus to agree to the terms:

> *Come, speak to him, my chains, for ye've a voice*
> *To conquer every heart that's not your kin?*
> *Oh! That ye were my son, for then at least*
> *He would be with me. How I loved him once!*
> *Aye, when I thought him good (I, iii, 67–71)*

---

11   Ibid., p. 36.

It must be noted that Lord Ernest's imprisonment represents a symbolic emasculation; his lack of capital becomes utterly disempowering, and he loses physical freedom as part of his loss of economic influence. Thus, much like Floribel, his only recourse is a kind of emotional blackmail, and his weepy pleading mirrors that of Floribel in the earlier scene. While Floribel's influence is derived from romantic love, however, Lord Ernest invokes male kinship as his persuasive device, implying that the 'good' son is one for whom the needs of the father are paramount. The laws of primogeniture, crucial to the maintenance of patriarchy, privilege the male-male familial connection over any others, and Lord Ernest uses that context to convince Hesperus of his duty to his father:

> But, if you recollect my name, bestow it
> Upon your best-loved child, and when you give him
> His Grandsire's blessing, add not that he perished
> A wretched prisoner. (I, iii, 88–91)

Unable to deny his father's pathetic entreaty, Hesperus makes another promise, one that is, of course, contradictory to the first: he agrees to marry Olivia.

Watkins reads *The Brides' Tragedy* as a dramatic rendering of the 'larger social and ideological deterioration . . . of the aristocratic ruling class' in the nineteenth century:

> All other actions and attitudes, though some are less explicitly class-
> bound than Lord Ernest's, are marked by class anxiety, by an attempt
> to preserve aristocratic hierarchy, order, and value, or by a desire to
> find some means of personal escape from certain class extinction —
> by the same needs and desires, that is, seen in the portrayal of Lord
> Ernest.[12]

Certainly, the aristocratic and patriarchal values represented by Lord Ernest include marriage, which traditionally involves a transaction between men. This constitutes one reason why Hesperus's and Floribel's marriage is unacceptable: neither Hesperus's nor Floribel's father knows of it, much less approves it. Lord Ernest and Orlando transact an engagement for their son and dependent sister, respectively, something clearly sanctioned by the social context. Hesperus, then, reverts to the masculine influence of that tradition in agreeing to the second engagement.

In addition, it is clear that, as Watkins points out, the traditional paradigm of father-rule is breaking down in the play for, like Lord Ernest, Floribel's father is ineffective and weakened. Mordred is bed-ridden before the play's action begins, described by his wife as having 'his sad smile upon his patient face, / Looking so dear in sickness' (III, ii, 71–72), and then promptly dies upon hearing of Floribel's death. Even Orlando, who wields the power of aristocratic and financial status

---

12   Watkins, p. 702.

inherited from his own father—the debt Lord Ernest owes was to Orlando's father, not Orlando himself—does so because he also wants to marry Floribel. With his father dead, Orlando would subvert traditional authority just as Hesperus does, with the same woman, using his powerful aristocratic legacy to bring about his own union with the 'brown damsel' of the forest (I, ii, 25).

With two young noblemen shrugging off the influence of the father in an effort to ally themselves with feminine ideals, *The Brides' Tragedy* could seem like a play about a younger generation's overthrow of the traditional masculine paradigm. As Hoeveler explains in her analysis of male Romantic heroes:

> *At times the hero, assuming the role of a young son, seeks to merge with a chthonic Great Mother, and his quest takes on the aura of a regressive search for origins or a primal struggle with the oedipal-capitalist father.*[13]

Unfortunately, Hesperus is no such hero; he staggers into Act II still searching for a promise he can keep. He wanders back to Floribel's wood, then away again, then returns, only to witness Floribel bestowing an innocent peck on a kindly pageboy. At this point, Hesperus appears to completely lose his grip on reality, behaving as if he discovered Floribel and the page *in flagrante delicto*, spitting, 'Why Floribel,—Girl! Painted fickleness! / Madam, I'm rude; but Hesperus did not think / He could intrude on—what was Floribel' (II, ii, 130–32). Donner argues that Hesperus is simply an example of Romantic character construction, about which he says, 'Its place was supplied by melodramatic incident and by the hysterical dialogue which in the days of Romanticism went under the name of tragic passion'.[14] Donner's perspective, however, fails to take into account the true cause of Hesperus's histrionics. Of course his reaction is ridiculous; it is just ridiculous enough to show that it is spurred not so much by what he sees, as by how it makes him feel. He is frightened by a sudden sense of helplessness and loss of control, brought about by the discovery that Floribel has the power to injure him and that she exists on her own terms, not merely as an extension of himself. After that, it doesn't matter whether Floribel is innocent or guilty; the damage has been done. In his final words of the scene, Hesperus acknowledges his wife's power over him, associating that power as specific to 'woman', and states his intention to liberate himself from it:

> *I will not go, for if I do, the flock*
> *Of her warm suitors will be toying here;*
> *Yet I'll not stay; for she will melt and pray*
> *Till I'm a fool again. Strain not your lungs*
> *With laughter when I'm gone. Oh woman, woman. (II, ii, 186–90)*

---

13   Hoeveler, p. 10.
14   Donner, *The Making of a Poet*, p. 95.

In the most fundamental sense, Floribel's crime is in shocking Hesperus out of his fantasy of 'what was Floribel'. She acts in a way that does not conform to his construction of her, behaving not like a possession but an independent other, and exposes Hesperus's Pygmalion project as a failure:

> Madam, we're strangers;
> And yet I knew some while ago a form
> Like thine, as fair, as delicate. Oh heaven!
> To think of it. But she was innocent,
> Innocent, innocent. (II, ii, 178–82)

As Hoeveler explains:

> The androgynous ideology . . . is a quintessentially artificial concept
> that on one level expresses the fantasy of sexual unity as a denial of
> death, but on the other and deeper levels expresses the inevitability of
> frustration and the limitations of all human art and artifice.[15]

In other words, Hesperus's attempt to assimilate feminine ideals must inevitably fail, because it is based on an unattainable, immature desire for absolute control of the object. He leaves the distraught Floribel and returns to Orlando's palace where she, as a commoner, cannot follow.

Floribel herself understands that, while she did not commit adultery, she did unearth some latent anxiety in Hesperus. After her fight with Hesperus, Floribel talks to her mother about their financial status:

> FLORIBEL   Dear mother, I will strive to be at ease,
> If you desire; but melancholy thoughts
> Are poor dissemblers. How I wish we owned
> The wealth we've lost.
>
> LENORA   Why girl, I never heard
> One such regret escape your lips before;
> Has not your Hesperus enough?
>
> FLORIBEL   Too much;
> If he were even poorer than ourselves,
> I'd almost love him better. For, methinks,
> It seemed a covetous spirit urged me on,
> Craving to be received his bride. (III, ii, 28–37)

---

15   Hoeveler, pp. 15–16.

Watkins views this conversation as indicative of Floribel's class anxiety:

> *These and other comments by Floribel, though prompted and colored by intense personal anxiety, describe perfectly her understanding of the class and economic forces that both push her marriage into secrecy and drive her husband to unpredictability.*[16]

Watkins is undoubtedly correct, and it is but a small step from his study of class conflict in the play to recognizing the gendered nature of that conflict. Floribel and her mother, in their Romantic femininity, can maintain a serene rural poverty in a way that male characters cannot; financial ruin feminizes Mordred and Lord Ernest to the point of extreme weakness and pathos. Floribel's worry that Hesperus turns from her because he believes her covetous is therefore symbolic of his castration fear, the fear that she threatens his masculinity, that she has become 'a usurping and castrating power'.[17]

Floribel then, like Psyche, is shunned by her husband after she exposes him in a way that makes him vulnerable. Moreover, both husbands deny the true reason for abandoning their wives. Cupid claims he abandons Psyche to punish her for disobedience but, in reality, he flees because Psyche dismantles the power dynamic he has so carefully constructed between them, unmasking his identity while wielding a knife, a castration image that underscores the threat of emasculation. He knows that the only superiority left to him is his godhood, so he sulks in Venus's divine palace, a place where the mortal Psyche will not be welcomed. At this point in the story, he is not yet mature enough emotionally to accept the vulnerability of a true union with Psyche, so he leaves her to the cruel torments of his mother, a regressive act. In the same way, Hesperus claims that he abandons Floribel because she kisses the page, when he is actually more compelled by the vulnerability exposed by his jealousy. His manhood threatened, Hesperus becomes eager to re-enter the paradigm of male supremacy, so he resigns himself to marrying Olivia and assures his father's reinstatement in society, returning the briefly deposed patriarch(y) to power.

An important difference between the myth and Beddoes's play is that Venus, Cupid's mother, is the one who punishes Psyche because she is jealous, both of her celebrated beauty and of her hold on her pampered son. While Venus tortures Psyche, Cupid languishes in the palace nursing the burn he sustained when Psyche held the lamp over him to reveal his identity, but it is he who ultimately comes to Psyche's rescue before Venus can kill her. The burn Cupid receives at that crucial moment is a physical manifestation of the emotional one, which also must heal before Cupid and Psyche can reunite. To grow emotionally he must remove himself from his mother's power and protection and dedicate himself to his wife.

Hesperus, in contrast, has no mother; she died when he was an infant. The role of disapproving parent falls, in part, to the feminized Lord Ernest. Also, however,

---

16   Watkins, p. 703.
17   Hoeveler, p. 7.

in Beddoes's tale, the angry jealous Venus is not separate from Cupid; Hesperus and Venus are one. Even the name Hesperus, as Eleanor Wilner points out, is an alternate name for the star Venus, 'the portal star to night and death'.[18] In a sense, Hesperus dramatizes the phenomenon that Barbara Schapiro outlines in *The Romantic Mother*:

> *Some Romantic poets attempt to come to terms with angry and aggressive feelings and allow the woman a concrete, if humanly imperfect, reality, whereas others portray her solely as an abstraction, as split between the ideal maiden and the monstrous witch.*[19]

The monstrous mother, a separate character in the myth, becomes part of the Hesperus/Venus androgyne in *The Brides' Tragedy*, representing a defensive instinct in Hesperus that will always fear the influence of the feminine. Like Psyche's divine mother-in-law, Hesperus's 'feminine side' is an abstraction of jealousy and possessiveness wholly incompatible with the idealized femininity he attempts to assimilate. Unlike Cupid, whose story chronicles his growth and maturity, Hesperus cannot remove himself from the controlling mother influence to bond with an active woman in a marriage of equals. He is like Norman Bates in *Psycho*, stunted by over-identification with the monstrous mother, and in the end he can only make his Psyche figure immortal by murdering her.

Thus, the most obvious difference between the myth and Beddoes's play lies, of course, in their endings: Cupid and Psyche join for eternity and produce Pleasure from their union, while Floribel and Hesperus do neither. Cupid and Psyche's tale is about growing through selfishness and self-interest to a point of emotional maturity that allows for true integration of a beloved Other. Beddoes denies this potential in his revision, mocking Psyche's joyful immortality through Hesperus's murder of Floribel: 'I could be content / If she were safe in heaven' (II, iv, 46–47).

Hesperus's utter lack of growth is confirmed when he searches for another Floribel in Olivia. Because her betrothal to Hesperus is politically arranged, Olivia's influence is weaker than Floribel's from the outset; she comes to Hesperus already objectified as a bargaining tool. In fact, when Hesperus arrives at the palace, Orlando presents Olivia to him like a door prize: 'Here is a living welcome, prithee know her; / Olivia' (II, iii, 10–11).

Unfortunately for them both, Hesperus does not want to know Olivia; he wants to create her from the same false image with which he constructed Floribel. In his first words to Olivia as her fiancé, Hesperus assigns her to the role of a goddess in a painting: 'Pray, lady? Didst thou ever see the goddess / Step from her dignity of stone, or leave / The hallow'd picture in its tinted stole / And crouch unto her suppliant?' (II, iii, 20–23). Again Hesperus appears to idolize a beloved, but the

---

18   Eleanor Wilner, *Gathering the Winds: Visionary Imagination and Radical Transformation of Self and Society* (Baltimore: Johns Hopkins University Press, 1975), p. 76.

19   Barbara Schapiro, *The Romantic Mother: Narcissistic Patterns in Romantic Poetry* (Baltimore: Johns Hopkins University Press, 1983), p. 5.

effect is a double deferral of her humanity, first as goddess and then as a work of art. This construction of Olivia denies her agency, objectifying her as a repository of aesthetic pleasure and serenity for Hesperus's consumption, reinforced by his pledge:

> Thou flower of love, I'll wear thee in my bosom;
> With thee the wrath of man will be no wrath,
> Conscience and agony will smile like pleasure,
> And sad remembrance lose its gloomy self
> In rapturous expectation. (II, iii, 130–34)

Obviously, Olivia cannot eradicate wrath, agony or sadness, nor can she exist simply as a decoration worn in Hesperus's lapel and, as with Floribel, Hesperus's self-interested idealizing of Olivia will destroy her. Continuing in his denial, Hesperus seeks to prevent another failure like the one with Floribel by embracing the impulse toward death, deciding his fantasy of love must be incompatible with the materialism of the physical world. He therefore tells Olivia that, though they will marry, they will have no physical relationship until they are dead:

> For when our souls are born then will we wed;
> Our dust shall mix and grow into one stalk,
> Our breaths shall make one perfume in one bud,
> Our blushes meet each other in a rose,
> Our sweeter voices swell some sky-bird's throat
> With the same warbling, dwell in some soft pipe,
> Or bubble up along some sainted spring's
> Musical course, and in the mountain trees
> Slumber our deeper tones, by tempests waked:
> We will be music, spring, and all fair things,
> The while our spirits make a sweeter union
> Than melody and perfume in the air.
> Wait then, if thou dost love me. (II, iii, 76–88)

Hesperus accomplishes several things by convincing Olivia to agree to this bizarre arrangement. For one, he forestalls any sexual power that Olivia might wield in their marriage; in death, fears of emasculation ostensibly cannot plague him. Moreover, he will avoid the ambivalence about Olivia's purity that Floribel, once no longer virginal, evoked in him. In Hesperus's mind, Olivia will remain uncorrupted, a virgin until they reach their 'bridal sheets of lead' (II, iii, 108).

Certainly, while the Cupid and Psyche narrative suggests that the lovers must move beyond shallow physicality to a mature spiritual union, the (P)leasure of the physical remains part of their happiness, their child being the ultimate proof of their successful marriage. Again, Beddoes gives Hesperus's motives a perverse twist, wherein Hesperus asserts that the key to proper male/female integration is to skip forward to the immortality (in death), bypassing the struggle for personal growth and understanding. As a result, Hesperus learns nothing and understands nothing, and he most assuredly does not join either bride in the afterlife.

In the end, Hesperus himself is defeated by his inability to coexist with the feminine. As Hesperus waits for his execution, Floribel's grieving mother, Lenora, presents him with a bundle of flowers:

> They grew upon the grave of Floribel,
> And when I pulled them, through their tendrils blew
> A sweet soft music, like an angel's voice.
> Ah! There's her eye's dear blue; the blushing down
> Of her ripe cheek in yonder rose; and there
> In that pale bud, the blossom of her brow,
> Her pitiful round tear; here are all colours
> That bloomed the fairest in her heavenly face;
> Is't not her breath? (V, iv, 85–93)

Hesperus breathes deeply of the flowers, saying, 'It falls upon my soul / Like an unearthly sense' (93–94), to which Lenora answers:

> And so it should,
> For it is Death thou'st quaffed:
> I steeped the plants in a magician's potion,
> More deadly than the scum of Pluto's pool,
> Or the infernal brewage that goes round
> From lip to lip at wizard's mysteries;
> One drop of it, poured in a city conduit,
> Would ravage wider than a year of plague;
> It brings death swifter than the lightning shaft. (V, iv, 94–102)

Thus it is the essence of Floribel, subsumed in beautiful flowers, which kills Hesperus, her 'breath' made poisonous through the legacy of femininity passed from mother to daughter.

And there is no question that Hesperus is damned. If the play ended with Hesperus's execution by the authorities, for instance, we would know only that they punished him for Floribel's murder, a socially sanctioned punishment for a socially determined crime. However, because Lenora breathes from the poisoned flower and dies alongside Hesperus, the play provides a comparison between their respective deaths, allowing us to see that while Lenora will be reunited with Floribel in heaven, Hesperus will not. Thus, Lenora dies witnessing:

> These banks of stars, these rainbow-girt pavilions,
> These rivulets of music—hark, hark, hark!

> *And here are winged maidens floating round*
> *With smiles and welcomes; this bright beaming seraph*
> *I should remember; is it not—my daughter?* [Dies. *(V, iv, 112–16)*

Hesperus, by contrast, is not redeemed in the end, as his dying words testify:

> *I see not those; but the whole earth's in motion;*
> *I cannot stem the billows; now they roll:*
> *And what's this deluge? Ah! Infernal flames!* [Falls.
> . . . .
> *The bloody hunters and their dogs! Avaunt—*
> *Tread down these serpents' heads. Come hither, Murder;*
> *Why dost thou growl at me? Ungrateful hound!*
> *Not know thy master? Tear him off! Help! Mercy!*
> *Down with your fiery fangs!—I'm not dead yet.* [Dies. *(V, iv, 117–19;*
> *121–25)*

Beddoes leaves us certain that Hesperus will not achieve the ideal union in death with either Floribel or Olivia. Instead, the play ends with Hesperus alone in a hell of his own creation, having destroyed himself and the feminine objects of his desires, a Cupid who allows the jealous Venus to slaughter his brides.

Dying with a Vengeance

Dead Brides and the Death-Fetish in T.L. Beddoes

Diane Long Hoeveler

I

> 'Tis now the moment still and dread,
> When Sorcerers use their baleful power;
> When Graves give up their buried dead
> To profit by the sanctioned hour.
>
> M.G. Lewis, 'Midnight Hymn', The Monk *(1794)*

One cannot read for very long the poetry or dramas of Thomas Lovell Beddoes without the sense of sinking, of being immersed in a murky underground landscape, a nether world where the living mingle comfortably with the dead, a place, in short, in love with death. Beddoes was not, of course, alone in his fixation on the question of death or, to be more precise, on the eroticization of Thanatos. Like other gothicists and late romanticists, Beddoes mediated a myriad of social, political, cultural, and religious anxieties through his poetry and dramas, depicting a realm that enacted on a microcosmic scale the larger ideological issues of his era. Clearly, Beddoes was imaginatively drawn in his works to the possibilities of creating something of an alternative locus, a city of the dead, a place where the dead would continue to exist in a world not radically unlike the one they were accustomed to inhabiting while living. And so, in some ways his poetry and two major dramas circle that city of the dead, imagining it and fantasizing about various ways to inhabit it and to live there with or (preferably) without women. I would contend that Beddoes's city of the dead appears, in some of its manifestations at least, as a world of men, a utopia beyond the realities of the flesh while its existence stands as a rabid denunciation of female fertility. In order to support this claim, this essay will explore some of the overlooked sources for Beddoes's death-fetish, focusing on his presentation of dead cities, dead women, and finally dead religious beliefs.

In many ways Beddoes's fixation on the city of the dead reminds one of Percy Shelley's dream landscapes in *Alastor*. For instance, consider this description of a city of the dead:

> I found him in a buried city I went by torchlight through
> I followed once a fleet and mighty serpent
> Into a cavern in a mountain's side;

And, wading many lakes, descending gulphs,
At last I reached the ruins of a city,
Built not like ours but of another world,
As if the aged earth had loved in youth
The mightiest city of a perished planet,
And kept the image of it in her heart,
So dream-like, shadowy, and spectral was it.
Nought seemed alive there, and the very dead
Were of another world the skeletons.
The mammoth, ribbed like to an arched cathedral,
Lay there, and ruins of great creatures else
More like a shipwrecked fleet, too great they seemed
For all the life that is to animate:
And vegetable rocks, tall sculptured palms,
Pines grown, not hewn, in stone; and giant ferns,
Whose earthquake-shaken leaves bore graves for nests.

(Death's Jest-Book γ variant at III, i, 40)

The reference here to torchlight is significant, given its identical use throughout the poetry of Johann Christoph Friedrich von Schiller (1759–1805), poetry Beddoes knew well. I would like to focus initially, however, on some material sources for Beddoes's monuments and underground tombs, namely the elaborate memorial built by Rigaud in memory of Vanbrugh, as well as the catacombs of Paris.[1] With those two locations in mind, let us consider this passage from Beddoes:

Throw up your monuments, ye buried men
That lie in ruined cities of the wastes! . . .
An earthquake of the buried shake the domes
Of arched cathedrals, and o'erturn the forests,
Until the grassy mounds and sculptured floors,
The monumental statues, hollow rocks,
The paved churchyard, and the flowery mead,
And ocean's billowy sarcophagi,
Pass from the bosoms of the rising people
Like clouds! Enough of stars and suns immortal
Have risen in heaven: today in earth and sea
Riseth mankind. And first yawn deep
Ye marble palace-floors,
And let the uncoffined bones, which ye conceal,

---

1   Illustrations of these monuments can be viewed as follows. The Rigaud pyramid in
     memory of Vanbrugh at: <http://www.stowe.co.uk/history/gardens_park/egyptian_
     pyramid.html>; and the Paris catacombs at: <http://triggur.org/cata/crypt.html>.

> Ascend, and dig their purple murderers up,
> Out of their crowned death. Ye catacombs
> Open your gates, and overwhelm the sands
> With an eruption of the naked millions,
> Out of old centuries! . . . guilty forests
> Where bloody spades have dug 'mid nightly storms;
> The muddy drowning-places of the babes;
> The pyramids, and bony hiding-places—
> > ('Doomsday', ll. 4–5; 10–26; 33–36)

It is necessary to begin, then, by noting that it is no coincidence that scenes of burial and literal graveyards are lovingly described throughout Beddoes's poetry and dramas. And although such an obsession may seem macabre to us, it is important to remember that from the 1780s and continuing through the 1830s, throughout the parishes of Paris, dead bodies began floating to the surface of the graveyards that encircled a number of city churches. In the marshy grounds along the Seine, bodies of the poor, who had been buried without coffins, simply appeared in spring as if in full bloom, like perennials that no one remembered having planted. In London, along the Thames, a similar problem occurred;[2] and it is the meaning of these dead but suddenly resurrected bodies, emerging and competing for space in the major urban capitals of Europe, that I think provides us with the first clue to Beddoes's concern with 'dead cities'. In particular, I want to interrogate what appears to be a strangely persistent leitmotif of dying brides or women clutching dead babies, or forms of blasted fertility in all their horrific manifestations, in selected works by Thomas Lovell Beddoes.

First of all, it is necessary to observe that the representation of the dead and living co-existing on one and the same plane, so to speak, was deeply disconcerting to the cultural and religious imagination of the late eighteenth- and early nineteenth-century European population. As you will recall, the Western religious imagination had constructed a 'great chain of being', and all of us had a particular place on this chain and were to stay in our assigned spaces. The reappearance of the dead, as if they were living, as if they had the power to will their reappearance on the surface of the earth, was unacceptable to the European mind, whether Protestant or Catholic. And so literature steps in, as it is wont to do, and mediates this phenomenon by depicting the nauseating mixture of the living and the dead and then resolving the crisis by consigning each to its proper sphere by the conclusion of the text.

Critics have been puzzling over the meaning of the death-fetish in Beddoes's works ever since he first entrusted his work for review to the ever-so-critical 'Barry

---

2   For informative discussions of burial practices in England, France, and Germany during this period, see Vanessa Harding, *The Dead and the Living in Paris and London* (Cambridge: Cambridge University Press, 2002); Craig Koslofsky, *The Reformation of the Dead: Death and Ritual in Early Modern Germany* (New York: St Martin's, 2000); and Richard A. Etlin, *The Architecture of Death: The Transformation of the Cemetery in Eighteenth-Century Paris* (Boston: MIT, 1984).

Cornwall'. Contemporary critical studies have addressed the theme by resorting to biographical, psychological, and literary source analyses, all of which I think are valuable and which I will employ where relevant.[3] Clearly, however, there are also what I would designate as buried and gothic levels of political and religious anxiety that have not been addressed or even recognized in reading Beddoes's works. Consider, for instance, one of the more famous, or perhaps more infamous, scenes in the gothic canon. Agnes, the fallen and pregnant nun in Lewis's *The Monk*, gives birth alone in her underground cell, and the premature baby soon dies because the new mother is unable to feed him. Agnes is later found and rescued, but she is clasping her dead baby in her arms, desperately trying to awaken and feed the hideously rotting child. The scene reads like a grisly and perverted parody of a Raphaelesque Madonna and Child, absolute beauty transformed into absolute ugliness. This scene, horrific and compelling as it is, also spoke to the increasingly anxious mixture of the living and the dead that was occurring throughout London and Paris. The dead, who should by all rights stay below ground, were instead dragging the living down below ground with them. Or, even worse, the dead were refusing to stay underground; hence the appearance of vampires or white worms in all their sickening permutations on the streets of London and Paris or the even British countryside.

But consider now another scene from *The Monk*, the famous meditation of Ambrosio in front of a portrait of the Virgin Mother, recently sent to him by an admirer who shows up shortly as a young man/woman/demon with the name of 'Rosario', the rose, the Virgin Mary's iconic flower. And in addition to the name's loaded associations, the young man bears a striking resemblance to the Virgin's portrait.[4] The youthful acolyte transforms first into a wanton seductress and then

---

3   For instance, one of the best of the early modern critics of TLB is, in my opinion, Northrop Frye, who observes about the death-fetish: 'The root of the conception of the grotesque [in TLB] is the sense of the simultaneous presence of life and death. Ghosts, for example, are at once alive and dead, and so inspire the kind of hysteria that is expressed equally by horror and by laughter. The grotesque is also the expression in literature of the nauseated vision, man's contemplating of himself as a moral body who returns to nature as "dung and death" . . . The most concentrated symbol of this aspect of the grotesque is perhaps the cannibal feast, the subject of two strategically placed lyrics in the play, one sung by Isbrand and the other by Wolfram, both in their character as fools.' On the question of ghosts in TLB, Frye observes: 'The question whether life drives to death or through it remains an unanswerable question. Beddoes answers, not that there is a life after death, but that life and death are different aspects of the same world, related as day is to night, summer to winter. Man, says Beddoes, is the seed of a ghost . . . so Beddoes presents us with a world in which a human life is a ghost's way of producing another ghost.' *A Study of English Romanticism* (New York: Random House, 1968), pp. 60–61 and 52–53. A more contemporary reading of the same theme can be found in Michael O'Neill, '"A Storm of Ghosts": Beddoes, Shelley, Death, and Reputation', *Cambridge Quarterly* 28 (1999), 102–15.

4   I am grateful to Fred Frank for his suggestions on *The Monk*. The most useful analyses of Lewis's use of Germanic ballad sources can be found in the work of Syndy M. Conger, *Matthew G. Lewis, Charles Robert Maturin and the Germans: An Interpretive*

finally into a demon, a curious line of anti-evolutionary descent suggesting that in the Protestant imagination the Virgin Mary should actually be understood as the Whore of Babylon. This demonization of the Virgin mother, as well as the almost uncanny obsession with her miraculous fertility, and then the need to blast this quality, repeats over and over again in Beddoes. Dying brides, thwarted fertility, dead babies, these representations permeate Beddoes's works, and the question for the literary critic is why?

First and most obviously, we could look at the medical trends and see a very clear pattern of male physicians infiltrating the obstetrical care of women, with nurse-midwives being removed from their traditional role of delivering babies. Although statistics show that deaths in childbirth actually declined very gradually throughout this period,[5] fictional literature would suggest otherwise. One could then examine attitudes toward sudden or lingering deaths, the anxiety about sewage, miasma, graveyards, and pollution, noting the increased outbreaks of cholera and influenza that swept across Europe and Britain during this period.[6] These medical or scientific explanations are tempting, but this essay will instead propose a religious explanation for the motif. In fact, in order to understand Beddoes, I would claim that we need to recognize the deeply anti-Catholic nature of much gothic literature, and understand that these texts served the blatantly ideological function of secularizing and reformulating the major tenets and representations of Christianity. Susan Griffin, as well as earlier critics such as Joel Porte and Sister Mary Muriel Tarr, of course, long ago recognized the virulent anti-Catholicism in gothic texts, and more recently Robert Miles has examined the theme in Charles Maturin's Irish tales, noting the nationalistic work that anti-Catholicism accomplishes for this Anglo-Irish writer, a descendant of Huguenots and a Protestant clergyman himself. Bostrom and Sage have also explored the theological and religious dimensions of gothic literature in direct retort to Montague Summers, who claimed 'it is folly to

---

Study of the Influence of German Literature on Two Gothic Novels (Salzburg: Institut für Englische Sprache und Literatur, 1977); and 'Sensibility Restored: Radcliffe's Answer to Lewis's *The Monk*', *Gothic Fictions: Prohibition / Transgression*, ed. Kenneth W. Graham (New York: AMS Press, 1989), pp. 113–49. The only extended (but impressionistic) discussion of TLB and the gothic can be found in Horace Gregory, 'The Gothic Imagination and the Survival of Thomas Lovell Beddoes', *The Dying Gladiators and Other Essays* (New York: Grove, 1961), pp. 81–95.

5   Irvine Loudon has documented that the female British population experienced a drop in deaths from 280 deaths in childbirth per 10,000 births in 1670, to 100 by 1800, and to 60 by 1850: 'Pre-industrial English deaths in childbirth were only a relatively small proportion of deaths amongst women of childbearing age. Even for mothers in the age of maximum childbearing, 25–34, maternal deaths accounted for only one in every five deaths in that age group'. Irvine Loudon, *Death in Childbirth, 1800–1950* (London: Oxford University Press, 1992), pp. 159 and 162.

6   For attitudes toward death during the period, see Philippe Ariès, *The Hour of Our Death*, trans. Helen Weaver (New York: Lane, 1981); also Christopher Daniell, *Death and Burial in Medieval England, 1066–1550* (London: Routledge, 1997), pp. 67 ff., for a discussion of anxieties about sudden death in the medieval period.

trace any 'anti-Roman [Catholic] feeling' in the Gothic novel'.[7] For Porte, gothic is a type of moral fable, with Protestant religious anxieties being displaced onto a Catholic setting. For him, figures such as Faust or Cain are 'guilt-haunted wanderers' inhabiting texts that are 'fable[s] of inexplicable guilt and unremitting punishment—in which [they] saw an image of their own condition and fate'.[8] And surely we can see throughout the works of Beddoes, particularly in his use of the doubled father-son configurations in *Death's Jest-Book*, just this sort of guilt-ridden angst and morbid religious dread. These specifically Calvinist fears are too narrow, however, to explain the eschatological fears that must have plagued members of all religious denominations during the nineteenth century. But rather than focusing on arcane theological disputes or issues of political legitimacy or nationality, which admittedly do appear in gothic texts, I want instead to examine one of the methods by which gothic literature spoke so effectively to the growing Protestant audiences of Germany and England. This essay will contend that Beddoes self-consciously used a variety of pre-Christian as well as Germanic literary sources in order to valorize the death-fetish, as well as to critique Catholicism and the female body. Much like earlier gothicists such as Matthew Lewis, Walter Scott, S.T. Coleridge, and Charles Maturin, Beddoes had a clear ideological agenda in presenting the lure and horror of death in his two major dramas. In order to understand his convoluted imagery, however, it is necessary to unpack the leitmotif of death eroticism by casting our eyes back to some of the earliest ballad forms, then their adaptation by Jacobean dramatists, and then finally to German poetry and *Märchen*.[9]

---

7   See Susan Griffin, *Anti-Catholicism and Nineteenth-Century Fiction* (Cambridge: Cambridge University Press, 2004); Joel Porte, 'In the Hands of an Angry God: Religious Terror in Gothic Fiction', *The Gothic Imagination*, ed. G.R. Thompson (Spokane: Washington State University Press, 1974), pp. 42–64; and Sister M.M. Tarr, *Catholicism in Gothic Fiction* (Washington DC: Catholic University of America Press, 1946). See also Robert Miles, 'Europhobia: The Catholic Other in Horace Walpole and Charles Maturin', *European Gothic*, ed. Avril Horner (Manchester: Manchester University Press, 2002), pp. 84–103. Irene Bostrom has noted that the number of Catholics in Britain had declined under the penal laws to less than 70,000, therefore, 'many English readers would have had only the slightest acquaintance with actual Catholics'. Irene Bostrom, 'The Novel and Catholic Emancipation', *Studies in Romanticism* 2 (1962), 155–76 (p. 159). More recently, Fred Botting sees 'the production of Gothic novels in northern European Protestant countries [as having] an anti-Catholic subtext'. Fred Botting, *Gothic* (London: Routledge, 1996), p. 5. In a similar vein, Victor Sage sees the Gothic genre as a caustic response to 'the campaign for Catholic Emancipation from the 1770s onward until . . . the Emancipation Act of 1829': see his *Horror Fiction in the Protestant Tradition* (London: Macmillan, 1988), pp. 28–29. See also Montagu Sommers, *The Gothic Quest: A History of the Gothic Novel* (1928; New York: Russell, 1964).

8   Porte, p. 50.

9   The most extended treatment of Germanic sources for the works of TLB can be found in Anne Harrex, '*Death's Jest-Book* and the German Contribution,' *Studia Neophilologica* 34 (1967), 15–37 and 301–18. She summarizes the earlier studies of Germanic influence on TLB and sees Novalis's theory of Magic Idealism and Tieck and the Schlegel

II

> *Cruelty is above all lucid, a kind of rigid control and submission to*
> *necessity. There is no cruelty without consciousness and without*
> *the application of consciousness. It is consciousness that gives to the*
> *exercise of every act of life its blood-red color, its cruel nuance, since it*
> *is understood that life is always someone's death.*
>
> Antonin Artaud, The Theater and Its Double[10]

In thinking about the gothic tradition of the eroticization of death or the dying bride herself, one could focus on Lewis's *Monk* or his poetic tale *The Dying Bride*, or the truncated bridal celebrations that abruptly conclude all of Ann Radcliffe's major gothic novels, or the murder of Elizabeth in *Frankenstein*, or Lucy in *Dracula*, or Lilla in *The Lair of the White Worm*. We could also have examined the theme in Wordsworth's 'The Thorn', Coleridge's *Christabel*, or Scott's *The Bride of Lammermoor*, whose heroine, Lucy Ashton, attempts to murder her bridegroom as he meets her in the bridal chamber and who then promptly sinks into insanity and death, a dead bride who takes her true love, the Master of Ravenswood, with her to the tomb as he sinks into quicksand, a particularly apt image of the soggy earth, part land, part water, unable to hold its dead permanently. Instead, this essay will ask why the motif of dying brides revives with such a vengeance in some selected poetry and dramas of Beddoes, whose *The Brides' Tragedy* (1822) and *Death's Jest-Book* (1825–49; pub. 1850) are filled with dying brides, rotting fertility, and a loathing of the flesh that verges on the pathological.

For instance, it is not simply the bride-figures like Sibylla, Floribel, or Olivia who die in the dramas of Beddoes; it is also the mother or her substitute who die in particularly sadistic manners. In his unfinished drama *Torrismond*, the eponymous hero addresses his father:

> *Tear all my life out of the universe,*
> *Take off my youth, unwrap me of my years,*
> *And hunt me up the dark and broken past*
> *Into my mother's womb: there unbeget me;*
> *For 'till I'm in thy veins and unbegun,*
> *Or to the food returned which made the blood*
> *That did make me, no possible lie can ever*
> *Unroot my feet of thee* (I, iv, 185–92)

---

brothers' concept of Romantic irony inconsistently employed throughout TLB's works (p. 37). See also Fred Burwick, 'Death's Fool: Beddoes and Büchner', *The Haunted Eye: Perception and the Grotesque in English and German Romanticism* (Heidelberg: C. Winter, 1987), pp. 274–300.

10   Antonin Artaud, *The Theater and Its Double*, trans. Mary Caroline Richards (New York: Grove, 1958), p. 102

A strange notion indeed, this intense nausea toward the physical body, this almost pathological desire to move behind the primal scene to the very origins of the parents' bodies and blood as a way of denying one's existence, of blocking one's conception. For Beddoes, life would appear to be the after-effects of a longed-for but botched abortion. In reverse fashion, however, the Duke as father presents his son Torrismond's life as an abjection:

> *Hear me, young man, in whom I did express*
> *The venom of my nature, thus the son,*
>
> *. . . . .*
>
> *Not of my soul, but growing from my body,*
> *Life thorns or poison on a wholesome tree,*
> *The rank excrescence of my tumid sins, —*
> *And so I tear thee off* (I, iv, 92–93, 96–99)

In a similar vein, we can recall the words of the poetic speaker who hates life so intensely that he thinks the happiest people are they,

> *Who have no body but the beauteous air,*
> *No body but their minds. Some wretches are*
> *Now lying with the last and only bone*
> *Of their old selves, and that one worm alone*
> *That ate their heart* ('Lines Written at Geneva, 1824', ll. 26–30).

The Brides' Tragedy builds on this nausea toward the flesh and was supposedly motivated by an historical event that was then popularized in ballad-form. Beddoes's version, however, contains a very curious addition by way of explaining Hesperus's murder of his bride Floribel. Like a pre-Freudian, Beddoes very conveniently provides us with a childhood trauma to account for Hesperus's bouts of madness, explaining that as a small boy he had witnessed the sudden violent death of his wet nurse-mother substitute as he lay on her breast. We are told that suddenly, out of nowhere, a huge bolt fell on her and crushed her head just inches from his face. This strange episode reads as almost a parody of the nursing virgin with the male infant on her lap, except in Beddoes's version, she dies a sadistic, horrific, and undeserved death that will continue to haunt Hesperus throughout his life. For Beddoes, the only permanent way to control a woman's fertility is to kill her, and women die all too frequently throughout his works. This is not to claim, however, that men do not also die with a vengeance in Beddoes, but in some way their deaths are less disturbing because they are described as welcome escapes from betrayal, treachery, and angst. Witness the poem 'A Dirge (To-day is a thought)':

> *And life is a death,*
> *   Where the body's the tomb,*
> *And the pale sweet breath*

Is buried alive in its hideous gloom.
Then waste no tear,
For we are the dead; the living are here.
In the stealing earth, and the heavy bier. (ll. 3–9)

Clearly, for Beddoes, life is a prolonged and torturous form of trying to live between two realms, the physical and the immaterial, while death is a return to our true unicellular essence, an embrace of the authentic material condition of dust.

Death's Jest-Book is filled with so many scenes of macabre death that one hardly knows where to begin. Suffice it to say that the drama's eroticization of death becomes manifest when a literal dance of death is performed as dead figures on a wall come alive and perform for the living and Isbrand sings in the persona of an aborted fetus: 'What shall I be? / Poor unborn ghost, for my mother killed me / Scarcely alive in her wicked womb' (γ: III, iii, 323–25). It appears that Beddoes would have known that the Dance of Death was first developed during the medieval period by German friars, probably growing out of their preaching tradition: during homilies on death the Dance may have been mimed or performed as a species of *tableaux vivants*, a sort of ecclesiastical dramatic performance in dumb show. It spread to France and England, but never was as popular in England as it was on the Continent. The most famous visual depiction of the dance was on the wall of the church of the Holy Innocents in Paris, but there are other depictions in England, including on the wall of Salisbury Cathedral.[11]

The medieval and faux-Elizabethan ambience that suffuses *Death's Jest-Book* conceals, however, a highly personal agenda that is biographical as well as anti-Catholic. For instance, one of the most curious incidents occurs when Wolfram is resurrected from the dead in place of Melveric's dead wife (a curious homosocial arrangement suggesting more than a hint of Beddoes's own sexual orientation).[12] Another occurs when Wolfram leads Melveric to the kingdom of the dead with him at the conclusion of the play, as if they were going out for a brief stroll:

Blessing and Peace to all who are departed!
But thee, who daredst to call up into life,

11   Leonard P. Kurtz, *The Dance of Death and the Macabre Spirit in European Literature* (1934; New York: Gordon, 1975) includes a discussion of TLB's use of the trope; while Geoffrey Wagner discusses the 'baroque' quality of death in TLB: '*Death's Jest-Book* satirizes a baroque world, a world fetid with the bourgeois illusion, disgraced by capitalist luxury'. Geoffrey Wagner, 'Beddoes: Centennial of a Suicide', in *The Golden Horizon*, ed. Cyril Connolly (London: Weidenfeld and Nicolson, 1953), pp. 543–61 (p. 560).
12   See Shelley Rees, 'Melveric and Wolfram: A Love Story', *The Thomas Lovell Beddoes Society Journal*, 8 (2002), 14–25, for a reading of the play that recognizes TLB's homosexuality; while Stephen Guy-Bray, 'Beddoes, Pygmalion, and the Art of Onanism', *Nineteenth-Century Literature* 52 (1998), 446–70, recognizes the masturbatory quality of his 'Pygmalion.'

And the unholy world's forbidden sunlight,
Out of his grave him who reposed softly,
One of the ghosts doth summon, in like manner,
Thee, still alive, into the world o' th' dead. (V, iv, 352–57)

Both incidents suggest that death is entered and exited through a revolving door, and that life, rather than being a blissful utopia, differs little from the underground vaults of death. For instance, Duke Melveric, in despair over his sons' defection, expresses the play's general attitude toward earthly existence:

Nature's polluted,
There's man in every secret corner of her,
Doing damned wicked deeds. Thou art old, world,
A hoary atheistic murderous star:
I wish that thou would'st die, or could'st be slain,
Hell-hearted bastard of the sun. (β: II, iii at 366; Works, p. 413, n.)

Certainly there is no escaping the feminization of the earth's body here, existing like some old mother-whore whose 'corners' (wombs) have been rooted around in by 'wicked' boys.

In an era that was negotiating political reform, gender relations, print culture and nationalism, colonialism and imperialist expansion, and all manner of issues connected with modernization, religion and secularization were highly contested and ambivalent, anxiety-ridden topics that were being fought out, literally, over the dead bodies that began emerging on the surfaces of Paris and London. If, as Protestantism asserted, there was no purgatory, then there was only either heaven or hell, not some murky purgatorial place (like quicksand) where the dead went to wait until the living prayed them into heaven. Anxieties about the rituals connected with Christian burial and the need to clearly define who could and could not be buried in a Christian church and the attached cemetery began to be played out, first in Germany, then in England, after the Protestant Reformation. In the absence of purgatory, it became crucial to determine where someone's soul was going to reside, and with the rise in population and the premium placed on space in urban centres, not everyone could be buried in a parish cemetery in the middle of a city. Competition, so to speak, for real estate in the afterlife (with a berth in a parish church or graveyard) was fierce. Proving that one deserved such a spot actually became an issue of great importance to all classes who did not own their own mausoleums. More importantly, however, if there was no purgatory, then the living no longer had any connection with the dead, except to fondly remember them.[13]

---

13   Changing attitudes toward purgatory are discussed throughout Christopher Daniell, *Death and Burial in Medieval England, 1066–1550* (London: Routledge, 1997). Daniel P. Watkins sees *The Brides' Tragedy* as enacting 'the conflict between a dying feudalism and an emergent industrial capitalism', an argument that, if extended into the

The new Chantries Act of 1547 not only closed chantry colleges, hospitals and free colleges, but it aggressively attacked Roman Catholic doctrines, particularly imposing a ban on the belief that anyone could be prayed out of purgatory. Theologically, it denounced the existence of purgatory and effectively ended one of the church's largest money-making schemes.[14]

Purchasing indulgences or buying masses for the dead in order to buy them out of purgatory became just so much nonsense, but if one no longer had a way of continuing to worry about and care for one's dead, then by necessity the living were cut off from their ancestors in an abrupt manner that the popular religious imagination could not easily accept. Such a sentiment is evident in Beddoes's 'Dream Pedlary':

> If there are ghosts to raise,
> What shall I call,
> Out of hell's murky haze,
> Heaven's blue hall?
> Raise my loved longlost boy
> To lead me to his joy.
> There are no ghosts to raise;
> Out of death lead no ways;
> Vain is the call. (ll. 38–46)

The poignant tone here, the defeated effort and grudging acceptance of being unable to bring back the dead, suffuses Beddoes's works. Gothic literature—and Beddoes's works are no exception—insists by the conclusion of its texts on a clear demarcation between the living and the dead, but the real work of ideology exists in those moments of slippage when the two realms reconnect and the dead and living speak to one another—negotiate—as in days of old.

It is necessary by way of further introduction, however, to point to a few representative examples of ballads, dramas, *Märchen*, and then the line of inheritance we see towards Beddoes in order to claim that the dying bride with an infant in her arms became a powerful way of reversing and secularizing traditional Christian iconography. Let me explain: if Christianity is predicated on salvation through the miracle of a mother who gives birth to a son whose conception is spiritual, and then both mother and son ascend bodily to heaven, where they have the power to intercede at the hour of death for their believers, then that constellation of representations—maternity, virginity, anti-body, eternal life—is of central importance in the understanding of the belief system. For Protestantism to effectively remove the mystique and power of a clergy who had set themselves up

---

religious realm, would see purgatory as a last vestige of a feudal world-view that had to be eliminated before Protestantism and industrialization could triumph: Daniel P. Watkins, 'Thomas Lovell Beddoes's *The Brides' Tragedy* and the Situation of Romantic Drama', *Studies in English Literature*, 29 (1989), 699–714 (p. 700).

14   Daniell, p. 198.

as celibate servants to such a powerful virgin mother, that representation had to be not simply dethroned but actually demonized for the process of secularization to continue to make the sort of progress that it needed to make. Besides removing statues and windows of Mary and the infant Jesus from churches, literature—like ballads, popular dramas, fairy tales, and gothic works—assisted in blasting that representation of its sacred associations. The defeat and desecration of the mother became vital steps in moving the population away from the earlier deification of such a woman and child.

It is worth remembering that, even at this late date, the mid-nineteenth century, the Roman Catholic Church understood what was at stake in the assault on the Virgin. After centuries of silence on her status, in 1854 Pope Pius IX declared the Virgin Mary to have been the only woman born without original sin, as the result of an 'immaculate conception'. Effectively elevating Mary to the status of a goddess, Pius IX knew that the Church's investment in Mary was crucial to holding its popular, lower-class base, and he was proved correct only four years later when the Virgin appeared at Lourdes to introduce herself to an illiterate peasant girl as 'the Immaculate Conception'.[15] As I have argued elsewhere, the gothic/Romantic aesthetic is a distinctly masculinist enterprise, Protestant, secularizing, capitalistic, and nationalistic. This new ideology is concerned with removing all traces of an earlier Catholic, feudal, communal, and ultimately matriarchal system in order to replace it with the liberal, sincere, secular humanist in full possession of a mind that combined the best of both sexes, although clearly this new androgynous psyche contained the feminine only as a colonized and subordinate category.[16]

III

Without an element of cruelty at the root of every spectacle, the theater is not possible. In our present state of degeneration it is through the skin that metaphysics must be made to re-enter our minds.
Antonin Artaud, The Theater and Its Double[17]

---

15   See Marina Warner, *Alone of All Her Sex: The Myth and Cult of the Virgin Mary* (London: Weidenfeld and Nicolson, 1976), ch. 16, for an historical overview of the history of the Virgin Mary's construction, as well as for a detailed discussion of the historical evolution of the notion of the 'Immaculate Conception'.

16   I have argued that the Romantic movement is, among many other things, a manifestation of what Paul de Man has called *dédoublement*, a self-duplicating system in which the canonical Romantic poets 'came face to face with the limitations of language, images, tropes, symbols, and all literary devices. They sought to use the imagination's capacity to transcend ontology, or 'being-ness', but they found themselves reduced to ironic postures, or non-being-ness': see my *Romantic Androgyny* (University Park: Pennsylvania State University Press, 1990), p. 22. This generalization holds true for TLB as well.

17   Artaud, p. 99.

Beddoes was keenly interested in the ballad form and used songs and snatches of ballads throughout his works; in fact, his revision of *Death's Jest-Book* consisted of adding nine new lyrics for the first act. As he wrote to Kelsall, 'songwriting . . . is almost the only kind of poetry of which I have attained a decided and clear critical Theory' (p. 649). *The Brides' Tragedy* is itself partially based on a ballad by Thomas Gillet that Beddoes read eighteen months before writing his first complete drama. More interesting than the specific Gillet ballad, however, is the larger ballad-cycle to which it belongs, beginning with the ironic, dark tone as well as the fetishization of the dead in the traditional ballad 'The Unquiet Grave':

> 'Tis I, my love, sits on your grave,
> And will not let you sleep;
> For I crave one kiss of your clay-cold lips,
> And that is all I seek.

> 'O lily lily are my lips;
> My breath comes earthy strong;
> If you have one kiss of my clay-cold lips,
> Your time will not be long.'[18]

Atkinson refers to 'The Unquiet Grave' as an example of a 'wit-combat' ballad in which woman's wit is tried in contest with various male figures in a ballad that joins sex and death. And surely the struggle between the living and dead that occurs in this ballad recalls the central situation in *The Brides' Tragedy*, as well as Floribel's doomed attempts to plead for her life before her murderous husband Hesperus kills her. The similarities between the Hesperus/Floribel relationship and those in the Grismond ballad-sequence are blatant.

The ballad 'The Downfall of William Grismond' recounts the tale of a young man who murders a neighbour's daughter in March 1650 in Hereforshire. The ballad is sung in the voice of William, who confesses that he promised marriage in order to have sex with the poverty-stricken, young woman. When she tells him later that she is pregnant and that he must fulfil his promises to her, he muses that he would rather marry 'another with Gold and Silver store'. He lures her to field, has sex yet again with her, and stabs her with a knife. After her body's discovery and his own attempt at escape, he eventually faces the gallows for his crime. Very similar in theme is the Scottish ballad 'William Guiseman',[19] as well as 'The Oxfordshire Tragedy; or, The Virgin's Advice or Rosanna's Overthrow', printed several times as a broadside ballad in England and Scotland during the eighteenth and nineteenth

---

18   'The Unquiet Grave' is quoted in Robert Graves, *The English Ballad: A Short Critical Survey* (London: Benn, 1927), p. 96; for a useful, contemporary discussion of this particular ballad tradition, see David. Atkinson, *The English Traditional Ballad: Theory, Method, and Practice* (Aldershot: Ashgate, 2002), p. 68.

19   Atkinson, pp. 186–88.

centuries,[20] and the version that we know Beddoes was to read before he wrote *The Brides' Tragedy*.[21]

In addition to *The Brides' Tragedy*, however, Beddoes also penned 'The Ghosts' Moonshine', a ballad that depicts another young man luring a woman out into a graveyard in order to murder her:

> *What dost thou strain above her*
>   *Lovely throat's whiteness?*
> *A silken chain, to cover*
>   *Her bosom's brightness?*
> *Tremble and weep not: what dost thou fear?*
>   *—My blood is spilt like wine*
> *Thou hast strangled and slain me, lover,*
>   *Thou hast stabbed me dear,*
> *In the ghosts' moonshine' (ll. 27–35)*

Both examples conform to what Anne B. Cohen has identified as the 'murdered girl' and 'criminal-brought-to-justice' formula-ballad:

> *The events of the murdered-girl formula are the following: wooing of trustful girl by artful man; luring of girl to lonely spot; murder of girl, who offers little resistance; abandonment of girl's body. Occasionally a fifth element—regret—is added, in which the murderer is sorry for his deed. The elements of the criminal-brought-to-justice formula are the following: youth, upbringing, or past deeds of criminal; crucial crime and events leading to it; pursuit, capture, and trial; execution.*[22]

Ballads stand as one of the earliest works of the oral literary tradition, and certainly in their original forms—sung poems on the topics of domestic violence as well as epic, dynastic themes—they precede Christianity. A dominant theme in the earliest ballads was the conflict of filial duty with ties of friendship, and certainly we see this theme in *Torrismond* (1824), a dramatic fragment about conflict between a father and son, *The Brides' Tragedy*, and later *Death's Jest-Book*, with the fratricide of

---

20   Atkinson, p. 195.

21   See H. W. Donner, *The Making of a Poet*, p. 84.

22   Anne B. Cohen, *Poor Pearl, Poor Girl! The Murdered Girl Stereotype in Ballad and Newspaper* (Austin: University of Texas Press, 1973), pp. 102–03. A twentieth-century Spanish adaptation of the ballad can be found in *Bodas de Sangre* (*Blood Wedding*), by Federico Garcia Lorca. Its refrain bears certain similarities to the tone of TLB's work: 'His hooves are hurt. / His mane is frozen. / And in his eye / A dagger of silver. / Down by the river, / Down by the river, / Blood is pouring / Stronger than water'. Federico Garcia Lorca, *Blood Wedding*, trans. Ted Hughes (London: Faber and Faber, 1996), p. 15.

Adalmar. Earlier, in Beddoes's dramatic fragment *The Second Brother* (1824–25), the brothers Orazio and Marcello stand as emblems of two different approaches to life, continually contending with each other until both sink into death. As Marcello, in the guise of a pauper, says to Orazio:

> *Let us shake hands; I tell thee, brother skeleton,*
> *We're but a pair of puddings for the dinner*
> *Of Lady worm; you served in silks and gems,*
> *I garnished with plain rags (I, i, 137–40)*

One can also see direct connections between such ballads as *The Cruel Brother* or *The Two Brothers*, and Coleridge's *Remorse*, or Beddoes's *Death's Jest-Book* with its two pairs of feuding brothers.

Another dominant ballad theme is the tragedy brought about by the false mistress, the false wife, or the false servant. Lewis's 'The Water King: A Danish Ballad' in *The Monk* tells the story of a water-fiend who, assisted by his all-powerful witch mother, leads a young woman out of the church and to her death in 'yellow sand'. In his ballad 'Alonzo the Brave and Fair Imogine', the bride is taken from her wedding feast by a mysterious stranger, who lifts his visor to reveal a skeleton's head: 'The worms, They crept in, and the worms, They crept out, / And sported his eyes and his temples about'. This ballad, a version of the demon lover tale used as well in *The Monk* in the Raymond/Agnes/Bleeding nun episode and reversed in Lewis's poem 'The Dying Bride', neatly connects the fear of dead rotting bodies suddenly emerging on the surface of the earth with blasted brides, in this case Imogine, who is forced four times a year (note the ancient reference to seasonal fertility) to dance with her Skeleton-Knight as they drink blood 'out of skulls newly torn from the grave'.[23] All of these motifs, of course, appear in Beddoes and in reversed fashion, for instance, with Hesperus killing Floribel in *The Brides' Tragedy* or Melveric, the false father-figure, betraying and murdering the son figure Wolfram in *Death's Jest-Book*.

The second large category of ballads—epics—concerns family and clan complications, one of which was the practice of bride-stealing. The ballad *Fair Annie* sings of the theft of fair Annie, who bears seven sons for her knight but then is replaced by her sister when he decides that he wants a legal bride. Along with 'Child Maurice', upon which Home based his drama *Douglas* and Scott based his *Douglas Tragedy*, the epic ballad relied heavily on the recognition plot, as well as the flight, pursuit, and fight to the death to save the bride, all of which are again reversed in Beddoes's play.

Finally, the funeral ballad with its supernatural or ghostly themes is pertinent to an examination of the thanatopic impulse in Beddoes. 'Sir Patrick Spens', 'Sweet William's Ghost', and 'The Wife of Usher's Well' are the most famous examples of this genre, but in addition to the understated, dignified, and pathetic tone of these

---

23   See Matthew Lewis, 'The Dying Bride', in *Romantic Tales*, 4 vols (London: Longman, 1808), II, 117–20; and *The Monk* (1796; London: Oxford University Press, 1992).

works, the theme of physical transformation can also be found most noticeably in yet another group of these funeral ballads about lost sailors who have commerce with mermaids or seals, or silkies in the sea ('Kemp Owyne', 'Allison Gross', and 'The Laily Worm' are all early examples of such ballads, while many of Anne Bannerman's gothic ballads are adaptations of these earlier works). Beddoes blatantly plays on these funereal ballad tropes in the dirge for Wolfram in *Death's Jest-Book* (II, ii, 1–18), considered by Frye and others to be the most beautiful poetry he ever wrote, while transformations of the dead who refuse to stay below ground recur throughout his works.

IV

> *Such ghosts as Marloe, Webster &c are better dramatists, better poets,*
> *I dare say, than any contemporary of ours—but they are ghosts—the*
> *worm is in their pages—& we want to see something that our great-*
> *grandsires did not know.*
>
> Beddoes to Kelsall, January 1825

Popular and folk ballads are generally believed to have provided the content as well as stylistic devices for the earliest European romances; for instance, 'King Orpheo', 'Sir Hugh', 'Hind Horn', 'Sir Cawline', and 'King Estmere' are all very close to the earliest Arthurian romances, as well as to *Tristan and Isolde*. It was but a short step from these romances to Elizabethan and Jacobean dramas, or the drama of blood as it has frequently been called, which in its own turn played out and exploited the ballad themes of revenge, incest, familial rivalry, kin and clan conflicts, and ghostly transformations and reappearances in order to tap into its audience's recognition of ballad tropes and expectations. In many ways, *Hamlet* is the embodiment of the ballad mentality brought to the stage. Beddoes, of course, self-consciously styled himself as a late Elizabethan or Jacobean, and certainly it has been traditional to see the influence of Webster and Cyril Tourneur, Beaumont, and Fletcher, as well as Shakespeare and Marlowe, on his two major dramas. William Congreve's *Mourning Bride* (1697) also comes to mind as a possible source, with its sixteenth-century Spanish setting and its heavy emphasis on prisons and tombs as the sites of most of the action. In this tragedy Manuel, king of Granada and a vicious and jealous father, is decapitated by his mistress by mistake, after he disguises himself as his enemy Alphonso in order to find out if his daughter has secretly married Alphonso (hints of incest and familial dysfunction permeate the play). The Moorish Queen Zara discovers his headless corpse in a cell and, believing mistakenly that the body is that of her lover's, promptly poisons herself. We have in this work a merging of the stolen bride motif along with the revenge gone wrong ballad, and other Jacobean dramas certainly play on the same themes that are then reworked and almost toyed with by Beddoes. In this vein it is interesting to recall the observation made by George Steiner, that drama is a central component of the romantic aesthetic, a 'dramatization' of their dialectical experiences:

In fact, romanticism began as a critique of the failure of the eighteenth century to carry on the great traditions of the Elizabethan and baroque theatre. It was in the name of drama that the romantics assailed neoclassicism. Not only did they see in the dramatic the supreme literary form, they were convinced that the absence of serious drama arose from some specific failure of understanding or some particular material contingency.[24]

For Beddoes, I would argue, that material contingency was an understanding and appreciation of the secularizing effects of science on what had been a primarily religious understanding of the world. If human life and reproduction can be dissected and reduced to chemical properties, then there can be no place in the modern world for the mystifications of religion: the divine mother cradling her immortal son in her arms. Beddoes's dramas are curiously dialectical in that they both mourn and at the same time mock the passing of such a world-view.

Dramas such as Beaumont and Fletcher's *The Maid's Tragedy*, John Marston's *The Malcontent*, or Tourneur's *The Atheist's Tragedy*, as well as *The Revenger's Tragedy*, along with John Webster's *The Duchesse of Malfi* (with its yew tree, which is clearly echoed in the tree under which Hesperus buries Floribel in *Brides' Tragedy*), as well as *The White Devil*, all reveal the mark of their origins in ballad motifs, particularly those dealing with the need for kin to avenge the father's murder in order to put his wandering soul to rest with his body. Ford's *'Tis Pity She's a Whore* is also worth mentioning as a possible source for *The Brides' Tragedy*, with its almost pathological suspicion about Floribel's supposed flirtation with a ten-year-old messenger boy employed by Orlando, Hesperus's rival. But in the wandering ghost theme we can see, I think, religious anxiety about the existence of an afterlife and the role that powerful men can play in ensuring that afterlife for their male forbears. Note that when women play a role in the ballads or Jacobean dramas, they are not virginal mothers with sacramental power to redeem a civilization. They are instead stolen brides, pawns, weak vessels in need of rescue by dominant and powerful men. The first step in desacralizing the Virgin Mary occurred when hymns to Mary were transformed into chivalric odes addressed to the singer-knight's out-of-reach queen, but the second step occurred when ballad materials were secularized into romances and, eventually, dramas and novels about women in jeopardy.

It is also necessary to recognize the overlooked link between Jacobean dramas and the German folk tradition, the *Märchen* or fairy tales and their influence on Beddoes. One of the most famous sources for much German fantasy writing was Schiller's *The Ghost-Seer* (1788; first English translation 1795), a fragmentary prose romance in which a mysterious, handsome stranger turns out to be an associate of the Holy Inquisition, a conspiratorial secret society engaged in trying to force important people to convert to the cause of Roman Catholicism. Set in Venice and written in fragmented letter and journal entries between two noblemen, *The*

---

24   George Steiner, *The Death of Tragedy* (New York: Hill and Wang, 1961), p. 108.

Ghost-Seer recounts the attempted conversion of an unnamed Protestant Prince to Catholicism. Part a seduction narrative and part hocus-pocus, the mysterious stranger (disguised as an Armenian with supposedly supernatural powers) uses all his wiles to persuade the Prince to join the 'cabal', which also includes a beautiful young woman with whom the Prince falls in love. Once converted, the Prince attempts to murder a man who stands in his way of gaining the throne, fails, and then is poisoned himself by the Armenian. In this blatantly anti-Catholic novel, the Prince dies 'in the bitterest agonies of contrition and remorse'.[25] Schiller's themes of betrayal, homosocial political maneuvering, secret cabals, and underground meetings can all be heard as echoes in Beddoes's two dramas, while clearly his anti-Catholic sentiments would become more and more blatant throughout his life.

In addition to Schiller, a figure like Ludwig Tieck is particularly important for Beddoes, who spent most of his adult life in Germany, knew and admired Tieck, and at one point thought he was forgetting his native language in favour of German. Tieck's tale 'The Blond Eckbert' (1797) presents the very strange history of the knight Eckbert, a ghost who actually haunts himself in the form of both his own wife and a visitor to the house where he currently appears to live. But Eckbert, we learn during the course of the story, married his sister only to watch her die of guilt. It may be faint, but strains of Beddoes's fragment 'Doubt' can be detected in his hero's similarities to Eckbert:

> Once I saw
> One who had dug for treasure in a corner,
> Where he by torchlight saw a trembling man
> burying a chest at night. Just so he stood
> With open striving lips and shaking hair;
> Alive but in his eyes, and they were fixed
> On a smeared, earthy, bleeding corpse—his sister,
> There by her murderer crushed into the earth' (ll. 5–12)

Another Tieck tale, 'The Runenberg', concerns a hunter who pulls a root from the earth and suddenly is aware of 'a horrid universe of putrefaction' just below the surface. Like some obsessed Swedenborgian, he is sickened by the existence of this other world below us, but he is nevertheless forced to return to it again and again. The hunter appears to be in thrall to the world of Nature as a destructive organism because he is seduced by a mysterious, shape-shifting Wood-woman, who lures him below ground through an old mine shaft. Never able to forget this hidden world just below ground, the hunter goes mad and finally disappears altogether with the Wood-woman. Like E.T.A. Hoffmann's hero Ellis Froeböhm, in 'The Mines of Falun', who dies wrapped in an underground root that bears an uncanny

---

25 Schiller, *The Ghost Seer or, Apparitionist: an interesting fragment, found among the papers of Count O******. From the German of Schiller (New-York: Printed by T. and J. Swords, 1796), p. 242.

resemblance to an umbilical cord, the German Romantic tradition displayed a ballad, blood, and folk loathing of fertility and women; or rather, perhaps it is more accurate to say that the fairy and folk tales advise their audiences of the uncanny and slippery slope between the world of the spirit (troped as male) and the world of the body (female). The recognition of such a gulf, horrific and purgatorial, leads directly to the sensibilities of Beddoes, whose works present the walking dead as inhabitants of an almost postmodern parody of purgatory.

V

> I am now already so thoroughly penetrated with the conviction of the absurdity & unsatisfactory nature of human life that I search with avidity for every shadow of a proof or probability of an after-existence, both in the material & immaterial nature of man. Those people . . . are greatly to be envied who believe, honestly and from conviction, in the Xtian doctrines: but really in the New T. it is difficult to scrape together hints for a doctrine of immortality. Man appears to have found out this secret for himself, & it is certainly the best part of all religion and philosophy, the only truth worth demonstrating: an anxious question full of hope & fear & promise, for w^h Nature appears to have appointed one solution — Death.
>
> Beddoes to Kelsall, April 1827

If we are to credit his best biographer, H.W. Donner, Beddoes suffered all his life from what Donner calls a 'skeleton complex',[26] and never psychologically recovered from watching his physician-father perform dissections on animals as well as humans, even going so far as to force his five-year-old son to pull out egg sacks from fertile fish. Further, Donner suspects that the father encouraged Beddoes to play with animal bones and dissected cadavers. Certainly we can see hints at such a traumatic memory in his poem 'Dream of Dying':

> . . . then I was dead
> And in my grave beside my corpse I sat
> In vain attempting to return: meantime
> There came the untimely spectres of two babes,
> And played in my abandoned body's ruins (ll. 5–9)

repeated almost verbatim by Wolfram, dressed as a fool, speaking to Isbrand and the rebels at the conclusion of *Death's Jest-Book* (V, iv, 197–202). Although it is not currently fashionable to speculate about the state of an author's psyche or his literary characters as psychological manifestations of his own unresolved traumas,

---

26   *The Making of a Poet*, p. 48 and passim.

Beddoes's work is difficult to assess without taking such recourse. The fact that Beddoes mutilated himself so severely that he had to have his leg amputated, and that he finally committed suicide by drinking poison (much like Hesperus) suggests an unresolved loathing of his own flesh, a desperate attempt to be his own dissector in a futile move to root out something diseased from his own body. His dramas are confused and at points odd and difficult, while the sense of nausea that Beddoes feels toward the human is never very far out of sight. His *Death's Jest-Book* finally has nothing but sneers for 'The bloody, soul-possessed weed called man' (III, iii, 454).

But also consider that Beddoes occupied himself in 1844 with writing a series of anti-Jesuit poems that were published in the Swiss newspaper the *Republikaner*. Vehemently anti-Catholic, his last political crusade was to work for the abolition of the Jesuit order in Switzerland. And to be fair, the Jesuits were not exactly innocent victims of persecution during the early and mid-nineteenth century. Perhaps one of the most dangerously political of all Jesuits was the Abbé Augustin Barruel, whose works proffered to expose Masonic, Rosicrucian, and Illuminati activities in France, tracing 'the origins of the French Revolution from the Illuminati in Ingoldstadt to the Freemasons, philosophers, and Jacobins, and then to the mobs on the street'. His *Mémoires* (first translated into English in 1798) depicted secret societies as 'precipitators of the French Revolution based on an anti-monarchical and anti-ecclesiastical conspiracy'. One can also recall that *The Wandering Jew* (1844–45) by Eugene Sue (1804–57) contains a long attack on the Jesuits, comparing them to the Thuggee Society in the East. In one incident, the Indian thug says to the Jesuit Rodin: 'you [Jesuits] kill the soul, and we the body. Give me your hand, brother, for you are also hunters of men . . . And what are bodies deprived of soul, will, thought, but mere corpses? Come—Come, brother; the dead we make by the cord are not more icy and inanimate than those you make by your discipline. Take my hand, brother, Rome and Bowanee are sisters.'[27]

Why would Beddoes choose the Jesuits, however, as his last target? I would suggest that his venom toward the religious order was simply a convenient scapegoat for his frustration at the death of God in his own lifetime.[28] Attacking the Jesuits, supposedly a politically reactionary force in European society, became a screen, a mask that concealed his long-standing anger at the decline of religious faith or tropes to provide him with the sort of final eschatological answers he demanded from life. And also there is the unacknowledged attraction to the Jesuits

---

27 Marie Mulvey Roberts, *Gothic Immortals: The Fiction of the Brotherhood of the Rosy Cross* (London: Routledge, 1990), p. 60; Eugene Sue, *The Wandering Jew* (New York: Burt, 1900), p. 370.

28 Michael Bradshaw has published the best full-length study of the relation between the body and existential anxiety in TLB's poetry as it explores 'the infinitesimal borderline between dead meat and living flesh' (p. viii). Seeing the issue of immortality as 'a secularized obsession' in TLB's poems (p. 16), Bradshaw eschews psychological readings of the problem and the poet in favour of historical, theological, medical, and political approaches. See his *Resurrection Songs: The Poetry of Thomas Lovell Beddoes* (Aldershot and Burlington: Ashgate, 2001).

as a secret and closed society, an all-male bonding unit, a group of men living together in legitimate isolation from all women except, of course, an oxymoronic virgin mother. Beddoes, however, ultimately worked in a secret society of one. Alone, isolated, and increasingly desperate, he compulsively wrote himself into and out of *Death's Jest-Book* until he was truly at the end of his tether by the time of his suicide in 1849. A drama that figures his anger, grief, melancholy, and mourning, it reads like a long scream of anguish and, finally, impotence. The ideological work of his plays was confused, I think, because his existential dread—manifested in a barely contained hysterical anger toward women, the body, and Catholicism—could never separate itself from his own self-hatred.

To be fair, there are critics who would differ, and for evidence point to Duke Melveric's celebration of his dead wife's body as the only avenue through which he knew and loved her:

> she was a woman,
> Whose spirit I knew only through those limbs,
> Those tender members thou dost dare despise;
> By whose exhaustless beauty, infinite love,
> Trackless expression only, did I learn
> That there was aught yet viewless and eternal;
> Since they could come from such alone. (III, iii, 227–33)

As Bradshaw notes about this speech, 'the human body is not being represented in Melveric's outburst as part of an internal-external dichotomy, but as the only means of human contact, the only comprehensible and reachable site of existence, and therefore the necessary locus of the most urgent investigation.'[29] But I would claim that this passage is the exception that in fact proves the rule in Beddoes. It is an example of 'protesting too much' and rings hollow or even shrill when placed alongside the preponderance of other passages that have nothing but contempt for the body. At times a dualist and at other times a monist, Beddoes is finally muddled as a gothic poet with theological interests.[30] Desiring immortality, escaping into a

---

29   *Resurrection Songs*, p. 139.
30   Frances Wilson notes that 'Beddoes oscillated between seeing the self as the affliction to be got rid of and writing as the impurity. Writing for Beddoes was a self-destructive and high-risk activity, staging a fight to the death between artist and art. This is why he chose to exile himself as soon as he had achieved poetic success—he turned to medicine to cure him of words and as protection from their powers'. Frances Wilson, '"Strange Sun": Melancholia in the Writings of Thomas Lovell Beddoes', in *Untrodden Regions of the Mind: Romanticism and Psychoanalysis*, ed. Ghislaine McDayter (Lewisburg: Bucknell University Press, 2002), pp. 127–42 (p. 128). Bradshaw argues that what TLB does in *DJ-B* 'is a de-theologized borrowing of the idea of resurrection—not an entirely secular version, but one wilfully torn from its inalienable doctrinal roots. Beddoes's frequent recourse to the concept of the immortal soul makes certain pagan Greek models interesting and valuable points of reference; but his combination of this

realm of bodiless mind and spirit, these impulses have haunted humanity, and they certainly haunted Beddoes's life and works. To celebrate the woman's body as the means of resurrection or redemption is as old a gesture as Genesis, while to blame the woman for not ushering in the Promised Land is equally as tired.

And so to return to those floating bodies in Parisian cemeteries, it is safe to say that the Parisian population wanted them buried once and for all. The old catacombs that the Romans had constructed close to two thousand years earlier were now used as convenient dumping grounds, and the dead were assembled parish by parish in artfully constructed cities of the dead. One can wander through these catacombs today, and to do so is to realize that they are all just directly below us, a foot fall away, living in a vast 'subterranean city of the dead', where the walls are inscribed with the words, 'Silence, mortal beings! Nothingness'. This macabre dance of death, this levelling of all of us by the material world, can also be understood as the defeat of the miraculous virgin and her divine child. When the Protestant imagination triumphed over Catholicism in England and Germany, it ensured that there no longer would be any virgin mother, no longer a powerful eschatological figure who would intercede for you with her son or who had the power to save you herself. The works of Beddoes perform this dialectical and ideological function: they both demonize the mother-bride, fertility, and the promise of new life, while at the same time they nostalgically mourn the demise of such a system of belief.

---

with Biblical and Talmudic bodily resurrection is not identifiably Judaeo-Christian, and creates a fraught doctrinal problematic all of its own'. Bradshaw, *Resurrection Songs*, pp. 36–37.

T.L. Beddoes's Terminable or Interminable End

Christopher Moylan

Thomas Lovell Beddoes wrote from his self-imposed exile in the German states that he hoped his gargantuan play *Death's Jest-Book* would 'come with its strangeness — it contains nothing else — like an electric shock among the small critics' (*Works*, p. 617). Despite the endorsement of a few larger critics — namely, Northrop Frye (1968), Harold Bloom (1962), and Christopher Ricks (1987) — the play has had few readers of any sort to shock. This is partly Beddoes's own doing. He is, as his own words suggest, the author of his own exclusion from the literary mainstream. Beddoes's resistance to reception is, in my view, a work that compels attention, a project of strength and complexity, not least in those places where it is most forbidding: his suicide, and, in the plays and other writings, his persistent investigations of subjects that are often disquieting, if not shocking. Yet, just how he inscribed his life and work with the obscurity of the little known, little read, and little understood, has not been examined carefully even by his defenders.

I would like to make a start at the subject of his obscurity by discussing Beddoes at his queasiest. I will briefly examine the suicide note, and devote the remainder of the paper to analyzing paradoxical aspects of death and the afterlife in his work. My analysis, although largely confined to close reading of the text, will involve a brief discussion of philosophical ideas concerning death and identity so far as they pertain to issues raised in the text. The essay will also involve a foray into Lacanian analysis, since Beddoes's concerns around death and identity, so closely bound with issues of language and meaning, call for such an analysis.

My thoughts in the area of death and identity in the *Jest-Book* and other writings were provoked by the poet John Ashbery's criticism that Beddoes has nothing of substance to say about death, and that his interest in the subject compelled decorative fragments and beautifully crafted lyric poems from him, but no insight or philosophy of substance. Ashbery, an otherwise sympathetic reader of Beddoes, puts the case against succinctly in his book *Other Traditions*: 'Somewhere, somehow, Beddoes in all his work is trying to make a point about death', Ashbery writes, 'but he never succeeds in doing so'.[1] Moreover, the failure to 'make a point' about death raises psychological questions — why the interest in death? why the failure to come to terms with this interest? — that the text fails to resolve. 'In truth', according to Ashbery, 'there is no rhyme or reason in Beddoes's death-haunted universe; one

---

1   John Ashbery, *Other Traditions: The Charles Eliot Norton Lectures* (Cambridge, Mass.: Harvard University Press, 2000), p. 41.

can end up feeling that he just likes to talk about death, that the sound of the word is comforting and that further comfort is beside the point'.[2]

This argument is persuasive in that it supplies an intention to the work—making a point about death—and a criterion for judging success or failure on terms Beddoes himself appears to have chosen. However, do the many references to death in his work necessarily mean that it was in fact Beddoes's intention to make a point about death, and do we have enough of his work to assess his intentions? The second question refers to the loss and deliberate destruction of a considerable portion of Beddoes's work after his death. References Beddoes made to now-missing texts suggest that he undertook projects on politics, social theory, theory of drama, and so forth, that may have provided some balance to his oeuvre, and to reception of it.[3]

In any event, we must work with what remains. Elsewhere, I have argued that the *Jest-book* and other writings are structured around coded allusions to alchemy, Judaic magical lore, psychology, and pneumatic medicine, among other things.[4] The hermetic symbols and colour references in the play, no doubt only partially identified at this point, suggest that Beddoes is often saying many things at once. The depictions of burial and entombment in the *Jest-book*, for example, involve symbolism of alchemical transformation, and all this entails themes of spiritual and psychological growth. In short, one cannot take for granted that when Beddoes uses an image of death he is referring merely, or at all, to death.

Nonetheless, Beddoes does at times consider death as such. In his early work, death is represented as seductively promising a resolution or cancelling out of inner tensions and conflicts:

> *And man, in whom are met*
> *Leopard and snake, and all the gentleness*
> *And beauty of the young lamb and the bud,*
> *Has let his ghost out, put his thoughts aside*
> *And lent his senses unto death himself.*[5]

Such lines, however, are delivered by characters depicted as insane (Hesperus in *The Brides' Tragedy*, for example), or duplicitous (the resurrected Wolfram in the *Jest-Book*), or otherwise unreliable (Mandrake and other fools in the in *Jest-Book*). The melting sensuality of the internal rhyme is masterful—one can well understand

---

2   Ibid., p. 41.
3   See *Works*, p. 711, and Donner, *The Making of a Poet*, p. 350.
4   See my *T.L. Beddoes and the Hermetic Tradition* (Belper: Thomas Lovell Beddoes Society, 1999); '"For Luz is a Good Joke": T.L. Beddoes and Judaism', in *English Romanticism and the Jews*, ed. Sheila Spector (New York: Palgrave, 2002), pp. 93–103; and 'In the Air: T.L. Beddoes and Pneumatic Medicine', *Studia Neophilologica*, 73 (2001), 48–54.
5   *The Poems of Thomas Lovell Beddoes*, ed. Ramsay Colles (London: Routledge, 1914), 306.

why Dylan Thomas admired Beddoes so;[6] but more often than not the text signals us, however ambivalently, not to listen, not to be entranced. Thus, as the resurrected Wolfram is about to approach Sibylla to woo her to an early death, he cries out 'My soul, my soul! O that it wore not now / The semblance of a garb it hath cast off' (IV, ii, 94–95). In other words, would that Sibylla could see through me—not as a ghost, but as an ambivalent and insecure lover, a man who wishes his beloved might have the better man of his past, if such a man ever existed. Beddoes here is making a point about the complexity and inconsistency of desire, not merely about death or its seduction.

When Beddoes was faced with his own death, his tone was as conflicted as that of his other writings. Within the space of several brief paragraphs in his suicide note he is by turns grim, solicitous, self-effacing, teasing, and bitterly humorous. He opens with a Shakespearian flourish—'I am food for *what I am good for*—worms'—and closes with a fond farewell to his friend Revell Phillips—'You are a good & noble man'. In the middle he bequeaths to his nephew William 'a *case* (50 bottles) of Champagne *Moet 1847* growth' to, as he puts it, 'drink my health in' (p. 683). A postscript with more farewells and instructions ends with a parting dig at his physician: 'Buy for Dr. Ecklin Reade's best stomach pump' (Beddoes poisoned himself). The cumulative impression of these shifts in tone and content is a blur, a brusque impatience of affect that partially effaces affect. This at times mischievous inconsistency—I am food for what I am good for, drink to my health—reclaims the text from the encroachment of deathbed eloquence or intimacy. Even the question of preserving his literary legacy is raised with ironic casualness, and dropped in the hands of a friend Beddoes has seen no more than half a dozen times in twenty years. Beddoes inscribes his final moments with half-formed gestures and partial erasures, a field of emotional deflections and erasures, through which he withdraws.

A similarly restless, paradoxical sense of identity emerges in Beddoes's personal writing when he considers the question of the afterlife. In a letter written during his medical training at the University of Göttingen, Beddoes describes his frustrated search for evidence of immortality. The passage is unusual for him in its personal candour, and in the length at which Beddoes discusses issues that dominate his dramatic writings and poetry. It provides a good illustration of his paradoxical approach to the self in relation to death and the afterlife. He writes:

> I am now already so thoroughly penetrated with the conviction of the
> absurdity & unsatisfactory nature of human life that I search with
> avidity for every shadow of a proof or probability of an after-existence,
> both in the material & immaterial nature of man. Those people, perhaps
> they are few, are greatly to be envied who believe, honestly and from

6   See Dylan Thomas, *The Collected Letters*, ed. Paul Ferris (London: Dent, 1985), p. 297, where Thomas lists TLB among his early influences, and p. 116, where he refers to 'my great Beddoes'. I also recall that somewhere Thomas cites TLB in response to an interview question concerning influences on his writing.

> *conviction, in the Xtian doctrines: but really in the New T. it is difficult*
> *to scrape together hints for a doctrine of immortality. Man appears to*
> *have found this secret for himself, & it is certainly the best part of*
> *all religion and philosophy, the only truth worth demonstrating: an*
> *anxious question full of hope & fear & promise, for w^h Nature appears*
> *to have appointed one solution—Death. (pp. 629–30)*

Here, as often in Beddoes's work, identity establishes itself through a process of negation. In figurative development of the passage, Beddoes presents himself as priest offering sacrifice to an emptiness, which is haunted by the absence of certainty. Like a lover, he is 'penetrated with the conviction' of life's absurdity and, as he writes later, 'haunted forever' by the 'dreadful importance' of doubt, one verb suggesting mock ecstasy and the other a mock Pentecost. The non-credo of the first sentence (life as absurd) and the non-transfiguration of the second (no 'proof' of an afterlife could be 'scraped' from the New Testament, the verb suggesting searching for a tissue sample), lead to a non-resurrection in the third (death).

Here, as in the suicide note, rhetorical and emotional shifts are the operative signifiers. Avidity in the search for a key to renewing life follows despair at the absurdity of Beddoes's current existence, even as an eschatological mediation of warring hope and despair—'greatly to be envied'—is dismissed out of hand. A pulse of alternating qualifiers and rhetorical emphases—perhaps, but really, appears, it is certainly—prefigures the climactic symmetry of 'the only truth worth demonstrating: an anxious question'. His 'avidity' is such that even disillusionment produces tropes of haunted eternity and dreadful importance. In the end, the wish that gives rise to the 'anxious question full of hope & fear & promise' is met with one 'solution'—not an answer, but a working out: life plus the negation of life equals death. In other words, death is death.

Death is the 'solution' in that it turns the 'anxious question' back on itself. That is, the tautological circle 'death is death' is not necessarily a semantic and emotional trap, as Beddoes appears to experience it in the midst of his search. The death of the self, as opposed to the fact of biological extinction, is nothing, a non-experience, a category without content. 'Death is indeed a void', writes the philosopher John Carse, 'but a total void—it is an emptiness so complete that it can show nothing of itself; instead it reflects back all that surrounds it in perfect detail'.[7] Death—our death—is a gap, a blank in which we lose and regain ourselves. It is the end of experience and subjectivity, and for this reason many writers have argued that it—"my death'—is not imaginable. Even those who have argued otherwise, Paul Edwards most notably,[8] have argued for a category or idea no more meaningful than 'my birth' or 'my invisibility'—tropes that Beddoes often employs, as I will

---

7   John Carse, 'The Philosophical Status of Death as a Fact', in *Philosophical Aspects of Thanatology*, ed. Florence H. Hetzler and Austin H. Kurtscher, vol. I (New York: Arno Press, 1978), p. 38

8   See Paul Edwards, 'Existentialism and Death', in *Language, Metaphysics and Death*, ed. John Donnelly (New York: Fordham University Press, 1994), pp. 43–79.

discuss below. Like invisibility, death shows through to what is there in the first place. To put it simply, the dead me, as opposed to whatever might return after death (a soul, a resurrected body, etc.) is the living me seen in different terms, terms that ordinary experience will not permit, for one reason or another. Thus, death is the self as mercurial and uncontainable remainder, as that which is turned out of, or spilled from its figurative representation.

Conversely, the person beyond death, and the environment it inhabits, can only be conceived now in terms of the living—as a projection of our experience in this life, this world. 'For references to the next world cannot be intelligible', writes Terence Penelhum, 'unless it is possible to use the language of our own world of things and persons to describe it'.[9] The afterlife, in other words, is reflexive, as is the blank face of death. Without contradicting religious belief, one can ask what emotional or psychological purpose is served by an afterlife. 'Or is some riddle solved by my surviving forever?' as Wittgenstein: puts it, 'Is not this eternal life itself as much a riddle as our present life?'[10]

Beddoes, unable to find the material evidence he requires for life after death, is left with the 'avidity' of a blind search, a search that finds no doctrine of afterlife in the New Testament, no lover or cause to provide an answer to the 'anxious question full of hope & fear & promise'. This avidity represents something other than a scholar's or a scientist's curiosity. That is, the avid questioning of death is associated with some unidentified, persistent desire and, so, with repression. Bruce Clarke, in *Allegories of Writing*, describes this as 'the dispossession of a given subjective relation and the displacement of its terms'.[11] In metamorphosis, the focus in his study, mind is separated from original body and projected to another form. Self and metamorphose suffer their individual fates, much as for Freud in repression affect and idea 'each undergoes its separate vicissitudes'.[12] This splitting of affect and idea has its creative and destructive sides; repression is not merely denial or loss; it is also a process of compensation and change.

In the *Jest-book*, the split of affect and idea takes the form of a repeated pattern of tragic love in which a woman withdraws or dematerializes at some point in a murderous love rivalry, leaving her suitors to join not her in a passionate death embrace, but each other. This embrace or meeting usually revises an earlier encounter, and with this pattern repeated in other couples there is an impression of sameness, of an endless, frustrated chasing of desire through different bodies in structurally similar encounters—thus analogous to metamorphosis. In the *Jest-book*, blood brothers or biological brothers clash over a love interest, the murdered brother eventually returning from the dead. Beddoes considered much the same pattern in dramatic fragments he wrote before the *Jest-Book*. In *The Second Brother*, Marcello in disguise embraces his brother Orazio and later, as the fragment breaks off,

---

9   Terence Penelhum, *Immortality* (New York: Wadsworth, 1973), p. 46.

10   Ludwig Wittgenstein, *Tractatus Logico-Philosophicus*, trans. Daniel Kolak (California: Mayfield Publishing, 1998), 48: 6, 4312.

11   Bruce Clarke, *Allegories of Writing: The Subject of Metamorphosis* (Albany: State University of Albany Press, 1995), p. 57.

12   Ibid., p. 57.

prepares to murder him. The love object, Valeria, is shown towards the conclusion of the fragment wandering in a trance-like state, convinced she is invisible to the crowd around her. The scene is an apt, if perhaps unintended, comment on women in Beddoes's work; they are so wan that whether they are opaque or translucent is incidental. Only men, in Beddoes's plays, matter, or have matter.

Yet, however strong and particular are the individual male characters—and certainly Isbrand and Melveric, among others, command their moments on the actual or closet stage—the relationships of man to man are so filtered and mediated that the eroticism is subsumed in great part by a process of occlusion. What we now reify as homosexuality is signified, in negative, as an absent consummation, or homo-eroticism effaced by the invocation of a woman and by the subject's physical death. Here, in a trope noted in various contexts by Irigaray, Sedgwick, and other feminist writers, 'women serve as the alibi and mediation of relations, economic as well as sexual, among men'.[13] The love triangle of Athulf, Adalmar, and Amala, with its blending of vowels and initials, reduces the woman to a vocal conductor between the two men, like a string vibrating between two mouthpieces. Similarly, Sibylla registers as a whisper between the merging liquids and hums of Wolfram and Melveric. In the context of this male consonance, fragile as it is, Homunculus Mandrake's role in the play is crucial: his antics centre the action of the play in an impossible *jouissance*. He queers the resurrection, in at least two senses of the word, twisting it in the direction of hilarity and bringing to light gender and sexuality identified as open and fluid categories.

It is perhaps because gender and sexuality are fluid and open that love relationships are so unstable in the *Jest-Book*. Sexuality is like death, in Beddoes's work, in that it holds out the false promise of consolidating identity. Part of the problem with sex, in this respect, is that Beddoes's characters misunderstand it, or fail to recognize its true object. The male-male encounter in the *Jest-Book* is simply a trope on failure to recognize one's pleasure, akin to the gay trope on homophobia as masking or repressing homosexual attraction. Men seek each other out for the wrong reasons, embrace for the wrong reasons, and kill for the wrong reasons. The details of how or why they are wrong—Wolfram and Melveric are pledged to each other, but really they have reasons before this to hate each other, and so forth—are too tedious to work out, and, I believe, deliberately so. Just how or why the reasons are wrong is less important, in the plays, than that they are wrong.

Thus, much as it is tempting to identify the thinly disguised homosexual encounters as offering the hermeneutic key to repression in the *Jest-book*, I believe this would oversimplify the disruptive quality of desire as such in the play. There are no 'right' unions in the play; attraction, it would appear, is perverse, in the sense of a turning away or misdirection, from the integrity and sufficiency of the self. When love or attraction enters, trouble comic or tragic ensues. A survey of the substitutions and reversals in *Death's Jest-Book*, for example, will give

13   Alice Yaegar Kaplan, *Reproductions of Banality: Fascism, Literature, and French Intellectual Life* (Minneapolis: University of Minneapolis Press, 1986), p. 26.

some indication of the mischief Beddoes makes with accidents and unfortunate coincidences involving desire and identity:

1.　　Melveric murdered the father of Wolfram and Isbrand in a love rivalry. His wife dies, one assumes of natural causes.

2.　　Melveric, trying to raise his wife from the tomb, calls forth by mistake his erstwhile best friend, Wolfram, whom he had stabbed to death in a love rivalry. He and Wolfram become inseparable after this accidental resurrection, eventually walking together into the tomb.

3.　　Athulf takes poison in despair over his unrequited love for Amala. Later, he is revived, only to stab to death his brother Adalmar (rival for Amala) and then himself.

4.　　Homunculus Mandrake, who may or may not be a person, is accidentally doused with a potion that may or may not make him invisible. Later, after an accident that knocks him unconscious, he is placed in the same tomb where Wolfram is buried. He emerges from the tomb as the unwanted third party in the reunion of Melveric and his Wolfram.

5.　　Blind Mario, the prophet of revolution, pledges his services to Isbrand, whom he stabs to death at the end of the play.

In short, it is not the form or object of desire that is wrong, but desire itself. Here, one can only read desire in its Freudian sense as a force or surge in the neural circuitry, a dynamic that precedes the discourse that would rationalize and control it. For men and men, women and men (women and women is a combination that does not occur in Beddoes's work), desire is so disturbing and destructive that it—that is, desire, and not the man or woman desired—is associated with otherness, monstrousness, and states outside of categorization or meaning. Thus the perplexity of Beddoes's work; the beckoning, and calling forth of desire or love turns inevitably to a calling forth from the grave or pit or charnel house, in short, from a profoundly alien otherness.

Homunculus is the key: visible-invisible, alive-dead, piebald and hermaphroditic, he represents a monstrous and uncategorizable otherness, an appearance from something beyond the symbolic order. 'Momus of hell', exclaims Ziba, the magus who resurrects him, 'what's this?' (III, iii, 583). But Ziba is also alive and dead, of this world and the other, as is every character, in varying degrees of explicitness. Perhaps there are only two characters in the play: the Fool and his shadowy other, and the two are simply following each other in and out of the tomb, into and away from desire. Women are merely instruments for exposing and bringing to light desire, desire that is in turn illusory to the extent that is centred on them.

The tomb, which gives a second birth to Homunculus and Wolfram and a second womb-like enclosure to Melveric, can be understood as the primal site of the strangeness or otherness that Homunculus and others temporarily embody. In Lacanian terms this otherness is identified as *das Ding*, the thing, 'a strange, traumatic element', as Slavoj Žižek puts it, 'which cannot be symbolized, [or] integrated into the symbolic order'.[14] It is 'the hard kernel' of the Real, 'that is both internal to our psyches and external to our subjectivities, a part of us of which we must remain unconscious and so unable to incorporate into our ego structures or manipulate as we can our own languages and narratives'.[15] *Das Ding* then is an appearance of something impossible yet quite possible, a thing emerging from a rupture in the signifying system, or discourse. It is a 'materialized emptiness', writes Žižek,[16] that is, nonetheless, in Lacan's phrase, 'in me more than me',[17] as an irreducible core of *jouissance* that is involved with experience of self even as it is resistant to conceptualization that might tame or reduce its horrific fascination. That which, initially, the mother desires in one remains outside the symbolic register, yet present, and liable to announce itself in relation to some paradox or knotted problem of signifying, of making meaning. As intermediary between living self and the Father (or Mother) awaiting reunion in paradise, the tomb lends itself to representing the fearful eruption of traumatic strangeness.

Beddoes's deployment of tomb imagery is intriguing in that it is so bound up with meaning, or the determination of the most fundamental coordinates of meaning; who is there, where is this place, what is this place . . . Thus, the tomb is such a pervasive presence in the *Jest-book* that one is never certain just when, or for that matter whether, characters emerge from it. As Northrop Frye demonstrated so persuasively in his essay on Beddoes, the characters in the play move in a 'Bardo world', ambiguously positioned between life and death, the tomb and the world beyond it.[18] The boat that takes Melveric and company *from* the island where Wolfram was murdered is named after Charon's ferry over the River Styx to the land of the dead.[19] Melveric and company may be alive or dead, or perhaps they were always in some state in between; Ziba was born of a dead mother, and Humunculus of an alchemist's crucible; Mario is an avatar of Roman Republican virtue, Sibylla a Proserpine-like wraith. And so it continues; there are no fixed points in the world of the *Jest-Book*, only the uncanny shimmer of indeterminacy over everyone and everything.

Das Ding is associated with what Lacanian theorists refer to as the 'second death', 'not the death of the so-called "real object" in its symbol, but the obliteration of the signifying network itself'.[20] The first death terminates biological life, the second terminates the relation of the self to the symbolic order. Last rites in Catholicism, for example, and deathbed settling of accounts accomplish this second death. In *Death's Jest-book*, the second death serves as both a severing of the symbolic order and as a corrective or redundant killing off of the physical person. Thus,

---

14   Slavoj Žižek, *The Sublime Object of Ideology* (New York: Verso, 1989), p. 132.
15   Thomas Foster, *The Souls of Cyberfolk: Posthumanism as Vernacular Theory* (Minnesota: University of Minnesota Press, 2005), p. 93.
16   *The Žižek Reader* (Malden: Blackwell Books, 1999), p. 43.
17   Žižek, *Sublime Object*, p. 180.
18   Northrop Frye, 'Yorick: The Romantic Macabre', in *A Study of English Romanticism* (New York: Random House, 1968), pp. 51–85 (p. 64).
19   The *Baris* is named in *DJ-B*, II, i, 46; commented on by Frye, 'Yorick', p. 63.
20   Žižek, *Sublime Object*, p. 132.

Melveric, who was entombed with his beloved Sibylla in the first act, is led into the tomb at the end of the play, as Sibylla has done more willingly earlier in the play. Athulf's second death, or murder after his failed attempt at suicide, resolves the hopelessness of his love for the wan Amala. Mandrake's exit to Egypt, land of the ancient cult of death, provides the natural conclusion to his cheerful satire of death earlier. Isbrand's crowning with a Fool's cap and bells after he is stabbed repeats the satirical message of Mandrake's end, only in a darker tone. These 'second deaths' intersect with the abortive, often redundant or repetitive, erotic meetings and couplings, rendering the structure of the play into a fractured mirror of stops and starts, deaths and rebirths without end. That is, the cycle of life and death is unresolved just as the process of identity formation is inevitably unresolved.

Mandrake, despite his brief interment in the tomb, represents problems of identity among the living. Wolfram, raised at the same time as Mandrake, represents the same among the dead. The New Dodo, the subject of the fool and would-be usurper Isbrand's ballad in Act III, represents a more cogent, if also more vicious, consideration of the problems of identity in and after death. Responding to the shocked reaction of a friend, Beddoes described the poem as 'almost necessary to the vitality' (p. 645) of the *Jest-Book*:

> Squats on a toadstool under a tree
>> A bodiless childful of life in the gloom,
> Crying with frog voice, 'What shall I be?
> Poor unborn ghost, for my mother killed me
>> Scarcely alive in her wicked womb. (III, iii, 321–25)

Early Christian theologians were perturbed by questions over the relation of soul to mortal body: would the elderly, say, resurrect as they were at death? Would someone born blind return as a person able to see? How would a drowning victim nibbled at by fish be reassembled if the fish were eaten by sharks? And so on. More recently, philosophers such as Anthony Flew, H.H. Price, Roderick Chisholm, and Paul Edwards have discussed the limitations of disembodied existence:[21] is it possible to conceive of a truly disembodied experience, that is, of experience disengaged from the senses? Would a disembodied soul deprived of information from the senses not be consigned to remembering previous experiences and, if so, could that memory state be considered an afterlife, or merely an endless rerun?[22]

---

21   See: Anthony Flew (ed.), *Body, Mind and Death* (New York: Macmillan, 1964); H.H. Price, 'Survival and the Idea of "Another world"', in Donnelly, pp. 278–302; Roderick Chisholm, 'The Recreation of the Psycho-Physical World', in Penelhum, *Immortality*, pp. 235–41; Edwards, 'Existentialism and Death'; see also Edwards's excellent bibliographical essay, pp. 31–17, for an overview of recent philosophical works on immortality.

22   See also Michael Bradshaw, *Resurrection Songs: The Poetry of Thomas Lovell Beddoes* (Aldershot and Burlington: Ashgate, 2001), for an important literary analysis of death in the works of TLB.

Moreover, what if the person never had a life to remember? The soul, one can infer, would exist in a pure state, transcending experience. This is something that Beddoes, student and devotee of the flesh in all its permutations, will not allow. His imagination returns insistently to the corporeal. So, here he cuts through the questions of what is conceivable, or what is possible in an immortal existence, to the question of desire; what do we want from an after existence? Beddoes's answer, given his play with various animal forms, is surprising but not inconsistent. No animal form, or identity, meets his desire; he or it decides instead to escape from the symbolic order into a place where something can be created from nothing, and nothing created from something. That is, the choice is not to choose, not to settle for an illusory form of closure. By rejecting various forms of mortality and immortality — disembodied afterlife, metempsychosis, resurrection — the self comes to 'life' in his work or, in Lacanian terms, comes into contact with the 'fantasmatic kernel of [its] being'.[23] Identity establishes itself not through affirmation, but through erasure and effacement.

Thus, after the nominal 'squats' and the temporally ambiguous 'crying with frog voice', the first particularizing verb is 'killed'. A series of optatives, conditionals, and sardonic imperatives follow as the fetus-ghost considers and rejects several choices in the animal kingdom to inhabit in the next life. At last it decides to become a grotesque combination of them all:

> I'll be a new bird with the head of an ass,
>> Two pigs' feet, two men's feet, and two of a hen;
> Devil-winged; dragon-bellied; grave-jawed, because grass
> Is a beard that's soon shaved, and grows again
>> Before it is summer; so cow all the rest;
>> The new Dodo is finished. O! come to my nest.
>>> (III, iii, 362–67)

'Finished' offers a reflexive and ambiguous answer to 'killed'. The new Dodo, like the fetus, is 'finished', as in done for; it is a stillborn species of one. To the extent that it has lived, it is through the mocking refusal of identity, in this case from an array of bird, beast and reptile. Yet the self does not die easily; it makes its ghostly, transfigured return in the double entendres of ass, pig, and egg-laying hen. These allude to the many fool characters in the *Jest-Book*, and, as I will explain in detail below, to that despised, ambiguously gendered creature, the author, busy hatching the egg of his creation. Moreover, these animal figures return the voice to itself in allusions to, among others, his own poems: 'A Crocodile' (*Last Man* fragment VI), 'The Oviparous Tailor' — this concerning a man who 'Crowed like a hen — but maler' (l. 31) and lays eggs under a witch's curse — and his scatological poem 'The New Cecilia', a satire of poets as hard-drinking, flatulent fools. In this light, 'The New Dodo' aptly represents Beddoes's literary self-negation, recapitulated not

---

23   *The Žižek Reader*, p. 96.

only in the terminal and interminable revisions of the text but also in the persistent resurrection of the totemic grotesques of the poet.

The post-mortem identity of the poet who is 'finished', lost and forgotten, is disembodied in the sense that its ties to the symbolic ordering or categorizing of the body—hetero-, homo-, or asexual, normal, or abnormal, and so forth—have been severed. Similarly, the poet's ties to commodity culture have been severed. Beddoes has no 'presence' in an ongoing cultural exchange. He no longer publishes and rarely visits England; in effect, he no longer exists professionally as a writer. To return to the image of author as egg-laying hen, he is, in his own view, an unsuccessful mother to his *magnum opus*. Over long years of revision he referred to the *Jest-Book* as 'stillborn' (p. 659); a grotesque fish' (p. 618), 'a new tragic abortion' (p. 594). The unwieldy narrative of the *Jest-Book*, so clumsy that at times it seems hardly a narrative at all, contributes to this dead, 'thing-like' strangeness. The plot, the characters, the Elizabethan-like diction, and the many genre references (Gothic, tragedy, comedy, satire, *danse macabre*, and so on) are eerily disassociated—Beddoes referred to the play as 'a strange conglomerate' (p. 676)—disassociated from each other and from a larger literary or social context that might ground them. The play, in turn, can be seen as a dismembered corpse, the remnant of a projected collection of stories and drama and drama criticism that Beddoes was unable to realize.

If *Death's Jest-Book* is an abortion or stillbirth, however, it is a prodigious one, recurring again and again over the course of twenty years of revision and perpetuating itself, ghostily, in the revisions and excisions of Jerome McGann's recent performance text.[24] Death is never complete in Beddoes, and disenchantment never conclusive; the aborted voice returns in the gloom. Beddoes gave himself the most un-Romantic of deaths, and subordinated his evident desire for notoriety, if not fame, to the pursuit of an impossible realization or, if you will, *jouissance*. Yet this drive to disenchantment perpetuates itself; the process of effacement casts its own spell.

---

24   See Epilogue.

Epilogue: *Death's Jest-Book* on Stage in 2003

Recollections by Jerome McGann and Frederick Burwick

The history of the adaptation of *Death's Jest-Book* for the stage: recollections and reflections on the occasion of the première at New York, August 2003

Adapting the Text[1]
Jerome J. McGann

Michael [Macovski] asked me to talk a bit about *Death's Jest-Book* and my involvement with it. I'm going to begin by saying something about why I have had anything to do with this play. That has to take me back to tell some little biographical information about myself.

I first read Beddoes and got involved with this play in about 1968. A few people at the University of Chicago, where I was at that time, and some people in the community at Chicago formed a company. Beddoes's play really illustrates what interested us a lot. We formed this company to put on what in a certain perspective were seen or thought of as unplayable plays. From another perspective they were great poems. What we wanted to do was to see if we could figure out some way to put these kinds of objects on stage and find theatrical equivalents to bring out their greatness as poetic events.

If some of you are anywhere near as old as I am, you will recall that in the mid-sixties there was a tremendous revival of interest in experimental theatre. The Living Theatre came through Chicago at that particular time, and I was sort of knocked off my feet by that particular event. Myself and a few friends began studying Artaud as well as Brecht, and we began thinking about theatre in completely non-realist theatre traditions. It seems to me that if you want to put on what are to me the most interesting Romantic dramas you have to absolutely jettison any commitment of involvement with realist conventions of representation. Tonight I think you saw in Fred's production a resolute effort to follow that kind of line. So in 1968 the company we put together was called Cain's Company because the first thing that we were going to do was Byron's *Cain*. I was resident adapter, and I set about ruthlessly cutting the play so that when we put it on it would only run for about

---

1   This account was delivered as a keynote address at the NASSR conference 'Placing Romanticism: Sites, Borders, Forms', immediately after the performance of *DJ-B*.

an hour and fifteen minutes. We put it on in Rockefeller Chapel at the University of Chicago, which was a perfect venue, because it had this neo-Gothic church—a great vast sort of thing. We put the play on in the chancel of the church. We would only allow sixty people to come, and sit around in the seats that surround the chancel; and it was sensational. It ran for a number of weeks, only on the weekend, and we were so pleased with the success of this particular staging that we decided, as we were people with jobs, people at university, or people in town, that we try to do this once a year.

The second year we put on a production of *The Marriage of Heaven and Hell*. That was a little bit more challenging as an adaptation job. The third year one of the company wanted to do Yeats, so we put on three short Yeats plays. We were then going to turn in the fourth year to either a production of Byron's *Sardanapalus*, or to *Death's Jest-Book*. The idea of doing *Death's Jest-Book* came out as our obligation, and it was my obligation to adapt it. I spent five months wrestling with this thing, and I just completely failed; I could not do it. And fortunately my failure was erased because the company had been so successful in the previous three years that everybody who was involved in it were all sort of pulled away to higher things. That sort of left me by myself, and that was the end of Cain's Company. At the time there were two things that stayed in my mind. I've always wanted adapt to *Death's Jest-Book*, and I've always wanted to put on what is for me the key Romantic drama in this fantastic tradition, *Manfred*.

It all stopped, and I went off and did what I was doing . . . In 1996 I went back to Chicago; I was teaching part-time at Northwestern. I was very much into memory trips, and one night it suddenly came to me how to adapt *Death's Jest-Book*! If you know the play, you know how complicated and absurd it is as a play, by any realist standards. Beddoes has got two plots that mirror each other, and in some senses the thing is quite symmetrical structurally. But it's incredibly too long, way too complex, and if you tried to put it on in the ordinary way you'd just fall asleep with boredom at the plot, as it were, because the plot is immensely in your face all the time. So there's this dumb plot that's going on, and then there's this gorgeous poetry, the gorgeous songs, the lyrics: there's a total collision between these two things. If you try to do what your initial impulse is, which is to cut the hell out of it, which was my initial impulse, you at that point destroy any possibility of structure in the thing. That was basically why in 1972 I couldn't cut it. I would hack away huge portions of the thing, and then it would sort of sit there like two or three separate scenes. But in 1998 (1996? I've forgotten now) it occurred to me what we had to do was to return the play to what it really was, which is a monodrama. We had to bring Beddoes into the thing explicitly, literally, because the play is in fact about Beddoes's mind, and make him a character, and therefore make everybody else in there basically his creatures, that are explicitly represented as his creatures.

So when we were watching the play tonight, you could see that happening all the time. Beddoes is there as a character on stage, Death is there, all as real or unreal as any of the other characters. Each of the spaces of the play, each of the persons, each of the events, and so forth, they're all non-real. They're completely artificial; they're completely beautiful. Footnote to this: back when we were talking to ourselves about these things we would always talk about opera. The model, it seemed to us, for what one had to do with this kind of work was to think about what opera was. When Coleridge talks about what poetry is, he goes through a series of analyses of theatrical representation. In doing this, he has a very famous passage, in which he speaks about the 'willing suspension of disbelief that constitutes poetic faith'. I understand and appreciate the importance of that way of thinking about it, but there's no doubt that we, Cain's Company, began to think about that phrase in a completely different way.

The approach to this kind of theatre, it seems to me, has to be, on the contrary, much more like *Don Giovanni*, much more like Mozart, and it has to be something like the willing *assumption* of disbelief that constitutes poetic creation. That's what Mozart does. That *is* what *Don Giovanni* is. And if you step back, and you apply any kind of standard of realist conventions to a performance of *Don Giovanni*, what you have is a serial rapist. And yet there is no-one who goes to *Don Giovanni* and sees it that way. What you see is the triumph of art over wickedness, sin, evil, illusion—all these things that in our ordinary world we make ethical judgements about. But in an artifice world, what art, and what music, and what poetry especially is able to do is to present an artifice that exposes these realities. You don't represent them as if they were there and then you had this sort of second order thing that was slightly lesser than what the reality of the world is. There's a certain sense in which the act of art is far more clarifying and in that sense real, than anything that we experience, it seems to me, when we move around the world. We move, as many poets and playwrights have said, in a dream, because we're so caught up in the immediate act of our living. But when you have a poet like Byron, say, or—we know how unique Mozart is, or Beddoes, they are tremendous artificers. And in those artifices that they create they expose things that interest us about ourselves and about our world. So that approach really dictated the way I have been thinking about, and a lot of people have who I have love and admiration for, when they (we?) approach these peculiar kinds of texts, and especially *Death's Jest-Book*.

I'm going to say really only one more thing, well two more things. First of all I want to thank Fred [Burwick]. I want to thank everyone, the musicians, the actors. It has been an amazingly thrilling event to actually see this thing brought into production. When I finished the adaptation of it I passed it around to some people I knew who were in the theatre, and they all thought it was completely crazy, as I knew they would. I had some vague hope that it might be put on, but it didn't go very far, and so I put it in a drawer, and that was that. I completely forgot about the play, until—I don't know when it was, about a year and a half ago, I get out of the blue a note from John Beddoes (which I can't believe—it's like some event on the stage itself), saying I understand that you have adapted *Death's Jest-Book*. I wrote back and I said, well yes, that's true, but how do you know that? And so he was all very excited about it, and he asked me to pass it on to him to publish in the Society newsletter, and I said you can do whatever you want with it. One thing led to another, and I ran it by Fred and he heard about it, and suddenly the next thing you know is, here it is—we're all here and we see the world première of *Death's Jest-Book*. And I'm very grateful to John and to Fred, and I hope you all enjoyed it.

Directing the Production
Frederick Burwick

Although I have directed many plays of the Romantic period,[2] have written fairly extensively about the drama, the acting, the stages designs and stage technology of the period,[3] and have even authored a few essays on Thomas Lovell Beddoes,[4] I would not have considered *Death's Jest-Book* as a play suited for a student production, perhaps not even for a professional production. My thinking was changed by a meeting with Jerome McGann in February, 2002. Jerry presented me with a script that effectively revised Beddoes's play for the stage, nevertheless holding rigorously to Beddoes's 1829 text—transposing passages, but altering no more than a dozen lines. He made two principle changes: 1) omitting the sub-plot, with Melveric's sons Adalmar and Athulf as deadly rivals in their love for Torwald's daughter Amala; and 2) giving the role of Isbrand to the playwright himself. The omission of the sub-plot, which echoes the rivalry of Wolfram and Melveric for the love of Sibylla, allows for a more compact structure. Introducing Beddoes as character in his own play, as explicit theatre of the Beddoesian imagination, provides for a fuller metadramatic exposition of the self-reflexive irony. For the Prologue,

---

2 Thomas Morton, *Speed the Plough*, Wordsworth Summer Conference, 2000. Elizabeth Inchbald, *To Marry or Not to Marry*, Wordsworth Summer Conference, 2001. Christian Dietrich Grabbe, *Jest, Satire, Irony, and Deeper Meaning*, UCLA and Scripps College, 2002. Joanna Baillie, *The Tryal*, Wordsworth Summer Conference, 2002. Thomas Lovell Beddoes, *Death's Jest-Book*, UCLA, Scripps College, Fordham University and Wordsworth Summer Conference, 2003. Elizabeth Inchbald, *Animal Magnetism*, UCLA, Scripps College, CSU Long Beach and Wordsworth Summer Conference, 2004. Hannah Cowley, *A Bold Stoke for a Husband*, UCLA and Chapman University, 2005.

3 'Stage Illusion and the Stage Designs of Goethe and Hugo', *Word and Image* 4.3–4 (1988), 692–718; 'On Stage Illusion: from Wordsworth's Marginalia to Coleridge's Lectures', *Wordsworth Circle*, 19.1 (1988), 28–37; 'Romantic Drama: From Optics to Illusion', in *Literature and Science: Theory and Practice*, ed. Stuart Peterfreund (Boston: Northeastern University Press, 1990), pp. 167–208; 'Science and Supernaturalism: Sir David Brewster and Sir Walter Scott', *Comparative Criticism* 13 (1991), 82–114; *Illusion and the Drama. Critical Theory of the Enlightenment and Romantic Era* (University Park: Pennsylvania State University Press, 1991); 'Illusion and Romantic Drama', in *Romantic Drama*, ed. Gerald Gillespie (Amsterdam and Philadelphia: John Benjamins, 1994), pp. 59–80; *The Boydell Shakespeare Gallery*, ed. with Walter Pape (Bottrop: Peter Pomp, 1996); 'The Paradox of Irrationality in Goethe's Classicism', in *A Reassessment of Weimar Classicism*, ed. Gerhart Hoffmeister (London: Mellen Press, 1996), pp. 11–33; 'John Boydell's *Shakespeare Gallery* and the Stage', *Shakespeare Jahrbuch*, 133 (1997), 54–76; 'Ideal Shattered: Sarah Siddons, Madness, and the Dynamics of Gesture', in *Notorious Muse: The Actress in British Art and Culture 1776–1812*, ed. Robyn Asleson (Yale University Press, 2003); and 'Joanna Baillie, Matthew Baillie, and the Pathology of the Passions', in *Joanna Baillie: Romantic Dramatist*, ed. Tom Cruchunis (London: Routledge, 2004) pp. 48–68.

4 See General Bibliography and essay in this volume.

McGann took advantage of Beddoes's own metaphor, always spoken by Isbrand, that life is a 'puppet theater'. I was at the time in rehearsal for a performance of Christian Dietrich Grabbe's *Jest, Satire, Irony, and Deeper Meaning* (1822), a play that had many similarities to Beddoes's work and may have influenced the style of grotesque comedy. As in Grabbe's play so also in Beddoes's, I saw a need to realize the musical dimension. To my mind, this was all the more important for Beddoes, who is an exceptionally gifted lyricist. My major changes were to restore the lyrics and the grotesque comedy of the tavern scene that had been omitted from McGann's version.

Having made the decision to direct *Death's Jest-Book* with its lyrics intact, I proceeded to restore, as well, those lines necessary to introduce the songs. Some of the songs already had musical settings, by such composers as Sir Hubert Parry and, more recently, by Benjamin Britten.[5] None of these songs, however, were written to suit their dramatic context. I needed a composer who was not only skilled in early nineteenth-century art songs and lieder, but also a composer who was well acquainted with Beddoes. I found that composer in Brian Holmes, Professor of Music and Acoustical Physics at San Jose State University. Between March and November, 2002, Brian set all thirteen songs for the performance, and then went on to write an overture and a choral reprise of Mandrake's Song for the finale.[6] Brian's musical interpretation of Beddoes's lyric is powerful and unerringly accurate. His melodies, as they should, fully merge with the words and become a part of their meaning. Brian served as Musical Director and attended all rehearsals for the performances at UCLA in March and in New York in August. Holly Replogle, who played the role of Sibylla, served as Vocal Director.

The impact of this play results not, as often assumed, from Beddoes darkening the Gothic elements into an extreme morbidity, but rather from presenting the afterlife as utterly bereft of religious meaning. As in the 'The Speech of the Dead Christ',[7] the passage from Jean Paul that Germaine de Staël translated in her *D'Allemagne* (1809–11), the afterlife is utterly godless, an existentialist eternity of unanswerable questions. Dramatically, then, the dialogue in the catacombs has to be played as in Samuel Beckett's *Waiting for Godot* (1949), and in the comic scenes as in Grabbe's *Jest* or Georg Büchner's *Woyzeck* (1834). The tavern scene, with the antics of Mandrake's invisibility, is raucous slapstick, but the theme of death persists, physically emphasized in my production by a tavern drunk all the while lecherously ogling Kate, whom he subsequently murders. Melveric, performed by

---

5   For musical settings to the lyrics, select 'Beddoes' at the website: <http://www.recmusic.org/lieder/>.
6   'Mandrake's Song' ('Folly hath now turned out of door'); 'To Sea, To Sea'; 'The Swallow Leaves her Nest'; 'The Phantom Wooer'; 'Wolfram's Dirge' ('If thou wilt ease thy heart'); 'The New Cecilia' ('Whoever has heard of St Gingo'); 'Dream Pedlary'; 'The New Dodo' ('Squats on a toadstool'); 'The Moon doth mock and make me crazy'; 'Mummies and Skeletons'; 'My Goblet's Golden Lips Are Dry'; 'Old Adam, the Carrion Crow'; 'We do lie beneath the grass'.
7   Jean Paul, 'Rede des toten Christus vom Weltgebäude herab, daß kein Gott sei', from his novel, *Siebenkäs* (1797).

Zachary Gallager, brings the play to a climax of existential *angst* in his monologue, 'Deceived and disappointed vain desires! / Why laugh I not, and ridicule myself?' The operative homosexuality results in the strained dynamics of male interaction and the suppression of male-female union. The women (Sibylla, Kate) exist only as vehicles for, not as recipients of, male passions.

To intensify these attributes on the stage, I imposed a 'no touch' rule. Throughout the play, with two exceptions, the characters never touch. The two exceptions: the act of penetration when Duke Melveric stabs his male companions—Wolfram, Mandrake, Ziba, and Beddoes—and is himself stabbed by Sibylla at the play's end; the mortal touch, when Death grasps Melveric's hand. To help the audience anticipate the stabbings, Melveric wears four ornamental daggers on his doublet. One by one they are embedded into the chests of Mandrake, Ziba, and Beddoes, leaving only the one dagger that Sibylla uses to 'point the truth'. A similar kind of anticipatory device is the golden goblet as a prop: it is used exclusively as a vessel of poison, given first by Ziba to Wolfram, and then by Melveric to Thorwald. Another significant prop is the fool's cap-and-bells, first worn by Beddoes, subsequently passed to Wolfram, to Death, back to Beddoes, and finally to Melveric. To underscore the sexual tensions of the play, Melveric is captured not by Pagans but by Amazons, female warriors who scorn the masculine pretences of their prisoner, but are driven off when Melveric is rescued by his male friend.

The supernaturalism of the play I chose to enhance through the simple expedient of a backlit scrim (simplicity is a necessity in a low-budget production). The first backlit scrim is Sibylla's tent, where the phantom of the 'dead' Wolfram rises from his corpse (a body double) lying in front of the tent and appears a shadow. Sibylla and Wolfram then engage in a shadow dance accompanying their duet, 'The Phantom Wooer'. The second backlit scrim is the 24-foot long 'wall' in the catacombs, the setting for the entire latter half of the play. The purpose of 'wall' was to give visual presence to Beddoes's evocation of 'The Dance of Death', the iconic representation of Death leading a procession of knights, ladies, merchants, and beggars. As each of the characters in the play is killed, he or she assumes a place along the wall. Behind the wall, however, are cut-out life-size silhouettes of each of the characters who are then animated by a moving hand-held backlight whenever the strains of 'Mummies and Skeletons' are played.

To re-emphasize the puppet-theatre motif of the Prologue, I had 'To Sea, to Sea', choreographed for chorus, dancers, and a puppet-ship to bear Mandrake on his journey. 'The New Dodo' was also choreographed as a puppet song, in which each of the creatures mentioned in the lyric is manipulated as cut-out figure. The choreography was directed by Francine Maigue, who also created the stunning dance interpretations of 'Dream Pedlary', 'Old Adam, the Carrion Crow', and 'Mummies and Skeletons'.

Each of the actors was assigned a specific manner of gesture, gait, and delivery. Ziba, performed by A.J. Rodriguez, was required to slither and lurk, always peering from behind the backdrops before making his S-curved entrances. As necromancer, Ziba also delivered as incantational spells the blank-verse monologues on conjuration and the occult arts. Beddoes, played by Daniel Zamani, is the metadramatic authorial persona created out of the original speeches of Isbrand. Costumed as a caped conjuror, he can comment self-reflexively on writing this play and playing in it, but he is nevertheless entrapped by it. Just as Melveric is irrevocably paired to his murdered friend Wolfram, Beddoes is linked to his comic counterpart, Mandrake. To his role as Wolfram, Stephen Pu brought a naïve sincerity, which irritates Melveric, forcing him to recognize his own self-centred failings and his friend's moral superiority. Similarly, the zany, would-be alchemist Mandrake, played by William Bibiani, possesses a wit and human compassion that seems to surpass that of his 'author'. The link between the two is visually dramatized in scenes where the movement downstage of the one seems to pull the other upstage as if by an invisible rope and pulley.

The production at the NASSR Conference in New York was made possible by Michael Macovski and the generosity of Fordham University, who provided housing for the UCLA cast during rehearsals throughout the two weeks prior to performance. A few substitutes in the cast were necessary: the role of Death, originally played by Tom Wheatley at UCLA, was taken over by David Damstra; the role of Torwald, the Duke's Minister, originally played by Greg Cragg, was assumed by Tom Fenaughty; Kate, tavern hostess and companion to Mandrake, played by Rebecca Wyrostek at UCLA, was performed by Kristin Crawford. Tom Wheatley and Kristin Crawford again played their roles, joined by a new cast, for the final performance at the Wordsworth Summer Conference, 22 August 2002. Credit for the entire production belongs to Jerry McGann for his stage-worthy adaptation, to Brian Holmes for his stunning score, to the entire cast and crew and musicians for their talent, time and energy. My thanks and gratitude also go to an extraordinary stage and prop manger, Vicki Leung.

General Bibliography

Manuscripts

Scaroni; or, the Mysterious Cave, A Romantic Fiction, Charterhouse School MS. *Songs*, British Library Add. MS 39674, F.f.9 (r. *Song*, 'Lady was it fair of thee'; v. 'If there were dreams to sell').

'An Earth is Born! an Earth is Born!' (copy of 'The New Born Star' written in the poet's hand, from the Donner Collection at the Bodleian library).

'There is a mighty magic tree' (copy of 'The tree of Life' written in the poet's hand, from the Donner Collection at the Bodleian library).

Published Texts

Anon., *Death's Jest-Book; or, The Fool's Tragedy* (London: William Pickering, 1850).

Beddoes, Thomas Lovell, *The Brides' Tragedy* (London: F., C., and J. Rivington, 1822).

—, *The Brides' Tragedy*, facsimile of 1822 edn, ed. Jonathan Wordsworth (Oxford and New York: Woodstock Books, 1993).

—, *Death's Jest-Book; or, The Day will Come*, ed. Alan Halsey (Sheffield: West House, 2003).

—, *Death's Jest-Book: The 1829 text*, ed. Michael Bradshaw (Manchester and New York: Carcanet/Routledge, 2003).

—, *Selected Poems*, ed. Judith Higgens (Manchester: Carcanet, 1976).

—, *Selected Poetry*, revd edn, ed. Judith Higgens and Michael Bradshaw (Manchester: Carcanet, 1999).

—, 'The Romance of the Lily', *The Album*, 6 (1823), 251–63.

—, 'The Oviparous Taylor', *Borderland: Dark Fantasy*, 1, 2 (1985), 12.

Beddoes, Thomas Lovell, *Resurrection Songs* (Chislehurst: The Gothic Society, 1992).

The Complete Works of Thomas Lovell Beddoes, ed. with a memoir by Sir Edmund Gosse and decorated by the Dance of Death of Hans Holbein, 2 vols (London: Franfolico, 1928).

Plays and Poems of Thomas Lovell Beddoes, ed. H.W. Donner (London: Routledge & Kegan Paul, 1950).

The Poems of Thomas Lovell Beddoes, ed. with an introduction by Ramsay Colles (London: Routledge, The Muses' Library, 1907).

The Poems Posthumous and Collected of Thomas Lovell Beddoes, with a Memoir, ed. T.F. Kelsall, 2 vols (London: William Pickering, 1851).

The Poetical Works of Thomas Lovell Beddoes, ed. with a memoir by Edmund Gosse (London: Dent, 1890).

The Letters of Thomas Lovell Beddoes, ed. Edmund Gosse (London: Elkin Matthews & John Lane, 1894).

The Works of Thomas Lovell Beddoes, ed. with an introduction by H.W. Donner (London: Oxford University Press, 1935).

The Works of Thomas Lovell Beddoes, ed. with an introduction by H.W. Donner (London: Oxford University Press, 1935; repr. New York: AMS Press, 1978).

'Bodes, E.D.' [Beddoes], 'The Comet', *The Morning Post*, 6 July 1819, p. 2.

Donner, H.W. (ed.), 'T.L. Beddoes to Leonhard Tobler: Eight German Letters', *Studia Neophilologica*, 35, 2 (1963), 227–35.

Lucas, F.L. (ed.), *Thomas Lovell Beddoes: An Anthology* (Cambridge: Cambridge University Press, 1932).

McGann, Jerome J., *Death's Jest-Book: a posthumous theatrical travesty, in three acts, translated by Jerome McGann, from the original dramatical fantasia by Thomas Lovell Beddoes* (Belper: Thomas Lovell Beddoes Society, 2003).

Wolfson, Susan J. and Peter J. Manning (eds), *Selected Poems of Hood, Praed and Beddoes* (Harmondsworth: Penguin, 1999).

Biography and Criticism

Abbott, Claude Colleer, 'Correspondence: Thomas Lovell Beddoes', *Times Literary Supplement*, 28 March 1929, p. 260.

—, 'The Parents of Thomas Lovell Beddoes', *Durham University Journal*, n.s., 3 (1941), 159–75.

Adler, Eric, *Thomas Lovell Beddoes: Studien zu seiner Lyrik* (Zürich: Juris, 1968).

Agar, John, 'Isbrand and T.L. Beddoes' Aspiring Hero', *Studia Neophilologica*, 45 (1973), 370–82.

—, 'The Brides' Tragedy and T.L. Beddoes' English Roots', *Studia Neophilologica*, 46 (1974), 175–201 and 338–69.

Angell, Leslie Ekberg, *A Dance with Death: Image and Theme in the Works of Thomas Lovell Beddoes* (unpublished doctoral dissertation, University of Massachusetts, 1974).

Anon., Review of *The Improvisatore*, in *The Monthly Review; or Literary Journal, enlarged*, 95 (1821), 218–19.

—, 'On Ancient and Modern Tragedy', *The Album*, 3 (1823), 1–31.

—, 'Reviews of Miscellaneous Publications', *The Gentleman's Magazine*, 93 (1823), 347.

—, Review of Kelsall's edn of *Death's Jest-Book*, *The Athenaeum*, 26 October 1850, pp. 1115–16.

—, Review of Kelsall's 2 vol. edn of Beddoes, *The Athenaeum*, 20 September 1851, pp. 989–90.

—, 'The Vision', *Times Literary Supplement*, 2 November 1933, pp. 737–38.

—, Review of Gosse edn, *The Athenaeum*, 3296 (1890), 879–81.

—, Review of a performance of *The Second Brother*, Norwich Maddermarket Theatre, *The Times London*, 2 Apr. 1935, 12.

Ashbery, John, 'Olives and Anchovies: The Poetry of Thomas Lovell Beddoes', in *Other Traditions* (Cambridge, Mass. and London: Harvard University Press, 2000), pp. 23–44.

—, 'Thomas Beddoes', in *Poets on Poets*, ed. Nick Rennison and Michael Schmidt (Manchester: Carcanet, 1997), pp. 10–11.

Baker, John Haydn, '"Georgium Sidus": Thomas Lovell Beddoes and the Discovery of Uranus', *Notes and Queries*, 49, 1 (2002), 46–47.

—, '"Tom Laocoön": A Newly Discovered Poem by Thomas Lovell Beddoes', *Victorian Poetry*, 40.3 (2002), 261–67.

Bamforth, Iain, 'Pickled Essence of Englishman: Thomas Lovell Beddoes—time to unearth a neglected poet?' *Journal of Medical Ethics*, 30 (2004), 36–40.

Bayley, A.R., Correspondence: Thomas Lovell Beddoes, *Times Literary Supplement*, 28 March 1929, p. 260.

Berns, Ute, 'The Politics of Revolution in Thomas Lovell Beddoes's *Death's Jest-Book*', in *Romantic Voices, Romantic Poetics: Selected papers from the Regensburg conference of the German Society for English Romanticism*, ed. Christoph Bode and Katharina Rennhak (Trier: Wissenschaftlicher Verlag Trier, 2005), pp. 97–107.

—, 'Thomas Lovell Beddoes and the German Sciences of Life', *Poetica* (Munich) 38 (2006), 1–2, 137–65.

Blain, Virginia, 'Browning's Men: Childe Roland, Homophobia and Thomas Lovell Beddoes', *Australasian Victorian Studies Journal*, 7 (2001), 1–11.

Bloom, Harold, *The Visionary Company: A Reading of English Romantic Poetry* (London and New York: Faber and Faber, 1962).

Blunden, Edmund, 'Beddoes and His Contemporaries', *Votive Tablets: Studies Chiefly Appreciative of English Authors and Books* (London: Coloden-Sanderson, 1931), pp. 292–303.

Bradshaw, Michael, 'Resurrecting Thomas Lovell Beddoes', in *The Influence and Anxiety of the British Romantics: Spectres of Romanticism*, ed. Sharon Ruston (Lampeter: Edwin Mellen, 2000), pp. 139–57.

—, *Resurrection Songs: The Poetry of Thomas Lovell Beddoes* (Aldershot and Burlington: Ashgate, 2001).

—, 'Review of the Performance of *Death's Jest-Book* (NASSR, August 2003, Fordham University)', *European Romantic Review*, 15.2 (2004), 387–90.

—, *Scattered Limbs: The Making and Unmaking of* Death's Jest-Book (Belper: Thomas Lovell Beddoes Society, 1996).

—, 'Beddoes and the Poetics of Fragmentation', *Agenda*, 37, 2–3 (1999), 264–80.

Brodsky, Gary H., *Metaphor in the Dramas of Thomas Lovell Beddoes* (unpublished doctoral dissertation, University of Nebraska, 1970).

Brown, Sarah Annes, *The Metamorphosis of Ovid: From Chaucer to Ted Hughes* (London: Duckworth, 2002).

Burwick, Frederick, 'Beddoes, Bayern und die Burschenschaften', *Comparative Literature*, 21 (1969), 289–36.

—, 'The Anatomy of Revolution: Beddoes and Büchner', *Pacific Coast Philology*, 6 (1971), 5–12.

—, 'Beddoes and the *Schweizerische Republikaner*', *Studia Neophilologica*, 44 (1972), 90–112.

—, 'Death's Fool: Beddoes and Büchner', in *The Haunted Eye: Perception and the Grotesque in English and German Romanticism* (Heidelberg: Carl Winter, 1987), pp. 274–300.

Bush, Douglas, 'Minor Poets of the Early Nineteenth Century', in *Mythology and the Romantic Tradition in English Poetry* (New York: Pageant, 1957), pp. 169–96.

'Mr Buttle's Review', *Blackwood's Edinburgh Magazine*, 80 (1856), 447–49.

Chew, Samuel C., 'Thomas Hood, Thomas Lovell Beddoes, and Other Poets', in *A Literary History of England*, ed. Albert C. Baugh (New York and London: Appleton-Century-Crofts, 1948; 2nd edn London: Routledge & Kegan Paul, 1967), pp. 1252–63.

Church, Richard, 'The Last of the Alchemists', *The Spectator* (London), 9 Feb. 1929, pp. 118–19.

Clark, Leigh '"The Skull Beneath the Skin": A Study of Beddoes' Poetic System' (unpublished doctoral dissertation, Kansas University, 1983).

Collier, William Francis, *History of English Literature* (London: Thomas Nelson and Sons, 1910), pp. 478–79.

Collins, Mabel, 'A Poet Not Laureate', *The University Magazine*, 4, 23 (1879), 513–25.

'Cornwall, Barry' [B.W. Procter], 'To the Editor of *The Athenaeum*', *The Athenaeum*, 7 July 1832, p. 440.

Coxe, Louis O., 'Beddoes: The Mask of Parody', *The Hudson Review*, 6 (1953), 251–66.

Crossan, Greg, 'Thomas Lovell Beddoes's *Death's Jest-Book*: An *OED* Oversight', *Notes & Queries*, 247 (2002) 486–89.

—, 'Unnoticed Words in Beddoes for *OED*', *Notes & Queries*, 248 (2003) 446–53.

Crosse, Mrs Andrew, 'Thomas Lovell Beddoes', *Temple Bar*, 101 (1894), 357–70.

Darley, George (as 'John Lacy'), 'A Sixth Letter to the Dramatists of the Day', *The London Magazine*, 8 (1823), 645–52.

Dearlove, Sharon Lynn, *The Kiss of Death: Thomas Lovell Beddoes'* Death's Jest-Book *and the Rosicrucian Quest* (unpublished doctoral dissertation, Massey University, 1993).

Dewsnap, Mary Anne Caporaletti, *Idiosyncrasy and Spirit: Five Tragedies of the English Romantic Period* (unpublished doctoral dissertation, University of Pennsylvania, 1978).

Donner, H.W. (ed. with an introduction), *The Browning Box: or, The Life and Works of Thomas Lovell Beddoes as reflected in letters by his friends and admirers* (London: Oxford University Press, 1935).

—, *Thomas Lovell Beddoes: The Making of a Poet* (Oxford: Basil Blackwell, 1935; repr. Folcroft, 1970).

—, 'Echoes of Beddoesian Rambles: Edgeworthtown to Zürich', *Studia Neophilologica*, 32 (1961), 219–64.

— (ed.), 'Two German Poems Attributed to T.L. Beddoes', *Studia Neophilologica*, 37 (1965), 360–66.

Eliot, T.S., *On Poetry and Poets* (London: Faber and Faber, 1957; repr. 1969).

Selected Prose of T.S. Eliot, ed. Frank Kermode (London: Faber and Faber, 1980).

Elton, Oliver, *A Survey of English Literature 1780–1830* (1912), 2 vols (London: Edward Arnold, 1928).

Forster, John, 'The Literary Examiner: *Death's Jest-Book, or The Fool's Tragedy*', *The Examiner*, 20 July 1850, 461–63.

—, 'Poems. By the late Thomas Lovell Beddoes, Author of *Death's Jest-Book, or The Fool's Tragedy*, with a memoir', *The Examiner*, 27 Sep. 1851, 611–14.

Forster, Leonard, 'T.L. Beddoes' Views on German Literature', *English Studies*, 30 (1949), 206–14.

Frye, Northrop, 'Yorick: The Romantic Macabre', in *A Study of English Romanticism* (New York: Random House, 1968; repr. London: Harvester, 1983), pp. 51–85.

Fugô, Shunji, 'Some Aspects of T.L. Beddoes' Style, *Studies in English Literature* (1933), 233–58.

Good, Donald William, *Thomas Lovell Beddoes: A Critical Study of His Major Works* (unpublished doctoral dissertation, Ohio State University, 1968).

Gosse, Edmund, *Critical Kit-Kats* (London: Heinemann, 1913), pp. 31–61.

—, 'Thomas Lovell Beddoes', *The Athenaeum*, 2921 (20 October 1883), p. 496.

Gregory, Horace, 'The Gothic Imagination and the Survival of Thomas Lovell Beddoes' in *The Dying Gladiators, and Other Essays* (New York: Grove, 1961), pp. 81–95.

Grimble, Ian, 'This Unfathomable Fever: An account of the Life and Writing of Thomas Lovell Beddoes' (BBC production script no. BDB475T559N, broadcast on Radio 4, 27 December 1983).

Guy-Bray, Stephen, 'Beddoes, Pygmalion and the Art of Onanism', *Nineteenth-Century Literature*, 52 (1998), 446–70.

Halsey, Alan, 'Beddoes: a Reconsideration', *Agenda*, 37, 2–3 (1999), 246–63.

—, *Homage to Homunculus Mandrake* (Belper: Thomas Lovell Beddoes Society, 1996).

—, *A Skeleton Key to* Death's Jest-Book (Belper: Thomas Lovell Beddoes Society, 1995).

—, '*Todtentanz*: from An Anatomy of *Death's Jest-Book*', *Fragmente*, 7 (1977), 49–53.

Hannigan, D.F., 'Thomas Lovell Beddoes: "A Forgotten Oxford Poet"', *The Westminster Review*, 149 (1898), 484–92.

Harrex, Anne, '*Death's Jest-Book* and the German Contribution', *Studia Neophilologica*, 39 (1967), 15–37 and 302–18.

Hearn, Lafcadio, 'Thomas Lovell Beddoes', in *Life and Literature*, ed. with an introduction by John Erskine (New York: Dodd, Mead, 1917), pp. 200–04.

Heath-Stubbs, John, 'The Defeat of Romanticism', in *The Darkling Plain: A Study of the Later Fortunes of Romanticism in English Poetry from George Darley to W.B. Yeats* (London: Eyre & Spottiswoode, 1950), pp. 21–61.

Hilliard, Kate, 'A Strayed Singer', *Lippincott's Magazine*, 12 (1873), 550–57.

Howarth, R.G., 'Two Poems of Beddoes', *Notes & Queries*, 192 (1947), 410–11.

—, 'Beddoes' Last Poem', *Notes & Queries*, 192 (1947), 475.

Hoyt, Charles Alva, *Studies in Thomas Lovell Beddoes* (unpublished doctoral dissertation, Columbia University, 1961).

—, 'Theme and Imagery in the Poetry of Thomas Lovell Beddoes', *Studia Neophilologica*, 35 (1963), 85–103.

Jack, Ian, 'Clare and the Minor Poets', in *English Literature 1815–32: Scott, Byron and Keats* (London: Oxford University Press, The Oxford History of English Literature, 1963), pp. 130–84.

Johnson, Hiram Kellogg, 'Thomas Lovell Beddoes: A Psychiatric Study', *The Psychiatric Quarterly*, 17 (1943), 446–69.

Joshua, Essaka, *Pygmalion and Galatea: The History of a Narrative in English Literature* (Aldershot and Burlington: Ashgate, 2001).

Keith-Smith, Brian, and Ken Mills (eds), *Büchner in Britain: A Passport to Georg Büchner* (London: Goethe Institute/University of Bristol, 1987).
Kelsall, Thomas F., 'Thomas Lovell Beddoes', *The Fortnightly Review*, 12 (1872), 51–75.
—, 'Original Papers', *The Athenaeum*, 18 May 1883, p. 313.
Kroeber, Karl, 'Trends in Minor Romantic Narrative Poetry', in *Some British Romantics: A Collection of Essays*, ed. James V. Logan, John E. Jordan and Northrop Frye (Ohio: Ohio State University Press, 1966), pp. p. 269–92.
Logue, Christopher, 'Air', in *Selected Poems* (London: Faber and Faber, 1996), p. 1.
Lucas, F.L., 'The Strange Case of Dr Beddoes', *Life and Letters*, 4 (1930), 55–73.
—, 'Death's Jester', *Life and Letters*, 5 (1930), 219–45.
Lundin, Jon W., 'T.L. Beddoes at Pembroke College', *Studia Neophilologica*, 41 (1969), 348–49.
—, 'T.L. Beddoes at Göttingen', *Studia Neophilologica*, 43 (1971), 484–99.
Meyerstein, E.H.W., 'Thomas Lovell Beddoes', *English*, 3 (1940), 8–15.
Meynell, Alice, *The Second Person Singular and Other Essays* (London: Oxford UP, 1922).
Miller, Barnette, 'Thomas Lovell Beddoes', *The Sewanee Review*, 11 (1903), 305–36.
Mirarchi, Margaret Klett, *A Study of the Grotesque in the Works of Thomas Lovell Beddoes* (unpublished doctoral dissertation, University of Pennsylvania, 1973).
Moldauer, Grete, *Thomas Lovell Beddoes* (Wien and Leipzig: Wilhelm Braunmüller, 1924).
Moylan, Christopher, '"For Luz is a Good Joke": Thomas Lovell Beddoes and Jewish Eschatology', in *British Romanticism and the Jews: History, Culture, Literature*, ed. Sheila Spector (New York: Palgrave, 2002), pp. 93–103.
—, 'T.L. Beddoes, Romantic Medicine, and the Advent of Therapeutic Theater', *Studia Neophilologica*, 69 (1991), 181–88.
—, *Thomas Lovell Beddoes and the Hermetic Tradition (Seeds, Bones, Bowls: T.L. Beddoes' Alchemical Recipe)* (Belper: Thomas Lovell Beddoes Society, 1998).
—, 'In the air: T.L. Beddoes and Pneumatic Medicine", *Studia Neophilologica*, 73 (2001), 48–54.
Muir, Edwin, *Some Uncollected Reviews and Essays by Edwin Muir*, ed. and intro. By P.H. Butter (Aberdeen: Aberdeen University Press, 1988), pp. 52–56.
Nickerson, C.C., 'T.L. Beddoes' Readings in Bodley', *Studia Neophilologica*, 36 (1964), 264–65.
O'Neill, Michael, '"A Storm of Ghosts": Beddoes, Shelley, Death and Reputation', *Cambridge Quarterly*, 28.2 (1999), 102–15.
Pierce, Frederick E., 'Beddoes and the Continental Romanticists', *Philological Quarterly*, 6 (1927), 126–32.
—, 'The Elizabethan Current in *The London Magazine*', in *Currents and Eddies in the English Romantic Generation* (New Haven: Yale University Press, 1918), pp. 186–211.
Potter, G.R., 'Did Thomas Lovell Beddoes Believe in the Evolution of the Species?', *Modern Philology*, 21 (1923), 89–100.
Pound, Ezra, 'Beddoes and Chronology' (1913), *Selected Prose*, ed. William Cookson (London: Faber and Faber, 1973), pp. 348–53.

Prickett, Stephen, *The Romantics: The Context of English Literature* (London: Methuen, 1981), pp. 152–53.

Procter, Bryan Waller, *An Autobiographical Fragment and Biographical Notes, with personal sketches of contemporaries, unpublished lyrics, and letters of literary friends*, ed. Coventry Patmore (London: George Bell, 1877).

—, Review of *The Brides' Tragedy*, *The London Magazine*, 7 (1823), 169–72.

Purinton, Marjean D., 'Staging the Physical: Romantic Science Theatricalized in T.L. Beddoes's *The Brides' Tragedy*', *European Romantic Review*, 14 (2003), 81–95.

Rees, Shelley, 'Gender and Desire in Thomas Lovell Beddoes' *The Brides' Tragedy* and *Death's Jest-Book*' (unpublished doctoral dissertation, University of North Texas, 2002).

—, 'Melveric and Wolfram: A Love Story', *Thomas Lovell Beddoes Society Journal*, 8 (2002), 14–25.

Richardson, Alan, '*Death's Jest-Book*: "Shadows of Words"', in *A Mental Theater: Poetic Drama and Consciousness in the Romantic Age* (University Park, Penn. and London: Pennsylvania State University Press, 1988), pp. 154–73.

Ricks, Christopher, 'Thomas Lovell Beddoes: "A dying start"', *Grand Street*, 1 (1982), 32–48; and 3 (1984), 90–102; repr. in *The Force of Poetry* (Oxford: Oxford University Press, 1984), pp. 135–62.

Rickword, Edgell, 'Thomas Lovell Beddoes', *The London Mercury*, 9 (1923), 162–74.

Ross, Gregory, 'The Cherub and the Bacchanal: The Poetry of Thomas Lovell Beddoes' (unpublished doctoral dissertation, UCLA, 1983).

Saintsbury, George, *A History of English Prosody*, vol. III (London: Macmillan, 1910).

—, *A Short History of English Literature* (London: Macmillan, 1925), pp. 722–23.

Sassoon, Siegfried, 'Beddoes: A Personal Approach', *The Listener*, 14.363 (1935), 1179.

Schmidt, Michael, *Lives of the Poets* (London: Weidenfeld & Nicolson, 1998).

Sharma, Virendra, *Studies in Victorian Verse Drama* (Salzburg: Universität Salzburg, 1979).

Snow, Royall H., *Thomas Lovell Beddoes, Eccentric and Poet* (New York: Covici-Friede, 1928).

Stafford, Fiona J., *The Last of the Race: The Growth of a Myth from Milton to Darwin* (Oxford: Oxford University Press, 1994).

Strachey, Lytton, 'The Last Elizabethan' (1907), in *Books and Characters, French and English* (London: Chatto & Windus, 1922), pp. 225–52; also published in *New Quarterly* (1907), 47–72; and in *Literary Essays* (New York: Harcourt Brace 1969), pp. 171–194).

Symons, Arthur, 'Thomas Lovell Beddoes' in *Figures of Several Centuries* (London: Constable, 1917), pp. 122–29.

Tandecki, Daniela, 'Die Totentänze des Thomas Lovell Beddoes—*Death's Jest-Book* und die Verneinung des Lebens', *Tanz und Tod in Kunst und Literatur*, ed. Franz Link. (Berlin: Duncker and Humblot, 2003).

The Thomas Lovell Beddoes Society, *Newsletter*, vols 1–8 (1995–2002).

—, *Journal*, vols 9–12 (2003–06).

The Thomas Lovell Beddoes Society Web Page: <http://www.beddoes.org>.

Thompson, James R., *Thomas Lovell Beddoes* (Boston: Twayne, 1985).

Thomson, Ian, 'Thomas Lovell Beddoes at Slaughterhouse', *Agenda*, 37.2–3 (1999), 281–86.

Todd, A.C., 'Anna Maria, the Mother of Thomas Lovell Beddoes', *Studia Neophilologica*, 29 (1957), 136–44.

Wagner, Geoffrey, 'Centennial of A Suicide: Thomas Lovell Beddoes', *Horizon*, 19 (1949), 417–35; also in *The Golden Horizon*, ed. Cyril Connolly (London: Weidenfeld & Nicolson, 1953), pp. 543–61.

Watkins, Daniel P., 'Thomas Lovell Beddoes's *The Brides' Tragedy* and the Situation of Romantic Drama', *Studies in English Literature 1500–1900*, 29 (1989), 699–712.

Weber, Carl August, *Bristols Bedeutung für die englische Romantik und die deutsch-englisch Beziehungen* (Halle: Max Niemayer, 1935; repr. Walluf: Sändig, 1973).

Wieselhuber, Franz, 'Thomas Lovell Beddoes', in *Beyond the Suburbs of the Mind: Exploring English Romanticism*, ed. Michael Gassenmeier and Norbert H. Platz (Essen: Verlag die blaue Eule, 1987), pp. 178–92.

Wilner, Eleanor, *Gathering the Winds: Visionary Imagination and Radical Transformation of Self and Society* (Baltimore and London: The Johns Hopkins University Press, 1975).

Wilson, Frances, '"Strange Sun": Melancholia in the Writings of Thomas Lovell Beddoes', in *Untrodden Regions of the Mind: Romanticism and Psychoanalysis*, ed. Ghislaine McDayter (Lewisburg: Bucknell University Press, 2002), pp. 127–43.

Wilson, John (as 'Christopher North'), 'Notices of the Modern British Dramatists, No. II, Beddoes', *Blackwood's Edinburgh Magazine*, 14 (1823), 723–29.

Wood, Henry, 'T.L. Beddoes, a Survival in Style', *The American Journal of Philology*, 4 (1899), 445–55.

Wolfson, Susan J., 'Representing some Late Romantic-era, Non-canonical Male Poets: Thomas Hood, Winthrop Mackworth Praed, Thomas Lovell Beddoes', *Romanticism On the Net* (2000), <http://www.users.ox.ac.uk/~scat0385/19hoodhtml>

Wooster, H.D., 'Thomas Lovell Beddoes', *The Bibliophile*, 3, 13 (1909), 21–25.

Other works

Apuleius, 'The Myth of Cupid and Psyche', in *The Transformations of Lucius; Otherwise Known as The Golden Ass; a New Translation by Robert Graves from Apuleius* (New York: Noonday, 1951).

Artaud, Antonin, *The Theatre and its Double*, trans. Victor Corti (London: Calder, 1970).

—, *Selected Writings*, trans. Helen Weaver, ed. Susan Sontag (Berkeley and Los Angeles: University of California Press, 1988).

Ariès, Philippe, *The Hour of Our Death*, trans. Helen Weaver (New York: Lane, 1981).

Ashbery, John, *April Galleons* (London: Paladin, 1990).

Atkinson, David, *The English Traditional Ballad: Theory, Method, and Practice* (Aldershot: Ashgate, 2002).

Auden, W.H., *Collected Poems*, ed. Edward Mendelson (London: Faber and Faber, 1994).

Bailey, Richard W., *Nineteenth-Century English* (Ann Arbor: University of Michigan Press, 1996).

Baillie, Joanna, *Plays on the Passions (1798 edition)*, ed. Peter Duthie (Peterborough, Ontario: Broadview, 2001).

Bakhtin, Mikhail, *Rabelais and his World*, trans. Hélène Iswolsky (Cambridge, Mass.: MIT Press, 1968).

Barker, Francis, *The Tremulous Private Body: Essays on Subjection* (London and New York: Methuen, 1984).

Barrell, John, *Imagining the King's Death: Figurative Treason, Fantasies of Regicide 1893–1796* (Oxford: Oxford University Press, 2000).

Beddoes, Thomas (Sr), *Alexander's Expedition down the Hydaspes & the Indus to the Indian Ocean* (London: J. Murray, James Phillips, 1792).

—, *Contributions to Physical and Medical Knowledge, principally from the west of England* (Bristol: Briggs & Cottle, 1799).

—, *Hygëia: or Essays Moral and Medical on the Causes Affecting the Personal State of our Middling and Affluent Classes*, 3 vols (Bristol: Mills: 1802–3).

Billinger, Robert D., *Metternich and the German Question: States' Rights and Federal Duties, 1820–1834* (Newark: University of Delaware Press, 1991).

Bleiber, Helmut et al. (eds), *Demokratie und Arbeiterbewegung in der deutschen Revolution von 1848/49: Beiträge des Kolloquiums zum 150. Jahrestag der Revolution von 1848/49 am 6. und 7. Juni 1998 in Berlin* (Berlin: Trafo-Verlag, 2000).

Blumenbach, Johann Friedrich, MD, *An Essay on Generation*, trans. A. Crichton (London: T. Cadell, Foulder, Murray, 1792).

Boase-Beier, Jean, *Poetic Compounds: The Principles of Poetic Language in Modern English Poetry* (Tübingen: Niemeyer, 1987).

Bombaugh, C.C., *Gleanings for the Curious from the Harvest-Fields of Literature* (Philadelphia: Lippincott, 1874).

von Bormann, Alexander (ed.), *Wissen aus Erfahrungen: Werkbegriff und Interpretation heute: Festschrift für Herman Meyer zum 65. Geburtstag* (Tübingen: Niemeyer, 1976).

Bohte, Johann Heinrich, *Handbibliothek zu Deutschen Litteratur mit einer Vorrede von A. W. Schlegel* (London: G. Schulze, 1825).

Börne, Ludwig, *Sämtliche Schriften*, ed. Inge and Peter Rippmann (Düsseldorf: Melzer, 1964).

Bostrom, Irene , 'The Novel and Catholic Emancipation', *Studies in Romanticism* 2 (1962), 155–76.

Botting, Fred, *Gothic* (London: Routledge, 1996).

Brewer, William D. (ed.), *Contemporary Studies on Lord Byron* (Lewiston: Edwin Mellen, 2001).

Bruhm, Steven, *Gothic Bodies: The Politics of Pain in Romantic Fiction.* (Philadelphia: University of Pennsylvania Press, 1994).

Büchner, Georg, *Complete Works and Letters*, ed. Walter Hinderer, ed. and trans. Henry J. Schmidt (New York: Continuum, 1986).

—, *Sämtliche Werke, Briefe und Dokumente*, 2 vols, ed. Henri Poschmann (Frankfurt a. Main: Insel Verlag, 2002).

—, *Werke und Briefe*, ed. Karl Pörnbacher, Gerhard Schaub, Hans-Joachim Simm et al. (Munich: Deutscher Taschenbuch Verlag, 1997).

Bunzel, Wolfgang, Peter Stein and Florian Vaßen, '"Romantik" und "Vormärz" als rivalisierende Diskursformationen der ersten Hälfte des 19. Jahrhunderts', in *Romantik und Vormärz: Zur Archäologie literarischer Kommunikation in der ersten Hälfte des 19. Jahrhunderts* (Vormärz-Studien, 10), ed. Wolfgang Bunzel, Peter Stein, Florian Vaßen (Bielefeld: Aisthesis, 2003), pp. 9–49.

Burke, Edmund, *Reflections on the Revolution in France: A Critical Edition*, ed. Jonathan C. D. Clark (Stanford: Stanford University Press, 2001).

Burroughs, Catherine B., *Closet Stages: Joanna Baillie and the Theater Theory of British Romantic Women Writers* (Philadelphia: University of Pennsylvania Press, 1997).

Burwick, Frederick, 'Ideal Shattered: Sarah Siddons, Madness, and the Dynamics of Gesture', in *Notorious Muse: The Actress in British Art and Culture 1776–1812*, ed. Robyn Asleson (Yale University Press, 2003).

—, *Illusion and the Drama: Critical Theory of the Enlightenment and Romantic Drama* (University Park: Pennsylvania State University Press, 1991).

—, 'Illusion and Romantic Drama', in *Romantic Drama*, ed. Gerald Gillespie (Amsterdam and Philadelphia: John Benjamins, 1994), pp. 59–80.

—, 'The Romantic Drama', in *A Companion to Romanticism*, ed. Duncan Wu (Oxford: Blackwell, 1998), pp. 323–32.

—, 'Romantic Drama: from Optics to Illusion', in *Literature and Science: Theory and Practice*, ed. Stuart Peterfreund (Boston: Northeastern University Press, 1990), pp. 167–208.

Carlson, Julie, *In the Theatre of Romanticism: Coleridge, Nationalism, Women* (Cambridge and New York: Cambridge University Press, 1994).

Cartwright, Frederick Fox, *The English Pioneers of Anaesthesia: Beddoes, Davy, and Hickman* (Bristol: J. Wright, 1952).

Clarke, Bruce, *Allegories of Writing: The Subject of Metamorphosis* (Albany: State University of Albany Press, 1995).

Clery, E.J., *The Rise of Supernatural Fiction, 1762–1800* (Cambridge: Cambridge University Press, 1995).

Cohen, Anne B., *Poor Pearl, Poor Girl! The Murdered Girl Stereotype in Ballad and Newspaper* (Austin: University of Texas Press, 1973).

Conger, Syndy M., *Matthew G. Lewis, Charles Robert Maturin and the Germans: An Interpretive Study of the Influence of German Literature on Two Gothic Novels* (Salzburg: Institut für Englische Sprache und Literatur, 1977).

—, 'Sensibility Restored: Radcliffe's Answer to Lewis's *The Monk*', *Gothic Fictions: Prohibition/Transgression*, ed. Kenneth W. Graham (New York: AMS Press, 1989), pp. 113–49.

Cowling, Mark and James Martin (eds), *Marx's 'Eighteenth Brumaire': (Post)modern Interpretations* (London: Pluto, 2002).

Cox, Jeffrey N., *Poetry and Politics in the Cockney School: Keats, Shelley, Hunt and their Circle* (Cambridge: Cambridge University Press, 1998).

— and Michael Gamer (eds), *In the Shadows of Romance: Romantic Tragic Drama in Germany, England and France* (Athens: Ohio University Press, 1987).

Crichton, Alexander, *An Inquiry into the Nature and Origin of Mental Derangement: Comprehending a Concise System of the Physiology and Pathology of the Human Mind, and a History of the Passions and Their Effects*, 2 vols (London: T. Cadell and W. Davies, 1798).

Crochunis, Thomas C. (ed.), *Joanna Baillie, Romantic Dramatist: Critical Essays* (New York: Routledge, 2004).

Curran, Stuart, *Shelley's* Cenci: *Scorpions Ringed with Fire* (Princeton: Princeton University Press, 1970).

Daniell, Christopher, *Death and Burial in Medieval England, 1066–1550* (London: Routledge, 1997).

Davies, Robertson, *The Cornish Trilogy* (Harmondsworth: Penguin, 1991).

The Collected Works of Sir Humphry Davy, ed. John Davy, 6 vols. (London: Smith, Elder, 1839).

De Almeida, Hermione, *Romantic Medicine and John Keats* (New York: Oxford University Press, 1991).

De Lauretis, Teresa, 'Becoming Inorganic', *Critical Inquiry*, 29.4 (2003), 547–70.

Deleuze, Gilles, *Difference & Repetition*, trans. Paul Patton (New York: Columbia, 1994).

Derks, Paul, *Die Schande der heiligen Päderastie: Homosexualität und Öffentlichkeit in der deutschen Literatur 1750–1850* (Berlin: Rosa Winkel, 1990).

Derrida, Jacques, *Dissemination*, trans. Barbara Johnson (Chicago: University of Chicago Press, 1981).

—, *Specters of Marx: The State of the Debt, the Work of Mourning, and the New International*, trans. Peggy Kamuf, intro. by Bernd Magnus and Stephen Cullenberg (New York: Routledge, 1994).

Dollimore, Jonathan and Alan Sinfield (eds), *Political Shakespeare: Essays in Cultural Materialism*, 2nd edn (Manchester: Manchester University Press, 1996).

—, *Radical Tragedy: Religion, Ideology and Power in the Drama of Shakespeare and his Contemporaries* (Brighton and Chicago: Harvester Press and Chicago University Press, 1984).

Donnelly, John, *Language, Metaphysics, and Death* (New York: Fordham University Press, 1994).

Selected Prose of T. S. Eliot, ed. Frank Kermode (London: Faber and Faber, 1975).

Eliot, T.S., *The Waste Land: A facsimile and transcript of the original drafts including the annotations of Ezra Pound*, ed. Valerie Eliot (London: Faber and Faber, 1971; repr. 1980).

Ellis, F.S. (ed.), *A Lexical Concordance to the Poetical Works of Percy Bysshe Shelley* (London: Quaritch, 1892).

Ellison, David, *Ethics and Aesthetics in European Modernist Literature: From the Sublime to the Uncanny* (Cambridge: Cambridge University Press, 2001).

Emerson, Donald E., *Metternich and the Political Police: Security and Subversion in the Hapsburg Monarchy (1815–1830)* (The Hague: Martinus Nijhoff, 1968).

Erdman, David V., 'Byron's Stage Fright: The History of his Ambition and Fear of Writing for the Stage', *English Literary History*, 6 (1939), 219–43.

Etlin, Richard A., *The Architecture of Death: The Transformation of the Cemetery in Eighteenth century Paris* (Boston: MIT, 1984).

Fährmann, Sigrid, 'Musik, Theater, Kunst und Vereine', in *Göttingen: Geschichte einer Universitätsstadt*, ed. Dietrich Denecke and Helga Maria Kühn, 3 vols (Göttingen: Vandenhoeck & Ruprecht, 2002), II: *Vom Dreißigjährigen Krieg bis zum Anschluss an Preußen: der Wiederaufstieg als Universitätsstadt (1648–1866)*, pp. 905–30.

Flew, Anthony (ed.), *Body, Mind and Death* (New York: Macmillan, 1964).

—, *Merely Mortal? Can You Survive Your Own Death?* (New York: Prometheus Books, 2000).

Forster, John, *Walter Savage Landor* (London: Chapman and Hall, 1869).

Foster, Thomas, *The Souls of Cyberfolk: Posthumanism as Vernacular Theory* (Minnesota: University of Minnesota Press, 2005).

Foucault, Michel, *Discipline and Punish: The Birth of the Prison* (1975), trans. Alan Sheridan (New York: Vintage, 1979).

Freud, Sigmund, *Beyond the Pleasure Principle*, trans. James Strachey (New York: Norton, 1961).

—, *Civilization and Its Discontents*, trans. James Strachey (New York: Norton, 1961).

—, *Writings on Art and Literature*, trans. James Strachey (Stanford: Stanford University Press, 1997).

Freund, Winfried, *Die deutsche Ballade* (Paderborn: Schönigh, 1973).

Garrick, David, *Harlequin's Invasion*, in *Three Plays by David Garrick*, ed. Elisabeth Paula Stein (1926; New York: Bloom, 1967), pp. 11–53.

Geckle, George L., *John Marston's Drama: Themes, Images, Sources* (London and Toronto: Associated University Presses, 1980).

Gilmore, David D., Monsters: Evil Beings, Mythical Beasts, and All Manner of Imaginary Terrors (Philadelphia: University of Pennsylvania Press, 2003).

Golinski, Jan, *Science as Public Culture: Chemistry and Enlightenment in Britain, 1760–1820* (Cambridge: Cambridge University Press, 1992).

Goltschigg, Dietmar (ed.), *Büchner im 'Dritten Reich': Mystifikation—Gleichschaltung—Exil: Eine Dokumentation* (Bielefeld: Aisthesis, 1990).

Gössmann, Wilhelm and Manfred Windfuhr (eds), *Heinrich Heine im Spannungsfeld von Literatur und Wissenschaft: Symposium anläßlich der Benennung der Universität Düsseldorf nach Heinrich Heine* (Düsseldorf: Hobbing, 1990).

Grab, Walter and Uwe Friesel, *'Noch ist Deutschland nicht verloren': Eine historisch-politische Analyse unterdrückter Lyrik von der Französischen Revolution bis zur Reichsgründung* (Munich: DTV, 1973).

Grabbe, Christian Dietrich, *Napoleon oder die Hundert Tage* (Stuttgart: Reclam, 2002).

Graves, Robert, *The English Ballad: A Short Critical Survey* (London: Benn, 1927).

Greenblatt, Stephen et al. (eds), *The Norton Shakespeare, based on the Oxford Edition* (New York: Norton, 1997).

Griffin, Susan, *Anti-Catholicism and Nineteenth-Century Fiction* (Cambridge: Cambridge University Press, 2004).

Grimm, Dieter, 'Verfassung (II)', in *Geschichtliche Grundbegriffe: Historisches Lexikon zur politisch-sozialen Sprache in Deutschland*, ed. Otto Brunner, Werner Conze and Reinhart Koselleck, 8 vols, VI: *St-Vert* (Stuttgart: Klett-Cotta, 1990), pp. 868–99.

Hansers Sozialgeschichte der Deutschen Literatur: Vol. V: Zwischen Restauration und Revolution 1815–1848 (Munich: Hanser, 1998).

Harding, Vanessa, *The Dead and the Living in Paris and London* (Cambridge: Cambridge University Press, 2002).

Hardtwig, Wolfgang, *Vormärz: Der monarchische Staat und das Bürgertum*, 4th edn (Munich: DTV, 1998).

Hein, Jürgen, 'Grabbe und das zeitgenössische Volkstheater', in *Grabbe und die Dramatiker seiner Zeit*, ed. Detlev Kopp and Michael Vogt (Tübingen: Niemeyer, 1990), pp. 117–35.

Heine, Heinrich, *Sämtliche Schriften*, ed. Klaus Briegleb (Munich: DTV, 1997).

Herford, C. H., *The Age of Wordsworth* (1897; London: Bell, 1960).

Hermand, Jost (ed.), *Der deutsche Vormärz* (Stuttgart: Reclam, 1967).

Hertz, Neil, *The End of the Line: Essays on Psychoanalysis and the Sublime* (New York: Columbia University Press, 1985).

Hetzler, Florence H., and Austin H. Kurtscher (eds), *Philosophical Aspects of Thanatology*, vol. 1 (New York: Arno Press, 1978).

Hill, Reginald, *Death's Jest-Book* (London: HarperCollins, 2002).

Hoagwood, Terence, 'Prolegomenon for a Theory of Romantic Drama', *Wordsworth Circle*, 23.2 (1992), 49–64.

—, and Daniel P. Watkins (eds), *British Romantic Drama: Historical and Critical Essays* (Farleigh Dickinson University Press, 1998).

Hobsbawm, Eric, *The Age of Revolution: Europe 1789–1848* (1962; London: Abacus, 1977).

Hoeveler, Diane Long, *Romantic Androgyny: The Women Within* (University Park: Pennsylvania State University Press, 1990).

Holmes, Terence Michael, *The Rehearsal of Revolution* (Bern: Peter Lang, 1995).

Huddleston, Rodney, *The Cambridge Grammar of the English Language* (Cambridge: Cambridge University Press, 2002).

Ingram, R.W., *John Marston* (Boston: Twayne, 1978).

Johnson, Samuel, *Lives of the English Poets: A Selection*, ed. John Wain (London: Dent, 1975).

Jokl, Johann, 'Heinrich Heine', in *Zwischen Revolution und Restauration 1815–1848*, ed. Gerd Sautermeister and Ulrich Schmid (Munich: Deutscher Taschenbuch Verlag, 1998), pp. 526–78.

Kaplan, Alice Yaegar, *Reproductions of Banality: Fascism, Literature, and French Intellectual Life* (Minneapolis: University of Minneapolis Press, 1986).

Kastovsky, Dieter, 'Words and Word-Formation: Morphology in *OED*', in *Lexicography and the OED: Pioneers in the Untrodden Forest*, ed. Lynda Mugglestone (Oxford: Oxford University Press, 2000), pp. 110–25.

Kerrigan, John, *Revenge Tragedy: Aeschylus to Armageddon* (Oxford: Clarendon Press, 1997).

Knowles, James Sheridan, *Virginius* (London (no pub.), 1820).

Koslofsky, Craig, *The Reformation of the Dead: Death and Ritual in Early Modern Germany* (New York: St Martin's, 2000).

Kristeva, Julia, *Powers of Horror: An Essay on Abjection*, trans. Leon S. Roudiez (New York: Columbia University Press, 1982).

Kucich, Greg, '"A Haunted Ruin": Romantic Drama, Renaissance Tradition, and the Critical Establishment', *The Wordsworth Circle*, 23 (1992), 64–76.

Kurtz, Leonard P., *The Dance of Death and the Macabre Spirit in European Literature* (1934; New York: Gordon, 1975).

Lacan, Jacques, *The Seminar of Jacques Lacan, Book VII: The Ethic of Psychoanalysis*, trans. Dennis Porter (New York: Norton, 1992).

Lamb, Charles (ed.), *Specimens of English Dramatic Poets* (1808) (London: Routledge, 1907, intro. James Dykes Campbell).

Lane, Joan, *A Social History of Medicine: Health, Healing and Disease in England, 1750–1950* (London: Routledge, 2001).

Laqueur, Thomas, *Making Sex: Body and Gender from the Greeks to Freud* (Cambridge, Mass.: Harvard University Press, 1990).

Latour, Bruno, *We Have Never Been Modern*, trans. Catherine Porter (Cambridge, Mass.: Harvard University Press, 1993).

Lawrence, C.J., 'William Buchan: Medicine Laid Open', *Medical History*, 19 (1975), 20–35.

Levere, Trevor, 'Dr Thomas Beddoes: The Interaction of Pneumatic and Preventive Medicine with Chemistry', *Interdisciplinary Science Reviews*, 7 (1982), 137–47.

Lévinas, Emmanuel, *Existence and Existents*, trans. Alphonso Lingis (Pittsburgh: Duquesne University Press, repr. 2001).

—, *Otherwise than Being; or, Beyond Essence*, trans. Alphonso Lingis (Pittsburgh: Duquesne University Press, repr. 1998).

—, *Totality and Infinity: An Essay on Exteriority* trans. Alphonso Lingis (Pittsburgh: Duquesne University Press, repr. 1996).

Lewis, Matthew, 'The Dying Bride', in *Romantic Tales*, 4 vols (London: Longman, 1808), II, 117–20.

—, *The Monk* (1796; London: Oxford University Press, 1992).

Liang, Hsi-Huey, *The Rise of Modern Police and the European State System from Metternich to the Second World War* (Cambridge: Cambridge University Press, 1992).

Lorca, Federico Garcia, *Blood Wedding*, trans. Ted Hughes (London: Faber and Faber, 1996).

Loudon, Irvine, *Death in Childbirth, 1800–1950* (London: Oxford University Press, 1992).

Luzatto, Sergio, 'European Visions of the French Revolution', in *Revolution and the Meaning of Freedom in the Nineteenth Century*, ed. Isser Woloch (Stanford: Stanford University Press, 1996), pp. 31–65.

Lynch, Deidre, 'Overloaded Portraits: The Excess of Character and Countenance', in *Body and Text in the Eighteenth Century*, ed. Veronica Kelly and Dorothea von Mücke (Stanford: Stanford University Press, 1994) pp. 112–43.

Marlowe, Christopher, *The Complete Plays*, ed. John Barry Steane (1969; Harmondsworth: Penguin, 1980).

Marston, John, *The Malcontent*, ed. George K. Hunter (Manchester: Manchester University Press, 2000).

The Selected Plays of John Marston, ed. MacDonald P. Jackson and Michael Neill (Cambridge: Cambridge University Press, 1986).

The Poems of John Marston, ed. Arnold Davenport (Liverpool: Liverpool University Press, 1961).

Marx, Karl, *The Marx-Engels Reader*, ed. Robert Tucker (New York: Norton, 1978).

Matthews, Harry and Alastair Brotchie (eds), *Oulipo Compendium* (London: Atlas Press, 1998).

May, Arthur J., *The Age of Metternich, 1814–1848* (New York: Holt, Rinehart and Winston, 1966).

Mayer, David III, *Harlequin in his Element: The English Pantomime, 1806–1836* (Cambridge, Mass.: Harvard University Press, 1969).

Mellor, Anne K., *Romanticism and Gender* (New York: Routledge, 1993).

Middleton, Thomas, *The Phoenix*, ed. Chris Cleary, in *Thomas Middleton (1580–1627)* <http://www.tech.org/~cleary/phoenix.html>

—, Cyril Tourneur, *The Revenger's Tragedy*, in Thomas Middleton, *Five Plays*, ed. Bryan Loughrey and Neil Taylor (Harmondsworth: Penguin, 1988).

Miles, Robert, 'Europhobia: The Catholic Other in Horace Walpole and Charles Maturin', *European Gothic*, ed. Avril Horner (Manchester: Manchester University Press, 2002), pp. 84–103.

The Dramatic Works of Mary Russel Mitford, 2 vols (London: Hurst and Blackett 1854).

Moody, Jane, *Illegitimate Theatre in London, 1770–1840* (Cambridge: Cambridge University Press, 2000).

—, 'Romantic Shakespeare', in *The Cambridge Companion to Shakespeare on Stage* (Cambridge: Cambridge University Press, 2002), pp. 37–58.

Moore, John David, 'Coleridge and the "Modern Jacobinical Drama": *Osorio, Remorse*, and the Development of Coleridge's Critique of the Stage, 1797–1816', *Bulletin of Research in the Humanities*, 85 (1982), 443–65.

Mulrooney, Jonathan, 'Keats in the Company of Kean', *Studies in Romanticism*, 42 (2003) 227–50.

Mulvey Roberts, Marie, *Gothic Immortals: The Fiction of the Brotherhood of the Rosy Cross* (London: Routledge, 1990).

Neumann, Erich, *Amor and Psyche: The Psychic Development of the Feminine*, trans. Ralph Manheim (Princeton: Princeton University Press, 1956).

Nicolai, Friedrich, 'A Memoir on the Appearances of Spectres or Phantoms occasioned by Disease, with Psychological Remarks. Read by Nicolai to the Royal Society of Berlin, on the 28th of February, 1799', *Journal of Natural Philosophy, Chemistry, and the Arts*, 6 (1803), 161–79.

Outram, Dorinda, *The Body and the French Revolution: Sex, Class and Political Culture* (New Haven, London: Yale University Press, 1989).

Pendleton, Thomas A., 'Shakespeare's Disguised Duke Play: Middleton, Marston and the sources of *Measure for Measure*', in *Fanned and Winnowed Opinions: Shakespearean Essays Presented to Harold Jenkins*, ed. John W. Mahon and Thomas A. Pendleton (London: Methuen, 1987), pp. 79–97.

Penelhum, Terence, *Immortality* (New York: Wadsworth, 1973).

Phillips, John A. and Charles Wetherell, 'The Great Reform Act of 1832 and the Political Modernization of England', *The American Historical Review*, 100 (1995), 411–36.

Porter, Dorothy and Roy Porter, *Patient's Progress: Doctors and Doctoring in Eighteenth-Century England* (Stanford: Stanford University Press, 1989).

Porter, Roy, *Doctor of Society: Thomas Beddoes and the Sick Trade in Late Enlightenment England* (London: Routledge, 1992).

—, *Health for Sale: Quackery in England 1660–1850* (Manchester: Manchester University Press, 1989).

The Cantos of Ezra Pound (London: Faber and Faber, 1964).

Procter, Bryan Waller ('Barry Cornwall'), *Dramatic Scenes*, introduction Donald H. Reiman (New York: Garland, 1978; 'Romantic Context: Significant Minor Poetry 1789–1830' series).

Purinton, Marjean D., 'Science Fiction and Techno-Gothic Drama: Romantic Playwrights Joanna Baillie and Jane Scott', *Romanticism on the Net*, 21 (2001) <http://www.ron.umontreal.ca>

—, 'Theatricalised Bodies and Spirits: Gothic as Performance in Romantic Drama', *Gothic Studies*, 3.2 (August 2001), 134–55.

Rajan, Tilottama, 'Theories of Genre', in *The Cambridge History of Literary Criticism*, vol. 5, *Romanticism*, ed. Marshall Brown (Cambridge: Cambridge University Press, 2000), pp. 226–49.

Reinalter, Helmut (ed.), *Die demokratische Bewegung in Mitteleuropa von der Spätaufklärung bis zur Revolution 1848/49: Ein Tagungsbericht* (Innsbruck: Inn-Verlag, 1988).

Richardson, Alan, *A Mental Theater: Poetic Drama and Consciousness in the Romantic Age* (University Park: Pennsylvania State University Press, 1988).

Richardson, Ruth, *Death, Dissection and the Destitute* (London and New York: Routledge and Kegan Paul, 1987).

Rippmann, Inge, 'Börne und Heine', in *Heinrich Heine 1797–1856: Internationaler Veranstaltungszyklus zum 125. Todestag 1981 bei Eröffnung des Studienzentrums Karl-Marx-Haus Trier* (Trier: Karl-Marx-Haus, 1981).

— and Wolfgang Labuhn (eds), *'Die Kunst–eine Tochter der Zeit': Neue Studien zu Ludwig Börne* (Bielefeld: Aisthesis, 1988).

Robinson, Fred C., *Beowulf and the Appositive Style* (Knoxville: Tennessee University Press, 1985).

Rose, Margaret Anne, 'A Political Referent and Secular Source for Heine's "Belsatzar"', *Heine-Jahrbuch*, 21 (1982), 186–90.

Ross, Marlon, *The Contours of Masculine Desire: Romanticism and the Rise of Women's Poetry* (New York: Oxford University Press, 1989).

Ruckhäberle, Hans-Joachim, *Frühproletarische Literatur: Die Flugschriften der deutschen Handwerksgesellenvereine in Paris 1832–1839* (Kronberg: Scriptor-Verlag, 1977).

Rudkin, Olive D., *Thomas Spence and His Connections* (London: Allen and Unwin, 1927).

Rupke, Nicolaas (ed.), *Göttingen and the Development of the Natural Sciences* (Göttingen: Wallstein, 2002).

Sage, Victor, *Horror Fiction in the Protestant Tradition* (London: Macmillan, 1988).

Saintsbury, George, *A History of Nineteenth Century Literature, 1780–1900* (1896; London: Macmillan, 1906).

Schapiro, Barbara, *The Romantic Mother: Narcissistic Patterns in Romantic Poetry* (Baltimore: Johns Hopkins University Press, 1983).

Schiller, Friedrich, *The Ghost Seer or, Apparitionist: an interesting fragment, found among the papers of Count O*******. From the German of Schiller (New-York: Printed by T. and J. Swords, 1796).

Shakespeare, William, *Measure for Measure*, ed. Brian Gibbons (Cambridge: Cambridge University Press, 1991).

Percy Bysshe Shelley: The Major Works, ed. Zachary Leader and Michael O'Neill (Oxford: Oxford University Press, 2003).

The Complete Poetical Works of Percy Bysshe Shelley, ed. Thomas Hutchinson (1905; London: Oxford University Press, 1943).

Shildrick, Margrit, *Embodying the Monster: Encounters with the Vulnerable Self* (London: Sage, 2002).

Simpson, Michel, *Closet Performances: Political Exhibition and Prohibition in the Dramas of Byron and Shelley* (Stanford: Stanford University Press, 1998).

Smith, Ginnie, 'Prescribing the Rules of Health: Self-help and Advice in the Late Eighteenth Century', in *Patients and Practitioners: Lay Perceptions of Medicine in Pre-Industrial Society*, ed. Roy Porter (Cambridge: Cambridge University Press, 1985), pp. 249–82.

Sommers, Montagu, *The Gothic Quest: A History of the Gothic Novel* (1928; New York: Russell, 1964).

Sparrow, John, 'Dr Beddoes', *Farrago*, 3 (1930), 135–48.

Stanley, Peter, *For Fear of Pain: British Surgery, 1790–1850* (Amsterdam: Rodopi, 2003).

Stansfield, Dorothy A., *Thomas Beddoes, MD, 1760–1808: Chemist, Physician, Democrat* (Dordrecht: D. Reidel, 1984).

— and Ronald G. Stansfield, 'Dr Thomas Beddoes and James Watt: Preparatory Work 1794–96 for the Bristol Pneumatic Institute', *Medical History*, 30 (1986), 276–302.

Stein, Peter, 'Operative Literatur', in *Zwischen Revolution und Restauration 1815–1848*, ed. Gerd Sautermeister and Ulrich Schmid (Munich: Deutscher Taschenbuch Verlag, 1998), pp. 485–505.

Steiner, George, *The Death of Tragedy* (New York: Hill and Wang, 1961).

Stock, John Edmonds, *Memoirs of the Life of Thomas Beddoes, MD, with an analytical account of his writings* (London: John Murray, 1811).

Stonyk, Margaret, *Nineteenth-Century English Literature* (London: Macmillan, 1983).

Strähl, Wolfgang, *Briefe eines Schweizers aus Paris 1835–1836: Neue Dokumente zur Geschichte der frühproletarischen Kultur und Bewegung*, ed. Jacques Grandjonc, Waltraud Seidel-Höppner, and Michael Werner (Vaduz: Topos Verlag, 1988).

Sue, Eugene, *The Wandering Jew* (New York: Burt, 1900).

Swinburne, A.C., *George Chapman: A Critical Essay* (London: Chatto & Windus, 1875).

Symons, Arthur, *Figures of Several Centuries* (New York: Dutton, 1916).

Tarr, Sister M.M., *Catholicism in Gothic Fiction* (Washington DC: Catholic University Press, 1946).

Taylor, Mark C. (ed.), *Deconstruction in Context* (Chicago: University of Chicago Press, 1986).

Thompson, G.R. (ed.), *The Gothic Imagination* (Spokane: Washington State University Press, 1974).

Tieck, Ludwig, *Werke in vier Einzelbänden. Nach dem Text der Schriften von 1828–1854 unter Berücksichtigung der Erstdrucke*, ed. Marianne Thalmann, II: *Die Märchen aus dem Phantasus. Dramen* (1964; Munich: Winkler, 1978).

Trotter, Thomas, *An Essay, Medical, Philosophical, and Chemical, on Drunkenness, and Its Effects on the Human Body* (London: Longman and Rees, 1804).

—, *A View of the Nervous Temperament; Being a Practical Enquiry into the Increasing Prevalence, Prevention, and Treatment of those Diseases Commonly Called Nervous, Bilious, Stomach and Liver Complaints; Indigestion, Low Spirits, Gout, &c.* (London: Longman, Hurst, Rees, and Orme, 1807).

Vickers, Neil, 'Coleridge, Thomas Beddoes, and Brunonian Medicine', *European Romantic Review*, 8, 1 (1997), 47–94.

Walker, Robert, *Eighteenth-Century Arguments for Immortality and Johnson's Rasselas* (Victoria, British Columbia: University of Victoria, 1977).

Walsh, William, *Handy-Book of Literary Curiosities* (Philadelphia: Lippincott, 1892).

Warner, Marina, *Alone of All Her Sex: The Myth and Cult of the Virgin Mary* (London: Weidenfeld and Nicolson, 1976).

—, *No Go the Bogeyman: Scaring, Lulling, and Making Mock* (New York: Farrar, Straus, and Giroux, 1999).

Watkins, Daniel P., *A Materialist Critique of English Romantic Drama* (Gainesville: University Press of Florida, 1993).

Watson, J.R., *English Poetry of the Romantic Period 1789–1830* (London: Longman, 1985).

Wehler, Hans-Ulrich, *Deutsche Gesellschaftsgeschichte II: Von der Reformära bis zur industriellen und politischen 'Deutschen Doppelrevolution', 1815–1848/49*, 2nd edn (Munich: Beck, 1989).

Wharton, T.F. (ed.), *The Drama of John Marston: Critical Re-Visions* (Cambridge: Cambridge University Press, 2000).

—, *Moral Experiment in Jacobean Drama* (London: Macmillan, 1988).

Wheeler, Kathleen M. (ed.), *German Aesthetic and Literary Criticism: The Romantic Ironists and Goethe* (Cambridge: Cambridge University Press, 1984).

White, Martin, *Middleton and Tourneur* (Basingstoke: Macmillan, 1992).

Williams, William Carlos, *Paterson, Books 1–V* (London: MacGibbon & Kee, 1964).

Wittgenstein, Ludwig, *Tractatus Logico-Philosophicus*, trans. Daniel Kolak (California: Mayfield Publishing, 1998).

Winkler, Mary G., 'The Anatomical Theatre', *Literature and Medicine*, 12 (1993), 65–80.

Žižek, Slavoj, *The Plague of Fantasies* (New York: Verso, 1998).

—, *The Sublime Object of Ideology* (London: Verso, 1989).

—, *The Žižek Reader* (Malden: Blackwell Books, 1999).

Index